Reprinted 1983 from the 1888 edition.
Cover design © 1981 Time-Life Books Inc.
Library of Congress CIP data following page 456.

This volume is bound in leather.

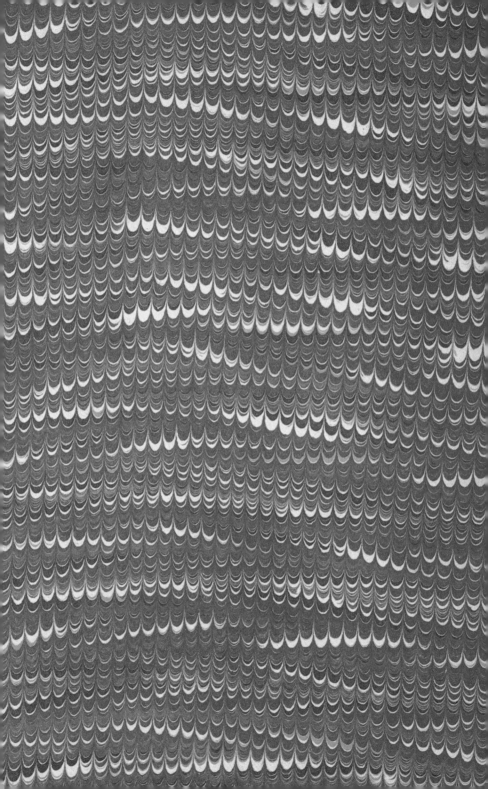

LIFE IN THE

CONFEDERATE ARMY

BEING THE

Observations and Experiences of an Alien
in the South during the

AMERICAN CIVIL WAR.

BY

WILLIAM WATSON.

NEW YORK:

SCRIBNER AND WELFORD,

1888.

TO

COLONEL JOHN SCOTT, C.B.,

1st Renfrew and Dumbarton Artillery Volunteer Corps.

Sir,

Having written a brief narrative of my observations and experience in the Southern States prior to and during the earlier part of the American Civil War, and as these observations touching the causes which led to the war were gathered from amongst the industrial and commercial classes, and my experience in the war being in a volunteer corps, I proposed to dedicate the simple narrative to you, as a gentleman who at once unites an extensive connection in the industrial and commercial world with an active interest and participation in the military defences of the country, and whose services in public affairs generally are well known.

I claim no merit for the work beyond a plain, honest, and truthful statement of what I actually saw and gathered from the general tone and sentiment of persons in the sphere in which I moved. I am, therefore, much gratified in having your permission to dedicate my humble volume to you.

I am, Sir,

Yours very respectfully,

WILLIAM WATSON.

Pea Ridge, Skelmorlie,
17th September, 1887.

PREFACE.

On the origin, progress, and issue of the American Civil War there has, no doubt, been much written from various sources, and from different points of view.

Assuming those accounts to be strictly correct and impartial, still it must be acknowledged that in general descriptions of events of historical importance the subject is generally taken in the abstract, wholly and collectively, and there is seldom room for any minute analysis of individual sentiment, personal views, or minor incidents, which might be interesting if given in a personal narrative, even though that narrative extended only to a limited portion of the general subject; and more especially if the narrator happened to be an outsider, having little or no direct interest on either side, but became a participant in the events through force of peculiar circumstances.

The writer resided for several years immediately preceding the war in the capital of one of the Southern States; and, though his occupation and station were more among the industrious, non-slaveholding, and less political class, still, as all classes took less or more interest in political

matters and politics was a general theme of conversation,
he had ample means of observing the working of the
political system.

The place being the seat of Government was the residence
or headquarters of the leading statesmen and politicians and
the centre of all political movements.

He had every opportunity of observing the movements
which led to the Secession of the States, and the manner
in which it was accomplished and carried through.

He had also a peculiar advantage of knowing the private
sentiments of a large body of the people when the Secession
movement began, and the change of sentiment which circumstances afterwards actually forced upon them.

That he got mixed up in the turmoil and came to take
part in the war he considered unavoidable ; and he trusts
the explanation he has given in the course of the narrative
will be sufficient excuse.

It may be a little disappointing to some that the narrative is confined to the early part of the war, and to
events which took place in the West and Centre, and do
not extend to the more brilliant campaigns in Virginia,
and the more sanguinary struggles in the later part of the
war.   But the writer presumes that much has already
been written from that field, while many things which took
place in the West and Centre were less noticed, and

sometimes entirely overlooked in the multitude of more exciting events at the time ; and, as he does not aspire to anything like a philosophic or historical account, but simply relates what he actually saw and experienced, he considers that the positions and places he happened to be in at different times, in and out of the army, afforded him more varied and better opportunities for observations, which would be of greater interest in a personal narrative than if swallowed up in the midst of a large army in one place or in one continued campaign.

In giving this account of his observations and experience, the writer sums up his observations from what he personally witnessed, and from the general feeling and opinions expressed by those around him of the more moderate class outside of the ring of fiery politicians ; and any opinions on the origin of the war he leaves to be deduced from what little testimony he has given, should anyone consider that to be of any value.

That the struggle should have been so sanguinary, should have continued so long and been maintained with such unanimity on both sides, and particularly on the part of the South, may have astonished many. He has mentioned one or two of the causes which he imagines contributed in some measure to prolong the struggle.

In relating his experience, any incidents he has tried to describe are given just as he witnessed them, and he

believes and trusts that many are still alive, who, if these
pages meet their eyes, will recognise the writer, and will
remember the incidents and that he does not attempt to
embellish them in any way.

The writer has no pretensions to literary attainments, and
possesses no great political or statistical knowledge, but
endeavours to give in a plain, blunt way this short narrative
of his observations and experience which he thinks, even
leaving out any political remarks, may be of interest in
showing something of the utility of the Volunteer system,
and how a nation may be strengthened in time of necessity
and large and effective armies raised upon that system, and
also in relating a test of the experience of citizen soldiers
and their capabilities in actual warfare.

CONTENTS.

SECTION I.—THE SOUTH BEFORE THE WAR.

CHAPTER I.

CHAPTER II.

CHAPTER III.

SECTION II.—THE SECESSION MOVEMENT.

CHAPTER IV.

CHAPTER V.

CHAPTER VI.

CHAPTER VII.

CHAPTER VIII.

CHAPTER IX.

CHAPTER X.

CHAPTER XI.

CHAPTER XII.

SECTION III.—LIFE IN THE CONFEDERATE ARMY.

CHAPTER XIII.

CHAPTER XIV.

CHAPTER XV.

CHAPTER XVI.

CHAPTER XXV.

CHAPTER XXVI.

SECTION IV.—IN THE SOUTH DURING THE WAR.

CHAPTER XXVII.

CHAPTER XXVIII.

CHAPTER XXIX.

CHAPTER XXX.

SECTION I.

THE SOUTH BEFORE THE WAR.

CHAPTER I.

STATE OF LOUISIANA IN 1860 — TOPOGRAPHICAL DESCRIPTION — SOIL — CLIMATE — PRODUCTIONS — POPULATION CLASSIFIED — INSTITUTION OF SLAVERY.

THE State of Louisiana comprises a part of that territory originally called Florida. It was settled by the French and sold by Napoleon to the United States in 1803. It lies to the west of the State which is now called Florida, and from which it is separated by parts of the States of Alabama and Mississippi. It has sometimes been called the sugar bowl of the United States, it being the principal State in which sugar is grown. It is one of the most Southern States in the American Union, and borders on the Gulf of Mexico. The Mississippi river runs through it, entering the Gulf of Mexico by one large volume at the Balize and by several small estuaries, or bayous as they are called, the most important of which are Bayou La Fourche, which branches off from the right bank at Donaldsonville, about 220 miles from the mouth, Bayou Plaquemines on the same side about 20 miles further up, and the Atchalafalia branching off near the mouth of Red river.

These bayous or small rivers flow through a rich and level country, and are navigable throughout a considerable part of the year.

The whole of the land along the right or west bank of the river as far up as the State extends, and to where the Ohio river joins it at Cairo, a distance of 900 miles, is flat alluvial land, and is below the level of the river when in flood at certain seasons of the year, and, before the country was settled, was overflowed when the river rose. To prevent this overflow, high embankments called levees have been formed all along the banks, which have to be kept in good repair and strictly watched when the river is high. Sometimes breaks take place which cause immense damage.

On the left, or east bank, this low alluvial land extends only about 260 miles from its mouth, where the high undulating land begins.

These flat lands are nearly level, but have a slight slope falling away from the river on either side, the drainage leading away from the river and falling into various creeks and bayous leading to the Gulf of Mexico. The lower part of the Mississippi river, for about 250 miles from its mouth, may thus be said to form an immense aqueduct flowing along the crest of a ridge.

These low lands, or bottoms as they are called, being entirely formed by the deposit from the overflow of the river, are very fertile and well adapted for the growth of sugar cane; and in 1860 all along the river as far as this low land extends on the east side, and as far as Red river on the west, the sugar plantations extended.

The high undulating lands produced cotton in abundance, Indian corn, sweet and common potatoes, with fruit, vegetables and live stock in abundance; but the great staple products of the State were sugar and cotton.

The State has also abundance of fine timber, on the lowlands there being enormous swamps heavily timbered with fine cypress, while much of the high and poorer lands are covered with excellent pitch pine, oak, ash, poplar, and other timber.

The climate is hot, though not more so than New York and the other Northern States in summer, but here the summer is longer, and there is very little cold weather. In winter the frosts are slight, and snow is very rare in the southern part of the State. There is a pretty fair supply of rain, though most of it falls in July and August, and in December and January.

The climate is on the whole healthy, although in the swampy districts there is a good deal of " chills and fever," but these are not of a serious nature.

New Orleans has the name of being a most unhealthy city, but this is on account of its being visited sometimes by that fearful scourge, the yellow fever. This disease is not supposed to be indigenous to the place, but is imported from the West Indies or Mexico. It generally appears in July and continues to the end of September, when the first slight frost puts an end to the epidemic, but it also too often proves fatal to any one afflicted with it when the frost appears. Its ravages are confined to New Orleans and the towns along the river, and it never extends into the country, and seldom to any of the towns back from the river. It is only in occasional years that the district is visited by this epidemic, which can be kept out by a strict quarantine.

At all other times the city is very healthy and the mortality much less than might be supposed from the low lying situation and its seeming insanitary position and surroundings.

New Orleans is the great emporium of the South, and is situated on the left bank, fronting the river, about 130 miles from its mouth, and upon the lowland.

The streets of this city are only a few feet above the level of the sea, and the drainage is led to Lake Pontchartrain, which is a branch or arm of the Gulf of Mexico, approaching to within six miles of the back of the city, the land intervening being low and level, the drainage is elevated and assisted along by water-wheels, driven by steam-engines.

At the time of which I write (1860) there was no through connection between New Orleans and the Northern cities by railway, and the whole of the traffic was by sea, and the Mississippi river; and although telegraph communication was established the mails took five or six days to come from New York by an inland route, and the railroads between the Atlantic cities and the Western States, not yet having been fully opened up, the most of the produce of the latter came down the river by means of steamers and flat boats to New Orleans, which was then the great outlet and market of the South-west.

In regard to population, the State of Louisiana had been originally settled by the Spaniards and French, and up till the end of the last century, had been a French colony, a large portion of the population were consequently of French extraction, still retaining their language, manners, and customs, and many of the oldest planters and merchants were of French descent. The great influx, however, from the Northern States and from Europe had considerably overtopped this, and the population of New Orleans became of a mixed character, and at this time might be said to represent every nation in the world.

The principal merchants and planters in the State were descendants of the old French families, men from the North, and other States, with a good many English, Irish, Scotch and Germans.

Of the other portions of the population throughout the State, there were what were called the Arcadians, or small settlers, something like the crofters in the Highlands of Scotland. These were of French extraction and were located mostly on the low grounds along the river and bayous. Interspersed among the larger planters they lived in rather poor wooden houses; they were not guilty of great ambition; they lived poorly; they cultivated nothing beyond a little Indian corn and vegetables, spent most of their time in hunting and fishing; their wants were small and they were regarded as a contented and inoffensive lot, and were often subjected to the taunting remark that they lived and ate the crawfish which they caught on the river bank and then died, and the crawfish ate them.

Then there were the small farmers who did not aspire to the name of planters. These were mostly located on the higher lands and owned tracts of from 10 to 160 acres, possessing oxen, cows, pigs, poultry, and other live stock, and the never failing supply of native ponies for saddle or spring cart. Part of the land this class cultivated produced Indian corn, fruit, and vegetables, and a few bales of cotton to meet their financial wants. They were mostly natives of the State or of some of the other Southern States. A few of them owned one or two slaves or perhaps a family which they had inherited from their forefathers, but the greater part of them did not own slaves but worked the land with their families or hired help.

Of the mechanic or artisan class, the greater portion of them were natives of the Northern States, or Europeans. These, with clerks and others of similar nationality, constituted a considerable portion of the population.

The labouring classes, of which there was a large number, were located chiefly in New Orleans and the other towns along the river, where they were extensively employed in loading and discharging the numerous steamboats, stowing cotton in ships, and employed about the cotton presses and other public works, and very largely on the river on barges and steamboats. They were composed mostly of Irish and Germans, and but few of them, after the requisite five years' residence, had failed to pass through the form of getting their naturalisation papers, and in becoming citizens, thereby obtaining the coveted privilege of voting.

But the great ruling power and interest was centred in the " peculiar institution," which was regarded or had at least to

be acknowledged as paramount to all other interests—the
" institution of slavery."

There has been a great deal said and written on this
" institution " for and against it, though I cannot see that on
either side much has been said or written from a truly
authentic or dispassionate source.

Those who have written condemnatory of it have generally
been actuated by a spirit of prejudice against those who
maintained it without having any practical or personal
experience, or observation ; but have based their criticisms on
testimony sought for and selected from prejudiced sources.
These have portrayed shocking outrages and horrible cruelties
which may have been mere tales of tradition or may have been
illustrative of something which actually did occur, but of
which the accounts were generally so much overdrawn as to
show too plainly that they were intended to create a sensation
rather than to set forth the actual truth.

If these writers had, with earnest philanthropic motives,
sought truly authentic information or taken a temporary
sojourn in a slave State where they would have witnessed
personally the working of the system, they could have produced
irrefutable arguments against slavery of a more practical, plain,
and reasonable kind, and which, properly used, could with the
general advancement of modern sentiments have had greater
effect towards producing a steady and gradual reform, culmin-
ating not only in its abolition but also in obtaining a means
whereby the negro might have been provided for either by
colonisation or by being trained in the habits befitting an
industrious freeman, and without being demoralised by a
sudden transition brought about by revolution.

On the other hand those who wrote or spoke in favour of
slavery were equally extravagant in the opposite direction, and
were either prejudiced by personal interest or in endeavouring
to please a party, by meeting fabulous reports and extravagant
arguments by reports as fabulous, and arguments equally
extravagant.

It might be supposed that any person of ordinary observation
and common judgment, residing in a slave State, without
having any connection or interest directly or indirectly with
slavery, and in every way neutral both in interest or opinion,
but having every opportunity of looking on and dispassionately
observing the system, would be likely to give an unbiassed

opinion. There were plenty of such men, and among them men of sound judgment and independent minds, well qualified to give straightforward and unbiassed views on the subject, and it seems strange that so many of them were averse to doing so. The general response to any suggestion of this kind was that the subject had become distasteful and disgusting to all calm-reasoning and moderate-minded men, and had already gone into the hands of extremists on both sides. At that time any production on the subject to be patronised must be extreme on the one side or the other. Any honest and truthful statements or calm and dispassionate views would not have been sufficiently sensational to meet the wishes of the extremists on either side. Men of moderate views had got satiated and disgusted with the subject, and took little interest in the matter, and refused to take the field against opponents with neither of whom any sensible man could wish to have any controversy.

Such was the invariable reply that I have often heard made to any suggestion to the production of any such work.

As one of the disinterested class but without the necessary qualifications, I cannot enter into the merits of this "peculiar institution," as it was then called, and as it then existed, or attempt any criticism of it from a philosophical or sentimental point of view.

I could never see in it the merits of a "Divine institution" for the amelioration and enlightenment of the negro race as claimed for it by those who supported it. Neither can I relate any of the horrible cruelties we read about because I never saw any of them or heard of them except in books or tracts. Nevertheless I do not put this forward as an argument that such things never took place. As for outrages on kindred ties I knew of one case : I happened to see it tried in court. A master had under somewhat exceptional circumstances sold a mother apart from her daughter, the latter having lacked some two months of the prescribed age, which by the law of the State was ten or twelve years (I forget which). For this he was convicted and sentenced to six months' imprisonment and to pay a fine of one thousand dollars ! This took place in 1855.

I have seen plenty of the "institution," however, which has not appeared in books, but which was in my mind sufficient to warrant some attempt being made towards a change as soon as possible in the system of labour and in the abolition of slavery; I will confine myself, however, to describing what impressions I formed from what came under my own observation and from my own simple point of view and its connection with the question which gave rise to the civil war. Slavery was at that time a remnant still existing of customs which prevailed in former ages, now happily a thing of the past, and not likely again to be a question for international or domestic legislation.

I have often heard it questioned—and I believe it is open to question—whether, when the abolition movement sprung up in the North, it arose out of pure sympathy for the negro, or whether it was more of a political move for party purposes.

If it arose from the former motives, their personal regard and affection for the negro were certainly not always strictly in keeping with their professed sentiments.

If from the latter motives, it effected its purpose, though at a fearful cost.

I believe it originated from the former motives, but the true sentiments were confined to a very limited number. The vote of this sect, however, became (like the Irish vote) a bid for political parties, and when the Republican party was originated just sufficient of the principle was cautiously ingrafted into its platform to secure the vote of the abolitionists without endangering the support of the greater body who had no sympathy with abolition.

It was an argument of long standing and strongly maintained, not only in the South, but over the whole of the United States, that the negro race were unfitted for any other position than that of the slave. There were undoubtedly some who expressed themselves otherwise and who were no doubt sincere in their convictions, but I question much whether even at the present day there are not a very large number who look upon the negro at least as an inferior race.

If there is any ground for this opinion I have often thought that it is not so much that the negro is unfitted for any other position than that of a slave, as the undoubted fact that there is not in the whole world any other race that is so fitted for the position as the negro. I believe that to take any other race of the most rude and savage nature and place them under the same bondage even with good care and treatment, they would never thrive, and, if they could not revolt against it, would give way to wretched despondency, pine away, and die. The negro can suit himself to the occasion, thrive under it, be contented and happy, " laugh and grow fat," and, under certain circumstances, show some pretensions to polish and even an attempt at gentlemanly manners. All this, of course, is of a kind.

How different with the American Indian who could not be subdued, and whose wrongs so few have sympathised with. I have sometimes in conversation with the Indians introduced the subject of the negro race and slavery, and the invariable response was—"The Indian has a birthright, which the negro has not. The Indian can die, the negro cannot die."

The Southern master made the whole of the negro his study. He studied his mental and physical nature, his wants and his passions, even to some extent to the humouring of his sentiments. They knew what were his pleasures and tastes, and they strove to turn them to the best account. It was the master's interest that the slaves should increase and thrive. They knew the negroes were possessed of human sentiments. They knew these sentiments must have play, and they endeavoured to cultivate those sentiments to suit the slave's position. They encouraged and cultivated his tastes for amusements, of which they knew them to be fond, songs, music, dancing, balls, and holidays at certain times. All these tended to gratify and smooth their rougher sentiments, occupy their minds, and absorb their thoughts, and leave no room for the intrusion of care or sad reflection.

Other or finer sentiments were no doubt trampled upon, but these were blunted by long usage, and the condition seemed to be accepted as a part of their heritage, and to this state of things their natures had become hardened. The slave was born to the position, he was educated for it, he knew he could not make better of it, and he yielded resignedly to it. The idea of being bought and sold seemed to be a part of his nature, inherited from his earliest origin in Africa, and transmitted with him and to his posterity wherever he might go.

There is certainly not in existence any other race of mankind that could so well have made the best of the unfortunate position, and the way in which they seemed to turn a life of bondage and misery from which they could not extricate themselves, into a life of comparative happiness, showed a certain amount of philosophy of no ordinary kind.

The Southern slaveowners were undoubtedly, of all men who ever had been slaveowners, the most humane, kind, and considerate in the treatment of their slaves, and especially the real old Southern families who had been settled in the South for generations. If there were cases of cruelty or oppression they were generally to be found among those who had come from the North and other places, with a view of enriching themselves in a short time and returning to their native country, and then, perhaps, becoming pillars of some philanthropic society or institution.

But the real old settlers, who had no ambition beyond making their plantation their home, and maintaining a comfortable independence, regarded their slaves as their families and it was a cause of considerable grief to a family if any of their negroes became such bad subjects as to require to be severely punished or sold. These planters and their negroes were born together on the plantation; they had played together in childhood. Surplus sons of the planter might branch off to follow some profession, the others as they grew up fell into their respective positions of master and slave (or negro, as it was more popularly termed). Both were contented, and, like many others, they saw themselves and their position in the light of their own eyes and not as others saw them, and they did not understand why any outsiders should interfere with them.

I certainly believe that the Southern planters in general, and particularly the class I have referred to, did not uphold the institution of slavery out of a cruel and heartless design of enriching themselves. They were, I believe, sincere in the belief, however erroneous that might be, that they were the benefactors of the negro in thus taking charge of and compelling him to labour honestly, and to maintain habits of morality in a class which they considered were unable to take care of themselves, and who would if left to themselves soon give way to indolence, immoral passions, and relapse into barbarity.

With regard to the more speculative class of slaveowners who had more recently settled, most of them were from the Northern States, a good many from New England, the seat of the abolition movement, and I have heard it naïvely insinuated that some of them had come as abolition agents; but thinking that slaveowning would be a better paying business,

they became converted to Southern ideas and thought they
would try a "spec" in the "peculiar institution." Of course
such things were said in joke, though there might be some
slight grounds for the insinuation. Be that as it may they
were not considered the kindest of masters, though in general
by no means harsh or cruel, still the negroes did not like the
idea of being sold to a Yankee master.

As to the question of the negro being an inferior race that
is a question for philosophers. By a long residence in the
British West Indies I had ample means of judging that the
negro as a freeman can be an industrious and faithful labourer
or servant, a thrifty and respectable member of society. But it
is most rigidly necessary that he must be made to understand

First.—That it is the destiny and duty of every man to earn
his bread by honest employment.

Second.—That he is in a country and among society where
this is a necessity and cannot be evaded.

Third.—That he is under a law that will be strictly enforced,
and which impartially executes justice betwen man and man
and between employer and employed.

Let such conditions be fully understood and enforced, and
no man need complain of the average negro as an industrious
man or a member of society.

But let the agitating self-styled friend of humanity stir up
his passions, set before him his great wrongs, his rights as a
freeman, the glorious liberty which he, the agitator, has
obtained for him, and means to defend him against those who
now seek to rob him of his rights; and thus feed his vanity
with a consciousness of his own importance, no ear is more open
to such seductive flattery. He immediately thinks that he is
wronged in having to work at all, and no class of men can so
completely set aside all reason and carry their imaginative
ideas to such an incredible extent.

I am well aware that from this cause chiefly arose all the
evils which followed the emancipation in the British West
Indies when the disgusting indolence, the unreasonable pre-
tension, and the bearding swagger and insolence of the negroes
disgusted the civilised world, took away much sympathy, and
cast a stigma upon the name of the negro race, which tended
to degrade the negro as a freeman, and added force to the
belief that he was fitted only for a slave, and to a great extent
neutralised the generous act of the British people in their gift

of twenty millions to emancipate the slave, by demoralising him at the same time.

Thus his pretended friends were his greatest enemies, and did more injury to the negro race than many years of slavery.

When we consider the excesses which our own working population, with all the advantages of civilisation and education can be led into at the present day by the same kind of agitators, we may well excuse the poor ignorant emancipated negro for listening to such flattery half a century ago.

I am fully aware that the well-known state of matters which followed the emancipation in the British West Indies stood greatly in the way of any movement towards the abolition of slavery in the Southern States; and, with the condition of Jamaica before their eyes, a belief that such a course would be disastrous was held not only by the slaveowners but by the population at large, particularly if no provision was made for the disposal of the emancipated negroes. And this belief was strengthened and resistance to such a measure was still more intensified by the attitude of the New England abolitionists who preached the equality of races and prescribed for the Southern people, politically and socially, perfect equality with the negro—an equality which they themselves did not accord to him in their own State; and in any case, if there was any aversion to contamination, they knew they were themselves beyond the reach of that contamination which they prescribed for others. There was no probability of the migration of the negro to starve in the cold climate of New England while he could revel in luxury in the more genial regions of the South.

The policy of the New England agitator I have often heard exemplified by the general people of the South in this way :—

"Allowing three different spheres of society and morals, numbers one, two, and three. Number one is completely beyond the reach of contamination with number three; nevertheless he is fond of adulation; he desires to ride high on the philanthropic hobby-horse; he conceives the idea of getting the honour of elevating number three by amalgamating him with number two, so that the better position and higher standard of morals so long striven for, worked for, and attained by number two may be taken from the patient and industrious number two and equally divided between him and the profligate and thriftless number three—and all this in order that number one may be adulated as a philanthropist, and thus claim to have been the benefactor of, and obtain the gratitude and praise of number three at the expense of number two."

How far such an exemplification may be applicable to this or other similar movements I will not pretend to say, but I have often heard such arguments brought forward by the non-slaveholding population of the South, with most bitter invectives against the Northern agitators, and I merely mention them because I have never seen them put publicly forward in political arguments or outside of the class who expressed them —a class which up to the time of the civil war seems to have been little known and little represented in the world at large— I mean the non-slaveholding population of the South.

I believe that a large portion of the population of the United States, both North and South, were in favour of abolishing slavery, but the question of disposing of the negroes and the bugbear of placing the emancipated slaves amongst them, with the example of the British West Indies before them, was the stumbling-block in the way.

While under a democratic government such as the United States, colour would most likely be adopted as a material for the manufacture of political capital, and it would be difficult to adopt a mild code of labour laws such as had been adopted in some parts of the British West Indies some years after the emancipation, and particularly in Trinidad, which, under the wise administration of Lord Harris, were strictly enforced, and tended compulsorily to elevate the moral character of the negro, taught him industrious habits, and greatly improved his condition in life.

So great was the fear of vagabondage by the increase of free negroes in the South that there were restrictions placed upon the emancipating of a slave. No master could emancipate his slave without in some way providing for him within the State or sending him out of it, and many slaveowners on dying bequeathed in their wills freedom to all or certain of their slaves on condition that they emigrated to certain specified countries. Thus, a number of years ago, a Mr. Stephen Henderson, a native of Scotland, died in New Orleans, making a provision in his will that his slaves should be set free and sent to Liberia.

From some dispute about the interpretation of the will, this case was not decided until some years after his death, by which time the slaves had been sold to other masters under the con-

ditions of the will still pending. When the decision was
finally given by the supreme court, it was to the effect that the
slaves should be set free on condition that they would emigrate
to Liberia. This was immediately made known to the slaves ;
but they did not care to avail themselves of it. I knew several
of the slaves. They seemed to have been the subject of good
treatment and were intelligent. They often talked to me on
the matter of their old master's will. Unconditional freedom
would have been very acceptable to them, but before they
would go all the way to Africa they preferred to remain with
their present masters.

There was said to have been many peculiar business transactions between Northern men, who posed as abolitionists and
philanthropists, and Southern slaveowners, which, if fully
enquired into, might have put a very different face on some of
the exciting tales put before the world in the gushing language
of fanatics. Of these I can give no authentic account, but
merely refer to them as current topics among the people
generally of the South, and, whether true or not, tended
greatly to disgust the non-slaveholding population and to
alienate them from the abolitionists of the North.

CHAPTER II.

Now as regards the connection of slavery with the question which gave rise to the civil war in America, I doubt much whether this has ever been regarded in its actual and true light.

If we are to accept the theory which some have presumptuously sought to advance that the South was fighting to maintain the institution of slavery, while the North was fighting to abolish it, it would be reasonable to suppose that the institution must have been very generally popular in the South and of universal benefit to all classes.

That this was not the case it is easy to show, for it was but a small minority of the people who derived any benefit directly or indirectly from the institution of slavery.

But a still more striking feature is, that it appeared to be maintained by a system which seemed strangely anomalous in a country and among a people whose chief boast was their freedom of speech and sentiment, while one word against this cherished institution would subject the utterer to the grossest maltreatment, banishment, or perhaps death. These retaliations, if not inflicted, were at least tolerated and endorsed by men whose interests were in no way benefited, but rather injured by slavery, and who were at the same time of sufficient number to have had it abolished within the State.

This state of things I have heard most justly and strongly commented upon, but never sufficiently accounted for. I found it to have originated from the following cause : While freedom of speech and sentiment was the acknowledged law of the land, the abuse of this privilege, which has sometimes been curtailed in other countries by an edict from the sovereign, could not in democratic America be suppressed except by the usual resources of a popular movement. From this popular movement arose the nefarious system of retaliation so justly condemned.

There is in all countries that pest of society, the unprincipled agitator, who, possessing some " gift of the gab," contrives to prey upon the credulity of the ignorant, and, to accomplish his own purpose, stirs up strife and discontentment among the industrial classes, and to these demagogues the ignorant negroes of the South offered a tempting field ; and had they been allowed to exercise their unscrupulous designs among the slaves, the consequences might have been serious ; and as by the statute nothing could be done to suppress the " freedom of speech," the people had no other way to prevent disturbance or insurrection than to have recourse to a system of popular repression, and to inflict summary punishment on the offenders.

Unfortunately the matter did not end here. These agitators when they saw before them what they dreaded most of all, the terrors of Lynch law, they as quickly turned round and became the champions and guardians of slavery, became loudest in their denunciations of the abolitionists, and with the view of obtaining the support and patronage of the slaveholders, were always ready to take an active part in inflicting punishment on anyone whom they could accuse of uttering an expression against the interests of the institution of slavery. Hence arose that terrorising system which became the curse of every community where slavery existed.

Many arguments had been raised against slavery beyond the limits of the States where it prevailed. Many books had been written condemnatory of it and detailing its horrors, but unfortunately most of these were absurdly exaggerated, and being more sentimental than accurate they tended rather to strengthen and maintain the evil than to pave the way for its abolition by those who had, or ought to have had, the immediate power to deal with it. These, I may say, were the population in the States where it existed.

The institution of slavery was recognised and provided for in the original constitution of the United States, and on the principle of State sovereignty had only been and could only be dealt with by the legislature of the State in which it existed; the Federal Congress had no power to deal with it or legislate upon it without first amending the constitution of the United States. This they could not do without a majority of two-thirds of both Houses, and this majority they had never been able to obtain.

The total number of States in the Union at the out-break of the war was thirty-three, and the total population about thirty-five million. The total number of States in which slavery was recognised and lawful, was fifteen. In one of these—Delaware—slavery was very little practised, and was gradually dying out. In three other States—Maryland, Kentucky, and Missouri—it was gradually being done away with, although they still maintained and upheld the principle. It may thus be said that only in eleven States was slavery in full power. These States had a population of about nine millions. Within these eleven States there was a total of a little over two hundred thousand of the population who owned slaves, and these included a large number who were not citizens, and who had no voting powers, such as females and unnaturalised foreigners of whom there were a considerable number. Though we may make every allowance for their families and adherents, and all others who might derive benefit, or were directly or indirectly interested in the "institution," there was still a large majority whose interests were in no way promoted but rather prejudiced by it. These latter were also largely composed of single men without families and without property, but who possessed the voting power, and the fighting power, if necessary.

How in the face of this could an institution so prejudicial to so great a majority of the population, and so distasteful to many, not only be so long maintained, but that to preserve it the people should withdraw from a union they had always cherished with an almost sacred reverence, and involve themselves in a desperate war, in which they knew the chances against them were as three to one, would puzzle many to answer, and I have never heard anyone give what seemed to me a proper explanation of it.

Slavery was detrimental to the interests of the small farmers and settlers, because in raising their cotton by free labour they had to compete against the wealthy slaveowner with his slave-grown produce. It was detrimental to the interests of the labouring classes, because they had at all times to submit to the employers' terms, otherwise their places would be immediately filled by hired slaves.

The institution was detrimental to the interests of the various grades of mechanics and artisans, insomuch that most determined efforts were often made by slaveowners to have the more intelligent negroes taught trades, which greatly enhanced their value, even though they should be but indifferent workmen.   It was also a common practice with master tradesmen to purchase likely negro lads, teach them trades, and so make them (the masters) more independent of free workmen, while planters, having a great desire to be independent of white or free skilled labour, would purchase a slave-mechanic, paying for him from three to four times the price of an ordinary hand.   Thus a master mechanic might purchase a slave for 800 or 1000 dollars, keep him four or five years, teach him his trade, have his work all that time, and then sell him for three or four thousand dollars.

This was particularly the case with such trades as coopers, carpenters and bricklayers, and led to frequent disputes between master tradesmen and their workmen.   Combination among workmen was not at this time very far extended but was increasing, and some of the newspapers were bold enough to cautiously approach the subject and to throw out mild words of warning.   In some of the larger foundries and engineering works a rule had been established that no slave should be employed in any capacity, and, in others, in no other capacity than that of a labourer.

The relation between the planter or wealthy slaveowner and the artisan was somewhat sensitive.   The slaveowner had no high regard for the artisan and would have been very glad if he could have done without him.   As that could not be, and the artisan class could be a powerful factor in the control of public affairs, it behoved the slaveowner to treat the artisan with all the deference and respect he could afford.

It might not be out of place, and perhaps not altogether uninteresting, for me to relate an incident and conversation in which I took part, as illustrative of the kind of feeling which existed between the mechanical or artisan class and the wealthy planter and slaveowner, and the views of the latter on and their objections to emancipation.

The following incident and conversation took place in 1859 : —Mr. C. was a wealthy sugar-planter; his estate and sugar manufacturing works were extensive ; he had superior vacuo apparatus for the manufacture of a high quality of sugar ; his large amount of machinery entailed upon him the necessity of employing skilled engineers, with whom he seemed to have had frequent controversies.   There would no doubt be faults on both sides, but Mr. C. had the name of being somewhat proud and arrogant, and not very popular among the artisan class, whilst he, perhaps not without some reason, had conceived a hearty hatred for all classes of mechanics in general. He at last, however, as he imagined, got over his troubles and was now happily independent within himself. He had been able to purchase, at an enormous price, a slave who was not only educated, but a thoroughly learned engineer, and a perfect expert in that class of machinery. Mr. C. was now jubilant, because he was at last independent of these professionals who had given him so much annoyance ; and the subject of a good deal of chaff and merriment amongst that class was of Mr. C. and his " scienced nigger."

Unfortunately, however, in the very middle of. the sugar-making season, Mr. C.'s apparatus got out of order, and in such a way that tons of sugar were being lost by escaping into the engine pond, and the cause of the disarrangement could not be discovered. Mr. C. and his engineer tried hard to find out the defect, but without success. As the loss was enormous, Mr. C. was in an awkward position. He disdained to apply to the regular practising engineers, who, he now feared, would turn the laugh against him. Eventually, he came to the senior partner of our firm, and consulted him as to getting an expert to try and find out and rectify the defect. I was immediately sent for as possessing some knowledge that way. I was ready to go at once, but having heard so much of the man, I stipulated upon a proper understanding before I went, which was that if I discovered the defect and rectified it, he should pay me a hundred dollars. If I failed to discover the defect and rectify it, I should charge nothing ; this was agreed to.

From my experience in such things, and from the description he gave, I had a very good idea of what would be the matter, having seen and rectified several similar cases before. On my arriving on the plantation, I found it to be, as I expected, a very trifling thing, which could be rectified in a few minutes, but away in a hidden part of the apparatus. I took care that no one should see what was wrong or what I rectified, and having ordered them to turn on steam and start the apparatus, everything was all right and going well within half-an-hour.

In the meantime Mr. C., who had been out of sight for some time, came up. When he saw everything going on well he looked surprised, but made no remark. He examined and tested again and again the discharge water to see that it was free from sugar.

"Is all right now?" he asked me. I nodded assent. He walked nervously back and forward for some time with a mingled expression of satisfaction and disappointment, while, I must confess, I stood with an ill-concealed look of triumph and suppressed merriment which no doubt slightly irritated him. Having examined everything carefully and satisfied himself that all was now right, he came up to me and handing me a roll of bank notes, said in a gruff tone, " Count and see if that is right." Having counted and found the hundred dollars all right, I asked if he wanted a receipt for it. " No," said he in the same tone, " I always trust to a man's honour."

" You are very prompt in your payment, Mr. C.," said I.

" Yes, Mr. W.," said he, in a more deliberate tone, " because when I make a bad bargain I always wish to get done with it as soon as possible." I saw from this that he was inclined for an argument.

" And do you consider," said I, " that the bargain you made with me to-day is a bad bargain ? "

" Well, if to pay a man a hundred dollars for half-an-hour's work is not a bad bargain I don't know what is."

" Oh very well," said I laughing, " I will give you back your hundred dollars and put your apparatus as it was, and you can send your sugar into the engine pond as before."

" Oh no, stop there," said he, " that is where you take the advantage. It is the same story with all you mechanical men ; that is where I say you are unreasonable."

" Oh now, Mr. C.," said I, " you wish to bring up that old vexed question between planters and mechanics, and I don't wish to enter into it ; so if you will order them to bring out my horse I will start for home."

" I shall order them to do nothing of the kind," said he ; " you shall come over first and take your dinner, and then after that you can go where you please."

" Is your dinner worth eating ? " said I.

" Well, it is just what I have for myself ; we hard-working men in the country can't afford to live as high as you gentlemen mechanics do in the city."

" Mr. W.," said he in a more serious tone as we walked towards the house ; " I know that I don't get a very good name among the artisan class, and particularly since I bought this man to take charge of my machinery. But you have no idea of the trouble I have had with workmen, and I know that all white mechanics have an ill feeling against planters who employ slave mechanics. I have no doubt you must be well aware of that feeling; but do you not think a man has a right to protect himself?"

"Oh for myself or for our firm," replied I, laughing, "it is all the better for us; we get the greatest part of our work from plantations where slave mechanics are employed, as it is there where the greatest breakage and damage to machinery takes place."

"But I mean," said he, "the working mechanics who are employed on the plantations."

"Oh I know," said I, "that such a feeling does exist, not so much against the planters as against the master mechanics in the cities and other places. That feeling is not very general yet, but it is likely to increase, as I see the newspapers have taken it up. No slave mechanics are allowed in our works."

"But what can they do? they can't help themselves; if the artisans can't find employment here and are not satisfied they will go elsewhere,—everything will find its level."

"That," said I, "would be applicable in ordinary cases or in a free State. But you must bear in mind that mechanics and artisans of different kinds are increasing and getting to be a powerful factor in the government of the State, and that your 'peculiar institution' is tolerated and supported by a large body of men who derive little or no benefit from it, and I should say it would be bad policy for slaveowners to make the 'institution' obnoxious to that class."

Mr. C. looked steadily at me for a moment as if he would read me through.

"Mr. W.," said he, "I understand you were some time in the British West Indies?"

I replied in the affirmative.

"And you have seen the condition into which these fine Islands have been brought by emancipation, and would you, or any man in his senses, desire to see these States thrown into the same state of ruin? Would that benefit the artisan class or any class? Where would your trade be then?"

I admitted it would be disastrous, and that the question was a serious one, and that the subject should be handled with the greatest caution. I admitted having seen the disastrous effects produced by the sudden emancipation in the British West Indies; "but this," I said, "was not so much caused by emancipation as by the unwisdom of the policy which accompanied it and followed it."

"Why, how do you mean?"

"I mean," said I, "that I think the negro might have been emancipated without being puffed up and made to believe that he was a god, and having his mind poisoned against his former masters and against anything like living by honest labour."

"You don't mean to say that the British Government did that?"

"No, but agitators were allowed to do it, and that brought on the ruin of both the negro and the planter."

"We are not much troubled with agitators here," said he, "they have made attempts, but we made short work of them; it got us a bad name, but it had to be done."

"I have often heard it condemned," said I, "but I believe that if something of the kind had been done with the agitators after the emancipation in the British West Indies, we would have heard less of fine colonies ruined, and you would not now have been so bitter against any idea of emancipation in these States."

"Things might not have been so bad," said he, "but they could never do much good; white labourers could not stand the climate, and a negro can never be made to work except as a slave."

"Oh, I beg your pardon," said I; "some parts of the West Indies have quite recovered. Would you be surprised to learn that I have seen in the British West Indies, fifteen years after the emancipation, a planter getting as good a day's work from a negro for forty cents as you get within ten hours out of any one of your slaves; and a task of field work for thirty cents equal to at least two-thirds of what you get from one of your slaves in the longest day; of course in addition to this they have a house and a piece of ground."

"But," said he, "the planters can't depend on them; they don't work steady."

"Oh yes, they are under compulsion; in the crop season they seldom lose a day. At other times of the year there are days and parts of days allowed by agreement for them to work their piece of ground."

"You astonish me. When, where, and how was that system carried out?"

"In the island of Trinidad, some ten or twelve years after

the emancipation, a law was enacted by the colonial legislature called 'The Master and Servants Act,' by which all
labourers—unless a special agreement to the contrary was
made—were deemed to work under a contract which could
not be broken or terminated by either party, without fourteen
days' notice being given, and any labourer absenting himself
from his work without a just and reasonable cause, or without
giving the fourteen days' notice, was subject to a fine of
twenty-five dollars or forty days' imprisonment, as a magistrate
might inflict."

"But why? What is that but slavery?"

"Oh no; it was just a penalty for breach of contract. The
masters were subject to the same penalty if they broke the
contract; but they knew the law, and did not break it. When
the negro got to know the law, and knew that it would be
enforced, he did not break it either. But then the words
'absenting himself from his work' embraced a good deal. I
have known a negro coming to his work twenty minutes late,
and then being insolent to the overseer when remonstrated
with, taken before a magistrate and punished by a fine of ten
dollars or twenty days' imprisonment."

"Well, that is surely rigid?"

"Yes; but it came within the Act, as absenting himself
from his work without a just and reasonable cause. This had
to be proved; but no employer would prosecute, and no
magistrate would convict for such an offence as this unless it
was found to be an aggravated case and against a very bad
subject."

"How did this law work?" asked Mr. C., becoming deeply
interested.

"It worked remarkably well. It enabled the employer to
carry on his work steadily without being subject to having his
whole works stopped or paralyzed by the whim of one or two
refractory malcontents to shew their importance. On the
other hand it protected the labourer from being made the
convenience of the planter or other employer. It insured him
steady employment and prompt payment, and though he might
grumble a little when the work was before him, he rejoiced all
the more when the pay day came. It was not the interest of
the employer to be too rigid. If a man wanted to be away
at any time he had only to ask leave,—it was seldom refused.
If a labourer was dissatisfied with his employer, he gave four-

teen days' notice and left. If an employer found that he had
a bad character among his people, he gave him fourteen days'
notice to leave. It had the effect of lifting the negro from
his demoralised condition: it gave him some idea of regularity,
law, and order. It stopped their wandering about from place
to place, caused them to settle on one estate, where they got
their house and ground. The wages now earned by them
were more than doubled, and as they were steadily settled, the
products of their grounds were realised; and as they were
temperate and did not spend their money in drink, a marked
difference took place in their dress and persons. They soon
had Sunday clothes and went to church. A marked improvement took place in their cottages. New and better articles of
furniture, and other personal and family comforts were added.
In fact, within four or five years after the passing of the
Act, many of them had saved sufficient to own considerable
property."

"But where were your agitators now?" said Mr. C.

"These agitating 'friends of humanity' had done all they
could do. They had preached the negro into degradation, vice,
and misery. They had got all out of them they could get, and
they sneaked out of sight. A wise governor and legislator
then determined by the firm hand of the law to save the colony
and the ignorant part of the population from the wreck and
degradation into which these agitators had thrown them."

"But," said Mr. C., "that act could never have been passed
if the legislature had been elected by the popular vote of the
whole people the same as with us."

"Most certainly it could not if the franchise extended to
the negroes, who would be led by agitators."

"Well, that," said Mr. C., "is just where our difficulty lies.
I believe every planter and slaveowner in the United States,
if he was promised compensation like the West Indian planters,
and a code of labour laws such as you describe, would advocate
emancipation at once. But that is impossible. Under our
system of popular government, agitators would then have free
run; they would work a greater wreck than even in the West
Indies; they would control the legislature, and a negro anarchy
of the worst kind would be the result."

Dinner was now over, we had smoked our cigars in the
verandah, and we both rose to go to our respective businesses.
Mr. C. had forgotten all about his bad bargain, and I felt

pleased that I had had another opportunity of laying before an American planter the system of labour laws as adopted and practised in Trinidad, although only as before to meet with the same objection, and to have the same obstacle pointed out.

And I could not help reflecting how often it happened that wise and temperate movements were so frequently debarred by the intemperate ravings of party demagogues who, while imagining or pretending to advocate some great reform or wise measure, managed by shameless effrontery to gain the ascendancy and supplant better counsels, and by their mad extremes or fanatical partisanism frustrated wise courses of legislation.

It has been set forth that books and pamphlets condemnatory of slavery and descriptive of its horrors were forbidden in the South. I do not know that there was any statutory law or penalty prohibiting their circulation, or, if there was, it was not strictly carried out. Plenty of such literature was to be seen, although it was mostly held up to scoff and ridicule. Indeed many of these publications were so far from the facts, and so silly, sensational, and absurd, that I believe the circulation of them was encouraged rather than suppressed by the votaries of slavery.

It seems to be a marked characteristic of all Americans to have what may be called a patriotic veneration for their country, amounting in many to enthusiasm. This was not only a love for the United States far above all other nations, but also an ardent love for their own geographical location, and their State, its society, its government and institutions. This was particularly marked among all the natives of the South of whatever class, and no matter how distasteful or oppressive any of their own laws or institutions might be upon themselves, or however desirous they might be to have them altered or repealed, they were exceedingly jealous of any encroachment by outsiders, and would brook no interference from the Northern States. This inherent feeling was very strong among the small farmers and settlers in the South, and when any of these sensational works were read by them they would regard them as an insult to their beloved South, and would probably throw them in the fire, with the exclamation that they, themselves, were no friends of slavery, and did not sympathise with the slaveowners; but would prefer them a thousand times to the lying hypocrites who wrote such fables.

This tended to embitter them against all abolition sentiments, and made the very name of an abolitionist hateful and disgusting to the people.

Nevertheless, they had no great sympathy with the overbearing manner of the slaveowner, and the terrorising system of slavery—not out of any sympathy for the slave; for, although they had no great hatred for the negro, yet they never regarded him as the equal of the white man, and considered that he was never intended or destined for any other purpose than that of a slave, and they dreaded most of all the bearding insolence of the negro if he should be set free amongst them. But they complained that legislation should be almost exclusively for the benefit of the slaveholding interest and restraint put upon the freedom of speech. These people did not venture to speak their sentiments openly in the face of the political mob, but in quiet conversations with those whom they thought they might trust they would speak their minds pretty freely on what they regarded as laws existing entirely for the benefit of the wealthy slaveowner, and to the detriment of the poorer non-slaveholder.

I found there, as I have found it elsewhere, that there is a very great difference between public opinion, or rather the pretended display of public opinion, extorted or carried by a *coup de main* from a body of men collectively at a public meeting or demonstration and the private opinion given by each individually in the quiet of his own fireside.

Political tricksters will, of course, pretend to scout this idea and say how should it be so; but no one. knows better than themselves that it is so, and they as well know how to pack a meeting, and arrange matters so as to make the apparent display of public sentiment show in the manner they wish.

Meanwhile, the mechanical or artisan class were getting bolder and less reserved in expressing their sentiments as they increased in numbers, as towns increased in size, and as the country became more thickly populated. A year or two before the war, I have heard it remarked, that sentiments were now spoken openly which a few years before would have made their authors liable to a ride on a rail or a coat of tar and feathers.

There is no question that a feeling of aversion to slavery was fast spreading amongst a numerous and powerful class in the South previous to the war. Unfortunately those foolish sensational books, and the gross intemperate ravings and offensive epithets of Northern fanatics did much to check that feeling, and tended to create antagonistic sentiments between the North and the non-slaveholding population of the South. I am quite certain that had not this ill feeling been stirred up between North and South slavery would within a very few years have been confined to very narrow limits, and would soon have been abolished altogether.

But reforms of any kind must emanate from the people of the State, and through the State Legislature. To such an extent had the strife and ill feeling been stirred up between the North and South by the untruthful and slanderous representations of the fanatics of the North, and the swaggering bullyism of the fire-eaters of the South, that any pressure brought to bear either by the Federal Government at Washington or by any party in the North would have been repudiated and rejected with scorn and contempt even by the strongest opponent of slavery in the South.

I may here state with some authority that the greater part of the men of the Southern army, who really fought the battles of the South, did not fight to maintain slavery, and the question of slavery was never before their eyes. So far as my observations went, slavery was only a minor point of little or no interest to a large portion of the population, and could never of itself have led to secession and war. Any interference in that or any other law of the State which did not conflict with the Federal Constitution involved a principle of much greater importance, almost unanimously cherished by the Southern people, which was, the sovereign rights of individual States to make and maintain their own laws and institutions, and it was upon this principle alone that slaveholders and politicians got the large body of the people to follow them.

But even with this powerful handle, it would have been difficult, and I believe almost impossible, to have brought about a dissolution of the Union by honest means.

To show how public sentiment was swayed or overruled and the people were led into this war, it may be necessary for me to say a few words on politics as they were at that time, and show how State legislation was conducted, and how secession was effected.

CHAPTER III.

THE interest taken in politics by the American people is well known, and requires no description from me; but I have often imagined that while the individual plumes himself in being a ruler, the individual has often, after all, very little control in the management of public affairs.

The boast of the American people is their freedom of government, where freedom of speech and sentiment and a voice in the legislation of their country is the acknowledged birthright of all. Their condemnation of despotic governments, where they allege a potentate holds the people in subjection by means of a standing army, is often freely expressed. But I have often wondered whether sometimes the American people, particularly in the South at that time, were not to a considerable extent held in subjection by a standing army, and that army of a most unscrupulous, depraved, and corrupt nature—I mean the army of professional politicians and their immediate followers, who called themselves "the people," composed chiefly of professional gamblers, café loafers, supported by street rowdies and others of a similar class who controlled public affairs. These assumed the leaderships of the different political parties, formed caucuses, nominated candidates, and controlled elections.

These political instruments always took care to strengthen their position by their loud plaudits of some popular statesman or leader who might for the time being hold sway over the minds of a large body of the people, and whom they sought to deify, and to whose principles they professed most rigidly to adhere; and though it was necessary for their occupation that there should be two or more parties divided upon minor points, those of the South were of course all united in the one Southern doctrine that the great fundamental principles of human rights and human liberties were based upon the Southern institution of slavery. One of their chief objects was to agitate, engender, and keep up an antagonistic feeling against the abolitionists of the North. In this they were strongly supported by the slaveholding planters and other pro-slavery fire-eaters.

In Louisiana, as in many other States, the incumbent of every public office in the State, from the governor to the village constable, was the issue of an election, and, as the terms of holding offices were limited, elections were of frequent occurrence.

These public offices did not seem to be regarded so much as actual requirements or the duties attached to them of so much importance for the public good as they were regarded as gifts in the hands of the people to be bestowed on such as they deemed deserving of them or whom they delighted to honour and reward. The capabilities of the candidate for the duties of the office were seldom taken into consideration. The only consideration was what claims the candidate might have, or be supposed to have, for services rendered to the State or to his party. I have known men holding high positions who could not read or write intelligibly. Each successful candidate had in his turn the appointment of his clerks and subordinates, whose claims were of course in proportion to the assistance they might have given in promoting his election.

There were, no doubt, occasional instances where some really deserving person, perhaps some industrious man with a large family, who, having been disabled or otherwise become unfit to support himself and family, might get elected to some minor office. Such instances were generally in country districts, where the political army did not thrive so well, or, if otherwise, it was more a stroke of policy intended to cover, and did cover, a multitude of sins.

There were what were called the fat offices in which the pickings were good. To these the incumbents were elected, but for short periods, and in which it was supposed that they and their followers were to make hay while the sun shone, and then come out and give some one else a chance, an opportunity of which they seldom failed to avail themselves.

Legislative offices were not so directly remunerative, the pay of a member of the State Legislature being eight dollars per day for the time the session lasted, which seldom exceeded sixty days each year, and each member had his obligations to fulfil to his followers.

It was generally considered an open secret that legislators

swayed legislation pretty much to suit the interests of themselves and their immediate followers. To effect this they had
many facilities.

A great source of wealth in the United States and also in
the individual States was the enormous revenue derived from
the sale of public lands.

These lands were originally the property of the United
States, but large grants of land were made from the Federal
Government to the Government of each separate State for the
purpose of forming a fund to promote various purposes, one
being public education, but the most important was internal
improvements. These comprised the making of roads, bridges,
canals, railroads, river embankments, draining of swamp lands,
etc., within the State.

The regulations of applying these funds and carrying out
these works being of course under control and sanction of the
State Legislature, some were carried out under the direction
of the State officers and engineers. But in the case of railways
got up by a company, I think the way in Louisiana at that
time was for the promoters to apply to the State Legislature
for a bill and an appropriation to carry out the enterprise. If
the bill was passed, a grant of money was voted out of the
internal improvement fund towards carrying out the enterprise,
and then the State became a shareholder in the railway to the
amount of the grant so voted.

When any of these improvements were carried out in
districts of rich productive lands hitherto unsettled and not
bought up, the attention of land purchasers and speculators
was quickly drawn to it, and the land was quickly entered and
rapidly increased in value.

The directing of these internal improvements, the passing of
bills for and voting of grants to enterprises, formed a considerable part of the State legislation.

A bill with the usual grant of money might be applied for
to construct a railway through a large tract of public land
hitherto unsettled. The promoters might be gentlemen who
had some interest in land speculation as well as railway
enterprise, and it required a little care and management to
pilot the bill through the House.

The bill was entrusted to the care of one or more influential
members who might be well up in that class of business, and
who in their turn became a little interested in its success.

They adroitly canvassed their fellow-members for their votes and influence. As it involved a grant of public money, the latter of course declined, asserting that they saw no reason why they should vote for the bill. "But, my dear sir, I can show you fifty *reasons* why you should vote for the bill." "I fear it will take a hundred *reasons* to convince me." A hundred, or as many *reasons* as might be agreed upon would be guaranteed, a sufficient number of votes would be obtained, and the bill would be passed.

Simultaneous with the passing of the act, large tracts of the best land in the vicinity of the proposed railway, amounting perhaps to several hundred thousand acres, would be applied for by those in the combination. This application did not amount to absolute entry or purchase of the land, and left sufficient opportunity for the applicant to resile from the purchase within a certain time. It gave merely a prior claim preliminary to entry, and the application was registered, but the applicant was not called upon to implement the entry till the books, which were generally about six months behind, were brought up to the date of the registration. The applicant was then called upon to complete the entry, and pay for the land at the present Government price. If he failed in that, he forfeited his prior claim, and the right to entry of the land passed to the next registered applicant. The Government price was at that time about one dollar per acre, paid on entering the land.

In the meantime the combination had made application and secured the prior claim on the land, and could dispose of it. As soon as the bill was passed, smaller speculators were ready to buy up the land in large tracts at from two to five dollars per acre, and if the enterprise had the appearance of being speedily carried out and the location good, there was generally a rush of settlers seeking to purchase, and the price of the land would be run up to ten or fifteen dollars per acre before the original combination were called upon to pay the one dollar per acre of entry-money.

Thus enormous sums were made off such enterprises by these combinations, which handsomely recouped all expenses they had been put to in furnishing "*reasons*" to legislators to induce them to vote for the bill. While this could not be called altogether honest procedure, the result of the whole, if successful, wrought out considerable good in the main—in a railway constructed, a valuable communication established, a large tract of country opened up, cleared, and settled, the products of the State increased, a great many benefited, and no one injured, at the expense of a wild tract of waste land which had hitherto lain dormant, unknown, and profitless.

Such legislative proceedings were not much inquired into or criticised, for, whilst it was this kind of legislation that was most profitable to the legislators, it was also the kind of legislation that was most profitable and useful to the public.

A considerable portion of the legislative body consisted of lawyers. These had for their main object to provide food for their fraternity.

This they contrived to do by constantly amending acts, inserting new clauses in acts, and passing new acts without repealing the old ones, and as there was a new legislature every two years, much confusion was the result; every act seemed to be counteracted by another act, no man could tell what was the law, and every lawyer could find a law to suit his notion and neither counsel nor judge could unravel the tangled web.

I have heard it said that such places as Louisiana, Arkansas, and Texas, were lawless places. No term could be more inappropriate or absurd. They were the very reverse of lawless, they had too much law. They were completely surfeited by overdoses of legislation. If a law existed to hang a man for murder, it seemed quite easy to find another which would get him off. Hence the necessity of having sometimes to resort to Lynch law, which was perhaps the only law that some of the most hardened ruffians stood in dread of. Another reason why law was so often set aside was because it was beyond the means of most men. The swarms of lawyers fostered by the lawyer-legislators so hedged round about and levied toll at the gate of the temple of justice as to make it unapproachable.

The carrying of weapons and the frequent resort to the bowie knife or revolver has been much commented upon, but I believe much of the practice of carrying arms arose from the impossibility of obtaining justice or redress by legal means. It no doubt seemed to many at that time, as it may seem to many at the present time, somewhat unreasonable that the temple of justice, established and supported by the nation to maintain order and equity between man and man, to which men should have recourse for the peaceful settlement of

D

unavoidable disputes, should have become a thing to be shunned and abhorred as uncertain in its issues and certain only in its exorbitant expenses and exactions upon both just and unjust.

It seemed in civil actions an absurd thing that a dispute about 100 dollars could not be settled without an expenditure of 300 dollars, and then the issue often left open to question.

In criminal cases it unfortunately happened that the rowdy element had too often a sway over the judge's election, and his decision was oftener influenced by the so-called popular feeling than by the enforcement of the law.

This state of things tended to bring law, or rather the administration of law, into contempt, and men were in a manner compelled to take law into their own hands. This, however, like other remedies, can be carried to excess.

To account for this state of matters it may be necessary to take a glance at the class who ruled the political system and how they managed their business.

These professional politicians, though nominally of some profession or business, seldom attended to anything but politics, unless it might be gambling, which was recognised among themselves as a legitimate and honourable profession. Many of them were office-holders, ex-office-holders, or office-seekers. The leaders among them were to outward appearance by no means of a depraved or degraded class. They were well dressed, affable in their manner, and somewhat courteous. They frequented largely the cafés, billiard rooms, or other public places. They were ever ready to shake hands and treat about election times, or introduce a country rustic or a working mechanic to his excellency the governor or to an honourable member of the legislature or other high functionary, and, as they were always strong canvassers for the candidate of their party, they strove to be bland and agreeable.

Their power in the political world lay not so much in their influence over elections as in their entire control in the nomination of candidates, which they managed something after this fashion :—On the time approaching for an election the matter was talked over among themselves, each " party " respectively, as to whose turn it was to share the spoils.

Some little regard is given to outward appearance, oratorical powers, notoriety, and political standing of the candidate, and how he would be likely to take. Thus : D. might have the highest claim, but he might lack oratorical powers, or his character might be too notorious to bring him forward as a candidate, and he might be defeated by the candidate of the rival party. Therefore, C. is agreed upon, with the understanding that if elected he will share the emoluments with D., who will assist him in his duties and in carrying out his arrangements. In like manner F., H., and J. are agreed upon for the other different offices.

A meeting must now be called to give effect to this, and the arrangements are made. Ten, twenty, or as many of themselves as possible will be forward early and take their seats close to the speaker's chair; fifty or sixty or more of their followers of the rougher or lower classes will be drummed up and got ready for the occasion. These will be placed where they can show or act to the best advantage, and the order of business is arranged. One or two members of the press, also of the clique and well paid for it, will be present and report as directed.

Next is seen posters on the street corners and fences announcing that a meeting of all true Democrats will be held in the court-house on   night at   P.M. for the purpose of nominating candidates for the offices of, etc. These posters, dated a week previous, will be posted perhaps a few hours before the hour appointed for the meeting.

The meeting takes place, few people know anything about it, and make little inquiry about it; it is filled up as arranged. Brown moves that Jones takes the chair. Jones is therefore unanimously appointed chairman, he appoints Smith secretary. C.'s nomination is now moved by Brown, seconded by Green, and ayed by the sixty followers. F., H., and J., are nominated, seconded, and ayed in the same way, and the voice of the people has been heard.

No time is lost making speeches at these meetings. The whole thing is over in half-an-hour, and all now flock to the *cafés* to have a drink at the expense of the nominees. Three cheers are given for the candidates—another and another learns the news—another and another drink—and the enthusiasm seems to arise spontaneously.

Next morning the party journals publish in glowing details, in a column headed by large type, " Great Meeting of the Democratic Convention ! Nomination of Candidates !" Then follows an eulogy on each of the candidates, and their high qualifications for the office, as compared to any candidate which has been or may be brought forward by the opposite party.

About the same time, perhaps the same day (as there is no danger of any hostile feeling between the parties) the other party would have their meeting carried through in precisely the same way, and heralded through the streets and cafés, and endorsed by the journals of their party, and from this time till the election the names of the candidates stand at the head of the leading columns of the journals of the respective parties as the nominees of the party convention.

In all of these proceedings the real or actual public had little or no hand or cognisance whatever, until the names appeared in the newspapers, and then they had the glorious privilege of voting for the candidate of which party they preferred.

It must not be for a moment supposed that this corrupt system arose and existed through the ignorance of the masses, or from their lack of interest or indifference. They were a quick, intelligent people, took great interest in politics, seldom neglected to vote at elections, were constant readers of the newspapers, and were often quite alive to the unworthiness of the candidate which they had to vote for. But they were so infatuated with their own national system, which they considered to be superior to anything else in the world, that they could not entertain the idea of any fault or defect, direct or indirect. When this state of things was clearly shown them they would allow there was something wrong, but this they regarded as the fault of the hour, not of the system, which must and would be put all right by and bye, by the people taking the matter into their own hands and putting down these rascals who were controlling nominations and elections, and corrupting politics and legislation. While this impracticable remedy was advocated by every one it was carried out by no one. What was everybody's business was nobody's business, and no one took the initiative. At the same time, what was everybody's property was nobody's property and became the prey of the vilest scum.

Meanwhile none were louder in denouncing this political corruption than the very candidates who had been nominated through its agency. They had now taken the stump in full voice. The candidates of each party against their respective opponents nightly declaimed from platforms in the open air, each avowing themselves to be the representatives of no clique, caucus, or faction, but that of the people—the actual and genuine people, the working, producing class, the backbone and sinew of the nation. They promised, if elected, great reforms, by putting down these hole-and-corner cliques and caucuses that usurped the name of the people. They would put legislation more directly into the hands of the people, and purify the ballot box. This latter phrase had at that time been remembered from earliest recollection by the oldest inhabitant as a parrot cry at elections, and I presume continues down to the present day without much affecting the purity of the box.

These harangues went on almost every night by the candidates or their supporters, and as the weather was fine, people were out walking, and stopped to listen; and as there was no lack of eloquence, and the orators well knew what key to touch, many who had before known and detested them, came away allowing that "there was at least a good deal of truth in what they said."

And so matters went on. People who had work or business to attend to did not interest themselves much in corruption in politics. It did not directly affect them. They felt taxation but little. The country was rich, and teeming with resources, and there was plenty for everybody. The people were fond of politics—liked to talk of them. "Corruption" gave them something to talk about. Elections were an amusement; they liked to attend them, and to talk of the chances of the respective candidates, of the number of votes they would get. Bet on them, odds or even, two, three, or five to one on so and so, just as a man would talk about or bet on a cock-fight or horse-race.

The people were proud of their government—their political system—laws and institutions which they maintained to be the best in the world, and believed this none might gainsay.

These office-holders, let them be what they might, when in office were always exceedingly courteous, civil, and obliging to all, and showed none of that gruff incivility which is too often met with among such functionaries in Great Britain.

But still, looking at the matter in the theoretical light which sets forth that the nation is ruled by the voice and choice of the people, it does seem ludicrous when you come to look at how the matter is carried out in practice.

As all this is more observable to an outsider, I may give as an illustration the substance of a sort of bantering conversation which once took place in my hearing.

Two Scotchmen, both employed or connected with an engineering establishment, whom we shall call Mr. B. and Mr. W. B. had recently become naturalised, and had thus become a citizen of the United States. W. had not been naturalised, and was an alien.

The early breakfast was over, and it was the time of going to work for the day when the following conversation took place :—

W.—So you are not going down to the works to-day, B. ?

B.—(Jocularly) No, sir ; I am to-day going to exercise that great and glorious privilege, the birthright of every American citizen. You see, W., if you had taken my advice and got naturalised like me, you might to-day have been exercising the same privilege.

W.—Some men will be thrown idle and lose their day, and the work will be kept back by your not being there.

B.—Can't help that, duties as a citizen must be attended to.

W.—So much for citizenship. The election to-day is for a town constable for one year, the emoluments about five hundred dollars, while the expense and loss caused by the election to you and me and others will amount to four times that sum.

B.—That is very true, but then it is the principle that I look to.

W.—Principle forsooth ! you have in what you call your great privilege to-day your choice to vote for one of two men, N. or C. ; do you think either of those men is a fit and proper man to fill the office, or would be your choice ?

B.—Certainly not, I allow that neither of these men is a fit or proper man for the office.

W.—Further, do you think if you was to search the town and country through you could find two bigger rascals ?

B.—That may be, but they are the nominees of the party.

W.—Why were they nominated ? Who nominated them ?

B—Oh, that I don't know. The party nominated them. It is the fault of those who so nominated them, but that don't affect the principle.

W.—Why did you not object to their nomination, or had you a voice at all in the nomination ?

B.—I never knew when or how they were nominated. I see what you are driving at. That is an evil, no doubt, but it is the fault of the people that don't attend better to these things.

W.—Then why is it never attended to? I suppose you are satisfied to be between the devil and the deep sea so long as you have the glorious privilege of choosing which you would prefer, but you must vote for the one or the other.

B.—Oh no, don't go so far as that. I don't need to vote for either unless I like.

W.—Well, be thankful for that alternative, it is certainly the best of the three, so I think you should consult your own interest and those of your fellow-workmen and go down to the works, and not be a party to putting either of such men into office, but let them fight dog, fight devil at the election.

B.—Well, to tell you the truth, I would much rather go to work and have nothing to do with it, but I promised H. C. that I would vote for C., and I do not like to break my word.

W.—No, you were bored night and day until you promised, and of course you would get into the black books with your party if you kept away. So much for your liberties and glorious privileges. I thank my stars I am not a citizen.

SECTION II.

THE SECESSION MOVEMENT.

CHAPTER IV.

ON the left bank of the Mississippi river, about 130 miles above New Orleans, is the city of Baton Rouge. This place is finely situated on the first point of high land which meets the eye on ascending the Mississippi. It stands on a pleasant elevation and is (or was at that time) a dry, clean town, and a somewhat pleasant place to live in.

The place was in 1860 the capital or seat of Government of the State of Louisiana. At the lower end of the city was situated the Capitol, or House of Parliament, or State Legislature, a somewhat imposing structure, and presenting a very fine appearance from the river. Here sat the State Legislators. Near to the Capitol, a little further down was another building of nearly the same size and design, and similar appearance from the river, but of a very different nature. It was the deaf and dumb asylum. There was also the State penitentiary and other State institutions. These buildings and a large part of the city were burned and levelled to the ground during the war. At the upper end of the city was one of the principal United States arsenals in the South, and a garrison with barracks for about 1000 men.

In this arsenal large stores of ordnance, small arms, ammunition, and army equipments were manufactured and kept, and the place was garrisoned by a detachment of United States troops, a part of the regular standing army of the United States.

This arsenal was the depot from which all the forts in the gulf States were supplied with munitions of war. The forts on the Indian frontier, the forts at Galveston, and along the coasts of Texas, Louisiana, Mississippi, Alabama, and Florida, were also supplied from this depot. There were several powder magazines, immense piles of shot and shell, about 1000 pieces of heavy ordnance, and about 200,000 stands of small arms, many of the latter no doubt were not of the newest patterns, with large stores of ammunition and cavalry equipage.

A number of men were constantly employed here in the manufacture of gun-carriages and other stores and equipments. It might be said to have been the Woolwich of the South.

This city, though not by any means a large commercial city, was a place of considerable importance, was a great rendezvous of the sugar and cotton planters, and being the seat of Government and the residence of the Governor and other State officials, it was the centre of politics.

It was in this place, after having been for some years engaged in engineering in different parts of the State, that I resided for several years immediately preceding the war, and I had become connected as a junior partner in an engineering establishment in the place. The same company also carried on a sawmilling and wood factory and a coal and steamboat business.

Though not a citizen of the United States, I had, partly for pleasure and partly for policy, been an active member of the town company of rifle volunteers.

In the summer of 1860 everything went well and prosperous in this place. The fluctuations of business were here not much felt. People in general were contented and happy, and the community had been greatly enlivened this summer by the first introduction of a state fair, or exhibition, which proved a great success. Permission to hold the fair within the spacious garrison grounds had been given by the United States officers, who vied with the citizens in their endeavours to encourage and promote the object. Visitors and exhibitors came from all parts of the United States. Many Northern manufacturers exhibited their goods and obtained orders, all tending to revive that friendly trade and communication which canting fanatics and strife manufacturers had done so much to impair. Many of the planters in the neighbourhood gave their slaves a holiday to visit the exhibition, and to see these sable gentry happy for the day, dressed in the height of fashion, meeting with friends from other plantations, gracefully pulling off their gloves to shake hands, or the "gentlemen" raising their hats to "ladies" at an introduction, was certainly a part of the exhibition not the least worth seeing.

Several companies of volunteers from different parts of the

State joined with the United States * troops stationed in the garrison in a grand review, and the several volunteer companies competed for prizes to be awarded to the best drilled companies, the officers of the army being the judges. The company of which I was a member won the second prize, which we carried off amid the loud plaudits of the officers and men of the United States army. We little dreamt at the time of the very different terms on which we were destined to meet ere one short year had passed.

The never-failing theme of politics, which during the excitement of the exhibition had partially been set aside by the population at this place, before the exhibition grounds had been cleared off, was renewed with a vigour as if to make up for lost time, and culminated in the dissolution of the Union, followed by the war and all its disastrous consequences.

To break up and dissever a great Federal Union, the very name of which was and always had been cherished with almost a sacred reverence by a great people, and had been held up by them as the pride of the world, may be regarded as a most striking instance of the instability of public opinion.

This was the more striking in this case when it is remembered that the section which had hitherto been apparently, and I believe sincerely, the most zealous in their desire to maintain the Union should make the first move to disintegrate it.

I well remember the storm of indignation which scarcely a year before passed over the whole South when the first idea of disunion was mooted in Congress—this was by a Northern abolitionist. It was when Mr. N. P. Banks, Speaker in the House of Representatives, at Washington, in a moment of excitement used the expression—" Let the Union slide ! "— " Let Mr. Banks slide," was the echo from nearly every

---

* It may be here explained that the term "United States army " or "United States troops " was always applied to the regular army of the United States to distinguish it from the forces of the individual States. The former was maintained by and under control of the central power at Washington, with the President as Commander-in chief, and was upon the same footing as the regular standing armies of Europe.

The State's troops were composed of militia and volunteers, and were maintained by each individual State, the Governor of the State being Commander-in-chief of the army of the State. The relationship between the governments of the respective States and the United States was often characteristically expressed by applying to the Federal Government the familiar *sobriquet*, taken from the initials U.S., of "Uncle Sam."

journal and man in the South.   Such a treasonable expression
coming from the leader of a party was denounced and regarded
as most damaging to that party, and liberally applied against
them by Southern orators.   Yet, strange to say, before two
years had passed, Mr. Banks was fighting against the South to
keep the Union from "sliding," and the South, which had
denounced Mr. Banks for the expression, was fighting to be
separated from the Union.

I may here observe that at the time Butler seized the specie
and closed up the banks in New Orleans, this same Banks
(then General Banks) was hard pressed by Stonewall Jackson
in Northern Virginia, and was the subject of the following
jeu d'esprit :—

> "While Butler plays his roguish pranks,
> And stops the run of Southern banks,
> Our Stonewall Jackson by his cunning,
> Keeps Northern Banks for ever running."

To fully account for what would seem to be a strange revul-
sion of sentiment, and how that revolution was brought
about and secession accomplished, would be presumption in
an obscure individual entirely outside of political or Government circles.

I can merely attempt to describe to the best of my recollection events as they happened under my own observation and
experience, and which were daily witnessed and commented
upon at the time by myself and others of my acquaintance and
associates, most of whom were better tutored and took more
interest in politics than myself.

To do this it will be necessary to advert to the political
subjects which then agitated the public mind, and give an
outline of the different parties how they originated and existed
in 1860.

The all-absorbing topic at this time was the election of a
President.   This is an election in which the general people
take more interest than any other.   It takes place every fourth
year, and is a national question equally interesting to all parts
of the Union, and may be taken as a test of the public sentiment on the leading political questions of the day.

It is an election which calls forth an enormous amount of
political oratory, and the influence of each party is strained to
the utmost.   Nevertheless, I believe there is less actual corruption either in the nomination or in the voting in this election

than in most other elections. But there seems to me to be a rather singular defect in the system of electing a President. The President is supposed to be elected by the popular vote of the whole nation (South Carolina excepted), every citizen giving his vote singly and individually for the candidate of his choice, which he does by dropping into the ballot-box a billet with the names of the candidates he favours for president and vice-president. The vote is taken in every part of the United States in one day. Notwithstanding this a candidate may be elected against whom by far the largest number of individual votes have been polled.

This does not arise from any corruption in the election, but by the system of carrying out the election by means of what is called the Electoral College.

Each State forms an electoral district, and each State, according to the number of its population, is entitled to a certain number of electors or electoral votes for president. This system, as generally described, would imply that the people only vote for a certain number of electors to whom is entrusted the power of electing a president; but this is not so. Electors are no doubt appointed by each State for their respective candidates, but these electors are merely nominal, and have no power whatever beyond formally presenting the vote of the State in favour of the candidate who has polled the greatest number of individual votes in the State.

The candidate who polls the greatest number of individual votes in a State carries that State with the whole electoral votes of that State, and any candidate to be elected must have a majority of electoral votes over all the other candidates combined should there be more than two. Notwithstanding, a discrepancy may arise in this way :—Take, for instance, the State of New York, allowing it to have, say, 300,000 voters, and is entitled in proportion to 45 electoral votes. Virginia has, say, 100,000 voters, and is entitled in proportion to 15 electoral votes. A. and B. are candidates for president. In the State of New York, when the votes in the ballot-boxes are counted, it is found that A. has polled 160,000 votes and B. has polled 140,000. Thus A. has carried the State and gained 45 electoral votes for president.

In the State of Virginia, when the votes in the ballot boxes are counted, it is found that A. has polled only 15,000 votes and B. 85,000 ; thus it will be seen that in those two States only 175,000 of the citizen voters have voted for A., yet he has obtained 45 electoral votes for president, while 225,000 have voted for B. and he has only 15 electoral votes for president. This, of course, is showing a possibility and an extreme case, and there is no doubt when the whole of the States come to be taken together the chances of the candidates become more equalized. Nevertheless the instance given shows the possibility of a president being elected by a minority, particularly if a political question arises affecting the geographical position, as was the case in 1860.

I understand that Mr. Lincoln, though having a majority of electoral votes over all the other candidates combined, was still very much in the minority by the popular vote. This of course could be easily accounted for, as the South was almost unanimously against him, and in some of the States his name never appeared at all ; while in some of the Northern States which gave him a large electoral vote, he carried the State by a very small majority. He was therefore what was called a minority president.

The long-standing political parties in the United States were the Whig party, which dated from the revolution and war of independence. The Democratic party sprung up shortly after the death of Washington, about the beginning of the present century, and during the administration of Thomas Jefferson, who has been called the father of democracy. It was strengthened some twenty-five years later by Andrew Jackson, and got into the ascendancy, and the Whig party began to go down.

In 1853 another party was started on the ruins of the Whig party, called the "Native American" or "Know-nothing" party. This party was somewhat hostile to foreigners and naturalised citizens, and lasted but a short time.

Another party then sprung up in opposition to the Democratic party, afterwards called the Republican party. This party was composed of different sects, all more or less opposed to slavery. This party in 1856 ran John C. Fremont as a candidate for president against James Buchanan for the Democratic party, and Mr. Filmore for the Native American party, when Mr. Buchanan was elected by a majority over Mr. Fremont and Mr. Filmore combined. One of the professed objects of the Fremont party was said to be the settlement of the negro question by establishing a negro republic in Africa or some other place. Hence it got in the South the name of the " Black Republican party."

In 1860, when Mr. Buchanan's term of office was drawing to a close, the position of parties was somewhat confused and complicated. The Democratic party having been long in power was now regarded by many, both North and South, as having become hopelessly corrupt. The Native American party having made such a poor show at the election of 1856 by carrying only one State (the State of Maryland) was now considered extinct.

The Republican party had considerably increased in the North, but as it was hostile to slavery, it was rigidly suppressed in the South, and as it increased in strength, so increased the hostile feeling between North and South. Dark hints as to the danger of a dissolution of the Union now began to be thrown out.

The alleged corruptness of the Democratic party, and the danger of disunion supposed to arise from the increasing power of the Republican party in the North, was the means of stirring up in 1860 a large portion of the more moderate men of all parties, both North and South, to organise a party whose avowed principles were to uphold the Constitution, the Union, and the enforcement of the laws. The Democrats opposed that party, considering such sentiments quite superfluous.

The Constitution, they considered, was embodied in the principles and platform of the Democratic party. The Union they considered to be in no danger, and they scouted the idea of a disruption. The only union they considered necessary to preserve was the union of the Democratic party. The enforcement of the laws, they considered, was quite sufficiently attended to, at least for their purpose. Probably some of their leaders supposed that if the laws were very rigidly enforced, they might not then have been enjoying that glorious liberty they were so constantly prating about.

There was, no doubt, a few of the leading politicians of each party who entertained a slight idea of this kind.

After holding a convention at Charleston, the Southern parties failed to come to any agreement upon a candidate, and the convention broke up, each determining to act independently, the Democrats nominating as their candidate John C. Breckenridge, who was vice-president during Buchanan's administration, and Mr. Lane as vice-president.

The Constitutional and Union party nominated as their candidate John Bell for president, and Edward Everitt for vice-president.

The Republican party, who held a convention at Chicago, nominated as their candidate Mr. Abraham Lincoln of Illinois.

There was also another candidate, a Mr. Douglas of Illinois, who came forward in the interests of the Northern Democrats, so that there were in all four candidates in the field for president, each party holding forth their respective views, and the political atmosphere was much troubled, a great many of the people not knowing or regarding much the different narrow points set forth by the leaders as questions of vital importance, and the result of the election seemed to depend a good deal upon chance.

Mr. Lincoln was not at that time regarded as an abolitionist or in favour of abolishing slavery within the States where it at the time existed. He was what was called a "Free Soiler," that is, he was against any further extension of slavery, and was for confining it to certain limits south of a certain parallel of latitude, and that it should be prohibited in any of the territories.

This view did not seem unreasonable to moderate men in the South, and I believe was privately acquiesced in by most reasonable men, but it was not the Southern politics of the day. The seeds of discord had been too thickly sown, and the strife and enmity so effectually stirred up between North and South by the canting abolitionists of the North and the bullying fire-eaters of the South, that every word was distrusted, and such doctrine dared not be even talked of in the South.

Mr. Lincoln's nomination, his election, and subsequent popularity I consider arose more from a train of circumstances than from any high qualification as a statesman. Some of these circumstances had a smack of the humorous or comical, which is a most powerful factor in American politics and elections. He was facetious in conversation, and his speeches were characterised by an amount of humour which never failed to bring him thunders of applause; and let a man get the name of being a humourist and every sentence he utters is considered as entitled to a laugh, although it may be difficult sometimes to see where the laugh comes in. The anecdotes attributed to Lincoln, some of which were not of the most refined nature, would have filled a volume.

I have always observed that some trivial incident or event coupled with a candidate's name or profession, and more especially if this has obtained for him some favourable sobriquet, is a most powerful agency, particularly with mob or bunkum at elections.

When Mr. Lincoln's name was put before the Republican party as a candidate for president at the Chicago convention, as a testimonial of his qualification a bundle of old fence rails was carried into the convention hall by some of his admirers and supporters, and displayed as having been split by him in his younger days. While this was used as a text in the speeches of his supporters, it called forth a good deal of joking and jeering from his opponents, and was the cause of some squibs appearing in the newspapers, such as—

"Mr. Editor. Please put down my name as a candidate for President of the United States. I split rails in this State thirty years ago; I am sound on the goose. Yours, Bill Stubbins."

All this, however, only tended to bring Lincoln's name more before the public, and whether he obtained the nomination on the strength of his skill in splitting rails or from some other qualification I don't know, but there was something in the matter so pertaining to rural or backwood life as to make the name savour of homely, honest industry, that it obtained for him the sobriquet of "Honest Abe."

This appellation was, perhaps, one of the chief agents that elected him to office, and gave him his high popularity; and I have no doubt that thousands voted merely for "Honest Abe" without knowing or considering what was the qualification or policy of the man himself. This sobriquet adhered to him and strengthened his popularity to the end of his days, and added greatly to the deep emotion and excitement caused by his tragical end. He was no doubt a good, honest, and well-meaning man, altogether too honest and simple for the trying position he had to fill and the artful wire-pullers around him. But I never could see that he possessed any extraordinary talent or sagacity as a statesman. Nothing in my opinion can be more absurdly ridiculous or traducive to the memory of one of the world's greatest men than the presumption of comparing even in the smallest degree Lincoln with Washington, if it was for nothing more than the respect for virtue that the very presence of Washington commanded.

It might be said that, while the most unprincipled jobbery
and corruption would revel in Lincoln's very presence, the
perpetrators of it hoodwinking him by flattery or using him as
a buffet, one stern look from George Washington, as he stood
forth a pillar of what was noble and good in man, would have
paralyzed them with terror.

When Mr. Lincoln was nominated I do confidently believe
that among the great masses of Southern people the thought
was not for one moment indulged that his election would cause
a dissolution of the Union.   Mr. Lincoln was not regarded by
the South as a man of extreme partisan views or a man of
great political powers, and he openly declared that his policy
was not to interfere in any way with slavery in the States
where it already existed.   Thus his nomination did not cause
much excitement among the great body of the real industrious people, and a very general expression that I often
heard privately made was, that they believed Mr. Lincoln
would make a very good President.   Unfortunately this was
only the heartfelt sentiments in the homes and domestic circles
of the quiet, industrious people who would have only to wait
until the political trumpet sounded.

If the South had any justifiable cause to rise in rebellion on
Lincoln's election it could not be attributed so much to him
personally or to his avowed policy, as to his supposed connection or alliance with a party who adopted an insidious
policy too common throughout the world, and who, while
pursuing aggression under the shield of fraternity and good
will, keep edging closer to get their knee on the throat of their
victim, and meantime reply in the blandest manner to any
remonstrance in this wise, "Oh, my dear sir, our intentions
are pacific, we would not injure you for the world," while
nevertheless they continue carrying on their encroachments.

CHAPTER V.

WHEN the election took place on the 5th of November, 1860,
Mr. Lincoln was declared elected. This was nothing more
than was expected even in the South, and caused very little
excitement in Louisiana, at least among the people at large.
But some excitement was created shortly afterwards by the
announcement that South Carolina had by an Act of her
Legislature seceded from the Union. This was regarded at
first by many of the sober-minded people as an act of braggadocio by a hot-headed legislature, South Carolina being unique
among the other States in the Union in granting to her legislature extraordinary powers, even to the vote for president,
which power is, or was at that time, vested in the legislature. The question was now, How would this proceeding
be regarded? Would it be ratified or endorsed by the people
of South Carolina; would it be recognised by any of the other
States; or would the secession be recognised or permitted by
the Federal Government?

It was remembered that South Carolina had on a former
occasion during Jackson's administration stood out against
the authority of the Federal Government and repudiated the
tariff imposed by Congress of duties on goods imported, defied
the Federal authority, and threatened to secede from the
Union and prepared for war against the Federal Government.
President Jackson took a strong position, and threatened war
against the State to coerce it to obedience. But Congress, to
avoid civil war, removed the grievance by reducing the tariff,
which satisfied South Carolina, and civil war was averted.
This precedent rather tended to weaken the Federal authority,
and left the question of the right of a State to secede from the
Union still in abeyance.

After some days' suspense there did not seem to be any
notice taken of the proceedings in South Carolina at this

time, nor any action taken by the Federal Government at Washington.

In the meantime it had been arranged to take the sense of the people in each of the Southern States as to whether the Southern States should act in co-operation or secede separately from the Union. This vote was construed to mean—whether the Southern States should remain in the Union and act as a body in Congress, or secede entirely from the Union.

In the meantime politicians had been holding their conclaves as to which side they should take.

In former presidential elections there had always been a goodly number of Federal offices to dispose of among the political spirits of each State, who had worked hard to secure the return of the president elect, which at this time would not fall to any of the Southern politicians, as there had been no workers for Mr. Lincoln in any of the Southern States. There were also the permanent Federal officials at the ports and in the department of customs within the States and others who held their offices from the Federal Government, but who had become so identified with the politics of the State that, even if allowed to retain their offices, they could not now with honour remain in them under the administration of a party which they had so lately denounced.

Influence was also said to have sprung up from another quarter outside of political circles.

A great many of the plantations and slaves in the South were heavily mortgaged to Northern capitalists.* The greater part of the cotton produced in the South was shipped to Europe in Northern-owned ships and through Northern agencies, and many of the Southern planters were entirely in the hands of Northern capitalists. It was also said that many of the merchants in the South were heavily indebted to Northern houses of business.

It was also held that the Northern States, having a majority in Congress, imposed tariffs, and so managed legislation as to cause the whole of the trade between the South and Europe to pass through Northern agencies, which secured from it heavy tariffs and commissions. It was also held out somewhat bitterly that, while the South did the hard work, took the responsibility or odium of being slaveholders, and produced the exports, and maintained the prosperity of the nation, the

---

* In these mortgages the plantations and slaves generally went together, but not always.

North derived the benefit, and pocketed the lion's share of the profits. Whether these allegations were just or partly so, they had no doubt considerable effect in causing some of the more influential men to regard with favour any movement for the dissolution of the Union, and perhaps, by some of them, as one way of getting rid of their liabilities.

In the town and county of Baton Rouge the public feeling and popular vote had been in favour of the Union and constitutional party, and the popular feeling was strongly in favour of Union, but the politicians and State Government were Democratic, and favoured secession.

When the secession of South Carolina became a certainty, some of the politicians began to appear about the cafés with tricolour rosettes in their hats. This was at first pretended to be a kind of frolic, but a day had now been fixed for taking the vote of the State on the question, and parties for or against secession had now taken the field, the political party going for secession, but the greater part of the people holding aloof.

Meetings were now held with audiences drummed up from every available source. Irish labourers, proud of their citizenship, fond of politics, easily led, and always ready to take part in any political agitation, were now in great demand, and were flattered, coaxed, and prevailed upon to attend the meetings and give their decision on the great question of the day.

The regular political gang, with tricolours in their hats, headed by the office-holders, occupied the front seats, the whole audience garnished with a few rabid slaveholding planters and merchants, many of them no doubt sincere in their belief in the justice and excellency of Southern institutions and the expediency of Southern independence; others, in the hands of and pressed by their Northern creditors, were willing to have their liabilities wiped off in a general smash-up.

These meetings were harangued by political orators with all the soul-stirring eloquence that political education and practice could produce. Blatant demagogues who supported the movement were magnified into men of the greatest genius and patriotism, while the name of William L. Yancy resounded from every platform, every café and street-corner crowd as the greatest living man of the day.

As a specimen of the rhetoric poured forth at those meetings I will give an instance of what I actually saw and heard at one of them.

Walking out with a friend one evening we went into one meeting just to see what was going on. The audience was being addressed by a well-known politician who was known as Judge B., and the following is a part of the speech which we heard and the words just about as he uttered them :—

"Fellow-citizens,—This is a white man's country ; we have formed a part of the Union of the great United States ; we have been one of the brightest stars in the great galaxy ; we have reverenced that Union ; we have been true and loyal to it, but when a treacherous phalanx within that Union seeks to crush us under their iron heel, seeks to trample us into the dust, rob us of our own birthright and set the black man over us, are we to submit to such degradation ? Fellow-citizens, will you submit to eat dirt ? I tell you if you submit to a black Republican President you do so. No, fellow-citizens, the blood of our noble forefathers runs in our veins ; we inherit the rights they have purchased by that blood ; they have bequeathed to us their beaming swords to defend those rights ; shall these swords rust in our hands ? Never ! Fellow-citizens, I say, Never ! Where are the men who call themselves Unionists ? Those submissionists who hanker after the flesh-pots of Egypt ? Fellow-citizens, before I would submit to such degradation, even if I cannot get a single man to follow me, I will arm myself and go to the frontier and take my stand there and fight while a spark of life remains within me, and these Northern hordes, the enemies of my country, before they shall put a foot on this sacred soil they shall have to pass over my lifeless body."

"Hold him," whispered my companion in my ear, as he pulled me by the sleeve to come away, and we retired, not caring to make any remark until we got out of the crowd, which we just effected as the tremendous cheering which greeted this last sally had died away.

On our way home we passed where several gentlemen of our acquaintance were seated in a verandah, and knowing them to be of the more peacefully disposed Union party, and that they had not been at the meeting, we began in a jocular way to rally them on their want of zeal and patriotism, and related what we had heard spoken at the meeting. They laughed in derision at what they termed balderdash, observing that there were plenty of sensible men in the country to overrule the ravings of a few unprincipled demagogues who, before six months had passed, would deny they had ever uttered such words or appeared with a tricolour in their hats.

To show what dependence may be placed in the integrity or patriotism of professional agitators, contrasted with what may spring from the more quiet and unassuming in time of necessity, I may mention that about two years after this, I happened to visit Baton Rouge ; New Orleans had then been captured and Baton Rouge was occupied by the Northern troops. I made inquiries after many of my old friends, amongst whom were some of the peacefully inclined men of Union proclivities with whom we had been talking in the verandah on the night of the meeting referred to. I found that every one of them capable of bearing arms had taken the field and were now in the Confederate army, their houses were deserted and their families had retired within the Confederate lines, preferring to abandon their homes and endure the privations within the Confederate lines to remaining in their homes under the Union flag, although food and all the necessities of life were there in abundance. How this great change in sentiment took place may be somewhat accounted for from what took place prior to the actual breaking out of the war, which I will endeavour to recount in its place. Whilst thinking over the cause which had produced this change in sentiment, and endeavouring to find out more of the course taken, and the present position and circumstances of some of my former acquaintances, I chanced to step into a café, within a hundred yards of where I had heard that exciting speech delivered two years previously. There the first thing that met my eye was our friend Judge B., who I might have supposed to have long before this been lying dead on the frontier, surrounded by the dead bodies of the Northern hordes whom he had slain ; but here he was, playing billiards and hobnobbing with some officers of the Northern army. I wondered whether he might not be on the secret service and acting as a spy. I was told, however, that he had never taken up arms, or joined the Southern army at all, but kept shuffling until the Federal troops entered the town, when he was one of the first to meet them—not armed and in a hostile way, but to make his peace with them and take the oath of allegiance, and was now trying to get under the Federal Government some safe and easy civil appointment. I do not think that ever in my life I felt such an inclination to go up to a man and kick him.

CHAPTER VI.

VERY shortly after this agitation commenced, the intelligence
came of the secession of the States of Alabama, Florida,
Mississippi, and Georgia, all within a few days of each other.
As the news came of each successive secession, it was hailed
with great enthusiasm by the political rabble and the pro-
secession party. Salutes were fired, and lone star flags
were borne through the streets in honour of each State
respectively amidst the cheering of the rabble, almost mad
with excitement.

In the meantime business was almost at a standstill, money
had become scarce, and confidence in business circles was gone,
the political commotion was increasing. The great body of the
more law-abiding people began to wonder how all this was
going to end, and as the Congress at Washington was about to
meet, they strained their patience to see what action it would
take in the matter.

When Congress met, President Buchanan in his message
pointed out that, while there was no provision in the constitution of the United States to give any individual State the
right to secede from the Union, there was no provision to prevent it from seceding, or to coerce it to remain in the Union,
should it elect to secede. There was a provision that no two
or more States should join in or form any coalition without
the consent of the United States, but if a State should secede
separately from the Union, he saw no power under the constitution to prevent it. He did not see the right of the Federal
executive to interfere, and left the matter with Congress.

Congress came to no decision on the point, and no action
was taken. This inaction of Congress was regarded by many

as virtually a recognition by the Federal Government of the right of any individual State to secede from the Union.

The leaders in the secession movement seem to have taken the same view of the constitution as Mr. Buchanan, and acted upon it, for they adopted the plan of each State seceding separately, and each forming itself first into a separate and independent power, and then as an independent power entering into coalition and forming a combination or union with other States, being also already independent powers. This was, no doubt, only a device to evade or avoid a direct violation of the constitution, or, as it was expressed, a mere "whipping of the devil round the stump." Nevertheless, the indecision of Congress, and the inaction of the Federal executive seemed to satisfy many who had as yet formed no opinion and had taken no part in the movement that the States had at least the right to secede.

When the plebiscite on the question was taken in Louisiana, it being different from an ordinary election, the Government executive took control of the polling, and announced the result to be in favour of secession. This was, of course, received with tremendous cheering by the secession party, and the demagogue mob which seemed to have been got ready to greet the announcement, and send it out over the land accompanied with such deafening shouts as would effectually check, smother, and drown any voice which might attempt to express dissent, doubt its accuracy, or dare to inquire into its correctness. It was said that the announcement was given out before the result was known and before some of the distant counties were heard from.

Some people, however, did express their doubts as to the correctness of the returns, and some Union papers were bold enough to insist upon the returns being published, each county separately. This, of course, could not be refused, and a statement was published giving the returns from each county. The vote was small, showing that many had refrained from voting, but showing in the aggregate a majority for secession. This was, however, criticised by some of the Union papers, which pointed out several discrepancies, and particularly where one populous county, which was known to be strongly in favour of union, was left out of the return altogether.

Such remonstrances, however, were soon clamoured down and declared as unpatriotic ; and now that the State had by the unmistakable voice of the people declared and asserted its independence, and was now a free and independent State, any one that should raise his voice against it should be denounced as a traitor.

Before this, however, and immediately after it was announced that the vote of the State was for secession, and in order to increase the enthusiasm, the old days of 1776 were re-enacted. A " Declaration of Independence," similar to that signed at Philadelphia in 1776 was drawn up and signed, and an Act passed by the Legislature repealing the Act of the Union of Louisiana with the United States, and Louisiana was declared to be a free and independent State.

All this was carried through so quick that the people in general had scarcely time to think. There was no time for remonstrance ; the people's minds seemed to be carried along with the current from one excitement to another.

What was lately a State was now declared to have become a nation, with all its accompanying responsibilities. To form a cabinet, organise the different departments, and appoint the necessary officials to each office, there could be no difficulty, at least from lack of men to fill them. The greatest difficulty was rather how to dispose of the surplus and satisfy expectants. But a more serious movement was now determined upon by the State Government.

There was, as I have said, at Baton Rouge a United States garrison with a large arsenal adjoining, containing a large stock of ordnance stores, small arms, and ammunition. Intelligence was received that at Charleston, South Carolina, the State Volunteer troops had seized Fort Moultrie, and that at Mobile, Alabama, the State Volunteer troops had seized Fort Morgan. Against these seizures no action was taken or remonstrance made by the Federal Government or War department. Major Anderson, in command of the United States troops at Charleston, had, upon his own responsibility, made a stratagetical movement by taking his forces from Fort Moultrie to Fort Sumter.

A deputation of the leading men in the secession movement now waited upon Governor Moore, of Louisiana, to urge upon him the importance and necessity of taking possession in the name of the State of Louisiana, of the United States garrison and arsenal at Baton Rouge.

The garrison was at the time occupied by a detachment

numbering about 80 men of the regular army of the United States, with some three or four light field guns, under the command of Major Hoskins. The place was no kind of a fort, or in any way a place of defence.

A demand was made upon Major Hoskins by Governor Moore, in the name of the State of Louisiana, to deliver over to the State the whole of the property with all arms and munitions stored in it belonging to the United States. Major Hoskins telegraphed to Washington for instructions. The position was one of extreme difficulty. The Federal Government at Washington was democratic, and acknowledged the doctrine of the supremacy of States sovereignty; the Secretary of War, Floyd, and several members of the Cabinet were Southern men, and General Scott, the commander-in-chief of the army was a Southern man, and all supposed to be more or less Southern in their proclivities.

After waiting for a day or two Major Hoskins stated that he could get no satisfactory reply or instructions, but he refused to surrender the place unless an overwhelming force was brought against it. It was afterwards agreed that he would deliver over the place to a force of not less than from 600 to 800 of the State Volunteer troops.

I may here say in regard to the standing army of the United States at that time it consisted of about 12,000 men of all arms; that in efficiency it should be up to the standard of any European army.

The officers were all graduates of that famous military training institution, West Point. The non-commissioned officers must be picked men of good education and thorough military training. A large number of the soldiers were Europeans, mostly Irish and German, and many of them had served in the British army and other armies of Europe.

The Governor now called out the State Volunteers, and amongst others was the Baton Rouge Rifle Company, of which I was a member, although it was known to be nothing more than to make a military display, and on any other occasion would have been much enjoyed by the men. On this occasion, however, the duty was very repugnant to the feelings of most of them. In our company the most of the men were strongly union in their sentiments, and as citizens were opposed to the whole secession movement. Nevertheless, as they were in the service of the State, it was their duty to obey the orders of the Governor, who was by virtue of his office commander-in-chief of the State troops. They therefore responded to the call, although I for one confess, and I believe I might say the same for many others, that I would much rather have been called upon to act with the United States troops to suppress the secession movement and maintain the Union.

A force of about 800 volunteers, including about 600 of a very efficient corps from New Orleans, called the Washington Artillery, who, like the United States troops, acted also as infantry, and some three or four local companies were marshalled on the Boulevards at Baton Rouge while the terms of surrender were being agreed upon, inventories of stores made out and receipts signed by the Governor, and the property formally handed over to the State. The United States troops then marched out with their arms and colours, carrying with them the United States eagle and emblem of Union which had been fixed over the gate of the garrison. They embarked on a steamer which was waiting to receive them at the landing place on the river bank.

The order was then given to the Washington Artillery alone to march up and take possession of the place, and to the other companies that their services would not be required.

What was the object of this dispensing with the services of other companies I never learnt; but the officers took great offence and considered that they had been slighted and disgraced at not being allowed to share in the honours of marching up, and they protested against what they considered a slur on their companies. In expressing their minds to the men, the latter became enraged, or pretended to be in a rage, and threw down their arms, most of them I believe, and I for one, only too glad to have some excuse for a dissension of some kind. They soon, however, took up their arms as something which they might yet want; and our captain, who appeared to be in a towering rage, ordered us to break ranks, take our arms and go and put off our uniforms, and not to put them on again till we came out as an independent company.

I, for one, did not require to hear this order a second time, for in a very short time I was home, my arms put away, and dressed in my citizen clothes.

On going toward the works I met my partner's daughter, a girl of about ten years of age, accompanied by a friend, a girl of about the same age, who said they were going down to the steamer to take good-bye with Major Hoskins' children, who had been their schoolmates. I agreed to accompany them, as the streets were thronged with an excited crowd. I also wished to have an opportunity of bidding a friendly good-bye to Major Hoskins and his officers, with whom I had a slight but pleasant acquaintance.

The boat was still at the landing-place coaling for the passage up the river, and the soldiers were busy getting on board their luggage. I observed many of the most respectable people of the place taking an affectionate adieu with the Major and his family and the other officers. They had been much respected during the time they had been at Baton Rouge, and it was plainly to be seen that there were a great many of the most respectable citizens who regarded the movement with sorrow and indignation, although they dared not openly express their feelings. On getting a word with the Major I saw he deeply felt the situation, but maintained a dignified reserve.

Just at that moment the Pelican flag, the emblem of the State, was being hoisted on the flag-staff at the garrison amidst tremendous cheering. On my calling his attention to it, he pointed to the Union flag which was then waving over the steamer, and said with some emotion, "You take my word for it, you will see that flag waving there again before six months." "Sooner, I hope," said I, as I took my leave. "So say I," also cried five or six voices around me, as we walked ashore.

Having taken the children to their homes I sauntered along the streets to see what might be the outward display of public feeling. But few people were now to be seen in the streets; the sounds of drunken orgies proceeded from some of the cafés, while bands of politicians of the Government party were congratulating each other on the glorious event, and joining in loud cheers for the "Independent State of Louisiana;" while small groups of more thoughtful men might be seen in secluded corners talking in a lower and more serious tone, and quiet whisperings were rife within doors of fears of this being a black day for Baton Rouge.

Many looked upon it as an act of war against the United States, as a plundering raid, which, if the Federal Government did not take prompt measures to resent, they would be unworthy of the name of a Government and not entitled to the respect of the people.

I may observe that the term " Federal " was what applied
to the Central Government at Washington over the whole of
the United States, as a nation in its relation with foreign
powers, etc., and is controlled by the President and Congress,
each State having again its own Government and laws called
the State Government. Afterwards during the war, the
Northerners were called the " Federals," and the Southerners
were called the " Confederates."

CHAPTER VII.

PREPARATIONS TO ORGANISE AN ARMY—AFFAIRS BECOME SERIOUS—SHAMEFUL
INACTION OF THE FEDERAL GOVERNMENT—SECESSION UNOPPOSED GAINS
STRENGTH — THE PEOPLE, HAVING NO OTHER RESOURCE, ACCEPT THE
SITUATION—OFFICE HUNTING—DEPRESSION OF BUSINESS—AN INTERVIEW
WITH GOVERNOR MOORE.

THE Washington artillery volunteers, having done the part
they were called upon to do, returned to New Orleans. The
local volunteer companies were sullen and disaffected. The
garrison and arsenal, with all the large stores of ordnance,
small arms, and ammunition, having been taken possession of
by the State Government, were still unguarded. The State
Government had a war department on paper, with plenty of
officials, but they had neither troops nor commissariat. It now
became necessary to adopt some means to garrison and guard
the place. A movement was set on foot to raise a force by
enlistment, to constitute the regular army of Louisiana, and
great inducements were held out to men to enlist; first, a
provisional force for three months, then for longer periods—
one year, and three years. As all trade and business was
about a stand-still, there was abundance of idlers and unemployed, and a body of recruits was soon raised and stationed
in the garrison.

In the meantime people began to look upon the state of
matters more seriously. The passing of the formal act of
secession, and the declaration of the independence of the State,
was regarded by many as a mere piece of political bounce,
carried out with the view of compelling from the Federal
Government some guarantee against any encroachment on
what they termed Southern rights. But the seizure of the
United States arsenal, and driving the United States troops
from the State, was considered a high-handed act, which they
expected the Federal Government would immediately resent;
and many and various reports were whispered of immediate
action to be taken by the Federal Executive, and that large
forces of Federal troops were on the way to retake and hold
possession of the garrison and arsenal.

This at least could have been very easily effected. The garrison and arsenal stood on a level plateau about 40 feet above the level of, and bordering on, the Mississippi river. They stood on a plain field without any kind of defensive works, and could have been completely swept by the fire from a vessel on the river. The Mississippi river, which bounded the garrison on one side, was navigable for the largest ships in the United States navy, and the forts near the mouth of the river were not yet in a condition for defence, while it was perfectly open to an approach from above. And so completely did this great river form the main highway and artery throughout the South, that had the Federal Government acted promptly and sent up the river one or two of their small steam frigates, and if at the same time one or two armed transports with 500 troops had been sent down from above, the garrison and arsenal would have been re-occupied without resistance, while a couple of gunboats stationed on the Mississippi would have crushed secession in the bud.

There would no doubt have been a howl of indignation from blatant politicians about coercion, violated rights, and suppression of the freedom of the people by force of arms.

But a very large proportion of the people—I believe a considerable majority of them whose freedom was suppressed by a less legitimate power—would have approved of the action of the Federal Government, and would have hailed with gladness some appearance of a sovereign power, and felt a sense of security, and realized that they were living under a government that would enforce the laws, and protect the true liberties of the people. For, even allowing the right of the State to secede from the Union to be admitted, the Federal Government was bound by the constitution to provide in each State a Republican form of Government, and it was considered their duty in such a question to see that the will of the people was freely and clearly expressed.

In any case the Federal Government would have been justified in resenting what might be called an outrage, and in immediately enforcing the restitution of the forts, arsenals, arms, and property. Had this been done, secession could have made no headway.

" The precious hour was passed in vain."

The Federal Government took no action. The loyal portion

of the population who had been waiting in breathless suspense to see what action would be taken, were now disheartened, while the secession party increased in numbers, and became more arrogant and noisy.

The question now asked among the loyal and law-abiding people was, whether the proceedings were constitutional and lawful, and if the Federal Government recognized the right of the State to secede. The question had to be answered by the action they took. Had the Federal Government repudiated the right of secession, followed up Major Anderson's movement, sent a war vessel into Charleston harbour before the Secessionists had time to mount a gun, and supported Major Anderson in Fort Sumter, secession would have been checked where it begun and gone no further. It could not have been called an excessive warlike demonstration, as it would only have been a movement in the army and navy, such as is often done in ordinary times of peace. It was therefore considered obvious that they did not consider it politic to make any such movement. They had before them an easy and simple method of checking secession if they had considered it unconstitutional and unlawful. As they did not do so, it was to be supposed that they recognized the action as legal.

Such were the comments at the time among many respectable Southern people ; many regretted and disapproved of the action, and what appeared to be the decision of the Federal Government. But as the party in power was the party that had almost unremittingly governed the United States for fifty years, their authority was considered valid, and very many of the Southern people accepted very reluctantly the situation, and gave in their adherence to the new Government.

Could these people be blamed for thus acting, and could they afterwards be blamed for showing a determination to resist an attempt by the same central Government administered by a man of different opinions to chastise them for acting as they did.

There has been various reasons assigned for this inaction or supposed connivance of the Federal Government. But I think the most probable reason was that the Democratic Government then in office, seeing that their power was overthrown in the election of a president by their opponents, and saw also that, although Mr. Lincoln had got a majority of the electoral votes, he was still very much in the minority by the popular vote. That is, throughout the United States there were more individual votes against him than for him, although by the electoral college system he had obtained a majority by states.

They, therefore, as is too often done in popular Governments, cast aside honour and duty, to favour, as they thought, the source from which would come the largest number of votes.

All business, except political business, or what was connected with the State Government, was now nearly at a stand-still.

The State now being out of the Union, and declared an independent power, there was great confusion and alteration in the departments — creation of offices, and, of course, a great rush and struggle among office-seekers to obtain lucrative appointments under the new *régime*.

In the commercial and ordinary business circles money had become exceedingly scarce, credit was about stopped, creditors sought payment, debtors were unable to pay.

It happened about this time that our firm had a pretty large account against the State of Louisiana for work done for the different engineering departments; also against the United States for work for the Ordnance Department, and whose liabilities the State had assumed. And, though the State accounts, and the United States accounts, had always been considered as the best and surest class, still, after the events that had taken place, and the uncertainty of what might follow, and the fearful drain upon the State treasury, it was thought advisable, if possible, to secure payment before matters became more deeply embroiled. We well knew that the heads of departments—such as Engineer Department, Auditor and Treasury Departments—through which we had formerly to get our accounts settled were undergoing changes, and certain to be in confusion; and as each would have their own friends to serve, it would be almost useless at the time to think of getting a settlement through them in the usual way. It was therefore thought best under the circumstances to see the Governor direct on the subject.

The Governor, who had only been about a year in office, was a planter on Red river, and with whom, in his private capacity, we had formerly done a good deal of business, and whom we always found to be a just and honourable man. I accordingly sought for a favourable opportunity to have an interview with him, and obtained it.

Governor Moore was a tall spare man between fifty and sixty years of age, of a quiet, unobtrusive manner, and of rather a kindly and homely disposition, and very different from the fiery spirits that surrounded him. He seemed very careworn, and was evidently impressed with great anxiety with the responsibility of the act which he had taken, or rather which had been forced upon him. He received me very courteously, and when I had stated my business and explained the difficulty of the position, he examined the accounts, and, having satisfied himself that they were just and correct, he subscribed his approval on them, recommending that the accounts might be settled without going through the usual formalities in the then disorganised state of the departments.

Having done this, he motioned me to sit down if I had no pressing business to call me away. I think that, satiated with politics, he wanted to have a little respite from the worry he was enduring in the political turmoil, and the constant importuning of office seekers, and while he was reported "engaged," could have a little rest, and have his mind refreshed by a change of subject, and a talk on matters more congenial to his home tastes and non-official business.

He now entered into a long conversation on rural subjects, and engineering in all its branches, sugar and cotton machinery, sawmills, steamboats, his own works, river overflows and embankments, swamp draining, piling, railroads, bridges, canals, timber, the different qualities of wood produced in the State, and their capabilities for different purposes.

He seemed to enjoy the conversation, and to feel as if in a change of atmosphere, and showed no disposition to terminate it, whilst I must confess I could not help enjoying a chuckle at the impatience which would be felt by the expectant office seekers who, I knew, were sitting in rows in the adjoining rooms, each with his credentials for services rendered, and letters of recommendation to the Governor, waiting his turn for an audience.

After sitting for upwards of an hour, a peculiar knock at the door seemed to be a signal quite understood by the Governor, for he promptly called out—" Come in, Major."

The door opened, and in walked Major H., Secretary of State.

It must be here observed that the term of major, colonel, or general, or judge, so often applied to many in the South, was purely honorary or self-imposed, without any claim or origin whatever beyond courtesy; the term major, however, was regarded with a little more respect than the others. The higher ranked titles of colonel and general had been adopted by so many that they had become common and vulgar.

Major H. was in appearance and manner the very reverse of Governor Moore. He was a stout man, of ruddy complexion, with an open jocund countenance, and the plump jovial expression of his face indicated that he took matters easily, and certainly did not neglect the wants of his body as far as meat and drink were concerned. Major H. was a well-known and exceedingly popular man, possessed of great tact and considerable talent. He had for a long time held the office of Secretary of State, and though many had tried to oust him at the periodical elections, he still held his office against all competitors. He was an able stump orator, could tickle an audience, and ridicule an opponent, and always managed to be at the head of the poll. He had the peculiar ability of being "Hey fellow, well met," with everyone, without making himself too cheap, and always commanded respect.

On his entering I made a motion of rising to leave, but he tapped me familiarly on the shoulder, saying, "Oh! it is you, W.; sit still."

He handed to the Governor some papers, and what I took to be an extract from a newspaper, which the Governor read over carefully, and looked thoughtfully for a moment, while the Major gave a sort of derisive laugh, saying, "Well, what do you think of that, Governor?" The Governor replied in a more serious tone, "Well, I suppose it matters little; the thing is done now, and they must just accept it."

The Major, seeming not to wish further talk on that subject, turned round to me and said in a jocose manner, "Well, W., how do things get along in your line of business?" "Very depressed indeed, Major," said I. "O that will be only for a short time; but you will see before long that business will be better than ever. What do you think of this movement?" "O you know, Major," said I, "that I am a regular John Bull, and take nothing to do with politics!" "John Bull or no John Bull, you take our money all the same." "O yes!" said I laughing, "I take as much of that as I can get, but just in the same way as you take John Bull's money for your cotton."

"That is so, Mr. W.," said the Governor, "but you get the full amount for your services, but look at what we in the South get for our cotton, a mere remnant of its value by our trade being hampered by having to pass through Northern agencies."

"But that is no fault of John Bull," said I.

"O certainly not," said the Governor, "there are worse men than John Bull with all his faults."

"Who do you mean, Governor," chuckled the Major, "is it the Yankees?"

"I mean," said the Governor, "those Northern capitalists who command our trade, and manage to control legislation to suit their purposes."

"But you are not in that position yourself, Governor," said the Major, "you are not in the power of any Northern capitalist."

"Not directly," said the Governor. "I am not personally like many others in the power of any Northern capitalist. But then all suffer indirectly. Only the other day I got a consignment of hardware from England, it had to come through a Northern agency, and the charges over and above the freight and duties amounted to about 30 per cent. on the invoice."

"Well we have got rid of all that now," said the Major in a congratulating tone.

The Governor seemed to muse on the subject, but said nothing.

It was now evident that there was a crowd outside waiting for an audience, so I rose and took my leave.

From this interview simple as it was, I could see that the Governor, who was not a great politician, but a man of considerable standing in the State, had no great heart in the movement, but was altogether overruled and goaded on by those around him, and had to go with the political current.

But I could see that he had a strong sense of the position in which the South stood with the North in regard to trade, and it was no doubt a little irritating. The Southern planters were the real producers of the country. They were enduring the toils and privations of a backwoods life. They were bearing the odium of being slaveholders. The North was pocketing the lion's share of their labours, living in ease and luxury, and maintaining an exterior of virtue and sanctity, and it did seem like adding insult to injury that they should stigmatise the Southern people as slavemasters, nigger drivers, etc.

I heard it very often said in the South at that time, that the 1000 dollars paid for a pew in Beecher's church, and the 1000 dollar dresses which adorned the godly dames who occupied them, were often derived in a pretty direct way from the products of the Southern planter with all the horrors of slavery upon it, which they had come there to denounce. How far these assertions may have been correct, or how far they may have been applicable to the question, I do not pretend to say, but I often heard them expressed; and I did know of similar instances which came pretty direct. And although I could see nothing to justify the secession movement, still the remarks of the Governor reminded me that a question may be looked at from many points of view. And it was questionable if the Northern Abolitionists came into court with clean hands.

CHAPTER VIII.

ONE of the first steps taken by the new Government was the organisation of the War Department. A Secretary for War had been appointed, and there was abundance of officers, and a considerable number of recruits had been enlisted, and were undergoing drill in the garrison.

A party of professed engineers were employed making surveys round the garrison, and preparing plans with a view to throwing up works on the side next the river, and forming the garrison into a place of defence.

These works, however, were not carried out to any great extent, but the proposals and preliminaries with the attendant expenditure, if they did not serve to repel enemies, might at least have been the means of creating friends.

A good many of the official appointments in this branch of the service were given to Germans, who were known to exercise considerable influence over their fellow-countrymen among the labouring and other classes. The latter, though citizens, and forming a considerable part of the population, had not hitherto shown any marked zeal in the secession movement.

A similar policy was adopted throughout the Government Department in general. Offices, both civil and military, were offered to such men as were known to possess influence over the public mind, or were capable of swaying the minds of any particular class of the population, and every means was devised to make the new Government popular.

Explanations, apologies, and flatteries, were applied to win back the disaffected volunteers.

These devices all tended more or less to strengthen the new Government, and as there was no appearance of any interference on the part of the United States Government, more of the people began to acquiesce in the new order of things.

The Government was now called the Republic of Louisiana. The other States which had seceded had also declared themselves Independent Republics, each regarding the other and the United States as foreign powers.

About the end of January, 1861, the result of the general plebiscite throughout the South had become known, and although different accounts had been circulated, the fact had now to be admitted that only six States had decided on secession. These were—South Carolina, Georgia, Florida, Alabama, Mississippi, and Louisiana.

Early in February, 1861, and shortly after the result of the general plebiscite throughout the South had become known, a convention of the six States was held at Montgomerie, Alabama, and the old days of 1776 were again re-enacted. A Federal Constitution was drawn out after the form of the constitution of the United States, and a Government formed to be called the Confederate States of America. Mr. Jefferson Davis of Mississippi, a man supposed to be possessed of great talent and strength of mind, was appointed President, *pro tem.*, and Mr. Alexander Stephens of Georgia, a man also of great talent, and of somewhat milder views, was appointed Vice-President.

These appointments were regarded as a sort of compromise to meet the views of both parties who had been in the Southern States at the time of Lincoln's election, Jefferson Davis being to suit the tastes of the rabid secession Democrats who supported Mr. Breckenridge, and Mr. Stephens to please the Union and Constitutional party who supported Mr. Bell.

Mr. Jefferson Davis signalised his inauguration by an inflammatory address, the violent and extravagant pro-slavery bounce of which did not add much to his general popularity.

Having established a Government, formed a cabinet, and appointed the heads of departments, they proceeded with great vigour to make preparations for defence by organising an army, and strengthening and garrisoning the forts.

The newly-fledged Government grew stronger every day. Departments were more fully organised, recruiting was pushed, the army was increasing, the forts were being strengthened, armed, and garrisoned. In the garrison at Baton Rouge, bands of recruits were being drilled and sent off to garrison the different forts, while in the Ordnance Department the greatest activity prevailed in getting gun-carriages completed, field pieces mounted, and caissons fitted up ready for use. Navy guns with their equipments were sent off to the different forts, while the road from the arsenal to the steamboat wharf on the river was cut up so as to be almost impassable with the carting of shot and shell which was being shipped to the forts at the mouth of the Mississippi, and along the coasts of Mississippi, Alabama, and Florida.

Meanwhile every possible means was adopted to rouse the enthusiasm of the people, and win over the disaffected portion of the population, and make the new Government popular.

A flag bearing three bars of red, white, and red horizontally, with a galaxy of six stars on a blue ground in the upper corner, had been adopted as the national flag of the Confederate States. This flag was floated over all the public buildings, displayed from windows, and paraded on the streets with bands playing patriotic airs got up to suit the occasion. Every steamboat calling at the landing place, or passing on the river, streamed with Confederate flags, and resounded with " Dixie's Land." This was done even by steamers from Northern cities, though it may be doubtful whether they did not as soon as they got out of reach and hearing, change their tune to " Yankee Doodle."

Enthusiasm seemed to be carried by a *coup de main*, females and children joining largely in it. Any attempt at remonstrance dared not now be uttered, and all misgiving expressions were drowned in the apparent hilarity and enthusiasm.

Notwithstanding all this outward show of enthusiasm, confidence was not by any means restored in private life or business circles.

It was now fully three months since the secession movement had begun, and it was evident that Buchanan's Government had to all intents and purposes acknowledged the rights of the States to secede, and meant to take no action. President Buchanan going out of office seemed either to acquiesce in the views of the secessionists, or wished to take no part in the matter, but leave the responsibility to his successor. In acting thus he by his delay rendered what might have been accomplished with a few hundred men and one or two ships of war without a drop of bloodshed a Herculean task, which could not now in any case be accomplished without an untold expense, and the sacrifice of thousands of lives.

The uncertainty of what policy might be adopted by Mr. Lincoln, when he came into office on the 4th of March, kept minds in constant suspense.

As to what Mr. Lincoln's policy might be there was nothing to indicate, and it was the subject of much speculation among the bulk of the people within the seceded States.

No one thought that he would adopt a coercive policy; it was now too late for that.

It had been pointed out by Mr. Buchanan in his message to Congress, that the executive of the United States had really no power under the constitution to coerce sovereign States.

The States had seceded separately from the Union, each remaining for a time a separate and independent Government, and afterwards formed themselves into a Confederacy, and all without any protest or hindrance on the part of the Federal Government. They had the sympathy of the Middle States, and also of a large number of the Northern Democrats. They were now well organised and had become powerful, and the President could not but see that any attempt at coercion would lead to further secession, and meet with the most determined resistance, and must result in civil war and bloodshed.

The seceded States had sent commissioners to Washington to make arrangements for the transfer and payment of the forts, arsenals, and other United States property within the seceded States, which had been seized by the State volunteer forces, and also for the evacuation by the Federal troops of Fort Sumter in Charleston harbour, and Fort Pickens in Florida.

These commissioners had been received at Washington, each party expressing a desire for a peaceful solution of the difficulty, but the negotiations made very little progress.

This, however, had allayed to some extent the apprehensions of the people within the seceded States. They now considered that secession, for the time at least, was a foregone conclusion, and would not now be undone; and it was hoped that by a little forbearance on both sides the whole thing would be peaceably arranged and war averted.

It must be remembered, however, that this was still during Mr. Buchanan's administration; and all now awaited with breathless anxiety the announcement of Lincoln's policy, as on that hinged the question of peace or war.

The generally accepted opinion of the greater portion of the people within the seceded States and outwith the political circle was, that Lincoln on taking office would recognise the defect in the Federal constitution. The late administration and Congress had considered they had no power under the constitution to prevent the States seceding or to coerce them back into the Union. That, although not altogether acquiescing in these views he would still have before him the broad principle that the foundation of the United States government was based upon revolution. That it came into existence through revolution. That revolution was embodied in its principles, and that it would be unprecedented and unconstitutional as well as a difficult and dangerous matter to make any attempt at coercion without some special and lucid provision being made for it in the Federal constitution. That those six States had now become fully organised and powerful, and any attempt to coerce them would lead to much bloodshed and most likely to a further breach in the Union ; and while as yet only six States had seceded instead of the whole South, as had been anticipated, he would let them go in peace, accepting an indemnity (which they were willing to give) for forts and other United States' property within the seceded territory.

With six States gone, and their representatives no longer in Congress, the President's party would be greatly strengthened. He would now be able to command a majority sufficient to enable him to amend the Federal constitution in respect to the right of States to secede, and also be able to deal with the question of slavery.

The slave States which still remained in the Union would be so much in a minority that they could no longer hold any sway in Congress on the slave question. In some of these States slavery had become nearly extinct; in most of them it was becoming less popular, and in a short time it would by an almost unanimous vote be abolished entirely in the United States.

The loss of the six States which had seceded and been formed into a separate Confederacy would, on the whole, have been no great price to pay for the peaceful and advantageous settlement of a question which had for years convulsed and divided the Union, and had kept it in a constant state of turmoil almost threatening its destruction. These views were particularly plausible when considering the enormous territories still at the command of the United States waiting to be settled up.

Besides this, the isolation might be only temporary, as the six States would find themselves almost alone in maintaining their peculiar institution in the face of the civilised world. They would be surrounded and hemmed in by the free States of the more powerful Union, and they would have no fugitive slave law to protect their institution. The largest portion of the population being non-slaveholders, their sympathies would be with the old Union of which many of them were natives, and they were bound to it by strong ties of traditional attachment. In short, there was a great probability of these States again seeking admission severally back into the United States.

The fundamental principles of the United States government being based on revolution, the Confederate States on the same principle maintained their right to secede severally and form a separate government.

Upon this admitted principle it was open for any of the Confederate States to secede from the Confederacy by a vote of the majority of the population and declare itself an independent State, and then apply for admission back into the old Union, under an amended constitution, having no longer the right or power to secede.

Thus in the end it might lead to a judicious plan of amending the constitution, abolishing slavery, and establishing the central government on a firmer basis than ever.

Whether with this view it would have been wise or practicable to have adopted such a policy, or whether Mr. Lincoln ever thought of such a policy, I do not pretend to know. It was talked of, and seemed to most sober thinking men in the South, as not only the wisest but the only constitutional course left open for him to pursue. It was further the conceded opinion of many able men both North and South, when they found that so few States had seceded that the wisest plan would be to let the rebellious States go in peace, and proceed to amend the constitution, and conserve the integrity of the Union in the States.

The hope that Mr. Lincoln would adopt this course got to be strongly entertained among the moderate party in the seceded States after it became known that the majority of the Southern States had decided to remain in the Union, and the fear of war was allayed, and confidence was in some degree restored.

CHAPTER IX.

THROUGHOUT the whole of this time Mr. Lincoln, the
President-elect, had given no indication of what his policy
would be. Several reports of interviews, or pretended interviews, had been published in the Confederate newspapers, but
these interviews (if ever they took place) showed nothing
in particular.

In fact, the pro-secession journals did not portray the new
President in any favourable light. Their object seemed to be
to prejudice the minds of the Southern people against him.

At length the time came for his inauguration, and it was
reported with great gusto by the Confederate newspapers that
such was his unpopularity that when on his way to Washington
he had to pass through the city of Baltimore clandestinely,
sitting in a farmer's waggonette disguised in a Scotch bonnet
and plaid.

Whether there was any truth in this I do not know, but
when his inaugural address came to be published it was
certainly disappointing to the moderate party, not only in the
Confederate States but throughout the whole of the South in
general, which had been expecting to find in Mr. Lincoln a
man whose wisdom and sagacity would have been equal to the
occasion. The speech contained a great deal of meaningless
rhetoric. He repudiated the abolition doctrine, and distinctly
avowed that he had neither the wish nor the intention to
interfere with the institution of slavery in the States where it
existed. He affected to treat lightly the serious state of
matters, and in a somewhat silly and jocular manner congratulated his audience that there was "nobody hurt." He
advocated the preservation of the Union, and declared that
the constitution must be enforced at whatever cost. This

was, of course, the stereotyped text of all inaugural addresses, but he refrained from giving his views on the meaning of the constitution, or what powers he considered it embodied in regard to secession, or as to what policy he would adopt under its provisions. This was what the people eagerly desired to know, and it was very important and essential at the moment having regard to what Mr. Buchanan had said in his message to Congress. It was evident that Mr. Lincoln had no fixed policy of his own, and that he would in a great measure be guided by his cabinet.

There is always in politics a party of zealots who are ever ready to magnify into greatness every action or utterance of some particular public man whom they admire and support. In this case the Lincoln journals and party set forth their high approval of the address, and lauded it in the highest terms as a production of great force and talent. Thousands, I believe, did so who neither read nor heard it, and neither knew nor understood anything about it but took it for granted. It was not reassuring to many in the north and South throughout, and to the moderate party in the Confederate States it was disappointing and disheartening.

In the Confederate journals it was treated in the most derisive way, and described as a piece of meaningless buffoonery, whilst the Confederate leaders and political orators turned it to every possible account, and indulged in the most extravagant and insulting abuse of Mr. Lincoln and everything pertaining to the North ; all this, while intended to intensify the feeling in the South against the North, could not fail to alienate much of the sympathy and good feeling which up till now was still entertained by many in the North toward the South.

For some time after Lincoln's inauguration he gave no indication of what his policy would be in regard to the seceded States. But the appointment of Mr. W. H. Seward as Secretary of State, whose well-known hostility toward the South gave rise to grave apprehensions, and again rumours of war became prevalent.

The representative members from the seceded States had now all retired from the Federal Congress at Washington, and the Confederate Commissioners who had been sent to negotiate during Buchanan's administration, had returned without effecting any arrangement.

Commissioners were again sent from Montgomerie to nego-tiate with Lincoln's Government, and more especially in the meantime to treat for the evacuation of Fort Sumter, the holding of which by the Federal troops was considered dangerous to the preservation of peace, and might lead to a rupture at any moment.

These commissioners were neither received nor repudiated, but their hearing put off from time to time, or as it was put before the people in the Confederate States, they were desired by Mr. Seward to " wait a little."

In the meantime the suspense among the general population within the Confederate States became intolerable. A month had now passed since Lincoln came into power, and yet he had taken no action, nor given the slightest indication of what his intentions were. Rumours of all kinds were constantly being circulated, now that hostilities had actually broken out. " Fighting at Fort Pickens " — " Fighting at Baltimore " —" Fighting at Charleston," and at other times that peace was likely to be preserved ; that a joint-commission from all the States was to be appointed to arrange all matters in dispute, and devise some means of settlement. Every day some new report was circulated, to be denied the next.

It soon got to be the general belief among all classes in the Confederate States—and there seems to have been good grounds for the belief—that Lincoln's cabinet was shuffling. No kind of reply or statement of their views, favourable or unfavour-able, would they make to the Confederate commissioners. Still less favourable was said to have been the reception of some representatives of the loyal or Union party in the South, who were said to have privately requested an interview with regard to their position.

It was the opinion of many quiet but wise and intelligent men in the South, that although Mr. Lincoln might be an honest, upright, and simple man, and had no bad feeling or intention towards the South, still he had as an adviser in Mr. Seward, a subtle and deceitful man possessed of great ability, and having an intense hatred toward the South.

As matters had now become so critical that hostilities might break out at any moment, and as the eyes of everyone both North and South were watching with breathless suspense the impending crisis, and as the onus of the war would lie on the side which struck the first blow, Mr. Seward's desire was to crush the South by a war, but in order that he might have the popular feeling on his side, his object further was to make the South the aggressor.   He therefore sought to goad them into striking the first blow.   He knew the feeling this would produce throughout the country at large, that it would set the nation in a blaze and rouse the North to a man.

He knew from the vain and arrogant pretensions of the rabid secessionists, and the fiery impetuosity of their leaders, that he could easily provoke them into striking a blow, while the intemperate swagger and insulting braggadocio of some of the Southern newspapers was fast alienating the good feeling which had hitherto been displayed by the people of the North in general towards the South, and creating a feeling amongst them of just indignation at the unreasonable and hostile attitude taken up by many of the Southern papers.   Thus by stirring up a hostile feeling in the North, and then provoking the South to strike a blow he would thereby accomplish his object and effectually crush the South out of existence, so that it would never again have a voice in the Government.

That those who entertained such opinions might have been right in their conjectures seems to have been somewhat substantiated by what immediately followed, and by many discussions which I heard during the war between parties of Northern and Southern soldiers when opportunities offered, such as at truce meetings, or with prisoners of war, when the Southerners asserted that all they wanted was to be let alone, the invariable reply was, Who began the war?   Who struck the first blow?   Who battered the walls of Fort Sumter?

It may be said that such arguments were only the opinions of soldiers who knew nothing of the higher theories of statesmanship or diplomacy ; but, when it is remembered that these men were intelligent citizens, and it was from these opinions that Mr. Lincoln and his cabinet obtained their support and positions, it was necessary for them to use every device to mould public opinion, and turn it so as to enable them to carry out their designs.

Fort Sumter, in South Carolina, was now the critical point, situated as it was in the middle of Charleston harbour, and occupied by the Federal troops, and blockaded by the Confederate forces.

Fort Sumter, being situated on an island near the centre of Charleston harbour, commanded the entrance to the harbour and also the city of Charleston. It was a strong and powerful work, and being surrounded by water could only be approached by means of boats.

Fort Moultrie was situated on a point of the mainland more seawards, and commanded the passage leading from the harbour out to sea.

When South Carolina seceded from the Union, Fort Sumter was unoccupied by any force, but Fort Moultrie was occupied by Major Anderson with a force of about 80 United States troops. Major Anderson, seeing that he could not hold Fort Moultrie against the State troops, should they approach by land and make a demand on him to surrender it, made a sudden movement into Fort Sumter, which could not be approached by land.

This movement irritated the secessionists; they had not taken the precaution to secure Fort Sumter before it was occupied by the Federal troops, and it would be a difficult matter now to get the Federal troops to retire from Charleston by a mere display of force and without a conflict.

Nevertheless the Confederates speedily occupied Fort Moultrie, and cut off all communication with Fort Sumter by sea; and, although it was known that Major Anderson had taken considerable stores with him from Fort Moultrie, it was a mere question of time that the garrison of Fort Sumter would be starved into submission, unless the Federal Government should force a passage past Fort Moultrie and relieve it.

In the meantime the friendly intercourse between the officers and men of the garrison in Fort Sumter and the citizens of Charleston was not broken. They were allowed to come and go in their boats, and purchase in the city what goods and fresh provisions they required as before.

The commissioners which had been sent to Washington by the seceded States during Buchanan's ministry insisted on the evacuation of Fort Sumter by the Federal troops, and a censure on the conduct of Major Anderson.

General Scott, who was commander of the United States army, considered the movement as strategetic, and commended the conduct of Major Anderson as an officer.

Mr. Floyd, Secretary of War, recommended the withdrawal of the garrison as a safeguard against any immediate outbreak of hostilities.

President Buchanan, who by virtue of his office was com-

mander-in-chief of the army and navy of the United States,
had refused to take any action in the matter, but left it first
to be decided by Congress whether South Carolina and the
other seceding States should be acknowledged as independent
powers or not.

As Congress took no action in the matter, the commissioners
had returned without anything being effected.

In the meantime an attempt had been made to provision
Fort Sumter; a steamer, the *Star of the West*, had been sent
with supplies; but as she approached the entrance to Charleston harbour a gun from Fort Moultrie was fired across her
bow, and she immediately put back and sailed home. I have
heard it insinuated that this was only a kind of form—a mere
show of an attempt to relieve the garrison, and a mere form
of resistance, a mere feeler to find if the Confederates would
actually resist any attempt to relieve the garrison. In any
case the attempt made to relieve the garrison was a very
weak one, and a very slight hint was sufficient to cause them
to desist.

Some attempts were made by the extreme parties and
newspapers, both North and South, to manufacture political
capital and strife out of the event.

The Southern fire-eaters attempted to make a boast of the
pluck of the Confederates and their determination to resist
any aggression; while the Northern abolitionists and fanatics
seemed to gloat over what they described as a gross outrage
and cause for war—"The rebels firing into a United States
steamer."

After Lincoln came into power, and while the Confederate
commissioners at Washington were waiting for an audience,
General Scott advised that, without prejudice to any view that
the Federal Government might take in regard to the seceded
States, or what action they might afterwards take, that in the
meantime the troops should be withdrawn from Fort Sumter
as a military necessity. Their presence there could in no case
be of any advantage to the United States, but rather an
embarrassment. No action was taken on this advice. It was
evident that Mr. Seward, who was now the master spirit in
Washington, was formulating some scheme of his own. Some
attempts had been made to throw supplies into Fort Sumter;
and the Confederates, irritated at what they considered the
shuffling of Mr. Seward, cut off the supplies which the garrison

had been receiving from the city of Charleston, strengthened Fort Moultrie and placed heavy guns to command effectually the entrance to the harbour, thus stopping any approach from the sea, and preventing the Federal government throwing in reinforcements or supplies to Fort Sumter.

General Scott is said to have again advised the withdrawal of the troops from Fort Sumter as a military necessity.

Mr. Lincoln again declined. It was evident that Mr. Seward, who was the real head of affairs at Washington, saw very well that the vanity and pugnacity of Jefferson Davis and his cabinet, and the defiant and warlike attitude of the Confederate leaders, would soon overcome their patience and wiser judgment, and cause them to commit themselves by striking a blow somewhere which would thoroughly rouse the indignation of the North and make the war against the South popular.

Nor was he wrong in his conjecture.

The Confederate government, if they now wished to avoid the responsibility of striking the first blow, acted with a rashness quite uncalled for and amounting to stupidity.

The troops in Fort Sumter were, undoubtedly, kept there by the Federal government for no other purpose than to provoke and irritate the secessionists. They were there of not the slightest use to the Federal government. They could act in no way—they were entirely blockaded and cut off from receiving any support or supplies.

When Major Anderson abandoned Fort Moultrie, he spiked the guns and moved into the stronger position of Fort Sumter, which commanded Fort Moultrie and the whole harbour and town of Charleston. The secessionists could not approach him as the fort was entirely surrounded by water, and they had no armed vessels or any power on the water whatever. In making this movement he no doubt expected that the Federal government would send him immediate support. Had the Federal government at the time supported the movement by sending a single ship of war into Charleston harbour, and reinforcing and strengthening Fort Sumter, they could easily have prevented the secessionists from mounting a single gun at Charleston, and the town and harbour at least must have remained under the power of the Union. But it was now too late. Three months had passed away, and the secessionists had had it all their own way.

General Beauregarde, who commanded the Confederate forces at Charleston, saw the position, and had been most indefatigable in his exertions to strengthen it. He had mounted heavy guns at Fort Moultrie, and so strengthened the fort as to be able successfully to resist any attack by sea which the United States could make upon it, and thus rendered impossible any immediate attempt to relieve or reinforce Fort Sumter.

He had also erected land batteries of heavy guns against Fort Sumter, and all supplies being now cut off from that fort, the garrison was reduced to extremities, and its inevitable surrender from starvation was only a question of a few days' time.

It was therefore very natural that General Scott, a military man of great ability, should advise the withdrawal of the troops as a military necessity while an opportunity still existed, for had hostilities broken out while the Federal garrison would have been prisoners of war and so much loss to the United States.

But Mr. Seward knew his own game; he had effectually measured the patience, prudence, and sagacity of Jefferson Davis and his cabinet.

While it seems inexplicable that the Confederate leaders should without any apparent necessity act so precipitantly, and incur the onus and responsibility of the war by bombarding the fort and actually commencing hostilities, I have never heard any satisfactory reason given for the rash act. Of course the excuse set forth by the Confederate leaders was the importance of the fort and the great danger to be apprehended to the Confederate cause should the Federal Government be able to send an expedition to force an entry into Charleston harbour and occupy and strengthen Fort Sumter.

But there was not the slightest grounds for this apprehension, and the Confederate commanders had no such apprehensions. The time was now gone past for this. It would have been impossible for the Federal Government to have got ready an expedition in less than three months which could with any chance of success attempt to force a passage into Charleston, whilst it was well known that the garrison could not hold out for more than ten days at the very utmost.

The real and direct cause, so far as I ever could see, was a vain desire on the part of Jefferson Davis and some of the

Confederate leaders to gain notoriety, fame, or glory, and stir up a warlike feeling throughout the South, and to gratify the vanity of a number of young newly-made officers who paraded the streets and shone forth at balls with jewelled swords and handsome uniforms, making great professions of zeal and impatient to be led on to battle, and other fiery demagogues who thirsted for war, but who all disappeared from the scene after the war broke out in earnest.

To illustrate this I believe I cannot do better than relate one single instance of what I saw and heard.

CHAPTER X.

IT was in the beginning of April, 1861, a few days before the bombardment of Fort Sumter. At this time great activity was being displayed at Baton Rouge arsenal in preparing and sending off heavy guns, shot, shell, and other munitions to Fort Jackson and the other forts commanding the entrance to the Mississippi river, when I chanced one evening along with a friend to step into the café of the principal hotel at Baton Rouge, where some of the chief officers were putting up.

Standing near the bar was a group of officers in uniform in conversation with some of the leading citizens of the place. Conspicuous among them was a Mr. D., formerly known as captain, but the jumps at that time from captain to general were so rapid that their toes seemed scarcely to touch the intermediate steps, so that I do not know what rank he may have held on that particular day, but I presume from the way he was addressed that it may have been " Major."

The subject, of course, was the great revolution, and the centre to which all eyes were turned was the critical position at Fort Sumter. The following is about the substance of the conversation :—

" I hope," said Dr. P., " that our leaders at Charleston will act cautiously, and not be led into the trap Mr. Seward has laid for them."

" What trap do you mean ? " said Mr. T. J.

" Why, into striking the first blow, and throwing upon us the onus and responsibility of the war."

" Confound the onus and responsibility," said Judge R., " they have been the aggressors, and with them rests the responsibility."

" Well, we consider them the aggressors," said Mr. S., " but the world at large may not be of that opinion."

" What do we care for the opinion of the world at large ? " said Mr. H., as he drained off his glass and looked around to see who was likely to stand treat next.

" Well, I do not mean so much the opinion of European powers," replied Mr. S., " though that may be something, but that of the other States is a very great matter. We have now the sympathy of the powerful States all around us,— Virginia, Kentucky, Missouri, and all the other Southern States sympathise with us, and would resist any force being sent through their territory to coerce us. But we know they are all wishful to avoid war, and for us to strike a blow unnecessarily would be against us, and considerably alienate their sympathy."

" S. and the Doctor were always Unionists and submissionists," said Judge R., " and I suppose would submit to be crushed under the feet of Lincoln and his abolition crew ; for me, before I would submit to such degradation, I would mount my horse and go alone and fight against the abolition hordes !"

" I admit," rejoined Mr. S., " that I have been always in favour of Union, if that is possible, and due respect is paid to Southern rights and interests. But if those are unduly encroached upon, then I advocate secession and accept it ; but I prefer that it should be done peaceably, and I see no reason why it should not. I am certain that a large majority of the population of the whole States, both North and South, although opposed to our secession, are still opposed to any coercion against us, and that if no arrangement can be made to persuade us to remain in the Union, we should be allowed to go in peace. But if we, without any just cause, strike a blow and commence hostilities, then we turn the tide of popular feeling against us, and we just play into the hands of that unprincipled man, Seward, who is known to be the bitter enemy of the South, and who is just leading by the nose that simple and ignorant man, Lincoln, and playing his own cards so as to provoke us to strike in order to rouse the indignation of the North and turn all the other States against us, which would not only strengthen his hands but give him good grounds for swooping down upon us in all his fury, and enable him to gratify his long pent-up revenge upon the South. He is just, as Dr. P. has said, ' Laying a trap for us by keeping those troops in Fort Sumter to provoke us into hostilities.' "

" Then why not blow them to h—ll ? " roared T. J. " He is keeping them there to insult us by waving their detested Yankee flag in the middle of our harbour and before our eyes. Is that not a just cause for striking a blow ? "

" Discretion and caution is better," continued Mr. S.

" Discretion and caution be d——d," roared Mr. H.   " Let us have another drink."   Mr. S. immediately ordered drinks all round to keep Mr. H. quiet.

" It is not so much discretion and caution as good policy and strategy," continued Mr. S.   " We have nothing to apprehend from the United States troops in Fort Sumter. They may wave their flag there for a few days longer, but for a very few days only.   They are virtually our prisoners.   Beauregarde has so strengthened the forts guarding the approach to Charleston that it is quite impossible for the United States to force an entrance to relieve them, nor will they attempt it, and in a few days they will be starved out and they will be quite in our power, and we will have the fort in good condition without having it damaged by a bombardment, and the defences of Charleston will be complete and nothing done to provoke a rupture.   We would then be in a position to stand on the defensive without making any advance toward war, and we would still have the sympathy of a large portion of the people both North and South ; and there are plenty of sensible men, North and South, to settle this matter without war."

" It is all nonsense now to talk of peace," said Judge R. " War must come, and the sooner it comes the better ; and I denounce any man who would talk of Union or advocate peace or submission to Lincoln's rule."

" As to that, Judge," replied Mr. S., " I do not exactly understand what term you would apply to me.   I am not an advocate of peace at any price, and I am ready to stand out for the rights of the South as you are.   I have a son a midshipman in the United States navy, and I have written to him to resign and come home if a rupture takes place.   I have other two sons who have already joined volunteer companies, and are preparing themselves to join in the defence if it should become necessary and war is the ultimatum.   As for myself, I trust to do my duty as far as lies in my power.   But I do not aspire to the Herculean task of fighting the Northern hordes single-handed, and I regard such language as idle balderdash."

Major D., who had till now preserved a dignified silence, now spoke up with all the pomp of a military dictator. " Gentlemen," said he, " it is neither possible nor desirable that this matter should be settled like a common law plea, and without a clash of arms. It would be a paper agreement, patched up by a set of political lawyers. Our revolution would not be worth the name of a revolution, and our independence not worth having if it was not baptized in blood. We have now gained the position over the enemy ; we must show them our power ; we must strike terror into them. We can now present to them a strong and unbroken front, and show them that we are in earnest, and this we will do, and it matters little who likes and who don't like it, and I hope to see Beauregarde open fire on Fort Sumter before this week is out."

"What is the last news, Major ?" cried several voices "There is a report just come in that—"

"The last news," cried the Major (interrupting lest anyone should anticipate him), "is that Beauregarde has, by order of President Davis, demanded the surrender of Fort Sumter. He has given Major Anderson three days to surrender, and if he don't surrender in that time he will open fire upon the fort. Major Anderson has replied that he has supplies for six days only, but if he gets no instructions from Washington he will hold out while he has a single biscuit left."

"Then I think," said Mr. S., "that they should let him eat his last biscuit, and then let him surrender quietly."

"No," replied the Major ; "we must give them a taste of Southern fire; we must show them that we are not to be trifled with. Beauregarde must not lose the chance of striking terror into them. I only wish I had the chance."

"You may get the chance in good time, Major," said Mr. S., "if war breaks out, for depend upon it, if it does, it will not be long before they make an attempt to get control of the Mississippi river, and it would be a gone cause with us if they got that."

"That is what I would not like to see them get," said Mr. T., an old veteran, and now one of the chief men in the Ordnance Department.

"That is just what I would like to see them attempt," said Captain J., a newly-fledged Confederate officer in shining uniform, who was in command of the troops in the garrison.

"Attempt it !" said the Major with an air of self-satisfaction ; "that is just what I am afraid they will not attempt; if they do, I am there."

"And if they do, I am there too," said Captain J.

"And I will be there too," said Mr. H., as he looked around, taking care to show that his glass was empty, "and we will fatten the cat-fish in the river on their abolition carcases."

At this time Mr. T., of the Ordnance Department, having recognized us, left the party and came over and joined us, and we walked out together.

Mr. T. was a veteran who had served in the Mexican war, and he had been over twelve years a foreman in the Ordnance Department; he was a respectable man, and we were both acquainted with him, his son being a member of the same volunteer company as myself.

"He seems to be a terrible warrior that Major D.," remarked my companion as soon as we had got out to the street.

"Bosh," said Mr. T., "he is a squirt, he is freezing for a fight, and I doubt much if there would be much fight in him if put to the test."

"Has he got command of the forts at the mouth of the river?"

"Yes, I believe so; he has got charge of the mounting of them anyway."

"Is he a graduate of West Point?"

"O, I suppose so, and I believe he has been in the regular army."

"What is he that Captain J.?"

"O, he is no military man, he is just learning; he got his commission and that post because he took an active part in the secession movement."

"He seems to have plenty of confidence in himself anyhow," observed my companion.

"Ah! they all have plenty of confidence in themselves, these fire-eaters. I only wish they may be up to the mark when the time comes."

"Do you think there is any truth in what Major D. was saying about Beauregarde going to bombard Fort Sumter?"

"Well, I would not doubt but there is."

"Well, I think they are going mad altogether."

"It is certainly madness, but that is between ourselves," and Mr. T. put his finger to his lip as a sign of the times.

My companion, who was a citizen and a man of some standing in the place, observed the motion and bit his lip. "Well, I think," said he, "that old S. gave them his mind pretty freely there to-night."

"Yes," he did, said Mr. T., "and spoke good sense too.

Old S. does not care for one of them. They can't cow him ; he has more brains and more fire too than all that was there put together. I only wish we had more men like him amongst us."

" I believe if we had," said my companion, " we would have had no secession."

" We would not," said Mr. T. " Good night." And Mr. T. took his leave, and we went home.

I might here anticipate a little, and give a short sketch of the characters who took part in this conversation, and the parts they afterwards took.

Dr. P. was a man well advanced in years. He had been in early life a physician, but became a planter, and owned a large number of slaves. He retained his Union principles as far as it was possible for him to do so ; he kept very quiet, and took little or no part in the secession movement.

When New Orleans and other parts of the State were subdued by the Federal forces he exerted himself as a mediator, and by his influence got some of his old friends released and paroled who had been imprisoned by Butler and other Federal commanders.

Mr. S. was also advanced in years, was also a planter and slaveowner and a merchant.

When Lincoln issued his proclamation he became an active supporter of the Confederacy. His sons all joined the Confederate army. One of them was in the same company with me, and was brave to recklessness.

Judge R. was a younger man. He had followed law and had been a judge, but was now a planter and slaveowner. He continued to make warlike speeches, until told that warlike words were no longer wanted but warlike deeds, but he could never be prevailed upon or even shamed into joining the army. He vanished from the scene.

T. J. was a planter and slaveowner; he was also a comparative young man. He had made himself so conspicuous as a votary of war and a fire-eater that he was constrained to take some part, and obtained an appointment as a commissary, which he held for some time while the commissary department was fat and healthy; but when that got lean and unhealthy so did T. J., and he retired on the sick list.

Mr. H. had also been a planter and slaveowner ; but, being also a good judge of brandy, his plantation and slaves got heavily mortgaged to Northern capitalists, and ultimately became the means of converting to Southern principles one or more of the Northern abolitionists who came South and took possession of his plantation and slaves, and quite abjured their abolition sentiments. Mr. H. then adopted the less successful method of making converts by becoming a politician and advocating Southern rights from the stump until his coat and his subject alike became threadbare. He continued to be a frequenter of the cafés, and throughout the war always contrived to be on good terms with either Confederates or Federals, just as the one or the other happened to be in possession of the place.

Major D. speedily became a general, and was entrusted with the defence of the Mississippi and commanded the forts near the entrance of the river. Great confidence was placed in him. He was called the gallant D. by the newspapers and the ladies. He commanded the forts and defended the river very bravely until the enemy made their first appearance, when of the defence he made there are many conflicting reports, but it was not what was expected of him. The Federal fleet sailed past, occupied New Orleans, and got control of the lower Mississippi, which was the first and most fatal blow to the Confederate States. The gallant D. surrendered himself a prisoner of war, accepted a parole and went and took his residence quietly in the North, and that was the last of the gallant D.

Captain J., who had been so wishful to see the Federal forces attempt the Mississippi river, got the opportunity of having his wish gratified. He did not, however, wait to see them, but quickly abandoned his post. It is true he could not have held it against the Federal fleet; but the precipitancy of his retreat without reconnoitering or taking some observation of the enemy's movements caused some comment.

He afterwards came to our camp at Corinth, and was recounting with great gusto his feat of destroying some of the garrison property so that it should not fall into the hands of the enemy, and was describing how he had taken down the flagstaff and broken it into pieces.

"Did you break it over a Yankee's head," jeeringly said little A. B., a lad in our company not yet seventeen years of age.

Captain J. turned fiercely on him, and recognized in him a boy whose head he had threatened to break for some little offence about the garrison gates at Baton Rouge about a year before.

That lad was now a veteran, having fought in three battles, and had been once wounded.

Captain J. had little more to say, cut the conversation short, and sneaked off.

On the morning after I had witnessed this scene, the newspapers gave an account of the communication between General Beauregarde and Major Anderson something similar to what had been related by Major D. General Beauregarde, in the name of the Confederate States, had given Major Anderson a certain time to surrender the fort, and if he did not surrender it in that time, he would open fire upon it. To which Major Anderson replied that he could get no instructions from Washington, but that he would return the fire and defend the fort as far as it was in his power, and if Beauregarde did not batter him to pieces, he would in any case be starved out in a few days.

It has been stated that General Beauregarde and Major Anderson, who were both men of the highest honour and integrity, were upon the most friendly terms with each other; that Beauregarde was pressed by the impetuosity of Jefferson Davis and his cabinet, and Major Anderson was disgusted with the mean and deceitful shuffling of the Government at Washington. And there was a mutual understanding between them that the bombardment should take place. It would on the one hand gratify the vanity and ambition of Jefferson Davis and the Confederate leaders, and on the other hand relieve Major Anderson from his awkward position, and afford him an honourable pretext for surrendering the fort.

CHAPTER XI.

ON the 12th of April, 1861, Beauregarde opened fire upon Fort Sumter ; his force was about 8,000 men, and about 200 heavy guns.

Major Anderson's force in Fort Sumter numbered about 83 men, and they replied with as many guns as they could work to advantage.

The bombardment continued for about two days, when some wooden buildings in the fort were discovered to be on fire. Whether this was from the effect of the Confederate shells or from some other cause is not known, but the garrison worn out after a gallant defence displayed a flag of truce, a parley was gone through, and Major Anderson's force evacuated the fort carrying their arms and colours and with all the honours of war. Major Anderson for the time being became the honoured guest of General Beauregarde.

It has been facetiously remarked that the gunnery on both sides must have been exceedingly good, as this tremendous cannonade was kept up for two days without a single person being hurt on either side. This was supposed to have been the object of the combatants, but how it was carried out without accident seems almost a miracle; and, notwithstanding the serious state of matters, it was humorously remarked throughout the South that Mr. Lincoln would still be able to express, as before, the only views he had ever given of his opinion or intended policy in regard to the situation, which was a congratulation " that there was nobody hurt."

The ceremony (for it was nothing more) was thus over, and Fort Sumter was now in the hands of the Confederates.

Bloodless and farcical as this performance seems to have been, it was the great factor in, and originator of, the devastating war through years of bloodshed which followed.

Truly did General Banks say two years afterwards, in his proclamation at New Orleans, that the first gun fired at Sumter proclaimed emancipation.

A little prudence on the part of Jefferson Davis and his cabinet, and a little patience, was all that was now required. They might have sat in perfect security, and in a week's time the garrison would have surrendered. They would have got possession of the fort sound and entire. That "first gun at Sumter" would never have been fired, war might have been averted, and emancipation in due time have come through a bloodless path. Mr. Seward would not yet have had a just cause to declare war against the seceded States; he would not have had the undivided sympathy of the North in attempting to coerce them, and he would not have been justified even by the bulk of the Northern people in declaring war without first making at least some attempt at a peaceful settlement.

The news of the bombardment and fall of Fort Sumter spread like lightning throughout the whole States, North and South. The vainglorious triumph of Jefferson Davis and the Confederate leaders knew no bounds; it was paraded as a great victory for the Southern arms, and was made use of in every possible way to rouse a warlike feeling in the South. A great many, however, regarded the affair in a more serious light, and saw the chances of peace getting less and less.

While Jefferson Davis and the Confederate leaders were triumphing over their *imaginary* victory and flooding the country with speeches about the prowess of Southern arms and threatening all opponents with a taste of Southern gunpowder and Southern steel, Mr. Seward was chuckling over the much more important victory he had gained.

His plans had succeeded completely. He had obtained the *casus belli* he had sought, and had manœuvred so that the Confederate States should strike the first blow, and give him cause to wreak his vengeance on the South, and he did not fail to avail himself of the opportunity.

The Lincoln newspapers of course made the most of it. The Northern people, few of whom knew the position or understood Mr. Seward's game, were fired with indignation, and the feeling against the Confederate States was general throughout the North, and the bombardment of Fort Sumter was declared to be the opening of hostilities and the commencement of war.

H

Mr. Seward took care to take the tide at the flood. He did not give the Northern people time to reflect, or allow any pro-Southern papers time to comment on his shuffling game or plead any extenuating circumstances on behalf of the Confederates, few as there were to plead, but followed up the news of the bombardment so quickly with an exposition of Mr. Lincoln's policy by his proclamation and declaration of war that it was obvious he must have had it all prepared and ready before the bombardment took place. He at the same time turned to the commissioners whom he had kept waiting for an audience and gave as his reply—"No compromise with traitors."

I may observe that any opinions I may express on these subjects are the summing up of sentiments I heard privately expressed on the rapidly occurring events during that critical period by men of sound wisdom and integrity who kept entirely out of the political circle. And I think it is unfortunate, and must be disastrous to popular governments, when so many of the wisest and most virtuous men show such apathy in public matters and allow public affairs to get into the hands of a few unprincipled demagogues who usurp the name of the people, and to which usurped power the most respectable of society must, as in this case, in the end become slaves and victims. To the apathy of the honest and respectable people, and to the usurpation of power by unprincipled political demagogues, may be ascribed the whole consequences of this fratricidal and devastating war.

Mr. Lincoln's proclamation, which was issued immediately after the bombardment of Fort Sumter, was a declaration of war against the States said to be in rebellion against the United States, and a call for 75,000 men to crush the rebellion. To each State outside of the Confederacy was issued an order to furnish its quota of men. And an imperative demand was made upon these States in rebellion to lay down their arms and submit to the authority of the United States within 10 days.

The purport of this proclamation was so sweeping and imperative and so menacing in its tone, that it caused the greatest excitement not only within the Confederate States but throughout the whole of the Southern States. It seemed to outdo even the arrogance and pugnacity of Jefferson Davis and his cabinet. It left no opening for any peaceful settlement, and it entirely ignored the existence of any loyal or

peaceful citizens within the Confederate States. It made no
appeal to them. It held out to them no guarantee or promise
of protection or amnesty. It gave them no alternative but
unconditional surrender or the sword.

This was what was called Lincoln's proclamation, and he
had to bear the name of it, and against him was kindled the
anger of every man, woman, and child in the South. It was,
however, the opinion of many, and this opinion was freely
expressed with what justice I do not pretend to say, that
although Lincoln's name was appended to it, it never emanated from him with the full knowledge of its purport, but that
Mr. Seward was in every word of it. The Federal Executive
well knew that such a proclamation would never be obeyed;
and Mr. Seward had so arranged matters that he had got his
Southern enemies duly convicted, and the powerful North
fully aroused to execute the punishment. He gloated over
the blow he was about to strike. The mere punishment of
the leaders and actual perpetrators would not satisfy him,
but, like Haman of old, he must have a glutting revenge.
Every one within the Southern States must yield to his grace
at the point of the bayonet.

Such was the construction put upon the proclamation by
the great body of the people within the seceded States ; and
such was the light in which it was regarded, and the way it
was commented upon. How far the proclamation itself, or
the construction put upon it may have been warranted or
justifiable it is not for me to say, but this sudden development
of Lincoln's policy, as it was called, took every one by surprise,
because it was so sudden and unexpected.

The so-called bombardment of Fort Sumter, though no
doubt a high-handed act, and might be called an outrage, yet
it was no more than many similar acts already done by the
seceding States of which the Federal Government had taken
no cognizance.

It was known to be nothing more than a mere demonstration,
with a careful avoidance of bloodshed previously arranged
between the two commanders, a harmless glove fight on the
same principle as the seizing of the arsenal and garrison at
Baton Rouge by a mere display of force; but, as in this case
the fort could not be approached by infantry by land, a form
of a bombardment was gone through, the result of which will
speak for itself.

The Confederate Government, if they really desired a peaceful settlement, must have seen afterwards their error—although they never admitted it—and how they had been outwitted by Mr. Seward in thus letting him get the handle which he so quickly made use of.

It has been stated that secession was not the unanimous act of the States, but that a large portion of the population was beguiled or coerced into the act. In refutation of this it is said that this is disproved by the unanimity with which the Southerners took up arms and fought so determinedly for their independence.

So far as my observation went at the time the Act of Secession was passed, the population was not unanimously in favour of it, and in most of the States the majority of the people were opposed to it. The act was carried through chiefly by the machinations of politicians, and some of the more rabid pro-slavery men who had extreme views on the subject. But the inaction of the Federal Government and their seeming acquiescence in the movement caused many to accept the situation, and when Mr. Lincoln was inaugurated, his seeming indecision and imbecility, followed by the supposed shuffling and deceitful policy of Mr. Seward, caused a still greater number to adhere to the secession party. But when Mr. Lincoln's war proclamation was issued calling for troops to crush the seceded States into obedience, then in reality did unanimous secession take place. The people within the Confederate States, especially those who had been favourable to union and opposed to secession, were now face to face with the situation.

Many of them would have given half of what they possessed to have preserved the Union. They would have been ready to take up arms to support the authority of the Federal Government, if that Government had at the proper time shown the slightest disposition to afford them any support or protection. The Federal Government had neither by word or act given them the slightest encouragement, it had rather seemed to point out to them that it was their duty to obey and submit to the secession Government.

The Federal Government had with every seeming acquiescence, and without resistance and without protest on the part of the administrative, handed over to the secessionists the forts, arsenals, arms, and munitions of war, to be used if need be in coercing into submission any part of the population who might be opposed to secession. The Buchanan Government had abandoned them and left them no other resource but to submit to the secession Government.

The secession Government had gained strength, and become firmly established, and they had as a matter of necessity accepted it for the time being.

Mr. Lincoln's Government had come into power, and had been in power for more than a month, without giving any indication of its policy. That Government had shown no friendly disposition towards or recognised the existence of any Union or loyal party within the Confederate States. It had made no attempt to settle the matter by a conference and avoid war. It had used the most insidious means to provoke a rupture, and in this it had succeeded.

Whatever might be their sentiments, they could no longer remain passive. To submit to Lincoln's terms they could not, even if they were inclined. They were hopelessly in the power of the Confederate Government, which was strong, determined, and unscrupulous.

If the secessionists fought and resisted Lincoln's proclamation, the Union party could not remain neutral, they would be coerced and pressed into service, and compelled to take part in the resistance, or they would be persecuted or banished, their goods and properties confiscated, and their homes desolated. They considered that the Federal Government by its weakness and inaction had placed them in this predicament, and now the same Government, under a different leader, sought to chastise them for being in the position they were.

They did not long hesitate, however. They had sought to be loyal but received no support. They had been cast off and abandoned, and they would not now submit to be whipped back into and under a Government which they considered had forfeited all claim to their respect or allegiance.

The whole population within the Confederate States was now roused to a man, and the last vestige of Union sentiment was now cast off. Those who had hitherto been the most earnest in their desire to maintain the Union and preserve peace, were the first to take up arms. Nothing was now thought of but war, and resisting to the utmost the aggressive invasion threatened by Mr. Lincoln. Volunteer companies were raised in every community, armed and drilled with great perseverance.

I must again observe that whatever may be said or has been said on the abstract principles which led to this war, particularly where it has been set forth that the North was fighting to abolish slavery, and the South was fighting to maintain it; I must to such an assumption give an unqualified denial. Whatever may have been the question from which the quarrel originated, it had now been entirely departed from and lost sight of.

Of the thousands who at this time rushed to arms, I believe very few had in their minds the question of slavery. Many had before them the question of "States' Rights" *versus* "Federal authority," but the greatest number were animated only by a determination to resist Lincoln's proclamation.

I can also assert that when the Northerners took up arms in obedience to Lincoln's proclamation it was only to avenge the bombardment of Fort Sumter, put down the rebellion, and maintain the integrity of the Union. Anything like emancipation, or interfering in any way with the institution of slavery, was no part of the programme, and was most emphatically repudiated. The abolition of slavery which afterwards followed, was altogether an after consequence of the war; and Mr. Lincoln's very questionable policy in issuing, in January, 1863, a proclamation of emancipation, but extending emancipation *only* to the slaves in the States or parts of States in rebellion against the United States, was called forth more as a military necessity, and as a means of subduing the South, than from any philanthropic motive. This will be shown in the course of events as they happened.

I mention this because I think there has been altogether too much said about the North fighting to set free the slaves, and the South fighting to hold them in slavery. Such assertions were no doubt put forth by the Northern agencies to obtain the sympathy of the world, and restrain any European or foreign power from recognizing the Confederacy. It must be remembered that the North had free intercourse with all the world, and could put their side of the question to the world unchallenged; while the South was blockaded and secluded from the world, and the real feeling and sentiment was never known except through limited and restricted channels.

CHAPTER XII.

THE storm of indignation which was aroused by Lincoln's proclamation was not confined to the six States now forming the Confederacy. It spread like wildfire throughout all the other Southern States. The sympathy which the Confederate States had lost by their rash act in bombarding Fort Sumter, was now recovered and increased tenfold.

Texas, which up till now had been undecided, and had been more inclined to fall back on her former independence and "Lone Star Flag," at once joined the Confederacy. Virginia, Kentucky, and Missouri sent a most peremptory refusal to furnish men to coerce sovereign States. And in a few days the exciting and joyful news was received in the Confederate States that Virginia had seceded from the Union. This was followed quickly by the news that North Carolina, Arkansas, and Tennessee, had also seceded, and that Maryland, Kentucky, and Missouri were preparing to follow.

It was now thought that Mr. Lincoln, seeing the serious state of matters, and the gigantic proportions the rebellion had assumed, would make an attempt at some conciliatory measures by proposing negotiation through some convention or meeting of commissioners appointed by North and South respectively, to come to some arrangement and avoid war, or perhaps have the matter referred to the decision of the supreme court of the United States.

Whether, as· has been supposed, Mr. Lincoln entertained such an idea but was overruled by Mr. Seward, I do not know. Certainly his position was now one of great difficulty.

It was too late to adopt the policy of letting the six rebellious States go in peace, and then proceed to amend the constitution. There were now 11 seceding States and three more preparing to follow. It was improbable that any proposal to negotiate would be accepted by the South, which by the sudden acquisition to its strength, had become more defiant and arrogant than ever, and would accept nothing but total severance from the Union.

The first movement of the Federal Government was to station an army at Washington under pretence of protecting that city, and by extending a force along the Potomac cut off Maryland from the other Southern States, and so prevent that State from seceding. At the same time a large body of United States troops under General Lyon, was sent into Missouri. Thus by holding command of the Missouri river they cut off the northern part of that State, including the city of St. Louis, from joining with the South.

Kentucky had in the meantime declared her intention to remain strictly neutral.

Mr. Lincoln now issued another proclamation, declaring the Southern ports to be in a state of blockade, and at the same time placing a blockading force in the Mississippi at Cairo, where the Ohio river joins the Mississippi. This was calculated to have a very paralyzing effect on the South, as it cut off all communication with the outer world, and stopped all additions being made to their supplies or resources. It was, however, to some extent gratifying to the Confederate leaders in so far as the act of blockading the seaports was concerned, as it would bring the Federal Government into conflict with foreign powers. It being considered a breach of international law for a nation to blockade its own ports, and that it can only as a belligerent blockade the ports of a foreign enemy, it seemed plain that if the Federal Government wished to avoid a conflict with foreign powers it could no longer claim the South as an integral part of the United States, and must either withdraw the blockade, or recognize the South as a foreign power and an enemy. These views were paraded before the Southern people as a proof of Mr. Lincoln's incapacity.

In the meantime the last seceded States had joined with the six States which had previously constituted the Confederacy, and a new and more powerful Confederacy was thus formed, consisting of the States of Virginia, North Carolina, South

Carolina, Tennessee, Georgia, Florida, Alabama, Mississippi, Louisiana, Arkansas, and Texas. The seat of Government was removed from Montgomerie, Alabama, to Richmond, Virginia; Jefferson Davis and Stephens remaining respectively president and vice-president as before.

The States of Maryland and Missouri being now kept by the Northern troops from joining the South, several collisions had taken place between the Northern soldiers and the populace at Baltimore and other parts of Maryland, and in Missouri.

The Confederate Government now gave notice to all parties who sympathised with the North, to leave the Confederate States within 10 days, and all communication with the North was cut off, war was declared, and a call was made for volunteers to serve the Confederate States for a period of one year.

I must now return to my own personal position, as the time had now come when I could no longer remain passive.

I had no sympathy with the secession movement, and had always been opposed to it. But matters had much changed since secession first took place, and I now certainly sympathised with the many who had at first been opposed to it, but afterwards became disgusted and indignant at the action, or rather inaction of the Federal Government, at the imbecility of Buchanan's Government, and the shuffling and· deceitful policy of Lincoln's cabinet.

Still I have no doubt, should there be any who may consider these pages worth reading, they will very justly question the consistency of my action in taking "act and part" in a movement in which I had so little interest, and a cause in which I had so little sympathy, and which I considered had at first been brought about by such corrupt and unfair means as I have attempted to describe, and that I, a disinterested foreigner, and an alien without kith or kin in the whole Western world, should forsake peaceful pursuits and embroil myself in a war the consequences of which it was impossible to foresee, and on a side against which the chances were at least three to one.

These questions I put to myself then, and have often put to myself since.

Was it selfish policy? Was it heartfelt sympathy? Was it a sense of honour, or love of adventure?

I have no doubt that the very idea of such reflections from
one of my sphere of life might cause a smile from many whose
aspirations soar to a higher sphere of philosophy, but I merely
mention them as they may tend to show how hundreds of
others situated like myself were led away by the same
impulse.

I may say that each of these motives contributed more or
less to my decision.

First, Policy had its part in a business point of view. I
had since I came to the community considerably improved my
position. I had as a working man, and recently as a partner
in a business, been kindly received and well patronized by
the people of the place. My two senior partners were both
foreign to the country (one English and one Scotch). Both
were married men with families and domiciled in the place;
and as the community from which we derived our support had
now unanimously, and we supposed justifiably, gone in for
the cause, and other firms composed of foreigners had lent
it their aid, our firm would have seemed singularly plodding
and selfish, and perhaps been regarded with suspicion had we
held aloof and not contributed at least one man to the service.

Second, Sympathy. I had been strongly opposed to secession,
and I could scarcely denounce strongly enough the one-sided,
unjust, and corrupt means by which the secession of the States
was effected; and, though my opinion on that point was still the
same, I now shared with the large body of loyal, law-abiding
and Union-loving people, in the disgust and contempt justly
invoked against the Federal Government, both under the old
and the new administrations, for the base and deceitful manner
in which they had treated the loyal and law-abiding people in
the South. For, to say the least of it, they had failed to
afford them at the proper time that help and support which
was within their power to give. They had in the most imbecile
manner withdrawn or allowed to be driven from the South
every vestige of their authority. They would not listen to
any representation which might come from any loyal portion
of the inhabitants of the South. They had not in the least
way tried to check the action of the clique which had gone
through the form of withdrawing the States from the Union,
and declaring them independent. They had not shown the
slightest indication that they would protect and support
the law-abiding people of the South in maintaining the

constitution and the Union. The trifling and imbecility of Buchanan's Government, followed by the deceitful shuffling of Lincoln's administration, could not but provoke the disgust and contempt of every law-respecting person in the South, who now seemed unanimously to come to the conclusion that a government which would not assert its authority by maintaining its laws and protecting its citizens from the dominance of unprincipled politicians was no longer entitled to respect or allegiance. In this I agreed with them.

Third, Honour. I had been, an active member of, and taken considerable interest in, the town volunteer company of riflemen ; and to have resigned and withdrawn from it in the hour of danger would not have been very creditable to myself or gratifying to my countrymen in the place, who, I am proud to say, that, in whatever part of the world they may be, generally maintain their proud national feeling and veneration for the honour of old Scotland.

Fourth, Love of adventure. Perhaps there was a little of that feeling as set forth by Sir Walter Scott—

> "That if the path's to danger known,
> The danger's self is lure alone."

I therefore concluded to remain with the volunteer company of which I was a member to see what action they took.

The volunteer company of which I was a member, as I have related at the seizure of the arsenal, showed disaffection and marched off the ground—had since that time continued as an "independent company" to maintain and increase their efficiency, and had been still more active in drilling and attaining proficiency and in preparing for any emergency.

When Mr. Lincoln issued his war proclamation, a meeting of the company was held to consider the matter. The proclamation was read calling upon them to lay down their arms and submit unconditionally to his authority before the invasion of 75,000 men.

There was also read and considered a call by the Confederate Government for volunteers to serve for a period of one year in order to resist the invasion.

The two propositions were before the volunteers, and they must accept the one or the other.

They unanimously agreed to offer their services as volunteers to the Confederate Government for the period of one year.

The offer was promptly accepted by the Confederate Government; and this decision and prompt action of the company was received with great applause by the populace as the pioneer company from the district which volunteered their services. And now commenced preparations in earnest for outfit and departure. The dress uniforms with tinsel and feathered hats were thrown aside, and fatigue or fighting uniforms and foraging caps substituted. To assist in the equipment and outfit handsome donations were freely given, many of them by ladies, so that the company was able to volunteer for service fully armed and equipped, and requiring only to be supplied with camp equipage and ammunition.

I may here say that as the matter has reference to a volunteer movement, and a power, or nation, going to war or preparing to resist invasion with an army composed entirely of volunteers (on this subject I will hereafter speak), nothing could exceed the avidity and enthusiasm with which the cause was taken up. Every other object and consideration was set aside, the whole thought and conversation was centred in the one subject. Every man, woman, and child seemed to vie with each other in their efforts to aid and support it. Aged men and women furnished donations in money according to their circumstances. Poor families set to work in preparing shirts, underclothing, stockings, and other necessaries. Wealthy merchants and employers, whose employees and clerks would volunteer for service, made provision for their families or dependents by continuing their salaries during the time they volunteered for service.

Mothers with tears in their eyes came up with their sons of 15 and 16 years of age, who had been carried away with the enthusiasm, and requested that they might be accepted as volunteers, and handing them over to the care of the orderly sergeant, with no doubt many a sincere prayer in solitude for the divine care and protection over their offspring. During the few days of preparation the strength of the company was augmented from 62 to 86, while other two companies recently formed had volunteered their services and were preparing to follow.

As several members of the company were men with families, and many were connected with business, they had been busy for the last few days in making arrangements and provision for their households during their absence. Much also had to be done by those connected with business, such as straightening up books, squaring accounts, signing powers of attorney, wills and testaments not being forgotten.

On the morning of the 29th of April, 1861, the Baton Rouge Rifle Volunteer Company embarked on a steamer for New Orleans. As may be imagined there was a large crowd gathered to see them off, and a unanimous, and, I believe, sincere expression of a wish for their success, preservation, and happy and speedy return. There were many surmises as to their future fate. Some were still confident in their belief that there would be no war, that it was quite impossible that a civilized and highly enlightened country possessing so many wise and talented men of sterling integrity, should be dragged into a gigantic and bloody civil war, through the instrumentality of a few bloated politicians. As a proof of this confidence, I will relate a little incident :—

As we were preparing to go on board the steamer, I said to one of my partners who was standing on the wharf with some other gentlemen of the place, that I was annoyed at the watchmaker who had been doing some repairs to my watch, and had not got it ready as he had promised, and I asked if he would get the watch when ready, and try and send it on to me as I could not well do without it. Upon this an old gentleman who was with him pulled out a handsome gold watch and handed it to me, saying, " Here, I will lend you mine."

" Lend me yours ! " said I, " when on earth do you expect to see it again ? "

" When you come back," said he, pressing the watch upon me, " and that will be in about four months. This thing," continued he, " will never be allowed to go on ; there are plenty of sensible men both North and South to put a stop to this madness ; Congress meets in July, and then means will be taken to put things right."

" I wish they had done it sooner," said I, taking the watch and joining the company who were now forming to embark.

I may say that some eighteen months afterwards, I had the pleasure of handing my friend back his watch, when he said he would value it the more for the services it had seen, and also as a reminder of events which had made him a wiser and a much sadder man.

We were soon on board, and the steamer backed out into

the middle of the stream amidst the deafening cheers of the crowds on the wharf and river bank, amongst whom there were no doubt many anxious hearts.

As this company may be taken as a pretty fair sample of the material of which the Southern army was composed, I may give a slight description of its composition, as my position afterwards in the company enables me to do with some exactness.

Of the calling or occupation of the different members there were : planters, or sons of planters, 9 ; farmers, or sons of farmers, 11 ; merchants, or sons of merchants, 11; merchants' assistants, clerks, etc., 13 ; lawyer, 1; engineers, 4; carpenters, 4 ; painters, 3; compositors, 3; bricklayers, 2; ironmoulders, 2; gasfitters, 2; sawmillers, 2; gunsmith, 1; tailor, 1; druggist, 1; teacher, 1; carriage makers, 2; cabinetmaker, 1; law students, 2; marble cutter, 1; miscellaneous, 8.

The total number of the above who owned slaves, or were members of families who owned slaves, or were in any way connected with or interested in the institution of slavery was 31 ; while the number of those who had no connection or interest whatever in the institution of slavery was 55.

Of the nationalities of the above there were : natives of Louisiana or other Southern States, 47 ; Northern States, 13 ; Canada, 4; England, 2; Scotland, 4; Ireland, 5; Germany, 6; uncertain, 5.

As we proceeded down the river it was evident that our presence on the steamer was well known. It being one of the regular line of steamers on the station, notice seemed to have been sent to the different places along the river where the vessel was to call. This was no doubt with the view of showing a precedent and increasing the enthusiasm, and stirring up others to emulate us. Of course wherever the steamer called we were greeted with hearty cheers, and in any of the places where volunteer companies existed these turned out to salute us, and to announce that they would be ready to follow us in a few days.

When night came on we were treated, though in a very slight degree, to one of the privations which we were to undergo as soldiers. Our meals had been furnished at table in the saloon with all the usual luxuriance for passengers on those fine steamers. But state rooms of course could not be furnished, therefore we must pass the night in soldier fashion by rolling ourselves in our blankets and lying down on the floor of the saloon. This was of course made the subject of many a laugh and joke, but it was evident before morning that some felt the deck a little hard, and not quite so comfortable as the soft beds they had been accustomed to. Some were a little put out at the want of the usual convenience for their morning ablutions and toilet. But like Midshipman Easy, they were reminded that it was "all zeal." As we approached New Orleans, another company of volunteers was taken on board, and we arrived at the city about daybreak.

The morning was wet and stormy, and very unusual weather for New Orleans at this season of the year, and it seemed to be in accord with the times. Several other steamers had arrived during the night with volunteer companies from other parts of the State, and we waited our turn to be mustered into service, which ceremony was to take place on the steamer.

We did not require to wait long before Brigadier-General Tracy, who was in command of the troops in New Orleans, came on board.

Brigadier-General Tracy was a veteran of the Mexican war. He was a little cross-looking man dressed in uniform, and wore a little red laced foraging cap. He had been busy mustering in volunteers all morning, and his voice was almost hoarse with calling out names amid the howling of the wind.

He took the roll-book from the captain and cried out, "All you that volunteer for the Confederate service answer to your names." He then proceeded to call the roll, the men answering to their names. He then closed the roll-book, and retained a copy of the muster-roll, and addressing the men said : "You are now mustered into the service of the Confederate States for a period of one year, unless sooner discharged, and subject to all the rules and regulations of war"—this last sentence being delivered with great emphasis.

Our boys, as the members of the company were called and by which term I shall sometimes hereafter designate them when referring more to the younger members, did not at once realise the importance of this short ceremony, and had to be reminded that they were now under authority, and that they were no longer citizens but soldiers ;— that all questions pertaining to public matters and all political subjects and civil matters should now be set aside, and every attention given to studying and becoming proficient in their duties as soldiers, and that military matters alone should now engross their attention.

Being now no longer a civilian but a soldier I will finish up to this time the account of my observations of the political movements which led to the secession of the States and the outbreak of the war, and devote myself entirely to military matters.

SECTION III.

LIFE IN THE CONFEDERATE ARMY.

CHAPTER XIII.

To give a simple narrative of my experience in a war campaign may be supposed to be but a repetition of many similar narratives given by individuals of their personal experience, and though such narratives may be more the personal feeling and observation of the narrator than descriptive of the campaign, and may picture more the real than the ideal, still they are necessarily limited, and often of a very different nature, and may appear tame and commonplace compared with the carefully prepared reports and the more glowing accounts furnished by Special Correspondents at the time, and which may contribute in some degree to the material out of which history is afterwards composed.

The individual soldier is swallowed up in the midst of the turmoil, and knows only what is going on around him; his duties are confined to a certain place or post, and beyond that he is supposed to see or know nothing ; and he can only describe minutely and in detail the movements of a small part of the campaign.

The correspondent is supposed to look down upon the whole from a distance, observing and describing each body of men as units collectively, and armies and detachments as they are moved about apparently with as much ease as men upon a chess-board.

There was, however, in this war some exceptional circumstances, which tended to favour the individual narrator more than the general reporter.

In the first place, the armies on both sides were composed of citizen soldiers who, although having for the time resigned their freedom as citizens and submitted themselves as soldiers subject to all duties and obedience under the rules and regulations of war, nevertheless there was even among the rank and file a large number of highly-educated and intelligent men who took a lively interest in every movement, and through personal friendship with staff or field-officers generally knew all that was proper to be known of the plan of the campaign, and took opportunity of observing how every movement was carried out; in short, men from business circles, whose intelligent and active minds required something more to exercise them than the simple duties of the soldier, and from want of having anything else to occupy their attention, applied themselves to the study of the art of war. They generally knew anything that was open to be known of their own army, and often had a good knowledge of the whereabouts and strength of the enemy, and could understand and account for the different movements.

The face of the country was a serious obstacle in the way of obtaining a bird's-eye view of the scene. This was also a serious impediment to generals in the way of observing the progress of the action, and in directing the movements of their troops. Most of the fighting was done in rough and broken country, covered with forests or tall brushwood; and although some eminence might be found from which an outline might be ascertained of the relative positions of the forces, still the movements of the men could not be seen, and could only be judged from the crackling of the musketry and the smoke rising from among the trees or brushwood, and the noise and smoke indicating the position of a battery of artillery. It was sometimes very difficult to distinguish friend from foe.

I have heard it jocularly expressed in camp-fire criticisms, that the plan of a battle as given in the official report was sometimes formed after the battle was over to bring it in accord with the result, and that the accounts given by the special correspondents were but the breath of the general commanding.

As regards the first of these insinuations, I do not know whether there may be any just grounds for the assertion, but I think there were in this war often cases where the face of the country rendered it extremely difficult for any general to ascertain precisely the movements of the enemy's forces, or to have completely under his eye the movements of his own troops. It is therefore inevitable that a good deal must be left to chance, and to the judgment of subordinate officers, and a good deal to the men themselves, who very often did good work independent of their officers.

With regard to correspondents, in cases where no letter or communication was allowed to go outside the lines without being first read and approved by the provost-martial, the thing must speak for itself.

One of my reasons for venturing upon a short sketch of my personal experience in this war is that it might be a little interesting to some on account of the material of which the armies were composed. It may be said to have been somewhat different in this respect from other great wars. The armies of both North and South, at the commencement and throughout the greater part of the war, were composed of volunteers, not altogether of raw undrilled recruits suddenly picked up for the occasion, but a large portion of them were of the numerous well-drilled and well-equipped volunteer companies which had been in existence and training for many years previous to the outbreak of hostilities.

The regular standing army of the United States consisted only of about 12,000 men. Some of them were stationed in forts, and those who took the field were soon lost sight of in the immense provisional armies that suddenly sprung up, and were never known after the first campaign, in which they were mostly all killed off.

Perhaps I might plead my experience with volunteers in actual warfare as an excuse for expressing my opinion on the volunteer system.

Those fastidious critics who speak disparagingly of volunteers, and can see efficiency only in precise movements, or neatly performed evolutions on a smooth lawn or open park, might do well to consider how far these accomplishments are of practical use in the rough and ready movements required in actual warfare, or how far the parade movements can be carried out in a wild country, amongst hills and ravines, swamps, trees, brushwood, and other obstructions.

Count Moltke is said to have spoken contemptuously of the armies of the American Civil War as being armed mobs, of which he knew nothing, and wished to have nothing to do with.

Count Moltke is no doubt a great military scientist, but it must be remembered that military science, although a leading essential in warfare, exists only so far as pre-arranged plans can be executed. And it may be questionable how far Count Moltke could have filled the place of Lee or Grant, or whether he could with his *grande armée* of levied troops have carried out with success a campaign planned upon his highest conception of military science, amidst the forests and swamps of America, in the face of even the smaller armies of rugged volunteers who fought in the American Civil War; or whether he could ever have kept his army together for four years under the same trying circumstances as the American generals did, without finding out that one ounce of makeshift was worth many pounds of military science; and that mutual willingness, enlightened zeal, and dogged determination, were better qualifications than forced training, be that training ever so precise and efficient.

I believe, and I think it has been sufficiently proved, that there are no better troops in the world than the regular army of Great Britain. But what is the composition of that army?

The British soldier is in a certain sense of the word a volunteer. He is not forced into the service, he enlists voluntarily, under no other compulsion than a taste for military life and a desire to be a soldier, and it is reasonable to suppose that such men will make the best soldiers. But such men are few in number, and the percentage to be got in a population is but small, while the remuneration to a private soldier is also small compared to what is obtainable in other pursuits. Therefore it cannot be supposed that a large army can be raised upon the enlistment system, at least an army sufficiently large to cope with the great masses brought into the field in modern warfare.

As the system of popular government extends, the question may arise as to how such large armies are to be raised and maintained.

In Great Britain the day is gone past when clans follow their chiefs to the field, and although the regular army under the voluntary-enlistment system maintains itself well and is good and efficient, still the army so raised is small in numbers, and could hardly be brought up by voluntary enlistment to a numerical strength sufficient to cope with the armies of the day.

The empires of Europe, under their different systems of maintaining their armies, can still enforce their levies, but the question arises, How long may they be able to do so?

As popular governments extend, men may become too

cunning to serve compulsorily as soldiers, or be subject at any moment to be called out to shed their blood to gratify the whim or ambition of a despotic ruler, and they may rebel against such a system.

Imagine the Czar of Russia who can now keep all Europe on the constant *qui vive*. His power rests entirely upon the obedience of the masses to his sovereign will. Suppose he should suddenly find his subjects acting upon their rights as men in other nations, and would no longer respond to his call, what a weak power his would become!

The immense levies brought into the field under the service system of the great European powers must be composed largely of men who have neither taste nor desire to serve as soldiers, but having no other alternative must obey the sovereign edict. Though for form's sake making a pretended show of enthusiasm, still they are in reality driven like sheep to the slaughter, and unless through a semi-barbarous ignorance they can be fired with some fanatic idea, there can be no great dependence placed in them. A victory obtained over an enemy may inspire them with temporary enthusiasm, but their mind is not with their duty, and the thought of most of them is how they can get clear of the service. I have much satisfaction in the belief that a chief part of the strength of Great Britian and America lies in their volunteers, and although the system is yet but in its infancy it seems destined to become the strong arm of all civilised nations, not only against foreign aggression but against despotism or anarchy at home.

Volunteers are not composed of the residuum of society, but rather of the elite, or of that part which may have a taste or liking for the precision which regulates the duties and habits of the soldier—men who take a pride in undergoing the training, and who would be ready to take up arms to serve or defend their country in case of need, but who would not in peaceful times abandon other pursuits and resign their freedom by enlisting for permanent service. It is natural to suppose that such men make the best soldiers, and from this class powerful armies of volunteers might be raised as provisional armies for any emergency. They might not attain that clock-work precision which looks so well on parade, but which is quite unnecessary in actual warfare, but they could be made thoroughly efficient for every practical purpose.

In the volunteer is the material for the soldier. Their zeal prompts them to study and learn the tactics of the field. Their intelligence gives them a sense of duty, and they know that strict obedience is indispensable, and that obedience to command is not servility. They come to know how to handle their arms. They are well drilled in the Manual, and in the evolutions of the company and the battalion, and can perform them quickly without confusion, and a few months or even weeks of active service will make volunteers the best of soldiers. Volunteers come to have a pride also in their corps. It takes its name from their place of residence. The honour of their corps is identified with the honour of their homes in town or country. From this cause, should they sustain a defeat or a reverse, they burn until they get a chance to retrieve their lost honour.

I do not for a moment mean to say that constant drill, strict training, and the attainment of precise movements and neatly performed evolutions are of no value. I consider them of great value, and particularly in a standing army, as being conducive to the health and physique of the soldier, as well as inspiring him with a military taste and pride in his profession, while the nature of the exercise fits him for more arduous duties. To say nothing of the moral effect drill may have on promoting general habits of smartness and self-respect and sense of duty, to men who have no other business or occupation drill becomes indispensable.

Care should be taken, however, that the soldier should understand that very strict precision is not a *sine quâ non* in actual warfare, and that although in a severe struggle, or in a rough country or difficult position soldiers may lose their places, or their company get mixed in the battalion, or the battalion in the brigade, they are not to consider themselves demoralised or out of command. I have seen a brigade as completely mixed up as if showered from the clouds, and still preserve a line, repel cavalry, and hold their position. My opinion may be of little value, but I think volunteers are destined to be the army of the future. The system is based upon the principle of giving effect to the military spirit of the land, and in training for military service, at a trifling cost, the best men to be found for soldiers, without compromising their liberty or interfering with their regular avocations as citizens. A powerful army may thus be kept up at little or no expense, composed of men of good moral standing who possess a taste for the use of arms, and who could, in a case of emergency, be made a strong defence of the nation, and thus dispensing with the necessity of forcing into service against their will men who have neither the spirit nor the inclination to act as soldiers.

To such men as possess a desire to become volunteers, this narrative of my experience may be a little entertaining if not instructive.

CHAPTER XIV.

HAVING now been mustered into the service, and having
become a part of the army of the Confederate States, a copy
of the army regulations was handed to us, and we were ordered
to Camp Walker, the camp of instruction.

Our baggage, which consisted of a company mess chest and
some boxes of company property, was sent ashore, and it was
arranged that we should remain for a few hours in the city to
give time for camp equipage being sent to Camp Walker for
the different companies which had that morning arrived.

The company was then formed, and we landed from the
steamer to march to the City Hotel, where we were to wait
until things were ready for us. As we proceeded towards the
hotel, one was reminded of Scott's picture of Edinburgh before
Flodden, for—

> " As through the bustling streets we go,
> All was alive with martial show."

On every side all was preparation for war. On the day
previous the first regiment from Louisiana had departed northwards to join the army of Virginia, and a second was being
organised and preparing to follow. All commercial business
was suspended. The extensive wharfs along the river which
were wont to be crowded with vessels discharging cargo or
loading with cotton were deserted. The ships had all cleared
out in consequence of the " notice of blockade."

The extensive cotton presses fronting the wharfs were all
silent and shut up, and nothing seemed in motion but the
preparations for war. The streets resounded with the sound
of the fife and the drum as different volunteer companies proceeded to the camp of instruction. Carts and waggons moved
hither and thither laden with army stores. Newly erected or

extended factories were busily manufacturing gun carriages, caissons, and tumbrils, and converting cotton waggons and drags into army waggons.

The constant rattle of steam-driven sewing machines from many buildings announced the extensive manufacture of saddlery equipments, tents, and army clothing, while officers and men in plain uniforms and thoughtful countenances—many of them accompanied by their wives—were seen going in and out of shops purchasing a few articles to take with them which they supposed would conduce to their health and comfort during their life in camp. Some officers were to be seen of the more dandified type, in gaudy uniforms and gay expressions in their countenance. These were of the zealous and gallant fire-eating class, who had got appointments in the different departments, and were more generally seen in the cities kissing their hands to ladies, than in the camp or field ditching a tent, or digging a rifle pit.

Having marched from the wharfs and through several streets we arrived at the City Hotel, where a sumptuous breakfast was prepared for us, and a large room, or hall, provided for our accommodation until ready to proceed to camp.

While here it was thought expedient before going into camp to have the company fully organised.

The standard complement of officers and non-commissioned officers for a company of infantry was : one captain, two lieutenants, one orderly-sergeant, four duty-sergeants, and four corporals. It had always been the rule among volunteer companies for the members of the company to elect their officers. But now by the "army regulations" it was pointed out, that although the members of the company might still elect their officers, yet no appointment would be confirmed unless the candidate passed an examination, and was found duly qualified and approved of by the brigade commander. This, however, did not apply to officers who held their appointments before the company was mustered into service.

It so happened that our orderly sergeant was the son of the captain, and as the latter carried on an extensive business, it was necessary that he should remain at home to attend to the business ; he therefore had not volunteered, but he had continued to act, and had accompanied the company thus far, but was now about to take his leave and return home. The office of orderly-sergeant was therefore vacant. In the American service this is rather an onerous position in the company, and I who was then third-duty-sergeant was selected for the post, and was examined for competency before a board of officers. I passed satisfactorily, but in the course of the examination it came out that I was an alien, and not a citizen. This was against me, but after some consultation it was considered that as the office was not commissioned I might pass, and the appointment was approved. I was, however, given to understand that I could attain no higher position, and could not hold a commission until I became a citizen; and they advised me to get the preliminaries done at once, as it would take some time to consummate it, unless a special dispensation of the rules was granted.

They then handed me a copy of the "army regulations" for my guidance as orderly-sergeant, and specially directed my attention to a clause which read thus : " No foreigner shall hold any office under the United States Government, either by commission or otherwise, unless he be a citizen of the United States;" the same regulations being adapted for the Confederate States, with the simple alteration of the word " United " being obliterated, and the word " Confederate " substituted.

I had already determined that I would never forswear or renounce my allegiance to Queen Victoria, to become a citizen or subject of any foreign power, nor would a commission in the Confederate service now tempt me. I had volunteered my services for one year, and that I would fulfil as far as lay in my power. I will now give a slight description of the duties of an orderly-sergeant as it was in the United States service at that time.

He held the rank of sergeant-major, his pay was equal to one-and-a-half that of the first duty-sergeant. He was the general executive officer of the company. He was secretary of the company, and was allowed a clerk. He went on no special detachments, or guard duty, except in cases of emergency. He kept the roll-book, and all other books, papers or accounts of the company. He was accountable for the men present or absent. He returned every morning to the adjutant a report of the state and effective force of his company.

He made out all requisitions for rations, ammunition, arms, or camp equipage, and all other requirements. He had charge of all the company property, and reported on its condition. He inspected the tents and company camp ground, and saw that it was properly formed and ditched, and inspected the sanitary arrangements. His signature must be the first, and followed by that of the captain, on all company requisitions and reports. He called the roll at reveille, and noted absentees and delinquents, punished for slight offences, and reported more serious offences. He gave certificates to men who wished to apply for leave of absence. He detailed all men for guard, and detachments for special service, and appointed police guards for the day. He reported the sick to the surgeon, and saw them attended to. He marched up to the colour line, and handed over to the adjutant all details for special service and guard duty. He drilled all squads, and the company in absence of the commissioned officers. He took his place on the right of the company, and acted as guide. He went to the front and centre at parade and heard the orders read. When in front of the enemy, he was generally informed privately of the programme, and of the movements to be made. While the duty sergeants were designated by their respective names as Sergeant T. or Sergeant H., he was designated as *the* Sergeant, and was regarded as the ruling power of the company when on active service. With all these duties to perform, it may be imagined that I had sufficient to keep me from repining.

Our boys, who had been allowed a few hours to stroll about the city, had been ordered to report back at two o'clock, and the greater part of them reported at that hour ; in fact all of them except one or two who came up shortly afterwards, and we prepared to march out to the camp, which was about two miles out of the city.

Camp Walker, which had formerly been the racecourse of New Orleans, was situated on what was considered the highest level of the land in the neighbourhood of New Orleans, although it was very difficult to observe any difference from the dead level of the surrounding country, the very highest part of which was only a few feet above the level of the sea. The place was of an oval shape, and about a mile and a-half in circumference, and enclosed by a close-boarded wall about 12 feet high, with several gates and doors for admission. About 40 feet inside of this wall was the course, which was lined on each side by a low but strong wooden paling   The location might be deemed to be anything but healthy, surrounded by swamps teeming with rank vegetation, through which were deep ditches filled with the drainage from New Orleans, as it moved sluggishly towards Lake Pontchartrain. Within the enclosure the ground had been cleared of the rank grass, but the soil was soft and marshy, and, rendered more so by the heavy rain which still continued to fall and by the carting in of supplies, was stirred into a soft, tenacious, black mud.

Here were stationed some 3,000 men under canvas. One regiment had been organised and sent off, another was organised and prepared to leave, and fresh companies were pouring in daily.

Our company marched in through one of the gates at which there was a strong guard stationed, and through which no one could pass out again without a pass or countersign.

We were then joined by a quarter-master-sergeant, who conducted us to the spot which was to be our company camp ground.

It was not inviting. A black soft soil with mud and pools of water here and there. The plan of the camp was roughly laid out. The rights of companies were to rest on the inner side of the course, the left to extend towards the centre of the vacant ground inclosed by the course; the officers' quarters on the opposite or outside of the course, where were also the staff-quarter-master's and commissary departments. Everything had been got up hurriedly.

The company here stacked arms, and a look was cast from one to another as much as to say, How do you like it? Nothing was said for a little, but it was evident from the faces of many that they did not relish the prospect. Fortunately there are always some spirits who can turn the blackest side of things into a laugh, and our company was favoured with a fair share of such. After a short silence a loud laugh broke from several of the boys.

" Well, boys, how do you like it ? "

" What do you think of it now ? "

" Well, D., is your zeal beginning to flag ? "

" T., are you beginning to wish you were home again ? "

" This is the first of soldiering."

" But here comes the waggon with the tents, and, oh my, we are going to have carpets."

This last observation was in reference to a load of boards

which was thrown down to lay on the floor of the tents to keep the men off the wet ground. The tents were now being delivered, and the object of the boys was to get as many as possible for the company, and as orderly sergeant I was called upon by the past quarter-master to make out a requisition, signed by myself and the captain, for all tents and camp equipage required and received, which, by the army regulations, should be done before anything is delivered.

I had to remind him that I had neither material nor convenience to write, which elicited the rule that the orderly sergeant is entitled to a tent for himself which he is supposed to use as the office of the company and store for the company property. This procured for me a fine large marquee-tent, and as most of the other tents were not of a uniform size, the number of men to each tent could not be strictly regulated, so the company contrived to get a pretty fair supply of tents, including one for the cooking department. The men having already formed themselves into messes, the lines were marked off and the tents pitched, some of the men who were already drilled in the pitching of tents instructing the others.

In the meantime I had been to the quarter-master's department and obtained the necessary forms for requisitions, which I filled up for camp equipments: 20 tents, 86 bed-sacks, 10 camp kettles, 22 mess-pans, 12 water-pails, two picks, four spades, three axes, one saw. Many other requisites the company provided out of their own funds. As was afterwards experienced, the question was not so much the obtaining of the articles, as the difficulty of getting them carried along owing to the limited means of transport.

These articles being obtained, ditches were cut round the tents as far as possible to lead away the water, while boards were cut up and laid on the ground inside of the tents where the bed-sacks were to be laid. A load of hay was brought up—it could not have been very dry owing to the weather ; but the bed-sacks were filled with it and put into the tents, also the arms and knapsacks. The rain still continuing, it was evident that the first night in camp was likely to be rather cheerless.

Hunger beginning to be felt, the next question was the prospect of getting anything to eat. If rations were issued where were the means of cooking? Some mess-pans were there, but where was the fuel to make a fire, or would a fire burn on the wet, muddy ground under the drenching rain?

Such were the questions asked by some. Others would answer by crying out, You will learn how to shift before six months are past (and this was verified).

The next cry was water—

> " Water, water, everywhere,
> But not a drop to drink."

This created more laughter and joking, and it was astonishing to see how joking and banter kept away despondency. Some were soon over among the other companies finding out how they got on, where they discovered that carts were constantly going, supplying the camp with water and wood for fuel. Therefore, to keep a look-out for these carts was the next object. Soon a cart was turned into the camp with a load of firewood, and not long after another cart with a puncheon of water was espied and captured, and forced into the company parade ground against the protestations of the driver, who had designed it for some other company. As no rations were to be served out that night, a barrel of biscuits was sent, opened and placed in the kitchen tent, which the men might eat at will. All this passed off with considerable good humour as something of an adventure.

But the great grievance of the service was now realised. The greater part of the men, not yet quite relishing for dinner and supper a hard biscuit and a cup of Mississippi water, thought that now their camp was pitched and the duties of the day over, and being wet with the rain, they would take a walk into town, and, having plenty of money, they would be able to get a hot meal at a restaurant, but they were much taken aback when they learned that they could not pass out of the camp without a written pass during the day, or at night without the countersign, which was only given to commissioned officers. This seemed to be the greatest grievance of the service, and caused a great deal of grumbling, and many a device was adopted to get round it. It was a proper and a most indispensable regulation, but, like many other regulations, it was often oppressive upon the law-abiding portion, while the more lawless, on account of whom it was imposed, generally found some plan to evade it. It was less oppressive so far that a pass was seldom refused to a well-behaved man if no duties intervened, and there was no danger or outside cause to make it imprudent to allow men to go out of the camp at any time, however, but a limited number could get at a time. On this particular occasion all wanted to go, and the difficulty was to select who should be favoured without showing partiality. As it was given them to understand that leave of absence would go by rotation, many postponed their application to another time, on the understanding that as no sutler was yet in the camp, a few men would be detailed to go to the city and return immediately, and would purchase for the company what articles they might want to furnish a repast, including ground coffee, sugar, soft bread, boiled ham, some candles, and a suggestion was made to add four bottles of whisky, which was allowed. The men were detailed and sent off with injunctions to return quickly, and some got leave of absence.

It was now getting dark, the rain had ceased, wood was split up and a large camp-fire lighted, and two camp-kettles filled with water and set on to boil. In the meantime, staff officers had come round to inquire the strength of the company and give the usual orders. The commissioned officers having gone to the city, a copy of the "camp regulations" was handed to me, and another posted up at the officers' tent.

A sergeant-major shortly afterwards came round, and made a requisition for men for guard on the following day, one sergeant, one corporal, and six privates. I also received a form of "morning report" to be filled up every morning, and delivered to the camp adjutant, showing the full state and strength of the company — "present for duty," "absent," "sick," or on "detached service."

The men soon returned from the city with the provisions. The water in the camp-kettles was boiling, plenty of ground coffee is tumbled into it, and we have two large camp-kettles of coffee; spoons and tin-cups are got from the mess-chest, and we enjoy a good supper of hot coffee, bread, biscuit, and ham. The commissioned officers, who had now returned from the city, came and joined us. The bottles of whisky were opened, and each man had a dram, after which we were much revived; more fires were kindled, and round them we stood and dried our wet clothes, smoked and chatted, and were even happy on the muddy ground round the camp fires.

At nine o'clock the "tattoo" sounded, the company was formed, and the roll called. All answered to their names except those absent on leave. As lights must now be put out,

K

the men crawled into their tents, and stretched themselves on their damp hay pallets, with a thin board between them and the wet, muddy ground, each observing that they thought the carpeted floor of the steamer on the previous night to be hard, but it was a luxury compared to this. Laughing, joking, and chaffing each other, however, kept them in good humour.

Having with the commissioned officers walked along the rows of tents and seen that all lights were out, although we could hear plenty of laughing and noise within, we went to the right of the company where my tent stood.

" W.," said the captain, " I see you have got candles ; that is a thing that I forgot to get to-day, and the orderly sergeant is allowed a light in his tent after tattoo. Have you anything to sit upon ? "

" Yes," said I, " plenty of boxes with the company property. Come in."

I lighted a candle and stuck it into the neck of one of the whisky bottles, and placed it on a box, and we all found seats, and cigars were lighted.

The captain was a man about 50 years of age. He had long been captain of the company, and took some care over the younger members, many of whom, as will be seen, were mere lads. He was a Northern man by birth, but had been nearly 30 years in Baton Rouge, where he carried on an extensive business. The first lieutenant might be about 32 years of age. He was a native of Kentucky, an engineer by profession, but had devoted much of his study to military matters, had been long an officer of volunteers, was an excellent drill officer, and was well versed in military matters.

The second lieutenant was about 28 years of age. He was a native of Scotland, but had come to the United States when a boy. His father had been a sergeant of artillery, and had long held a post in the garrison at Baton Rouge.

" I think," said the captain, " the boys must have got a sickener to-day, but I am glad to see that they still keep up their spirits."

" I am glad," said I, " that they got it at the first start, when they are full of enthusiasm, as it will show them what they have to undergo, and what follows will come easier upon them."

"All will be easier in the way of camping at all events," said the first lieutenant, "for I do not think it possible that they can ever be in a worse place for camping, and I wonder why a better place could not have been selected for a camp than this soft swamp."

"There is no better place in the neighbourhood of New Orleans," said the captain, "all is low flats for miles and miles around, the nearest high and dry land is at Baton Rouge."

"Why could they not have made the camp of instruction there?" said the second lieutenant, "there are lots of fine high and dry land with fine shady trees, besides the beautiful garrison grounds."

"Oh! you want to be near home, John," said the captain laughing. "It would no doubt be a better place for a camp, but this is the centre and head-quarters, but I do not think we will remain long here."

"How long do you think we will remain here, Captain?" said the second lieutenant.

"Oh, I do not know," said the captain, "but I hope not long; that will depend upon our efficiency. I was talking with the adjutant-general to-day, the second regiment is made up, and leaves to-morrow or next day, and we are entered for third, but there are about 26 companies on the list for it, and the 10 most efficient will be selected."

"Then I am not afraid," said the first lieutenant, "for I don't think there is a company in the State can beat us, except perhaps some companies of the Washington artillery."

"I don't think," said the captain, "that there are any of the Washingtons on the list for the third regiment. A good many of them are gone already, but some of these companies from Red river are very good, and some of them are on the list. And there are some of our boys who last joined are still behind, so, Sergeant, you must try your best to get them drilled up to the mark."

"Where is the second regiment going to?" said the second lieutenant.

"Oh, they don't know themselves," said the captain, "and that we won't know when we go; we will be put on railway or steamer with sealed orders to be opened at a certain place, and then it will be to report to General So-and-So."

"What light is that?" said a voice at the door of the tent.

"Officers' tent," answered the captain.

" 'Tis in the wrong place, then," said the patrol officer. " It
should be on the other side of the colour line."

" 'Tis the orderly-sergeant's tent," said I ; " officers in it on
business."

" All right," said the patrol officer, and passed on.

" You were wrong, there, Captain," said the first lieutenant.

" Yes," said the captain, " that is true.   I have not seen
any camp regulations."

" I have got a copy of them," said I, " and there is another
pinned to the door of your tent.   There were none of you there
when the quarter-master sergeant came round."

" I did not observe them," said the captain.   " What are
they ?   Can you read them ? "

I produced them and read—

" REGULATIONS—CAMP WALKER.

" The reveille will be sounded at 5 A.M., and all beds shall
be folded up and tents aired immediately after roll-call.

" The breakfast call shall be at 6 A.M., which shall be the
hour for breakfast.

" The sick call shall be at 7 A.M., when all sick shall be
reported to the surgeon.

" Company parade grounds shall then be inspected, and put
in proper order.

" The call for guard mounting shall be at half-past seven, A.M.,
when the relieving guard shall assemble on the colour line,
and guard mounting shall be at 8 A.M.

" Squad drill shall commence at half-past eight A.M., and
company drill at half-past nine A.M.

" Twelve o'clock shall be the hour for dinner.

" Battalion drill shall be ordered at 4 P.M., and dress parade
at 5 P.M.

" The tattoo shall be at 9 P.M., and lights out at half-past
nine P.M.

" By order of Brig. Gen. Tracy."

" That is all plain enough," said the captain.

" There is one thing plain enough," said the second lieutenant, slapping the back of one hand with the other, and slapping
his forehead, " that we are going to be eaten up with these
cursed mosquitoes (the smoking having stopped they were in
the tent in thousands), they will be very bad, and I don't

see how we are going to stand them, we will get no sleep at all."

"We must just get bars," said the captain, "I see they have got them in most of the other tents."

"What kind are they?"

"Oh, you will get them of all kinds, some big enough to fill the whole tent, and may be suspended from the ridge poll. There are others for one person about 18 inches broad, with a stick across each end to keep them stretched out. You tie a string to the centre of the stick, and suspend them from two sticks stuck into the ground, these are very cheap, and I believe that by taking a number they could be got for less than half a dollar each."

"Then let us get some of them by all means," said I, "as I expect to-morrow morning there will be some fine complaints about the 'cussed varmints!'"

"Then," said the captain, "to-morrow you had better get a list of all the men that want them, and just go into town and get them. You better see to that, Lieutenant J., as I expect the sergeant will have enough to do about the camp to-morrow." And the officers left to go to their own tent.

Having laid two boards across some boxes, I laid my hay pallet on them, using as a pillow a box of ammunition which we had brought with us. (Our rifles being different from the smooth bore muskets then in use, we carried our own cartridges with us.) Having laid my coat on this I lay down, and, being well fatigued, would soon have been asleep, but the light burning in the tent had attracted the mosquitoes, and the tent had become a perfect hive of them. I tried to drive them out with my coat, but to no purpose. I tried again and again to sleep, but they swarmed in myriads on my face and hands, and even stung me through my clothing. At last I thought of the cartridges, and lighting the candle I unscrewed the lid of the box, and taking out two or three, I screwed on the lid again. Taking the powder of two of the cartridges, I laid it on a piece of paper on the floor in the centre of the tent, and taking a ramrod, tied a piece of paper to the end of it, and lighting the paper at the candle, I stood at the door of the tent and stretched out and touched off the powder. There was a soft explosion which flamed through and shook the whole tent, and put out the light in my hand, and left the tent full of smoke. I feared the guard would have been down upon me, as the smoke was rising from the tent. They did not, however, seem to have observed it. When the smoke subsided a little, I went in and lit the candle, saw there was no damage done, and not a mosquito to be seen or heard.

I blew out the candle and lay down, thinking that I had made a discovery for the destruction of mosquitoes worth a patent, and was considering whether I should not go and see how my poor comrades were faring, and give them the benefit of my discovery, when I dropped asleep, and seemed to be immediately afterwards awakened by the reveille.

It was just grey daylight, I had slept soundly and was much refreshed, the mosquitoes had not returned, but the tent had still the smell of the powder. I jumped up, loosened and shook well my clothes, put on my boots and coat, and, stepping out on to the parade ground, called out the order to "fall in." The men began to emerge from their tents, and form on the company parade ground. When the music ceased, I gave the order, "Attention to roll-call." When the roll was called, the names of those who were to go on guard were called, also those who were to be the "police guard" for the day. Ranks were then broken, and the men set to washing their faces; many of them had been fearfully bitten by the mosquitoes, some declaring that they had never closed an eye. Some were laughing at their comrades being marked, not knowing that they were as badly marked themselves.

The beds were rolled up, and the sides of the tents turned up, while swarms of mosquitoes issued from the tents. The rain seemed to be all over, and as it was the 1st of May, there was every probability of it being fine weather now for a while. The cooking utensils were divided among the different messes, and a corporal and two men of the police guard were sent with a requisition to draw rations at the commissary store. Fires were lit, and some rough boards knocked together to form tables.

It was astonishing how quickly the boys learnt to forage and make shift; some had already managed to procure frying-pans and other extras. The men returned from the commissary stores with part of the rations, having had their first quarrel with that curse of all armies, the commissary.

Some bacon was fried and coffee made, and a rough, but well-relished, breakfast was got through. The men were now

ordered to attend to the first duties of the soldier, and see that
their arms and accoutrements were in good order, as they must
have suffered from the wet on the previous day ; and there was
guard duty, squad and company drill, at all of which arms
would be inspected. By this time the men who had got leave
of absence on the previous evening returned. They had leave
to be out all night, but to report in the morning before
"guard mounting." It was rather an extended leave of
absence to be away all night, but in this case it was exceptional, it being the first night in camp, and want of due
provision for them. Those who had spent the night in camp
were facetiously claiming seniority over them, as having
passed one night in the "tented field," and received their first
scars, pointing to the mosquito marks on their faces.

It might, however, have been better for the peace of mind
of one of them at least who went out on leave had he remained
in camp that night, but of this I will speak hereafter.

At seven o'clock the sick-call sounded, but as yet we had no
sick to report.

At half-past seven o'clock came the call for guard mounting.
"Fall in guard" was now the order, and the men detached
for guard assembled on the company parade ground. Having
inspected them, I marched them up to the colour line and
handed them over, with a list of their names, to the sergeant-
major, who, seeing that the full number from each company
was there, handed them over to the adjutant, who inspects
them and hands them over to the "lieutenant of the guard"
in presence of the "officer of the day."

Guard-mounting over, I make out my morning report and
hand it in to the adjutant. I then take out the young recruits
for squad drill for about an hour, and then assemble the company for company drill.

Knowing that there is much to be done in camp to-day the
company drill is cut short, and they return to camp about
half-past ten o'clock. The weather is now beautiful, the sun
is strong, with a light breeze, and the ground is drying fast.
Tents are ordered to be struck, boards taken up to allow the
ground to dry, bed-sacks are opened and the damp hay turned
out to dry, and blankets and all other articles of clothing are
turned out to dry. Ditches round tents are dug deeper, and
the soil thrown upon the site of the tents and trodden smooth
so as to raise the floors a little above the level of the surround-

ing ground. This plan of striking the tents and exposing the site to dry was done often in good weather, and greatly improved the sanitary condition of the camp.

All the men wishing to purchase mosquito bars are desired to give their names to the second lieutenant, who goes to the city with some men of the police guard to purchase and bring out certain articles, and everyone is ordered to make arrangements as he best can for his personal comfort.

After dinner a sergeant-major came round with orders. No battalion drill to-day, but dress parade at 5 P.M. in front of the " Grand Stand."

There was now an hour or two of leisure, which the men employed as they pleased, and the mosquito bars and other articles having come they were distributed and got ready for use. I got a rough writing-table knocked together and a bench long enough to serve for both a seat and bed along one side of my tent.

At 5 P.M. the call was sounded for "dress parade." This of course could not be a regimental parade, as we had not yet been organised into any regiment, but merely a few companies got together to form a temporary battalion for the purpose of battalion drill.

As our company had had but little experience in training beyond the school of the company, manœuvring in a battalion would be comparatively new to us, and we knew the experience of the other companies would be still less ; we therefore expected to see a little confusion ; however, it was only a dress parade, and if the adjutant knew his duty it might be got through easy enough.

I had been earnestly perusing " Hardie's Infantry Tactics," and studying the "School of the Battalion," and preparing the company for battalion drill. I had another advantage. We had in our company three members who had formerly been in the " regular army of the United States." One of these was a thorough soldier, and had been a drum major. He was a Scotchman by birth, a native of Kelso. He had been nearly all his life a soldier by choice, and he had been about nine years in the United States army. This man knew every tactic and regulation, and, being my countryman, was always ready to instruct me or explain anything I wished to know. We marched up and took our place, and, so far as the limited evolutions of a dress parade gave us any opportunity of displaying our efficiency, we imagined at least that we had acquitted ourselves very well, and, though less in numerical strength than any of the other companies, we were more efficient in drill, and we had great hopes that we would be included in the next regiment to be organised and sent off, which was our main desire and object.

When the orderly sergeants went to the front and centre to make verbal reports of the state of their companies I had been instructed by my Scotch friend how to report, as some confusion and fun was anticipated. There were in all 10 companies, and my place was near the centre.

The adjutant addressing the sergeant on the right ordered him to report. The man, who had evidently never before been on a battalion parade, was somewhat confused, and did not seem to understand what was wanted of him. After some stammering he said he had sent in his report in the morning. This caused a little laughter, with the peremptory order of, "Silence in the ranks!" He was told that he must now make a verbal report of the state of his company. He could not exactly remember, but the adjutant helped him through, and told him he must be better prepared at next parade.

The second man had pulled out of his pocket his roll book, but was told he must not produce a roll book on parade, that he must have always the state of his company in his mind ready to report at a moment's notice. He was also helped over the fence by the adjutant, and cautioned to be better prepared in future.

The third man boldly stepped forward.

"Keep your place," said the adjutant.

The man stepped back into his place, bowed an apology, and began to explain that as this part of the duty was not a part of the company duty, and as no notice that such a——

"I don't want a speech," cried the adjutant, who was now beginning to lose his patience. "Let me have your report."

"But," said the man, determined to vindicate his position.

"Let me have no 'buts,' but report."

"What will I say?"

"Say anything you like, but report."

"Well, Sir, if you will just allow me——"

"That fellow must be a lawyer," I heard some one whisper in the ranks behind me.

"And the adjutant a judge," said another.

A titter passed along the line.

"Silence in the ranks!" thundered the adjutant, as he passed on to the fourth man not wishing to create a scene.

The fourth was little better prepared, but was helped over and instructed like the others. I guessed number three was a lawyer or a politician, and the conjectures were correct, he was a lawyer, and a glib one too.

All this time I was conning in my mind how well I would make my report, which was ready on my tongue; and saluting, I said, "Baton Rouge Rifles, aggregate 85, present 78, rest accounted for."

"That is the right kind of report to make," said the adjutant, turning to the others.

He then passed to number six, the man on my left, who reported with an ease and precision which showed him to be a thorough military man.

"That is better still," said the adjutant, passing to number seven.

The latter was a mere lad, just from a military school, but whose every look betokened frolic and mischief. He called out with a smile and an air of confidence—

"Company present and accounted for."

This, however, did not satisfy the adjutant, who perhaps thought he detected a trace of the regardless, and sternly told him it would not do; he must give the aggregate number, and the number present on parade. He quickly gave it, although he told me afterwards that he did not know but merely guessed it, as he knew that the adjutant would not take the trouble to count them. The remaining three got through tolerably well, and the next order was, "Attention to orders."

The "general orders" read out on parade were generally awaited with some eagerness, and were like the last news to the troops as to their future movements or destination. On this occasion, however, they were of little interest, being only something about how the "officer of the day" should wear his sash that he might be distinguishable, and pointing out a certain field outside of the camp to be used for battalion drill. The parade was then dismissed, and we marched back to camp.

It was now near six o'clock. It had been a beautiful day, and the camp ground and all our equipage had finely dried. Orders were given to pitch tents again; and everything being now dry was put back into its place. Beds again filled with the now dried hay, and the mosquito bars fixed up, and everything about the camp had a much more comfortable and cheerful appearance than on the previous night, the different messes got their fires lighted and proceeded to cook supper. I may here observe that at this camp, and at this time, the men fortunately did not require to trust entirely to the commissary ; they had money of their own, and plenty of articles of food, and other necessaries were now being exposed for sale in and about the camp and easily obtainable, although anything in the way of cooked food or pastries was not allowed, or at least not encouraged, it being desirable that the men should learn to cook and provide for themselves.

After supper, the time was pleasantly spent round the camp fires, smoking, talking on different subjects, story-telling, singing, joking, card-playing, and other amusements, and occasional visits from friends in other companies, until tattoo sounded, when the company was again formed, the roll called, and then lights out and off to sleep.

Such is a sketch of how our first day in camp was passed, and it may be taken as a general sample of them all.

I retired to my tent, which was now fitted up and comfortable, made up my roll-book, marked off the names of the men to be detailed for guard and other duties on the following morning, entered in the company-book list of the quartermasters' stores received, and names of the captains of messes to whom they were delivered, made out requisition for rations for the following day, and then got under the mosquito bar and slept soundly until reveille sounded.

On the second day the routine was pretty much the same, except that more time and attention were given to drill—our company getting outside of the camp to practise skirmish drill, in which it was tolerably proficient, and in the afternoon we had battalion drill.

On the third or fourth day of our camp life, an incident occurred of rather a melancholy nature, which cast for a short time a sort of gloom and reserve over the members, and checked for a time their joviality. I have already referred to one of the members who got leave of absence, and went into the city on the first night of camping, and for whose future peace of mind it might have been better had he remained in camp. In the earlier part of this book I gave an account of a conversation I heard in a café in Baton Rouge, on the eve of and regarding the proposed bombardment of Fort Sumter, and of some very able remarks made by a Mr. S., then a strong Union man, and one of whose sons joined our company after Lincoln issued his proclamation. Young J. S. was one of those who obtained leave of absence on the night referred to.

On the third or fourth morning after our encampment, he came to me immediately after roll-call, and asked me to give him a clear pass from duty or default in order that he might obtain leave to go to the city for an hour or two on some very urgent business connected with his father. As he was not on any detail or special duty, and had no marks against his name, I readily did so, as far as I was concerned, but I reminded him that it was but a short time since he had leave of absence, and perhaps the captain would remind him of that, and as the "coms." (as we called the commissioned officers) were still asleep, the "old man" (as we called the captain) might be cross and refuse him. He said he would plead the urgency of the case, and taking the pen and ink with him so that the captain might sign the pass without getting up, he proceeded to the officers' tent. In a few minutes he came running back with the pen and ink, thanked me, and said it was all right. I thought I saw a wildness in his eye. I asked if it was all well with his father; he said it was all well, and started off quickly towards the camp gate. About half-past nine he returned and reported to me as I was forming the company for drill. He got his rifle, and took his place in the ranks as usual.

In the afternoon the news was circulated in the camp that a duel had been fought that morning about a mile from the camp, and that a young physician of New Orleans, the son of an eminent gentleman in Baton Rouge had been killed by a volunteer from one of the companies at Camp Walker. The truth immediately flashed upon me, and it was not long before the report was confirmed.

It seemed that on the night in question when J. S. was out on leave he had met with this young physician at a café. There had been some feud between their families, and an altercation ensued and some offensive epithets applied by the physician to the father of J. S. led to a challenge, with the result as stated. The matter was quietly talked over among the officers, but they could take no action; he had not broken his leave. The affair took place outside of the camp and beyond their jurisdiction. It was a matter for the civil authorities. But such things were so common that the civil authorities seldom interfered, and the thing passed over and was scarcely noticed in the excitement of the times.

Our captain, however, was much put about; he had a great regard for the young man that was killed; he never forgave J. S., and wished him out of the company as a rash and impetuous young man who might give us some trouble, which was to some extent verified. J. S. returned to his duty without ever saying a word of the matter, and the subject was never mentioned in the company; but he was morose and silent, and seemed to conceive an idea that the company rather shunned him, and he was very apt to fly up at anything which he thought was like a slight or insult. He seemed to feel his position much, and I rather felt for him, and tried to show as little reserve and be as free and easy with him as possible. He seemed to appreciate this, and was exceedingly submissive and obedient to me and attentive to his duty.

We got very quickly inured to camp life. It was astonishing how readily the boys learnt to shift for themselves and continued to add to their conveniences and comforts.

All the while new companies of volunteers from all parts of the State were daily pouring into the camp. These were mostly newly-raised companies, and, of course, were raw and undrilled. They were composed chiefly of men of good and high standing, wealthy planters' sons, sons of merchants, bankers, and other business men from the other towns in the State, professional men and students in abundance, all intent on showing their zeal in the great cause by serving as private soldiers, which Mrs. Grundy for the time being had declared to be the highest and most honourable position that a man and a true patriot could fill. Aspirations to any higher office, even to that of a corporal, would in a measure detract from the zeal displayed. Their whole desire was to be trained, drilled, and made into good soldiers, and I must do them the justice to say that they applied themselves most earnestly to learn their duties.

Drill sergeants were now in great demand, and although a great many of the young men of the South were trained in military schools, still drill officers were at a great premium.

I had, besides my own company duties, often to assist in

outside duties in drilling raw companies. It was, however, a pleasure so far, as they were most assiduous in their desire to learn. Many had provided themselves with books of instruction, and, after being instructed in the different movements in the manual, would continue to practise them in their leisure hours.

I have already referred to a fine body of volunteers belonging to New Orleans called the Washington Artillery. I may here observe that in the American service all artillery corps also acted as infantry. A finer body of men than the Washington Artillery I have never seen, and for discipline and efficiency I have yet to see them surpassed even in the armies of Europe. I wonder where they are now. I fear few of them survived the war. Most of this corps had already gone to the front, and of those that remained the officers were most useful in assisting to carry out the staff duties of the camp. Besides the ordinary company and battalion drill, much had here to be taught in the way of field and staff duties, such as camp forming, pitching and striking of tents, rolling away and stowing into waggons, post and guard duties.

The number of men in the camp had now increased to six or seven thousand. The camp was enlarged and extended, and in order to train the men well to guard duty, a large number of posts were created so as to give employment to a large guard. Many of these posts were quite unnecessary, and were maintained merely with the object of training the men to guard duty.

So many men in the youth and prime of life, of high culture and education, of so many classes and professions, thus suddenly taken away from their ordinary business pursuits, and comfortable and luxurious homes, to be converted into soldiers, and thrown together within the limited space of a camp, with all its roughing experiences, was an incident of no ordinary kind, and it may well be imagined that many a device was resorted to to maintain levity and keep away ennui.

The eager desire to acquire proficiency no doubt absorbed a large portion of the men's time, and, though constant drill and frequent guard duty were imposed to keep them employed, even that must be intermixed with a little variety, and many different kinds of amusement were got up to pass the time and keep them all lively.

But by far the greatest hardship to endure was the confinement to the camp; beside this all others were joked at as trifles, and many a scheme was devised to get away from the place without going through the special formality of awaiting their turn and getting permission. The requisite to pass the guard was by day commissioned officer or written pass, and by night the countersign. The countersign being given at night to all commissioned officers, who, if granting leave of absence to any of their men in place of a written pass, at night furnished them with the countersign.

Of the many devices used to get out of camp at night, I will give one specimen.

I have said the camp had been extended. It embraced a large building which had been used as a hotel during the races, and was now used as staff head-quarters. From this building were several walks leading through various gates into the enclosed racecourse, which had formed the original camp. These gates had at first been closely guarded by sentinels, but now the whole of them with the outside buildings were enclosed in the camp, and the entire place was guarded by an outer line of sentinels. These posts were completely enclosed in the camp, and it was quite unnecessary to guard them. However, seemingly with the view of creating plenty of sentinel duty, they were still kept guarded during the day, and at night sometimes they were guarded and sometimes they were not, according to the whim of the officer of the day. .

In the company next to ours there was a scapegrace whom I shall call Ben. If ever this meets his eye he will know who I mean. Ben's demands for leave of absence had been so frequent, and his abuse of leave had been so marked, that his leave was stopped altogether. Ben observed one night that one of those inner gates had been left without any sentinel. He immediately goes to his tent, gets his musket, and takes his station at the gate waiting for a fish.

By-and-by a commissioned officer approaches going towards the staff head-quarters.

"Halt! who goes there?" exclaimed Ben.

"A friend with the countersign," was the reply.

"Advance and give the countersign." Ben comes to "arms aport," bends forward to receive the countersign, which the officer gives in a low tone—

"South Carolina."

"All right; pass on," said Ben, coming to "shoulder arms."

The officer passes on, and Ben having obtained the counter-sign, leaves the sinecure post to take care of itself, goes to his tent, lays by his musket, dresses, passes the outer guard by giving the countersign, makes for the city, taking care to be back to camp before reveille. Ben managed to carry out his plan for several nights, but was at last found out. The thing was not without its good effects, as it taught the officers to be more careful in placing guards at night.

Our company, which had been well trained in skirmish drill, bayonet exercise, and other accomplishments, had now been inspected, and declared not only efficient but a crack company, was entered for the third regiment which was being made up of the 10 most efficient companies in camp, and we were all rejoicing at the prospect of getting away from Camp Walker, although we had not the least idea of where we would be sent.

About 10 days after we went to Camp Walker, our captain came to my tent and told me that the third regiment had now been organised, of which we would be the right flank company ; that he would be leaving the company, having obtained the appointment of major of the regiment ; and that it would likely be a general promotion forward. The first lieutenant would be captain, the second lieutenant would be first lieutenant, and that I certainly should be second lieutenant, but for that stumbling-block about citizenship. Would I not alter my mind, and declare my intention to become a citizen, and the difficulty could be got over ? I still declined. He urged me to think well over the matter. In the meantime, he told me to let the first duty sergeant take my place to-morrow, and come with him into the city after guard mounting, as he wished to collect some money which had been promised as donations to the company fund by some of the wealthy merchants, and if I would reconsider my determination, and declare my inten-tions to become a citizen, he would go with me to General Tracy and see about getting the matter arranged.

On the following day we went to the city, and on calling at some of the offices of the merchants referred to, the principals were not there, business being about suspended. Some of them, however, were expected to be in about one o'clock, but the captain, having to go to head-quarters, could not then call. A note was left, and it was arranged that I should call about that time. I called as arranged, saw the principals, and got cheques for the money.

On coming out from one of those offices in Carondelet Street, something attracted my attention which called back old memories. It was the British ensign, waving from a building on the opposite side of the street, which, on looking closer at, I saw to be the office of the British consul. This flag I had not seen for some years, as it is never seen back from seaports, or higher up the river than New Orleans. There was something in the sight at this time which awakened in me strange feelings, and if ever I had entertained the slightest thoughts of renouncing my allegiance to Great Britain, they were now dispelled, and I determined to adhere to the old flag. This trifling incident, however, somewhat damped my ardour in the cause I had embraced; and the same day I heard of the Queen's proclamation warning all her subjects to remain neutral, and denying protection to any that should take up arms on either side. I felt a little dull, and on my way back to camp, I could not help reflecting on the rash step I had taken, which seemed to sever me farther than ever from any home associations, and to place me in a rather singular position. It was, however, now too late to retract, and I must take my chance for a year at all events. The active duties of my office gave me little time for reflection.

The same evening there was a dress parade of the newly-formed regiment, and the organisation of the 3rd Regiment of Louisiana Volunteers, with the names of the field officers to command it were read out in "general orders."

The colonel was a graduate of West Point, was a thorough military man, and had been General of the State militia, and also State engineer.

The lieutenant-colonel was a veteran colonel of volunteers who had served in the Mexican war. The major was our late captain. These constituted the field officers of a regiment according to the regulations. The commissioned staff consisted of an adjutant, a quarter-master, a commissary, and a surgeon.

The office of captain in our company was now vacant. The first lieutenant was promoted to captain, the second lieutenant to first lieutenant, and we were ordered to elect a second lieutenant. This office fell to a member of the company who was acting as private, a young lawyer, who, though not having great experience in military matters, had a good military education, and was a hard-working and intelligent man, and very popular in the company, and the appointment was

L

approved. The regiment was now fully organised, and battalion drill was gone into with great vigour.

Our company was much inferior in numerical strength and physique to the other companies composing the regiment. They were mostly from the northern part of the State and composed of fine stalwart men, and many of the companies were over a hundred strong. They were armed with smooth-bore muskets of the newest pattern, that being the arm then generally in use. Our company of lighter material was armed with Springfield rifles and sabre bayonets. They greatly excelled the other companies in drill and general training, and they were a little vain of their accomplishments and liked to display them. This, however, stirred up the other companies to exertion. They seemed determined not to be behind us, and they pursued their drill with great avidity, and in a few months it took us all our time to maintain our name as the crack company of the regiment. Being, however, the only company armed with rifles, we were distinguished as the " rifle company."

We had not long to remain in Camp Walker. We had got marching orders, and many were the surmises as to our destination.

It was now generally known that Lincoln had made a call for 90,000 men in addition to the 75,000 already levied, and that the Federal forces would invade the South by three main lines of attack—one on the east, by crossing the Potomac into Virginia ; one in the centre, by the Mississippi river and down the left bank through Tennessee ; and one on the west, from Missouri down through Arkansas.

The South was preparing three lines of defence—the Army of Virginia, the Army of the Centre, and the Army of the West. To which of these armies we would be sent we could not tell.

CHAPTER XV.

On the evening of the 17th of May, we received orders to
strike tents, pack up, and prepare to march. This was pleasing intelligence, and we were all glad to bid farewell to Camp
Walker, with its broiling heat, bad water, and mosquitoes.
We marched to the city wharf, and embarked on board a
steamer waiting to receive us. This showed that we were not
to join the Army of Virginia, but either that of the West or of
the Centre. The steamers, three in number, were of the
ordinary river passenger class pressed into the service.

This method of pressing into service is one of the arbitrary measures resorted to in time of war. The quarter-
master-general takes possession of whatever private property
he requires for the emergency in the shape of houses, stores,
railways, steamers, or other boats, horses, carts, waggons, or
any other property required for the public service. A certificate is given to the owner, and the price or value is determined
by fixed regulation, payment being generally made by a
warrant on the treasury department. This may seem somewhat arbitrary, but if the Government is solvent, it is not so
bad as might appear, a fair price being allowed, and the owner
gets his compensation direct, without having the greater part
of it swallowed up by arbiters and lawyers. While on this
subject, I might say a word or two on the quarter-master and
commissary departments, as far as they came under my observation. I do not know how these departments may be
managed now, in the United States or in other countries, but
in this war they were both in the North and South subject to
the grossest corruption and peculation.

In the quarter-master's department the plundering was from
the State more than from the soldier, although the latter

suffered much from it, but in the commissary department the robbing of the soldier was so open and barefaced that it is astonishing it was tolerated, or that it did not create a mutiny. In the South it is true it had less effect, as less was expected from the departments, and the men knew that they were often beset with difficulties, but they did not trust much to either department.

The army was furnished, through the quarter-master's department, with quarters, whether houses or tents, camp equipage, arms, ammunition, accoutrements, and clothing, and all means of transport. These the department obtained from contractors, and the shocking quality of the materials furnished showed corruption to a great extent. The soldier, of course, knew nothing about the contracts, and in the South they had always the excuse that good materials were not to be got; but the things which mostly affected the soldier personally were shoes and clothing, and these, to a great extent, they managed to provide for themselves, or they were sent to them by their friends at home.

The system pursued by the commissaries, even making allowance for the difficulties they were subject to, were simply disgraceful. I do not exaggerate when I say that on an average from every requisition of rations said to be issued to the troops, the commissary took off one-third and sold it, putting the proceeds in his pocket. The cause of this peculation lay greatly in the system of management. I might say that the system, as it then existed, was such that even a man of the most sterling integrity, and of honest and upright principles, if appointed commissary of a regiment on active service could hardly, after six months, remain an honest man. If so, he would deserve the greatest credit for it.

The system was this : The commissary received a supply of provisions from the depôt. He got with it an invoice detailing quantity and price. From these he issued to the non-commissioned officers and soldiers, on requisitions signed by the orderly-sergeants and captains of companies. He sold for money to all officers and men pertaining to the army. He had to account for the amount of the consignment (losses and casualties excepted) by money and requisitions. The practice was this : An orderly sergeant made out a requisition for his company—say for 100 men for one day—flour, 100 lb.; beef, pork, or bacon, 75 lb.; coffee, seven lb.; sugar, 14 lb.; rice or

pease, six lb.; candles, six; soap, two lb.; salt, pepper, vinegar, etc.
This requisition was signed by the captain, and men were
detailed to go to the commissary store to draw these rations.
The commissary takes the requisition and calls his assistant,
and says to the men, " Well, you can get three-quarter ration
of flour, half ration of pork, half ration of coffee, and half
ration of sugar, and that is all." The men would grumble and
say, " We only got half rations yesterday." " Can't help it, I
am short of provisions, and there are other companies to serve
as well as you, and all must get their share." He then sticks
the requisition on the file, and his assistant weighs out the
rations. " Will we get the back rations when the supplies
come up ? " some mischievous young rascal would say as he
dodged behind a barrel. The commissary would put his hand
on his revolver, but restrain himself, and pretend to take no
notice of a thing so absurd, and buries his face in his book,
while he credits himself with full rations issued to 100 men
as per requisition, while his assistant and the men would laugh
at the audacity of the offender, "no back rations" being the
commissary's watchword, and, what was more strange, no
requisition would be received unless it was made out for the
full amount.

Thus the commissary had a voucher for and was credited
with supplying a full requisition when he had only supplied a
small part of it, and he had the rest to sell for his own benefit.
I have frequently known instances of a company, after giving
the full requisition and being supplied with half rations on
the grounds that provisions were scarce, getting one of the
army waggon drivers, and giving him money to go to the
commissary store and purchase four or five pounds of coffee,
or other necessaries, which had been kept off them, which he
would obtain for money without the least trouble, and this
system was carried on quite openly. I more than once nearly
got into serious difficulty by insisting on marking on the
requisition the actual quantity of provisions delivered.

In the post-commissaries and depôts there was another
system of peculation.

In these depôts there were immense stocks of provisions
stored for army use. These were periodically inspected by
officers, generally of the sinecure kind appointed through
favour for such purposes, and there was always a considerable
quantity marked " condemned " as being unfit for use. The

ceremony of inspecting was generally done in this way : The inspecting officers would come to the depôt, where they would be met by the post-commissary, who would receive them in the most friendly manner, and conduct them into the large stores. On each side along the wall would be piled up on the top of each other with their ends exposed, a great many barrels of beef, pork, flour, biscuit, etc.

"These," says the commissary, "are what I have myself picked out as being bad. Those on this side are good, but you can inspect for yourself. Cooper, open one or two of those barrels." The cooper opens a barrel which of course had been already selected. The unsavoury brine spurts out. The officers stand back to save their handsome uniforms. Other barrels are examined of flour, biscuit, etc., similarly selected. Then all on that side, the bulk of which were probably the best provisions, are ordered to be marked condemned. The officers would take a list of the number to make their report, and then go and inspect the hospital stores of wines, brandies, etc., of which they would acknowledge they were better judges. A few days' notice would then be given of a sale of " condemned army stores," and they would be auctioned off for a mere trifle. The commissary of course has an agent present who knew what lots to purchase.

Thus it was said large quantities of the very best stores were often marked " Condemned," and sold off at a mere trifle, the commissary having an agent on the ground to buy them in.

This system was more common in the North than in the South, as in the South, after the first year of the war, there were not the stores to work upon and no outside market for them. But in the last year of the war I saw in one of the seaports of Mexico a large quantity of mess beef and pork which bore the mark, " Condemned U.S. Stores," and which were of the very best quality, and sold at a high price.

The 3rd Regiment of Louisiana Volunteers, 1060 strong, left New Orleans on the night of the 17th of May, 1861, amidst the loud cheers of the populace.

No special fitting up had been made on the steamers for the conveyance of troops. On our steamer there were three companies, under command of the major, our former captain. A certain space of the boat was allotted to each company, and the men were allowed to make themselves as comfortable or as uncomfortable as they chose.

The steamers proceeded up the river, and on the afternoon of the following day they approached Baton Rouge. The men of our company were now told that the steamer would stop there for about an hour that they might have a short interview with their friends, and that notice had been telegraphed to Baton Rouge of the steamer's approach, so that their friends might be at the wharf to meet them. As the vessel came near to the landing-place it appeared to be less like the tearful parting of a few friends than a great public demonstration. The whole front of the town, the wharf and banks of the river were crowded with people. Flags floated on the Capitol and the public buildings and almost every other place where a flag could be stuck up. The steamer came to the wharf just as it was getting dark. Salutes were fired from the garrison and the river bank. A band of music welcomed the arrival. The governor and his suite stood on the wharf to greet the officers and men. All this was of course to create enthusiasm by honouring those who had already taken up arms, and to stir up others who had not yet done so ; and it was not without its effect.

The Baton Rouge Rifle Company, now known as Company A, was granted leave to go on shore for an hour. The meetings with friends, as may be supposed, were affecting, fathers, mothers, wives, sisters, younger brothers, and children gathering round and embracing the already slightly bronzed embryo warriors, while young ladies went through selecting such members as were known to have no family ties or relatives and presenting them, not with bouquets, but neat small cases containing pin-cushion, needles, thread, buttons, etc.—a most useful gift ; while the receivers, scarcely knowing how to thank the donors, and confused in the excitement of the moment at what was going on around them, quite forgot themselves, and some of them in their recklessness saluted the fair damsels with a kiss. The young ladies, under the circumstances, forgave the rashness—indeed I am not certain whether in the confusion I did not myself commit the offence.

Having no tender relatives of my own, I passed from one to another. Mothers, one after another, came up to me, holding their sons round the neck. "Now, Mr. W., Charlie is more directly under your charge than any other officer ; I hope you will take good care of him and make him do his duty. And, Charlie, you must always be obedient to your officers, you know it is your duty." I would affect to treat the matter lightly, and answer gaily, " Oh, never fear, Charlie is getting on very well; he will make a good soldier; he knows if he don't do his duty, I will take a stick to him;" and I would laugh and give Charlie a poke on the shoulder. " All right, sergeant," Charlie would say, with a manly and happy expression. The anxious mother would seem pleased and assured, and reply, " Oh, yes; I know you will take care of him, but you know what is before you, and he is only 16. May God protect you." The good woman would break down, and could say no more, and I turned to the next. My partner in business, who had come down to meet me, and who had been talking with the major, came up and told me that the leave ashore had been extended to two hours, and that I might come up and have tea. I must, however, learn this from some authority, and I saw the major walking up town with some of his family. I ran and asked him. He told me we would leave at nine o'clock as the steamer was going to take in wood.

It was now only a little past seven, so we walked up town. It was a lovely evening; the streets were fragrant with the flowers of the chinaberry trees which lined the pavements. What a difference from Camp Walker ! Every person, male and female, seemed to be in the street, and all wishful to stop and speak. The excitement appeared to have greatly increased since we had left, or rather the people had begun more to realise the situation. From everyone we heard expressions such as, " Is not this terrible ? Heaven knows what it is all going to come to ! War, I suppose, and a bloody war too ; there has already been fighting in some places." " Where are you going to ?" I would be asked. " I do not know." " I hear you are going to Cairo," says one. " I cannot tell ; all I know is that we proceed up the river under sealed orders." " I rather think," said another, " that you will be going to Missouri. General Lyon, with an army of United States troops, has overrun that State, laying it waste with fire and sword ; " and there were many conjectures and rumours on the subject. We reached my friend's house, and had tea and some conversation. At length the steamboat's whistle blew as the signal for all to be on board again.

I was soon on board, mustered the company, and found all present and two additions of men who had been carried away by the excitement, and sought to share the honours without thinking of the hardships. Provision was made for them, and they were enrolled without much ceremony.

The steamer was at last cast off and proceeded up the river. The boys were greatly elated with the reception they had got at their native town, and were now more ready and determined than ever to endure any hardship and fight for the cause to the last.

The part of the boat allotted to our company was the hurricane deck, with the blue canopy of heaven overhead. It was, however, fine weather, mild and clear, with a bright moon. There was no tattoo on the steamer, and the men could stay up or lie down as they chose. There was not much inclination to sleep. Some were talking and happy; others were silent and absorbed in their own thoughts. I was sitting on the forward rail about an hour after we had left Baton Rouge chatting with others, when some one called my attention to a commotion abaft the pilot-house. I looked in that direction, and I saw the flash of steel in the moonlight and heard the clash of sabre bayonets. I had just time to run aft, draw my sabre, and throw myself between the combatants before serious mischief was done. One of the combatants was J. S., who, from some real or imaginary slight or insult from another high-blooded member of the company, thought fit to resent in such a way as speedily led to a conflict. Both were furious and seemed bent on mischief. I had them disarmed and taken to different parts of the boat and placed under guard. The commissioned officers having gone to bed in the lower saloon, I could do nothing further in the meantime. I thought it probable that when ashore at Baton Rouge the combatants had been paying a visit to a café, and were thus a little excited. About an hour afterwards a deputation of the company came to me and said that the parties had agreed to settle the matter amicably, and if I would release them and say no more of the matter they would pledge their word of honour as soldiers that the disputants would not renew the quarrel. I did so, and the matter dropped.

We soon came up to the other two steamers, which had been wooding higher up the river, and the three vessels proceeded in company.

It cannot be good for soldiers, either morally or physically, to undergo long voyages on transports where they have not

their usual duties, drills, or exercise to perform, and unless
there is some special provision to keep them in proper employment they are apt to lounge, play cards, hatch mischief, and
quarrel. I have no doubt that the more complete arrangements for transport, as in the British service, these things are
provided for, but in this voyage of a few days on a crude system
and with crude material I could observe its bad effects.

Some three days after leaving Baton Rouge the steamers
left the Mississippi and proceeded up the Arkansas river, which
indicated that we were destined for the "Army of the West,"
and the following day we were landed at "Little Rock," the
capital of the State of Arkansas. Here we learned that our
first destination was "Fort Smith," about 250 miles further
up the river on the border of the "Indian Territory;" but, as
the water was now too low for the steamers to go there, we
must remain at Little Rock until the river rose, or, if that did
not take place in time, we would march by land as soon as
army waggons could be provided.

A newly-raised regiment of cavalry was drawn up to receive
us, but as we marched up the town preceded by a fife and
drum band their horses, though splendid animals, were not
used to that sort of thing, and became restive and plunged
fearfully, threatening to throw their riders. The animals were
well managed, however, and the riders kept their seats.

In the meantime our lieutenant-colonel ordered the band to
stop playing for fear of accident. This, however, the troopers
would not hear of, and their colonel (Churchhill) riding up
said he wished their horses to be trained to the sound of the
fife and drum, and was glad he had now got the opportunity.
Although he had been able to raise 1000 men and horses,
he had not yet been able to raise a single fife and drum. The
street was very wide, and the troopers formed column by
troops and preceded us up town, their horses rearing and
plunging violently, to the no small amusement of our men,
and I could just imagine that the drummers sometimes gave
an extra rub-a-dub to see if they could not awaken a
catastrophe.

It was of no use, the men could rein their horses, and they
kept their seats. We proceeded out to the large city park
where we were to encamp.

The park was a tract of undulating land not much improved,
but cleared and covered with good grass, and interspersed

with many fine shady trees, some cattle and sheep grazing upon it, and in appearance it was not unlike a nobleman's park in the old country.

Our tents and other baggage having been brought up from the steamer under care of a guard, the camp was soon formed, tents pitched, fires lighted, rations drawn and supper prepared. We were now getting used to this kind of duty. The sergeant-major came round to order the quota of men for guard to report immediately. The guards were posted and the camp guarded round, and, as it was facetiously expressed, no one could pass out unless they could say, "Natches."

This expression arose from an incident said to have occurred at Camp Walker.

A raw recruit, said to be a German (as these were generally the butts for such stories), was placed at one of the posts, with orders to let no one pass unless they could give the counter-sign, and the countersign was "Natches." Hans took his position, and shortly afterwards some one approaching, Hans cried out, "Halt! you can't pass here unless you can say, 'Natches.'"

This was said to have occurred at Camp Walker. But the story may be as old as guard mounting itself, and many other stories, such as the sentinel who was questioned for not salut-ing the officer of the day, while the latter was going the night rounds, replied, that he thought the officer of the day had no authority in the night.

Being now a regiment we felt better satisfied ; we were more like a family, or rather a moving community ; our home was the regiment, and the farther we got from our native State, the more we became attached to it.

Having passed the first night in our new camp, we were glad to find that there seemed to be no mosquitoes in the place, which was a great pleasure to realise.

The several morning duties and company drill being over, orders were given to shift camp.

A more suitable place had been selected in the park, and a camp laid out in the true regulation form. Tents were quickly struck and carried to the new site, and a new camp formed with all modern improvements, and the training was now con-tinued with great energy—company drill in the forenoon, and battalion drill in the afternoon. The place was in every way favourable for manœuvring.

Our company, with not a little vanity, liked to show off its accomplishments in skirmish drill, under the eyes of hundreds of spectators who came out from the city to look on.

This prompted some of the other companies to learn the drill, and eventually one other company got tolerably proficient, and was placed on the left flank of the regiment, our company being on the right. The other eight companies, being stronger in number and physique, formed the four divisions of the square, and the other two companies acted as right and left flank skirmishers.

The zeal and diligent application of the men tended greatly to accelerate their progress towards efficiency, and, on the whole, the regiment was progressing fast, and promised to be an effective corps. A school had been established for the instruction and special drill of the sergeants, under the direction of the sergeant-major, who was a thorough soldier, and a graduate of a military institute.

I mention these matters as descriptive of the mode adopted in time of need of organising and speedily bringing up to a state of tolerable efficiency a young regiment of volunteers.

When we had been here about eight days, a rise in the river took place, and steamers being ready, we broke up camp and embarked for Fort Smith.

Fort Smith is situated near the right bank of the Arkansas river, about 500 miles from where it joins the Mississippi. It is about the head of the navigation, and on the line which bounds the State of Arkansas with the Indian Territory. It had always been garrisoned by the United States troops, but had, like the other forts in the South, been surrendered when the State seceded.

The adjoining town, which takes its name from the fort, contained at that time about three or four thousand inhabitants. The fort was of some strength and advantageously situated.

It was now well known that we were to form a part of the Army of the West under Brigadier-General M'Culloch, and Fort Smith was for the present to be the base of operations. Several other bodies of troops were encamped in the neighbourhood.

We marched out to a suitable place about three miles from the town, where our camp was roughly pitched for the first night. On the following morning a suitable place was selected on a fine, dry ridge along the border of the Indian Territory. This place we were ordered to clear and prepare for a camp, and as it was probable that we would remain here for some time, a regular and proper camp was required. Here the men were initiated into the more common and practical duties of the soldier, which many of them did not so much relish. Large details were ordered with axes, spades, and pick-axes to do the necessary work. Trees were cut down, brushwood cleared away, ditches cut where necessary for drainage, and along on the side next the Indian Territory, and on the left where most exposed, earth-work defences were thrown up. This latter was no doubt intended more to exercise and instruct the troops in that kind of duty than out of any necessity for defence of the place. A regular camp was now formed, and a large piece of clear prairie land adjoining served well for drill and manœuvring. Here constant drill was persevered in, and every attention given to have the regiment made efficient and ready to take the field.

The regiment, since leaving New Orleans, had been in command of the lieutenant-colonel, Colonel H. not having accompanied it.

He now arrived and took up his head-quarters in the town of Fort Smith, having been temporarily appointed to the command of the post, General M'Culloch being busily employed in examining the country northwards towards Missouri, through which the campaign was to be conducted. The latter had already visited our camp, inspected the regiment, and expressed himself highly satisfied with it, but enjoined the strictest attention to drill and also to the more practical parts of a soldier's duty, as the campaign would be an arduous one and through a rough country.

Colonel H. visited the camp about three times a week, put the regiment through battalion drill or dress parade, and issued what orders he thought necessary from his head-quarters at Fort Smith. Here happened one of these ludicrous incidents which sometimes arises from oversight or from a careless or inexplicit way of giving orders.

In the large armies of volunteers which were raised in America at this time there was much less of that deference to rank and military formalities and ceremonies which exists not only in regular armies, but pervades also the military society in little garrison towns and military stations in Europe in times of peace. Respect to rank was certainly observed and enforced so far as it was essential to discipline and efficiency and the good of the service; but the American armies, being only provisional, and there being many privates in the ranks whose position in civil life might be higher than that of their field officers, this deference could not be carried to anything like servility. This was more applicable to that respectable class of volunteer regiments which composed the armies in the earlier part of the war than to those raised by draft or conscription towards the end of it. It cannot be gainsaid that in point of discipline, efficiency, bravery, and general worth the latter could hold no place with the former. Nevertheless, men who become soldiers, no matter what sphere of life they may come from, or under what circumstances they may join the army, will all, I believe, acquire that propensity to get out of camp and have a little freedom in towns near where they may be quartered. The restriction of this liberty was always a bitter pill to our men, and it was considered no breach of honour to evade the rule or outwit the guard.

It so happened that the spring which supplied water within the camp was not quite sufficient, and now, that midsummer was setting in and the weather dry and hot, it became altogether insufficient. Another spring was discovered some distance beyond the lines, to which it became necessary to go for water, and it was understood that a man going for water carrying a water pail would be allowed to pass the sentinel. Some, however, got into the habit of taking a pail and, getting past the sentinel, would hide the pail in the bushes and proceed to the town and enjoy themselves for a while, and then return and take up their pail and go into camp with the water, calling forth the remark sometimes that it must be a long distance to that well.

Colonel H., who was something of a martinet, imagining one day that there were more of his men on liberty than should be, stopped some of them and demanded to see their passes. Some had none. This enraged the colonel, who, meeting with the major who happened to be in town, demanded in a rather imperious manner an explanation of such lack of discipline. The major replied that it was not easy to prevent it, as the men had to go out of the camp for water, and they often hid their pails and ran into the town.

"And why don't you make a corporal accompany them," cried the colonel.

"It will require a special order for that," said the major.

"You will soon have it," said the colonel. And calling his secretary said, "Write a special order at once, and send it out to the adjutant to be read on parade this evening, that no person shall be allowed to pass in or out of the camp unless accompanied by a non-commissioned officer."

The order was read on parade that evening, and a copy of it stuck up at the guard house.

Shortly after guard mounting next morning, the major came laughing into my tent which was close to post number three, which commanded the road that led into the town.

"W.," said he, "I want to take my station in your tent to see the fun."

"What is up?" said I.

"Did you not hear the order read last night?" said he. "I want to see them carrying it out. Captain G. is officer of the day, and he is going to carry it out to the letter."

He then directed my attention to the word "person" in the order.

I saw the mistake, but remarked that it was not much. "But," said he, "there are some that would consider it a degradation, and I know two officers are now dressing to go to town, and they are two most pompous formalists, and I want to see them passed out, and then I want to pass out myself for the fun of the thing, and when stopped by the guard I will apply to you for a non-commissioned officer to pass me out; and I wish you to send the youngest corporal you have—has not little B. been made a corporal?"

"Yes, he has."

"Then send him to pass me out. Had the mistake occurred through any one else," continued he, "it would not have been so much, but you know Colonel H. has such pride in his military knowledge, and is such a stickler for military form and precision in everything. Oh! here they come," and he placed himself in a corner where he could see the post, and sat chuckling.

I looked out, and saw two handsomely dressed officers going towards the road that led into the town. As they approached the sentinel, I imagined I could see a smile of mischievous satisfaction in the fellow's face ; while the major was watching with extreme eagerness.

"Halt !" exclaimed the sentinel coming to the charge.

"What do you mean, sir ?" was the reply. "Shoulder arms till officers pass !"

"I mean," said the sentinel, taking a firm position, "that you cannot pass."

"How is this ? Explain, sir !"

"Corporal of the guard post number three," shouts the sentinel.

The corporal of the guard who had been hiding behind my tent came round, and as he passed the door I saw the major make him a sign, and he hastened towards the post. He told the officers that they would have to be accompanied and passed out by a non-commissioned officer, but other than a non-commissioned officer of the guard. Such were his orders. They demanded to see the officer of the day, but he would only call the sergeant of the guard. The sergeant of the guard having arrived at the post, he could only reiterate what the corporal had spoken. They then demanded to see the officer of the day, but he would only call the lieutenant of the guard, determined that they should pass through the whole routine. The lieutenant of the guard came, but he directed their attention to the order, and said his orders were imperative. They still demanded to see the officer of the day, and the corporal of the guard was sent to call him. The corporal knew very well where to find him, and the officer of the day soon made his appearance. I was wishful of hearing the row between them and the officer of the day, and had gone down towards the post, but when the officer of the day came along, he came alongside of me, and gave me a push, saying, "Go away out of that, man ; they will perhaps ask you to pass them out, and that would spoil the fun."

I now understood the thing better, and retired out of sight. They remonstrated with the officer of the day, and protested that it was a mere clerical error in the order. But the officer of the day was inexorable, and told them that they could easily get over the difficulty by asking a corporal to pass them out. This, however, they declined to do ; and they returned to their quarters in high dudgeon. These officers were not very popular in the regiment on account of their rather high pretensions, and the thing was much enjoyed by the other officers, none of whom, however, sought to go out of camp that day.

The major, however, determined to have revenge on the colonel for his hauteur of the previous day, was resolved that the order should be carried out, and mounting his horse rode up to the post and was of course stopped by the sentinel. He then rode back to my tent, and asked for a non-commissioned officer to pass him out. I called Corporal B. to go and take the major past the sentinel, which he did amidst the laughter and cheers of a large number of officers and men who had gathered round the post.

But the best of the fun was still to come. In about three hours afterwards the major returned, and a call was made for a non-commissioned officer to pass him in, and Corporal B. was ordered to go and pass in the major, which he did.

The major was in great glee. He had learned that Colonel H. and General M'Culloch were going to visit the camp in the afternoon, and how about passing them in. The order was plain, but the question was, Could not Colonel H. revoke the order when he came to the post? The officer of the day thought not, and he was determined to enforce it.

The lieutenant-colonel, being that day confined to his quarters from sickness, knew nothing of the affair till it was all over.

As the time approached, battalion drill was over (I believe it was got past a little earlier that day on purpose), and it was difficult to keep a crowd from gathering near the post. At length the general and colonel arrived, and were stopped by the sentinel, who had been specially selected and instructed for the occasion. The colonel was furious, but the general requested him to be calm, and the officer of the day was sent for. The latter, with the written order in his hand, explained that his position was one of great difficulty, but the general rules were, that the orders to the guard should not be broken so far as referred to the passing of a sentinel, even if the person desiring to pass was the commander-in-chief himself, and as the officers were often sorely tempted and tried on such occasions, he had resolved to abide by his orders, even if he should afterwards be court-martialed for doing so; and he added that no one would be more ready to punish for laxity of duty than they, the general and colonel now before him.

The general admitted the position of the officer of the day,

M

and that he was justified in having doubts on the subject, and
therefore the best way would be to carry out the orders, and
asked him to call a non-commissioned officer. The officer of
the day turned towards our company ground. I could see he
had a sore struggle to contain himself ; he could not speak for
laughing, but made a sign for a non-commissioned officer.

"Corporal B.," said I, "go and take the general and the
colonel past the sentinel at post number three."

Corporal B., who could perform his part very well, and to
the great amusement of the by-standers, walked with a dignified
air to the post, and passing the sentinel, went up to the general
and colonel, who were seated on their horses about 10 yards
outside of the sentinel, and respectfully saluting, looked up to
their faces and said in the simplest and most compassionate
manner, "Come and I will take you in," and he conducted
them past, just as a servant would conduct a stranger past the
watch-dog.

This ludicrous position quite overcame the general, and he
laughed outright, and was joined and cheered by the officers
and men who had gathered near the post.

The colonel's countenance betrayed anything but pleasant-
ness. He felt ashamed at the unmilitary style of the wording
of the order, which had occurred, not from any want of military
knowledge on his part, but from his precipitancy and careless-
ness in not reading the order before it was sent to the adjutant,
and also from the ignorance of his secretary, who had been
some lawyer's clerk, and, being newly appointed, wrote more
in a legal than military style.

A dress parade was ordered, the blundered order was revoked,
and a new "special order, number ———," was read out, which
was worded, " Soldiers passing out of the camp for water shall
be accompanied by a non-commissioned officer."

When the officers marched to the front and centre the
colonel, in saluting, slightly apologised to the officers for the
mistake, and explained that his secretary was newly appointed
and green to the business, and that he, being exceedingly busy
and hurried at the moment, omitted to examine the order
before it was sent to the adjutant, and for which he was to
blame. " But," continued he, " we are all apt to make little
mistakes at first, and I hope this incident will tend to show
both you and me the great importance of being precise and
exact in everything and in fulfilling our duties strictly to the

letter. I commend the officer of the day for his strict sense of duty and firmness in strictly carrying out the order."

General M'Culloch was a man about 40 years of age, of a well-proportioned, wiry frame, with a piercing blue eye, and a contemplative but firm expression of countenance. He had held the rank of major in the United States army, had served in the Mexican war, and had been much engaged in warfare with the Indians. He was a thoroughly practical general. He gave much attention to the nature of the country in which he was going to operate. He made himself acquainted with every road or passage through which an army with trains could pass or operate in. He examined every river, creek, ford, or bridge where an enemy could be checked or met to advantage. He took care to know where forage and supplies were to be procured readiest, and noted where a pass could be guarded, defended, or stopped up, or where a bridge could be burned or blown up. He was an excellent horseman and a most able leader of rangers or irregular cavalry, and could take them through and over almost impassable barriers of rivers, swamps, hills, rocks, woods, or copses. He was not so particular about clock-work movements in drill or in having the ranks dressed straight as an arrow, but he was particular in brigade movements, that proper distances were kept, and that corps passed regularly in order without any doubling up or confusion, and, above all, that the men knew well to handle their arms and were good shots. Of this latter he had little to doubt, as few of the men, even the youngest, had this to learn after joining the army. He had an utter abhorrence of all red-tape and bureau government. Had the latter not been against him, and had he lived, he would have made his mark as a daring general and leader of a flying column.

Towards the end of June it became well known that the Federal General Lyon had raised a large army and was overrunning Missouri. That State had been divided, part of the population favouring the North and part favouring the South. General Price, the Southern leader in command of the State forces, had retreated to the southern part of the State, where he was amassing an army and was awaiting assistance from the Confederate Government.

It was also reported that Federal agents were stirring up the Indians against the Confederates and promising them large grants if they would assist in putting down the rebellion ;

also that a notorious leader from Kansas named Lane had raised a force of about 3000 in the Indian Territory, composed of Indian half-breeds and white desperadoes, and was meditating an attack on Fort Smith.

Of course great vigilance was exercised, guards and outposts strengthened, and orders given for the troops to be ready to fall in at a moment's notice; and, as it does not take much to raise an alarm, several alarms did take place during the night; the long-roll was beat, and the regiment was quickly out and under arms. I believe, however, this was intended to test the alacrity of the men in falling in and to train them in that sort of thing.

I afterwards learnt, by conversation with some men of good standing among the Indians, that there was not the slightest foundation for the report that the Federal Government had tried to stir up the red men against the Confederates at that time.

CHAPTER XVI.

ABOUT the beginning of July, the regiment had got quite efficient for every useful purpose, and we received orders to march.

Army waggons having been prepared for transport, at a very early hour on the morning of the 4th of July (the great American anniversary day), the waggons were brought to the camp, and one was allotted to each company. Tents were struck and packed into the waggons, with all company stores, cooking utensils, camp equipage, spare arms, ammunition, and other company property. Orders having been read out on parade the previous evening that the line of march would be by way of Van Buren, crossing the Arkansas river there, and proceeding northward by the Evansville road, the men should on leaving take two days' cooked rations in their haversacks, and on halting for the night, the troops should not pitch tents but only bivouac.

When the men went to draw rations, the commissary insisted on having requisitions and issue for four days. This the men rebelled against, which led to another squabble between them and the commissary. The object of the latter was to give the men a larger share of the provisions to carry, and so lighten his own waggons that he might be enabled to carry more goods for his own speculative purposes.

Where we were to proceed to we had no information, but we understood that the Confederate Army of the West would assemble at Camp Walker, near Maysville, in the north-western extremity of the State of Arkansas, a place about 80 miles distant in a direct line, but about 110 miles by the road we would have to travel. The name Camp Walker seemed strange and unpleasant, and we hoped it would not be like the last Camp Walker. But why the name? Who or what were the two camps named after? The only noted personage of that name that we knew of was the late Filibuster Walker of Nicaraguan notoriety, but we did not consider him of sufficient fame or importance to have camps named after him. Who the camps were named after was of little importance to us, and we never knew or took the trouble to inquire further.

The hay being taken out of the bed-sacks, and with other light material which had gathered, was set fire to according to custom. It was said at this time that an effigy of the commissary was burned in the flames, but I did not see it.

While the refuse of the camp was burning in the dark morning, we formed and took up our line of march at the first dawn of day. We marched down the river bank until opposite Van Buren, which was on the other side of the river and some miles from Fort Smith. Here we waited while the waggons were being ferried over.

The trains consisted of the 10 company waggons, officers' waggon, staff waggon, quarter-master's and commissary waggons —in all about 20 waggons, with four or six mules to each. Forage would be found on the road as we proceeded.

The trains having crossed, we were ferried over two companies at a time, that being about as much as the boat could conveniently carry.

All having crossed, the regiment formed on the other side and proceeded up the bank from the valley of the Arkansas river. The road lay uphill, and was very rough and stony, while the sun poured down with such force that the granite boulders by the side of the road were so hot that they could not be sat upon if a halt for a few minutes was called.

The country on both sides of the road was cleared but of rather a poor appearance, divided into patches of Indian corn, enclosed by rail fences. There were no trees to afford any kind of shade. At length the call was sounded to halt for the night near a farm-house, about nine miles from the river and about 16 miles from the camp at Fort Smith, which we had left in the morning. The men having two days' cooked rations in their haversacks, the waggons were not unpacked or fires lighted. The men rolled themselves in their blankets and lay down to sleep on the side of the road.

About half-past three the reveille was sounded, and the line of march was taken up at four. The object now was to get the march accomplished before the intense heat of the day set in. The men were in no great spirits; they had been a good deal fatigued, had got but a poor night's rest, and thought they might have been allowed to make themselves at least a cup of hot coffee before marching. They were given to understand that, as far as possible, this would be provided for in future; that this was merely a halt for rest and no camp at all, there being no proper place to camp.

The second day's march was worse than the first. It was not all uphill, but the road was very rough and the sun was intensely hot. Canteens were soon empty, and water was scarce at times, but, on the whole, the country was fairly supplied with water. As the sun grew hotter some of the men began to drop out. Always as one would show signs of giving out the others would laugh and cry "Played out," "Played out," which would induce the wearied volunteer to make an effort to struggle on. It was now evident that the men were too heavily loaded for the first start at least, not being yet inured to marching over such roads in such intense heat. A good many fell out in spite of every effort to make them keep up, but these men always came up an hour or two after we got into camp. About 2 P.M. we got to the end of our second day's march, about 18 miles from where we started in the morning. This place was more pleasing than that of the previous night; a fine shady wood grew on the banks of a gravelly creek, down which ran a stream of beautifully clear water. The men were soon divested of their heavy load of knapsack and accoutrements. Many of them were suffering from sore and blistered feet from marching on the hot stony roads, and most of them had their boots and stockings off and were bathing their feet in the stream. The camp, however, had to be guarded to prevent the stream from pollution by the men washing or bathing above a certain point. Below this point there were some fine deep pools, which were soon filled with bathers and men washing parts of their clothing, which were saturated with dust and perspiration.

In about two hours the waggons came up, every company looking out for their own waggon, which they brought up as near to their bivouac as possible. Cooking utensils were got out, rations drawn, fires lighted, and the cooking of supper commenced.

The men complained of the heavy loads they had to carry,

and, piling up the total of rifle, sabre, belt, and accoutrements, 40 rounds of ammunition, knapsack, blanket, one day's rations, and canteen of water, the whole was taken to the commissary's scales and found to weigh 42 lbs.; but as these were the scales by which the commissary weighed their rations, they declared the result a cheat to the extent of 20 per cent. at least. They therefore allowed 8 lbs. off; still 34 lbs. was rather much to carry on such rough roads under a broiling sun.

Arrangements were then made that the knapsacks and blankets might be put into the company waggon and the men allowed to march without them. This was a great relief, and as there would always be some means of cooking at night, they were allowed to take in their haversacks just what provisions they chose. Tattoo was now dispensed with, and the men were allowed to go to sleep as soon as they pleased. Reveille was ordered to be sounded at 2 A.M., and the order of march to be taken up at half-past three. Very early in the night the men were wrapt in their blankets and fast asleep. A little before midnight our company was disturbed by a commotion in the next company, and some of the men coming over and lying down near our bivouac. We asked what was the matter. It appeared that they had formed their bivouac under a very large shady tree, and imagined they would be very comfortable for the night. But this proved no exception to the rule that "the best laid schemes of mice and men gang aft aglee." It seemed the tree had been already occupied by another tenant in the shape of a "skunk" (or pole cat), which, considering that he had a prior claim, threw out his fumes among the intruders on his domain with such effect as to cause a speedy retreat.

"A pretty set of fellows you are,' said our men, "to be driven from your position by a skunk." "Go over there and try it," said they. Our men, however, were not inclined to encounter such an enemy, and soon all were fast asleep again.

At half-past two reveille was sounded, the men turned out, and the roll was called. The men had had a good night's rest, but many of them were stiff and their feet so swollen and sore that they had to crawl up to answer to their names. Fires were quickly kindled, coffee made, and breakfast partaken of; while some of the men fomented their feet in hot water to enable them to get on their boots.

Cooking utensils, spare rations, knapsacks, and blankets

were packed into the waggons and all covered over carefully and strapped down. The line was formed, and at half-past three the bugle sounded the advance. The morning was cool and pleasant for marching, but it was very dark, and that was a great disadvantage.

The road, if it might be so called, was full of deep ruts, stumps, and large stones. Of course the men marched " Route step " and " Arms-at-will," but the darkness did not allow them to see the stumps and stones, and their feet, sore and tender, often struck against them, causing some poor fellows to suffer the most excruciating pain, which was made more vexatious by the laughing taunts of their comrades, such as, " Kick that stump again, man ;" " You haven't knocked it out yet ;" or, " Give that stone another kick and knock it out of the way."

As daylight set in the men could see their way better, and their feet got a little easier as they got seasoned by walking, and camp was reached about one o'clock.

This was also a fine place for camping on the banks of a creek considerably larger than the last. The banks of a creek were always selected, if possible, for camp, as it afforded a plentiful supply of water ; due precaution being taken to encamp on that side which would be most favourable for the army to be on, should a rise of the water take place during the night and render it unfordable, as frequently took place in this part of the country. The marks on the banks of this creek, as in most others, showed that it was subject to sudden rises and overflows.

The same routine was here gone through in cooking, washing, bathing, etc., and some of the boys succeeded in catching some fine fish, with which the stream abounded. The men were now beginning to learn the business and suit themselves to the work, and were making great progress in foraging and cooking. The rations served out was flour, which they had to make into bread themselves, for which purpose they had to provide themselves with skillets, which they used as ovens ; and they soon learned to make excellent bread or biscuits, as they were called, the quality being, no doubt, greatly improved by a sharp appetite, with which they were all particularly well supplied by the fine air of the country and the marching and exercise.

Having here enjoyed another good night's rest, the men were in better condition than the previous morning. Boots had been eased or changed, and their feet had somewhat recovered, but a toilsome march was this day before them—to cross Boston Mountain. This was a high mountain, probably the lowest one of a range which extends along the north-western part of Arkansas, and over which the road passed.

About 10 o'clock we reached the foot of this mountain, and were about three miles from the top. The ascent was steep and toilsome. The sun was intensely hot, and the road was very bad, with deep holes, rocks, stones, and stumps, and we wondered how the waggons would ever get over it. A number of men had been detailed to assist in getting them past the worst places, but it was a heavy task to get them over. We at length reached the top, hot and fatigued.

The descent on the other side did not begin at once. There was a considerable extent of undulating tableland, and, as soon as the left of the regiment had got up, a halt was called for rest and to be ready in case more men were wanted to assist in getting the waggons up the hill. The mountain was wooded to the top, and, there being some shade, a little rest was enjoyed. After great toil and exertion the waggons were got up, and we marched on and descended on the other side. We were later of getting into camp that day, but were all pleased that we had got over one bad part of the journey. Our next day's march showed a little difference in the appearance of the country. As we got more northwards vegetation seemed to be a little later, and the country was getting to have a more northern appearance. Wheat and oats were now to be seen in the fields. The large, rich brambleberries, which grow in great abundance along the roads, which we had been enjoying, and which on the south side of the mountain range were dead ripe and falling off the bushes, were on this—the north side—scarcely ripe. The country, however, seemed more fertile and was more thickly settled. The woods were mostly of oak trees, and great numbers of pigs, in a semi-wild state, roamed in them at large. These animals had belonged to the different settlers, but being turned into the woods to feed on roots and acorns, with the optional order, as it was said, to "Root, hog, or die," these animals had bred in these woods and had become partially wild, and were strictly the property of no one, or, as it might be said, they had with a true American instinct disavowed their allegiance to anyone and declared their independence.

Day after day the march now became pleasanter, and we were getting used to it, and marches of from 15 to 20 miles a day we accomplished easily.

The country now was beautiful; interspersed with fine woods and small prairies, through which ran many fine streams and pebbly brooks; and many fine springs of water ran from the mountain sides.

That part of a soldier's duty which implies a regard for number one the boys learned very rapidly, and generally one or two provided with money would contrive to drop out of the line and visit the farm-houses and make purchases. The farmers being far from a market, produce was plentiful and money scarce, and they were glad to sell; and such things as fowls, eggs, butter, milk, potatoes, venison, etc., could be bought cheap. I have seen a fine turkey bought for a quarter of a dollar. This was the first time that an army, or indeed any large body of men, had visited the country, and the rustic settlers little knew what was to follow.

In the meantime the strictest orders had been issued against any plundering, damaging of property, or molesting the inhabitants in any way.

About this time the first violation of this order took place, and the transgressors were quickly punished, although in rather an odd manner.

A few days after passing Boston Mountain we camped in a wood near to which was a large field of oats, part of which had been cut down and was in shocks. The ground where we lay was covered with stones and gravel and a little hard to rest upon.

Some of the boys, unlike Jacob and less honestly disposed, were not inclined to use stones for their pillow, and, casting a longing eye on the shocks of oats, thought that a sheaf would answer the purpose much better.

Accordingly when darkness set in one or two of them sallied out and securing one or two sheaves soon made themselves a comfortable bed; and as one sickly sheep infects the flock, the temptation was great and many others followed their example and lay down on the fragrant oats, and soon afterwards all were in silent repose.

Some time before midnight I was woke up by a loud cry from a man near to me, and springing up I saw him struggling as if to retain hold of something, and he was dragged off seemingly by the neck by some unseen foe. I sprang to his assistance, but ere I discovered who his assailant was something gave way and some monster disappeared in the darkness. Before I had time to think, my attention was attracted by the whole camp in commotion. And there was such a tremendous rustling, struggling, grunting, squealing, swearing, intermixed with imprecations, exclamations, and loud shouts of laughter, and such expressions as "Oh, man, don't hurt the pig, you might be a pig yourself one of those days." I knew from this that it was nothing serious. Some of my comrades began to wake up and rub their eyes, when suddenly a pig in a state of frenzy rushed into the circle in which we lay, and running over some of the sleeping men dashed right up against me, showing that pigs don't see well in the dark. Half stupified and scarcely knowing what I did, I dealt the brute a tremendous blow with my fist, which sent it reeling away from me. Whether the animal had been previously wounded, or whether the blow fell upon some vital part, I do not know, but it staggered back and fell dead right across the neck of our captain, who lay snoring near me.

"What the devil is that?" roared the captain, as he struggled to get up from under the load.

"A pig," said one of the men, as he pulled the dead animal off him; "and it is dead, too."

"A pig," said the captain. "Where did it come from? Who killed it?"

"I don't know," said the man; "it ran over the top of me and up against the sergeant, and he struck it a blow with his fist and killed it."

"Killed it with his fist! Impossible."

"Yes, he did," said the man; "I saw him do it."

"Killed a pig with his fist! Well, now, that's good," said the captain. "If the sergeant killed that pig with his fist, I would just advise you to take care of that fist, that's all," and he rolled over and went to sleep again.

The cause of the whole disturbance can be easily explained. A herd of pigs, which had been roaming in the woods, attracted by the smell of the fresh oats which the men were lying upon, and probably by the dirty garb and loud snoring of the men imagined in the darkness that they were of their own species that lay upon the oats. They therefore, without ceremony, began to feast upon the oats, inserting their snouts under the sleepers, and rolling them over to get at the provender. Many of the men, being considerably fatigued, slept so soundly that they never woke up, but were rooted over and over by the pigs, and had their bed eaten up without their knowing anything about it. Others, waking up, attacked and drove off the pigs, which, in their fright, ran against other sleepers and woke them up, until the whole camp was in commotion. A young man in our company was the possessor of an exceedingly good appetite, and to gratify it was one of his greatest cares. He was the son of a small farmer, and one of his greatest luxuries was corn bread, to which he had no doubt been much accustomed in his childhood. As yet this had not been a part of the army rations, and Preston, or Press, as he was called, seemed much to miss his favourite food, and when he could get an opportunity would purchase it at some of the farm-houses along the road. Press was, however, subjected to much annoyance from some of the younger members of the company who, partly out of a similar fondness for the article, and partly for mischief, took delight in making raids into his haversack. It seemed that on that day Press had succeeded in obtaining a fine supply of corn bread, and fearing that some of his mischievous comrades would be making inroads into his haver-sack, he took the precaution, when lying down to sleep, to keep it by him with the strap passed over the shoulder as usual. When the pigs entered the camp, the smell of the corn bread, once encountered, was no doubt the greatest attraction, and as the law of might is right even among pigs, a big fierce grunter soon drove off the smaller fry, and seizing the haversack in its jaws, endeavoured to carry it off, dragging the owner with it. The haversack was torn and the corn bread scattered on the ground, which Preston proceeded to eat forthwith lest some other attack should be made on it. The camp was soon quiet, and the men fast asleep again, but that night's disturbance created a hostile feeling between the regiment and the pigs which led to open war, and many a fine grunter was roasted in revenge for that night's aggression, and General M'Culloch once rebuking them afterwards for their action towards the pigs, told them he believed he would rather be a " Federal " than a pig in presence of the 3rd Louisiana Regiment.

About two days after this incident we reached Camp Walker, having had now a little addition to our training in the way of marching and bivouacking.

Camp Walker, like Fort Smith, was on the border of the Indian Territory. On a slightly rising ground in the middle of a fine open prairie several square miles in extent, there were some newly erected wooden buildings like a barracks, from which rose a very high flag-pole, carrying an enormous Confederate flag. On the edges of the woods surrounding the prairie were rows of tents showing the encampments of different regiments and corps from Arkansas and Texas, while on the prairie detachments of cavalry and artillery were manœuvring. We marched across the country greeted with the usual cheers of welcome, and our camp was laid out in the north-west corner of the prairie. A regular camp was here formed, waggons were unpacked and tents pitched. Here we were to remain for a few days until the whole army should be ready to march into Missouri.

The army waggons were now sent away to accumulate stores at Fayetteville, that town being now an advanced depôt for supplies.

Troops continued to arrive from different parts of Arkansas and Texas, and company, battalion, and brigade drill was persevered in, and various extended manœuvres on the prairie of foot, horse, and artillery were gone through, and several detachments of mounted infantry were reconnoitring the country northwards.

Here we learned that the Federal army had advanced into the south of Missouri, and had had some engagements with the State troops under General Price.

After remaining here about 10 days' drilling and preparing, we received orders to march. Tents were struck, waggons packed, and we were again on the move.

We proceeded eastward, passing through the town of Bentonville, other regiments proceeding by different routes. The object of different corps marching by various routes when not immediately in front of the enemy was to obtain forage and supplies easier and harass the country less by spreading the demand more over it. We bivouacked at night and proceeded in the early morning as before. After passing through Bentonville we turned northward and crossed the line into Missouri, and the second day after crossing the line we passed through the town of Cassville. Here we were received with loud cheering and great demonstrations of welcome. But I, for one, put very little faith in these demonstrations; they were things that were easily got up, and were generally composed of the scum and rabble, and, though that class might be sometimes fairly represented in them, yet they were often far from being expressive of the true sentiments of the people.

After passing Cassville we came up with a part of Price's army of Missouri State troops. These men seemed to out-demonstrate all the demonstrations we had yet seen; for, in their excitement of cheering and firing of salutes, they exploded a barrel of gunpowder, which blew some of themselves into the air. Whether this was by accident or intentional we never learned, but we considered such displays of zeal to be quite overstepping the thing.

Some three days after passing Cassville we halted and camped for a few days at a place called Sugar Creek. This halt was to allow the other forces to come up and concentrate.

While here we heard from the Missouri troops of their engagement with the Federal troops at Carthage, and of M'Culloch having captured 500 prisoners at Neosheo. We also heard here of the rout of the Federal army at Bull Run, and that the Federal General Lyon was at Springfield, about 35 miles distant, with a force of nearly 20,000 men, a considerable number of whom were United States troops and part of the regular army.

The different corps now began to come up, and the forces were kept closer together.

Our total force was now, of Confederate troops under General M'Culloch, about 5000 infantry, 2000 cavalry or mounted infantry, and two batteries of artillery of six guns each—in all, about 7400 of all arms. These were all efficient troops, well armed, and fairly disciplined.

Of Missouri State troops under General Price there were about 8000 men of all arms. Of these about 3000 were mounted infantry and one battery of artillery. About half of this force was well armed, the rest being supplied with flint-lock muskets, hunting rifles, and double-barrel shot-guns. They were very enthusiastic, but seemed to have more zeal than discipline.

All the forces and trains being now forward, we received orders to advance. Troops to bivouac at night; no tents to be taken except one for each company to keep arms and ammunition dry in case of rain.

We were now declared to be in the vicinity of the enemy,

and the strictest caution and vigilance were enjoined. Our regiment was assigned to the post of honour on the right, and our company on the right of the regiment acted as advanced guard.

About two days afterwards it was reported that the enemy was advancing to meet us, and we took a position at a place called Crane Creek. This creek was a fine clear stream, and along the banks was a good deal of level ground suitable for camping, the creek supplying abundance of water. The position was a good one for defence, surrounded by hilly land covered with wood. The approach from the north by which the enemy must come was by a broad road, on both sides of which was high ground, steep and rugged in many places and covered with small wood of oak, hickory, and hazel. On the high ground on both sides of this road our lines were to be formed in case of an attack. We found that the enemy had advanced to within seven miles of our position, and the advanced pickets of both armies were within a short distance of each other.

We were in an excellent position for acting on the defensive, but, being far from our base of operation, our supplies were getting short, and the army was subsisting chiefly upon green corn obtained from the neighbouring fields, and it soon became evident that we must force the fighting. Every device was tried to induce the enemy to make the attack, but they were not to be caught, and, seeming to guess at our position, tried every means to induce us to attack them, and skirmishes frequently took place. They made several feints and drove in our pickets, and once or twice every day we would be called out to take our position.

The enemy had some excellent cavalry—dragoons of the United States regular army. These would follow up our pickets almost to our lines, but managed, owing to the nature of the country, to keep out of the range of our artillery.

I had often heard my Scotch friend, P., who had been appointed drum-major, but still messed with and was a member of our company, speak in very high terms of a certain Captain M'Intosh, a captain of cavalry in the United States army, under whom he had formerly served. This gentleman he described as a most able and gallant officer, of Scotch parentage, but born in the State of Florida, who, when secession took place, resigned his commission and offered his services to the South. P. had learned that he was with the Army of the

West, and was colonel of one of the Arkansas regiments. P. was very anxious to see him, and wished he was here now.

A few days after we took up this position a call was made for a party of riflemen to go with a detachment to the front. Our company was selected; and the detachment was made up of the left flank skirmishing company, and three other companies of the regiment—in all about 500 men. When we were ready to march out great was the joy of P. when he saw that the officer going to take command of the detachment was Colonel M'Intosh.

Colonel M'Intosh was a true type of the real Scottish gentleman, such as might have been found about the beginning of the present century, free from all the adulterations and pedantic display of modern refinement. His every action betokened the officer and the gentleman. He was plain and affable in his manner, but his look was sufficient to command respect and obedience. Of the genuine clan of the M'Intosh, born and raised in the South, educated at "West Point" and trained in the United States army, and often engaged in Indian warfare, he seemed to have been selected by the general as his right-hand man. Having inspected the detachment, he examined our rifles, asked if we were good shots with them, and said he would give us an opportunity of trying our hands. He recognised P., for whom he seemed to have had some regard, and expressed his joy at seeing him. P., in the best manner he could, introduced me to him; and we marched out on the road towards the enemy's camp. My position was, of course, with the captain at the right or head of the company; and this was also the general position of the commander of the detachment.

Colonel M'Intosh, having dismounted and given his horse to an orderly, came and walked on the right and entered into conversation. He asked me how long since I had left Scotland, and much about it. He seemed to have great pride in his Scotch descent, and said he hoped that I and the other Scotchmen would do honour to our race.

When we had got a short distance beyond our pickets the report of a rifle was heard some distance in front. "What is that?" said Colonel M'Intosh; "that can't be the enemy's pickets, or else they have shifted them forward."

A party of mounted infantry from Price's division had been out reconnoitring that morning, and had been driven in by

N

the enemy's cavalry. Colonel M'Intosh ordered the detachment to close up and be in readiness. Another shot was heard, and, coming to a turn of the road, we saw a solitary man of Price's division standing on the road loading his rifle.

"That is one of Price's stupid fools," said Colonel M'Intosh; and, going up to the man, said, "What are you doing there? Was that you that was firing?"

"Yes," said the man, as he proceeded to ram a ball down into a rifle barrel nearly as thick as his arm with a bore that would scarcely admit a pea.

"What are you firing at?" said the colonel.

"At the enemy," said the man.

"Where is the enemy?" said the colonel; "I see no enemy."

"You go up to where yon scrub oaks are," said the man, pointing to a wooded hill about three miles distant, "and you will see plenty of them."

By this time the head of Churchhill's regiment of mounted infantry, which was in our rear, came up. Colonel M'Intosh laughed at the man's simplicity and ordered him back to the camp, as he might fire at some of our own forces.

We were soon after deployed among the brushwood of a rocky ridge which skirted the road on one side, while Churchhill's regiment moved up the road. The object, we were now told, was that Churchhill would make an attack on the enemy's outposts and drive them in, which would bring on their cavalry, while Churchhill would retreat back along the road followed by them, and they would thus be drawn under our fire. The difficulty would now be to distinguish friend from foe, but Colonel M'Intosh had given strict orders to each company not to fire until he gave the order, which would be when the rear of Churchhill's regiment had passed the left of the detachment.

I have often thought from this and other incidents that it is proper that soldiers, particularly volunteers, should know something of the programme that is to be carried out and what is the plan their commanders are acting upon, as no discipline in the world will provide against mistakes or accidents. The officer whose orders are awaited may fall at the first fire, or an order may be misunderstood, as after the firing commences it is difficult to make orders heard.

In about half-an-hour after we had taken our position we heard firing both of artillery and small arms, and soon after heard the sound of cavalry retreating down the road, and they were soon passing in front of us. It was Churchhill's regiment. They were in good order, and the enemy's cavalry was following them up. The rear of their regiment had passed our right and we looked for their pursuers. Fortunately there was some distance between the pursued and the pursuers, otherwise it would have been very difficult to distinguish between them on account of the dust. They did come, and whether they suspected anything or not I do not know, but before they were half way along our concealed line they halted and wheeled. Colonel M'Intosh nevertheless coolly waited until Churchhill's regiment had passed, and then gave the order to fire. The clouds of dust somewhat obscured the view, but the boys delivered their fire steadily and effectually, and a good many saddles were emptied. They wheeled in some confusion, some of the troops in the rear discharging their carabines amongst us. The bullets rattled among the bushes but did no harm, and in a few minutes they were off out of sight. Some of Churchhill's men returned to try and pick up some of the riderless horses, but most of them had followed their friends. They only got one or two that were not wounded. We were now ordered back to camp, quite pleased at having had a brush with the enemy. Some of the farmers in the neighbourhood were employed to bury the dead and attend to the wounded or take them back to their own camp.

Next morning the enemy advanced with artillery and shelled the woods on both sides of the road. From this it was supposed that they were going to advance in force, and we were drawn out in position to receive them.

Our company was posted to hold a narrow pass on the outside of the hill, to the right and a little in front of our position, through which a part of the enemy's force might pass and attempt to turn our right flank. When we had taken this position I was sent by the captain to place some pickets in front near the road. While engaged in this duty General M'Culloch came along, accompanied by a stout farmer-looking old gentleman dressed in a suit of white linen clothes, not over clean, who I took to be one of the farmers of the neighbourhood the general was often talking with about the roads, passes, and the country in general.

The general asked me what I was doing, and having told him, he gave me some directions about placing the pickets, telling me to keep them a little further back from the road and more out of sight, and, although the enemy passed on the road, to be certain not to fire unless they tried to enter the pass. The old gentleman then said something to the general which I did not hear, but the general turned to me and said, " Remember that there is a body of our own troops to come in first ; take care that you don't fire upon them."

" How are we to distinguish our own men from the enemy ? " said I. " The enemy's troops that we saw yesterday were so covered over with dust and dirt that we could not tell them from our own men."

" That is a compliment to your own men," said the old man, laughing. " But there should be something to distinguish them,—a piece of white cloth tied round every man's left arm would do very well."

" Yes," said the general, " that will do very well, and it should be done ; they can tear up a tent or something."

I did not like the idea of tearing up our only tent, and I asked the old gentleman whom I took to be a farmer, whether he thought we could not get an old white shirt or two.

" I can't give you any," said he, " unless I give you the one I have on, and it is not very white ;" and that was true.

" Tut," said the general to me, " that is General Price you are talking to."

I laughed and apologised. He laughed and said it was all right.

General Price had been Governor of the State of Missouri, but having taken part with the South, he was driven out by the Federal army, and had taken the field with the State troops, and such followers as he could raise.

He was a shrewd man and had some military experience, having served in the Mexican war. He was a good deal of a politician and courted popularity, and his object and policy were now to gather to his standard as many men as possible, and to win over the sympathy of the population of the State, and get the State to declare in favour of the South.

It was a part of his division that General M'Culloch referred to, when he said that a body of our own troops was to come in first, and we were to take care not to fire upon them. This was a body of some 2000 mounted infantry that had gone out to make a feint attack upon the enemy's forces, supposed to be advancing, and draw them on to attack our position.

Towards the afternoon we heard cannonading in the direction in which we supposed the attack was to be made; and not long after the sound of the retreating force was heard, and on they came—not in good order like Churchhill's regiment, but in a regular stampede. They had met a pretty strong force of the enemy who had thrown a few shrapnels amongst them which sent them back in confusion. They were in a sort of panic, and reported the enemy advancing at least 30,000 strong. They were laughed at and jeered for their precipitous retreat. Of course they could not have stood, nor was it expected they should, but it was suggested that they might have retreated in good order as Churchhill's regiment had done.

Not liking to be laughed at, and having recovered from their momentary panic, they were quite ready to face the enemy again, which, they assured us, we would all now have an opportunity of doing as they were advancing in tremendous force, and all awaited now the expected attack.

The artillery was in position and everything in readiness, but no enemy approached. Scouts came in about sunset and reported that the enemy had fallen back to their original position.

Strong guards and advanced pickets were put out, and the main body retired to their bivouacs near the creek, but no supplies had yet come forward. The men had had little or nothing to eat all day, and two ears of green corn served out to each was all they could get. This was roasted and a part of it eaten for supper, and part reserved for the morning's breakfast; and with a drink of water from the creek, and the ever-solacing smoke the men rolled themselves in their blankets and stretched themselves on the grass. We had one consolation, it was fine weather—the beginning of August. No rain, the nights warm; no mosquitoes; and never did we enjoy sweeter nights' rest than rolled in our blankets on the green grass under a tree with the branches just sufficient to break the bright glare of the moon or stars in our eyes.

At daybreak, we were aroused by a firing along the outposts of the camp, and the beating of the long roll. We were soon up and formed, and if we did not get our faces washed, we got our feet wet, in dashing through the creek in our sudden rush to the front, where we were soon in our position of the previous day.

It turned out to be nothing. A small force of the enemy's

cavalry had, during the dark of the morning, crept down the road, driven in the advanced pickets, and approached to the inner line, and were of course driven back ; and as one rascal who was taken prisoner coolly said, they had just come along to say good morning and see how we were getting on, apologise for not having visited us on the previous day, and hoped we had been put to no inconvenience.

It was now well known to the enemy that M'Culloch seldom kept prisoners, but took their arms, then their names and every mark for identification, and paroled them, saying he would rather fight them than feed them, and let them go, assuring them that if caught in arms again, unless previously exchanged, he would hang them on the first tree ; and it was supposed that this fellow was not such a fool as he pretended to be, and most likely he had contrived to make his horse stumble and himself fall and be made prisoner on purpose that he might inspect our force and position and take his chance of getting away with the information. What was done with the fellow I do not know, but no doubt good care was taken that he would not be allowed to make his escape until his information would be of no value.

We returned to the bivouac, but where was the prospect of getting anything for breakfast? Some had a little coffee which they had bought and preserved, some contrived to obtain at a very high price a small quantity of flour from some of the commissary staff, but the main food was green corn, which was brought in from the fields in waggons, and even that was limited ; and many had for breakfast nothing but the remains of the two ears of corn issued to them the previous evening, which they boiled and ate, and drank the water it was boiled in by way of a hot beverage in place of coffee, some declaring it was not so bad after all.

The men, however, were getting tired of this work, and no doubt M'Culloch saw that he must force the fighting. He had made some successful raids with the Texas Rangers, and cut off some of the enemy's detachments, but the enemy had now concentrated their forces and could attack him with their whole strength at any moment, and they were advantageously posted with Springfield, their base of operations, in their rear, only a few miles distant, with abundance of supplies, and they could quietly remain at ease and act on the defensive.

On the other hand, we were about 150 miles from our base

of operations, and had but few supplies even there. A wild country and almost impassable roads lay between us, and the animals for transport were giving out. The troops had thus to subsist on green corn, which was causing diarrhœa to break out amongst them.

The general had expected to get intelligence of the enemy's strength and movements through General Price, who was supposed to be very popular among the people, at least in the southern part of the State, and many of his political friends were often visiting him, professing great zeal in the cause, and that at great risk to their personal safety they gave information of the strength and movements of the enemy. M'Culloch began to find out that this information was not always to be relied upon, and it often conflicted with that obtained through his own scouts, and he had but little faith in the honour or integrity of politicians, and ultimately would not act on such information. The sequel showed that he was right, but this matter led to an estrangement between him and General Price which never was healed, but continued to increase, and was disastrous to the Confederate cause west of the Mississippi, and led to the abandonment of its defence by the Confederate Government.

CHAPTER XVII.

A DECISIVE battle was now the only thing that would alter this state of matters and make them either better or worse, and it was not without some shade of satisfaction that in the evening it became known that such a course was determined upon. Orders were quietly given to the captains and orderly sergeants of companies to have arms inspected and the men supplied with ammunition and be ready at nine o'clock to march forward and attack the enemy. It was evident that M'Culloch intended to surprise them by a night attack on their position.

There is something trying in the quiet solemn whisperings in the dark when preparing for a night attack, which might have tried the nerves of more experienced troops than ours, knowing as they did the hazardous nature of the undertaking; but they all seemed to be pervaded with a resigned and stern determination, and never did I see them take their places with more order and obedience and seeming sense of duty.

Our regiment, as usual, was to be on the right and our company on the right of the regiment. We formed and marched out of our bivouac and halted, waiting till the other companies were ready that we might form line. The strictest silence prevailed—not a word was spoken.

While we' stood there in the darkness the orderly sergeant of the left flank company (who, by-the-bye, was the same military sprig who had at New Orleans made such a ready and careless report to the adjutant, and who was full of mischief and animal spirits even at this time) left his position in the ranks for a moment, and running over to where I stood, and, pulling me by the sleeve, said in a half-joking way : " W., you are a very good fellow, but better you than me to be on the right to-night. Good-bye, old fellow."

It was very true that my place would be with the captain on the right of the company, and we would be the first to advance and approach the enemy, and had the Federals been aware of our approach and advanced one or two pieces of artillery down the road, or had infantry been awaiting in ambush, we stood a fair chance of being the first to be swept off. However, I expected that precautions would be taken to guard against that, and probably Price's division would advance by some other route and the troops would deploy into the woods, and by a preconcerted signal the attack would be made simultaneously.

A few minutes after 9 o'clock the column moved forward in silence. Not a sound was to be heard but the steady tramp of the troops, and never did I see them march so steady or soldierlike. Some clicking of canteens against the hilts of sabres was immediately checked and suppressed, and the silence and steadiness of that march in the dark night up that solitary road, lined on each side with the black frowning woods, seemed truly grand.

I could never lay claim to extraordinary courage, and could never be accused of exposing myself needlessly and recklessly to the fire of the enemy, and I may say that I was always on the whole happiest when I was out of danger ; but it seems to me that there are times when a man has not entirely free will or control over his sentiments. His courage may be stirred up by some great circumstance or necessity of the moment, and every other thought or consideration is forgotten ; and such, I thought, that night pervaded these men. For myself, it seemed plain, from my position, that I was going to almost certain destruction ; and yet, I think, I never in my life walked with such pride as I marched on that occasion at the head of the column.

By our side rode the colonel, who sometimes went back along the line to see if the files were keeping closed up, and occasionally the general came up and rode by us ; but the utmost silence was maintained, and anything said was in a very low tone.

When we had gone a certain distance we supposed we were near the enemy's pickets. The general quietly ordered a halt, and asked for about six men to act as scouts. I walked along the company, and asked for six men to volunteer to go to the front. More than a dozen were forward in a minute. The first was H., a man very low in stature and a tailor by profession. The general looked at him and said, " You will do fine as to size, but tell me this, my man, are you afraid of being shot by the enemy ?"

" No, d——n 'em," said H.

" You will do," said the general.

He then selected the rest, choosing men small of stature, who would not be so easily seen, and could creep softly through the brushwood. More wanted to go, but he would only allow six. He, however, allowed two more to go in rear of the others, so as to report back quickly anything they saw. He then gave them orders to go away ahead, three on each side— one on the very edge of the road under the dark shade of the woods, the other two to extend some distance from the road into the woods on each side. They proceeded on in front, and he ordered the column to advance very slowly.

I confess I now felt a little relieved, for I had for the last quarter of an hour been expecting a volley of grape-shot being sent down the road to greet our arrival, and, notwithstanding my pride at my position that night, I had a particular antipathy to grape-shot ; and if the enemy had lined the ridges on the side of the road with riflemen, and given us a salute as we passed, it would have been nothing more than a due respect to the compliment we had paid them two days previously.

We kept marching on slowly, the scouts reporting back that they had seen nothing. At length said the colonel, " This looks suspicious ; we must have passed their picket guard." This implied that they had been aware of our approach and drawn in their pickets, or that the picket guard had discovered us and retired in silence ; in either case they would be ready to receive us. The general, in the meantime, had gone back to give some orders about the artillery, as I supposed.

At length we came to an opening which looked down upon a creek about 80 yards distant. A quiet halt was made. The colonel looked puzzled, and turning to me he said, " Will you get a trusty man to slip quietly down to that creek and ascertain in which direction it runs ?"

" I will go myself," said I. And going softly down to the creek, I put my hand into the water to ascertain which way the current ran. Having satisfied myself, I looked around. It was an open space, not unlike Crane Creek which we had left. Suddenly I saw a dark figure moving a little way up the creek, and by the reflection of the stars upon the water I discovered our friend H., the scout, who was placing his foot on a stone to step over.

" Is that you, H. ? " said I.

" Yes.   Who is that ?   You, Sergeant ? "

" Yes.   Have you seen anything ? "

" Nothing at all," said he ; " but I heard a dog barking over there."

" Stay a moment," said I, " till I come back."

A strong smell of wood burning came from the opposite side of the creek, but all was quiet.   I went back to the colonel and reported : " The water runs from the right of the road to the left of the road."

" Are you sure of that ? " said the colonel.

" I am quite sure," said I.   " The creek is clearly defined, and cuts the road at right angles."

" There is a mistake somewhere," said the colonel.   " Come down with me."

The colonel dismounted and we went down to the creek together.   The colonel pondered : " There is something wrong somewhere.   But," said he, " this must be their camp ; don't you smell the rotten meat ? "

I did smell it and burning wood.   I now saw H., the scout, and motioned him to approach.   I went with him a short distance and found it was a camp but newly deserted.   The camp fires were still burning and the debris lay thick about. I went back and told the colonel.   He pondered and supposed they had withdrawn to a position in the rear of their camp, and he went back to see the general.

I followed up the bank to my place at the head of the column.   I there found the colonel in conversation with the general.   I heard the general say, "They must have retreated, for there is no other position they could take up of any value near that camp, or for some miles beyond it."

The men now drew a long breath ; the immediate prospects of a battle were again dispelled.

It was now long past midnight.   The troops were ordered to lie down on their arms and rest till daylight.

To be on the right of an advancing column, though perhaps attended with a little more danger, has some advantages.   In hot dry weather you are out of the crowd, have room for marching, and are free from the stifling dust.   You have also the first chance of getting clean water from the springs or creeks on the road, before it has been disturbed by the crowd in the crush to obtain it. You have also an opportunity of knowing what is going on by seeing clear in front and being amongst the leading commanders, observing their movements and hearing their conversation.

As soon as day dawned I got up, and with the captain went to have a look at the enemy's deserted camp. There, already minutely inspecting it, were General M'Culloch, Colonel M'Intosh, and our own colonel, H. Many of the camp fires were still smouldering, and the officers seemed to be making a survey of the whole camp and surroundings, with a view, I presume, of forming some idea of the composition and strength of the enemy's forces.

The site which had been occupied by each battalion could be traced, as well as marks which indicated the arms of the corps. The positions occupied by artillery or cavalry could be traced by the debris left behind, and which they in their sudden retreat had not burned or destroyed. Amongst the debris were a great many papers, such as newspapers, pieces of letters and envelopes addressed to men in different corps, such as "Sturge's Brigade, United States Army," "United States Dragoons," "Totten's Battery, U.S.A.," "Siegel's Brigade," "3rd Regiment Iowa Volunteers," and many others. The extent of their camp showed that the enemy had a strong force of efficient troops, of which a considerable number was of the regular army of the United States.

Their object in retreating was rather inexplicable, and from conversation which I heard among the officers it was deemed that they must either have overestimated our strength, or they were executing some manœuvre to draw us further away from our supplies or into some trap that they might completely annihilate us.

General Lyon was known to be one of the best generals the United States possessed, and it was not easy to surmise what strategy he might adopt.

General M'Culloch's decision seemed to be quickly taken. He ordered the column to advance at once.

Some mounted scouts were sent to scour the country in front and reconnoitre, and the column moved forward just as the sun was appearing above the horizon.

The country was now more clear, open, and level, and we

followed the line of the enemy's retreat. The brushwood or
crops for about 50 feet on each side of the road was cleared or
trampled down as if they had marched in column by companies.
They had left us a good road. They had felled no trees across
it, or placed any obstructions to retard our advance, as is
usually done in a retreat. They had destroyed no crops or
forage, so far as I saw, with a view of preventing our obtaining
provender. In fact, everything seemed to indicate an invitation to us to follow them. I presume our general saw this, for
he acted with great caution.

The men had had but little rest, no breakfast, little or
nothing in their haversacks, and hard toil and little to eat for
several days, and they were a good deal harassed and broken
down, but maintained their spirit and dogged determination to
have this matter out.

In the early forenoon the scouts reported that the enemy
was but a short distance in front. The head of the column
was halted for files to close up, but before this was done our
company was ordered to deploy in front as skirmishers, while
other companies deployed in line across the road. This was
scarcely done when a small body of the enemy's cavalry came
sweeping down upon us. A few shots from our rifles sent
them to the right about, and they went off as quickly as they
came. It was evident that this was only a rear-guard
reconnoitring party, probably trying to pick up some of our
advanced scouts.

These dashes were repeated several times, and the day being
intensely hot, it was becoming hard upon us. The cavalry
which was covering the retreat of the enemy began to appear
in larger numbers, and M'Culloch ordered up two pieces of
artillery to the front, and a few shrapnels sent amongst them
warned them to keep at a more respectful distance.

Shortly after mid-day some manœuvring took place, which
I did not understand. We had been wondering what had
become of the Texas Rangers, of which we had heard so much.
Why were not they, or some other of the mounted corps, sent
to the front to try their strength with the United States
Dragoons. They now did come, and went off on a detour.
Our regiment was ordered to advance quickly, and we were
led off the road through some fields and into a wood, until we
came to where the wood was opened by a large field which had
just newly been cleared of wheat. We were here deployed

along the edge of the wood, so far in as to be out of sight, and ordered to sit or lie down, and to keep quiet and concealed, and be ready to fire upon the enemy's cavalry, which would be certain to pass in front of us in a short time.

The men were very ready to sit or lie down ; it was pleasant to get a little rest in the cool shade, but the cravings of hunger were beginning to be severely felt. We remained in this quiet position for fully half-an-hour, but no enemy appeared, while the men were sorely tempted by a large flock of beautiful wild turkeys, which came quietly along in front of us within 30 yards, picking up and feeding upon the scattered fragments of the wheat, quite unconscious of our presence, or that so many loaded rifles were being pointed at them, and the officers had to use the most determined exertion and threats to restrain the men from having a shot at them. It was very tantalising to the men as they contemplated how soon one of the birds would have been roasting over a wood fire, and what a feast it would have made to starving men. I felt it more so as they came up closer, and a beautiful large gobbler strutted up with all the pride and dignity of a city alderman, and looked me straight in the face with a defiant air as much as to say, "You know you dare not fire." We were glad when they moved off.

The Yankee cavalry, however, were more 'cute, and had less faith in human forbearance than the turkeys, and they did not come near.

This ambushing was tried several times afterwards, but I never once saw it successful. We were now ordered back to take our place at the head of the column, and the troops, which had been having a little rest, moved onwards.

We were now warned to be careful of what we had in our canteens, as we had a march of over seven miles across a level prairie before we would come to a drop of water. At the end of that distance there was a roaring mountain spring, but the place would likely be occupied by the enemy. The sun was broiling hot, and our canteens were already nearly empty.

We toiled on, but before we got half way the pangs of thirst had become almost unbearable. The heat seemed to become more intense as the afternoon advanced, and the men were beginning to fag. Many would have dropped out, but for the intimation that we were likely to meet the enemy at Big Springs, as the place was called, and that there there were good shade and plenty of water. At last we began to approach the high and wooded land at the end of the prairie, and scouts brought word that there was no enemy there. This was pleasing news, for we were not in very good condition to meet them. The pace was quickened and we approached the mountain side, and soon reached the spring,—and a spring it was! An enormous fountain bursting out of the mountain side and rolling in a torrent down a stony creek. To dirty this stream was impossible, and the men let loose actually rushed into the torrent up to their knees. The water was clear, cool, and delicious, and what a luxury! It seemed the greatest of all gratifications. The men drank almost to bursting, then filled their canteens. We were allowed a short time here to rest, and the men took off their shoes and wrung their wet stockings, some of which were beginning to show so many holes that it was difficult to know which hole to put the foot into.

It was now near sunset and we had been manœuvring in the broiling sun since daybreak, besides a long march had been accomplished, and we hoped we would bivouac here for the night, but we were ordered to march on about two miles farther. We had just got to the place where we were to bivouac for the night, when the sky suddenly darkened and a violent thunderstorm came on, and the rain poured down in torrents. We were drenched to the skin. Why did not this come, thought we, when we were scorched with heat and thirst on the prairie? We then had too little water, now we had too much. The rain was soon over and we managed to get fires lighted.

There was one good thing at all those bivouacs, we could always get plenty of good firewood from the woods or old fence rails. We wrung our wet clothes and blankets, and set about drying them; but the great question was: Were we to get anything to eat? After a while a waggon-load of green corn was brought in, and two ears were served out to each man. Poor as this fare was, and tired as we were of the green corn, it was soon roasted and eaten with a relish, followed by a drink of water, and the ever-solacing smoke. We then dried our clothes and blankets as well as we could, saw that our arms and ammunition were dry, and lay down upon our arms among the wet bushes.

At daybreak we formed line again to proceed, and as we were ready to move forward an aide-de-camp rode up along the

line and, coming up to our company on the right, told us that
our march to-day would be but a short one, as we had not far to
go, and we might depend upon it that supplies would be up, as
M'Culloch had sworn that if supplies were not forward by this
evening he would hang every waggon-master and commissary in
the division upon the oak trees; whereupon there was a general
acclamation and a sudden stepping forward of the whole line
volunteering to draw the ropes. He also delivered an order
detailing our second lieutenant to proceed to the rear and act
for the time as waggon-master of the brigade. It seemed that
the waggon-master and several of the commissary staff were
reported on the sick list—sickness perhaps brought on by the
sound of the firing. The second lieutenant, grumbling and
protesting that he knew nothing about waggons, proceeded in
obedience to orders, being strictly enjoined by the boys to
remember the threat of the general, and assuring him that
they would have a piece of rope in readiness.

This appointment was no doubt owing to Lieutenant B.'s
name being first on the list for detached service, but, though
he was a smart and active young man, his occupation in civil
life was that of a lawyer, and what did he know about getting
waggons over bad roads? The appointment caused some
comment, and the boys thought it did not augur well for the
waggons being got up that evening. But again it was remembered that lawyers were strange varmints, and if there was
any possibility of a horse or a mule or a driver being cheated,
flattered, or beguiled into a little extra exertion it was they
that could do it, and it might be all right after all.

The column proceeded, and the march for the day, as had
been promised, was a short one. We came up to another
creek called "Wilson's Creek." This creek was about the
same size, or a little larger, than the others, but did not cross
the road at right angles, but ran for some distance nearly in
the same line as the road. The land on both sides was higher
and somewhat undulating. Here we halted. We had seen
nothing of the enemy since yesterday afternoon, and we were
told that they had fallen back to Springfield, which was about
eight miles distant. We were allotted a particular place
for our bivouac, and preparation was made for a camp, which
showed that M'Culloch intended to bring up and concentrate
his forces here before making a further advance. The place
was not a very advantageous position for defence, such as

Crane Creek, but it afforded space on both sides of the creek for the forces to concentrate. Throughout the day the remainder of the division came up.

I may here say that M'Culloch was only a brigadier-general, while the force under his command would comprise a division. He was far from, and could have but little communication with, the War Department at Richmond, and presumably had no great influence there. Not having full power to act or appoint, he had temporarily divided his forces into two brigades, commanding both himself, with Colonel M'Intosh as his assistant.

General Price, with the Missouri State troops not being in the Confederate service, was simply an ally, and the two generals had to act in concert.

Towards evening Price's forces began to come up, encamping on the opposite side of the creek. About sunset we were rejoiced at the arrival of some waggons with provisions. The general's threat had not been without its effect. Rations of flour, fresh beef, salt, and a little coffee and sugar, were served out; and some cooking utensils were obtained, and cooking and eating gone into with great vigour, and we enjoyed a fair night's rest.

We had lately been slightly annoyed by little insects, with which the grass in the woods abounded. They were called red bugs, a small kind of spider of a red colour. They fastened on the skin, and caused a good deal of scratching; but they were nothing to mosquitoes, the remembrance of which made all other annoyances of that kind seem slight. In this camp these red bugs were very plentiful; and the men slept on the banks of the creek, which were steep, sloping down towards the water. The banks were covered with large round pebbles, and the itching from the bites of these insects caused the men in their sleep to roll or welter (after the fashion of a horse or mule) on their backs, and the round pebbles on which they lay, rolling, caused them to work downwards, until several of them in their unconscious state rolled into the creek, which was here about a foot deep, to the great amusement of such as had been awakened by the splashing and exclamations of their drenched comrades.

By the morning all the forces were up, and the camp was put into some kind of order and position. On the one side of the creek were the Confederate troops under M'Culloch, each

o

company having one tent to keep the arms and ammunition dry. The general's tent and headquarters were close to our bivouac. Beyond that, on the extreme right, was Woodruff's battery of six guns. To the left of us were the different regiments of infantry of Arkansas and Texas troops, and on the extreme left was Reid's battery of six guns ; Churchhill's regiment of mounted infantry being somewhere on the left, also the Texas rangers. These mounted troops were often on the move reconnoitring.

On the opposite side of the stream were several grassy ridges, the principal of which terminated in a hill about half-a-mile from the creek. This hill, near the top, was covered with stunted or scrub oak trees, and it bore the name of "Oakhill." On the grassy ridges, forming the spurs of this hill, Price's division was encamped.

In this position we lay for about three days, rather inactive. Here J. S. got into another serious difficulty. He had all along been somewhat morose and sullen, but always prompt to duty. He was now charged with assaulting a field officer. I never learned the exact particulars, but it seemed he had been doing something about some of the waggons, and was challenged by the major and ordered away, and he had retorted or refused, which led to high words, resulting in the assault. This was a high offence, and he was put under arrest, to be tried by court-martial.

It was now known that the enemy had fallen back to Springfield, and were entrenching themselves there. Springfield was a place of some importance. It was the principal town in the southern part of Missouri, and there converged the roads leading from Kansas, from the Indian Territory, and from Arkansas, and leading northwards towards St. Louis. It was plain we would now have to force the fighting. The enemy was all right. They were resting upon their base of operations, in a commanding position, with abundance of supplies, and their force likely to be augmented.

We were far from our base of operations, deficient of supplies, our means of transport giving out, and, to say nothing of the distance and excessive bad roads between us and our base of operations, there were numerous creeks and rivers which, as winter approached, would be swollen and become impassable. We had no chance of reinforcements, and our strength was likely to be decreased by sickness. M'Culloch (as I afterwards learned) did not care to trust too much to information received from the country people regarding the enemy's strength or movements.

These people were apt to be deceived or to exaggerate; besides, they would have their own private sentiments in favour of the South or the North, or they might be indifferent; but, whatever their private sentiments might be, they would have to shape their outward policy according as the country was occupied by a Northern or a Southern army, and generally he put but little faith in outward demonstrations.

Price, on the other hand, considered that the mass of the population was in his favour and loyal to his cause, but was kept in subjection by a Federal army, and that their information might be relied upon.

About the third day after we camped here some ladies on horseback visited Price's camp. I do not know whether they had any friends in it or not, but they professed great zeal in the Southern cause. They conversed very graciously with the men as they rode through the camp, and wished them every success. They expressed a great desire to see the Confederate troops, and were shown over the camp, and expressed their admiration at everything they saw, bowing graciously to the men, and promising to pray for their success.

About sunset the same evening an order was quietly sent round precisely the same as the one at Crane Creek for the troops to be prepared to march at nine o'clock to make an attack on the enemy at Springfield, the only difference being that the troops should take three days' cooked rations in their haversacks.

The preparation was commenced drawing and cooking of rations, not for three days, but for one day, that being as much as the commissary had to give. Arms and ammunition pouches were examined and the number of rounds made up to each man. Each company's solitary tent was struck, and with the cooking utensils packed in waggons to be sent as might be ordered. Our captain had been detailed to command the skirmishers, which were to consist of our company and two others, and we were to advance in front.

It was near nine o'clock, the sky had become clouded, and a few drops of rain were falling. I was just going to form the company, when the major came along to say that the march would be postponed to see what the weather would do, and if the rain continued we were to pitch tents again and keep the arms dry. The reason he assigned for this delay was that a good many of the Missouri troops were armed with flint-lock muskets, and a still greater number of them had no cartouche-boxes, and they would be of little service if it rained, and it would take every available man and arm that we had for what we had to do. "And you see, W.," continued he, assuming the old citizen style of talking, "it would never do for us to attempt this job and make a botch of it."

The rain continued, but not heavy ; tents were again pitched, and, though the rain ceased about eleven o'clock and the night became fine, nothing was said about marching. Another post-ponement ? The suspense was becoming unbearable. The men sought the driest place they could find to lie down. The weather looked better, and it was supposed that we should march forward at dawn of day.

CHAPTER XVIII.

On the first appearance of dawn some of the boys got up and ran down to the waggon to get something to make a little coffee to drink before we started on the march.

There being now no drum beat at reveille a bugle was sounded for roll call. The roll was called, and the boys were trying to get some coffee prepared, when mounted men were seen hurrying up to the general's tent, and a young lad called my attention, saying, "There is something up !"

The general was out partly dressed and bare-headed, eagerly listening. I got near to listen. I saw the men pointing in different directions, and heard them say something about "coming round through the prairie," "cavalry," and "16 pieces of artillery." The general gave them some orders and they rode off. He then returned to his tent and immediately came out with his coat and hat on, and seeing us looking he cried out, "Fall in there !" and then walked over towards Price's head-quarters. I gave the order to "Fall in," and the company was quickly formed, amidst cries of "We are going to have it now, boys."

The other companies were as quickly formed, and the regiment was soon in line. Two of the other companies were joined to ours to be ready to deploy in front as skirmishers ; and we were ordered to proceed to the right of Woodruff's battery. As we passed the battery we saw it had got into position, and the artillerymen bringing water from the creek to fill their sponge-buckets and prepare for action.

Here we were halted for a few minutes. I looked along the company and saw every man was in his place. We stood upon an elevated spot and had a fine view of the greater part of the field. Price's army waggons, which had been taken forward for the march on the previous evening, were being driven furiously to the rear.

The enemy had possession of the Oakhill, where they were getting their artillery into position, and large bodies of their troops were extending out on their left wing, seemingly with the view of turning our right flank, and getting in rear of Woodruff's battery. The order of the battle, notwithstanding the hurried way it was begun, was upon a regular plan and well ordered throughout.

Upon our right was the 1st Brigade, consisting of the 3rd Louisiana Regiment, the 2nd and 3rd Arkansas Regiments, with Woodruff's battery of six guns—under command of Colonel M'Intosh.

Upon our left was the 1st Arkansas Regiment, Churchhill's Regiment, and a Texas Regiment (the two latter were mounted infantry but fought on foot), and Reid's battery of six guns —commanded by General M'Culloch.

In the centre a little advanced was Price's division with one battery of four guns—under General Price.

The lines of the battle were somewhat in the form of a crescent, the enemy being on the outside line and we upon the inside line.

Upon the enemy's right was Siegel's German Brigade, with one battery of six guns, commanded by General Siegel. Upon their left was Sturges' Brigade of United States troops, with, I think, one battery of three or four guns, commanded by Colonel Sturges. In the centre were several regiments of Iowa and Missouri Volunteers, with some United States troops, and one battery of six guns, under Colonel Totten, with a detachment of United States Cavalry which acted as reserve, —the whole commanded by General Lyon.

As we stood here it got to be clear daylight, and we saw that the enemy had gained a great advantage by getting possession of the Oakhill, and having his artillery planted upon it.

We had not long to ponder over it, for Colonel M'Intosh galloped up, and putting himself at our head, cried, "This way, boys." He led us out towards the front of our right, against the enemy's left. We had not proceeded far, when a shot from Totten's battery on the Oakhill, and a shell bursting over our heads, announced the opening of the ball. This was followed by others thick and fast, and they were beginning to come unpleasantly close. We were soon pleased to hear Woodruff's battery returning the fire, which showed the enemy they were not going to have it all their own way. This drew some of the fire off us. We now got on to a road which led across some level land, which was covered with a low copse or brush-wood. The skirmishers were now ordered to deploy in front, and fight their way up to a rail fence which formed the boundary between the copse and the corn-fields beyond, where the enemy was forming their line. This road led to the corn-fields, and a large part of the rail fence had been taken down to allow of the carting away of the corn which had been already gathered. Colonel M'Intosh, pointing to this opening, which might be about 60 feet wide, said, "I see the enemy's cavalry yonder in rear of their infantry, take care that they don't pass in through that opening; and mind, that is my regiment that is in front on your left, take care and not fire into it."

The copse was low and easily got through, and we could see the enemy's line advancing in beautiful order, with skirmishers in front.

The opposing forces approached the fence about the same time. As we got to within 20 yards of it on the one side, their skirmishers would be about 20 yards from it on the other side, the main lines on both sides being about 30 yards in the rear of their skirmishers.

"Who are you? What force is that?" cried a voice from our side, which I think was our colonel's. "United States troops," was the reply. This was said in a tone so authoritative that I confess it for a moment almost staggered me. It seemed to say, This is authority, so lay down your arms and go home. The sudden appearance close before us of the men and officers with whom we had always been so friendly, and had respected so much, and with whom we had paraded a year ago at the Baton Rouge fair, took me slightly aback. Others may have had, and did have, the same feeling, but it was quickly dispelled by the words which followed, which were, "Who are you? Volunteers?" This last word was uttered with such scorn and bitterness, and followed by some expressions of contempt for volunteers, that I believe it roused the spirit of every man in our ranks, who seemed to say, "I thank thee, Roderick, for the word." "Volunteers!" cried a United States officer, with supreme contempt, "pitch into them, boys, and clear them out of your way!" "Yes, we are volunteers," cried several voices from our side, "and we will let you know that before we are done with you;" and the fire opened from both sides about the same moment, and our first lieutenant, with whom I was talking at the moment, dropped at my feet, with the blood streaming from his neck. All hesitation now left me, and I was roused to the work. Our captain, being in command of the whole line of skirmishers, was of course absent from the company. Our second lieutenant, being still with the waggon department, was busy getting the waggons to the rear, and the first lieutenant having fallen, the immediate command of the company now fell upon me. The sergeant-major came up to me to deliver some order, but I could not hear it for the firing ; he was coming closer to repeat it, when he fell shot dead.

The order had been for the skirmishers to fall back on the main body, which had now approached to within 15 yards of them. The fire from our rear passing so close over our heads soon warned us to fall back upon the main line. About the same time and in the same way the enemy's skirmishers fell back on their main line, and the battle now began in true earnest. Both sides were piqued and determined. It was now a fair stand-up fight, and the question was who would stand it longest. The fire was heavy on both sides, and the bullets rattled like a hailstorm.

We had certainly the advantage of being in the brushwood, for, although it did not reach higher than our shoulders, yet the men stooped when loading, and for the time were hid from the aim of the enemy; but in a short time the smoke got so thick that sure aim could not be taken on either side. The enemy tried to work round on our right flank, but was there as vigorously met.

The fighting was desperate for about half-an-hour, when a sort of a lull took place as if by mutual consent, to draw breath and let the smoke clear away.

When the smoke cleared away a little we could see the enemy plainly. They stood as firm as ever, but their ranks were much thinned and their dead lay thick. The voices of their officers, who had been crying, " Pitch into them, boys ! " were now hushed. Some of them had been slightly wounded in the head, but they still stood in their places, while the blood running down their faces gave them a ghastly but fierce and determined look. They were evidently riled at having met with such determined resistance.

" How about volunteers now ? " cried several voices from our side.

This was answered vindictively by a volley, and the battle commenced again with renewed vigour. It seemed to have become a test of rivalry between regulars and volunteers; both sides were thoroughly roused, and the combat was furious. The enemy were better armed than we were. They were of good metal and well disciplined, and maintained their phalanx by closing up to the centre. They stood upright, and preserved their line well formed. This was fatal to them. Our line was not so well formed or the men so well disciplined, but they were as resolute and were better marksmen, and the fighting being at close quarters the difference of arms was not much felt. We had had the advantage of the brushwood, but that was now getting too much trampled down to afford much shelter.

The enemy had evidently suffered severely. Their ranks were fearfully thinned; their fire was beginning to slacken, and they were unquestionably getting the worst of it. They were mad with desperation, and began to cry, "Come out and meet us in the open field."

"Charge them with the bayonet!" cried a voice near me.

"Give them the steel, boys!" resounded along the line, and with a tremendous cheer we rushed out upon them. They broke, the greater part retreating towards their centre on Oakhill; but some still stood in line, seemingly dumbfounded, and were pushed down and run over by our men as they followed the retreating body. But I don't think a single man of them was bayoneted; our men were too much excited and exhilarated with their success to notice them. One young officer stood holding a small flag or marker on their line. I ran to seize the flag from him. He with his sword inflicted a slight wound on my wrist. I closed with him, but found the poor fellow was already sorely wounded, and he fell fainting on the ground, still holding on to the flag. I left him; and, not wishing to be left behind, ran up and joined my company, which had passed on, following up the retreating enemy. We followed them up towards the base of Oakhill, but we were there checked by a storm of shrapnel and grape, which was opened upon us from a battery on the enemy's left. Fortunately we were not in very compact order at the time, and not much damage was done.

We rallied behind a rising ground and took a breathing space. Here I looked at my wounded wrist and saw it was not serious, though bleeding profusely. I tied it up with the piece of white rag which we had tied round our left arms to distinguish us from the enemy.

Colonel M'Intosh now rode up and told us that we had made a good beginning, but the day was not yet won, and we were ordered to form line as quickly as possible.

We formed line, but we covered much less ground than we had done in the early morning ; our ranks had got a considerable thinning. On looking over our company I found about 20 missing. The skirmishing companies now took their regular places in the regiment, and our captain joined us. I also became aware of the presence of J. S. ; he had broken away from the guard and had got a rifle and joined in the fight.

While we stood here a few minutes awaiting orders we had a good view of the whole field, which showed that the battle was still far from being decided. Our right had beaten and driven in the enemy's left wing, but on our centre and left wing the battle, was raging furiously. The sky had suddenly darkened down, which showed the red flashes of the artillery through the smoke, while the hissing of shells and the continued crackle of small arms made the scene look grand, though not altogether pleasant.

Suddenly some one cried out that there was cavalry coming down upon us.

" Pooh ! " cried Colonel M'Intosh, " who the devil cares for cavalry ? Here, you rifles, take your position along that fence and send them to the rightabout." This was addressed to our company, and we ran and took up the position. We saw the cavalry advancing upon us, but before they came within range of our rifles a shower of grape and shrapnels from Woodruff's battery sent them to the rightabout.

Just at this moment General M'Culloch came galloping up, and, addressing the regiment, commended them for their bravery, and pointing to a battery on the enemy's right, said it must be stormed. The shattered brigade was then formed, and Colonel M'Intosh placed himself at its head and we moved towards the centre. My position was on the right as usual, and Colonel M'Intosh rode by my side.

Colonel M'Intosh, though very affable and pleasant in his manner, had nevertheless something so commanding in his deportment that he carried men with him in spite of themselves, and, although I would just as soon have been somewhere else than to be the first man marching up to that battery, yet I felt that I would rather die three times over than display the slightest fear under the eye of that man.

On our way to the centre we crossed the creek. In the stream were several dead and wounded horses, and at the edge of the water were several wounded men who had managed to crawl there. The sun was now out bright and hot, and the dust and smoke were stifling. Our men, parched with thirst, drank and filled their canteens. This delayed the column a little, when our major came along in great distress. He was on foot, walking lame and bareheaded. " Ho! what is the matter, major?" He was in a sad plight. His horse had been shot under him. It had fallen upon his leg and hurt his foot, having partly rolled over on him. He had struggled a long time before he could extricate himself. His clothes were all dirtied and torn, and he had lost his hat. The sun was burning his head, which he was trying to protect with his hand. " Here is a hat for you, major!" cried one of the boys, picking up a wretched old torn straw hat which had been lost by some of the waggon-drivers in the morning while hurrying back with their waggons to the rear. The major, seeming to think that at that time at least the nature of the hat was of less importance than the preservation of the head that was in it, said it would be better than nothing, and put it on amid the laughter of the whole regiment.

As we got to the centre we found that a large number of Price's troops were falling back down the hill in confusion. Colonel M'Intosh was immediately amongst them. " Back, back, men, and stand to your colours. Why, here is a brigade that has already thrashed the enemy's regulars and cut them to pieces, and they are now come to help you." The men immediately rallied round him, and he led them back up the hill.

General M'Culloch then rode up, and saying something to Colonel M'Intosh, the latter turned the 2nd and 3rd Arkansas regiments up the hill to the support of Price, while M'Culloch himself led our regiment towards the left and against the battery on the enemy's right.

As we moved onwards we passed Price's battery, which was silenced. The place here showed signs of rough work; the ground was much ploughed up by cannon shot, and the dead and wounded lay thick. The place was enveloped in smoke from the burning grass and debris, and the burning wadding which was falling on us, as the cannon shots passed over our heads from the battery we were going to storm. This was all the better for us, as it hid our approach from the enemy and enabled us to come upon them and take them unawares. " Keep down and trail arms," said M'Culloch, and we kept down along the bank of the creek. The battery was situated on a piece of high tableland overlooking and commanding a large part of the field, with a steep bank in front. The road led along the bottom, of this bank, which was covered with trees and brushwood. Up and along the bank we went cautiously, under cover of the smoke and keeping below the range of fire, the general leading the way. We got so close that we could see the muzzles of the guns and a body of infantry in a hollow place to the left of the battery.

" What force is this ? " cried General M'Culloch.

" Siegel's brigade," was the answer.

" All right," said M'Culloch. " Now, boys, give it to them."

A deadly fire was poured upon the infantry and the guns simultaneously, and our men rushed forward and drove the artillerymen from the guns. They were taken completely by surprise and broke in confusion. Some of the artillerymen did succeed in limbering up, but horses and men were shot down before they could get away. The infantry tried to rally and retake the guns, but were driven back by our fire, and they retreated away through some corn-fields.

We were now, almost to our own surprise, left in possession of the guns, and we could hardly believe that we had captured a battery which had been doing such damage throughout the morning.

On looking round, one of the first men that I saw at the guns was Colonel M'Intosh. That man seemed to be everywhere. After getting the two Arkansas regiments set to work in the centre, he had galloped over to join in the attack on the battery. But we had quickly to stand back from the guns. A shot from one of our own batteries killed two of our own men (one of them a captain), knocking a spoke out of a wheel, and making a deep dent in one of the guns. Reid's battery on our left was still playing on this battery, and did not know that it had been taken. Orders were immediately sent to cease firing upon it.

In the meantime where was the enemy ? It was known that

Siegel was not the man to be so easily defeated, and he would likely make an effort to retake the guns. We soon after saw a body of infantry coming up in the rear of the battery, and we prepared to receive them, but they made but a poor stand. They rather seemed amazed and stupified, and after a few shots they retreated.

It seemed that this was a regiment of infantry which had been placed to support the battery, and in the confusion into which they had been thrown by our sudden attack, they had retreated the wrong way, and were now trying to make their way back to join their own main body. As we had advanced some distance past the guns, they probably mistook us for a part of their own brigade from which they were now cut off.

As soon as the battery had been captured, and the infantry supporting it driven back and held in check by our regiment, our second brigade, consisting of the 1st Arkansas regiment, Churchhill's regiment, and the Texas regiment, which had suffered severely in the morning, made a fresh attack on the main body of Siegel's brigade, which they drove back and cut off from Lyon's centre. Meanwhile we were deployed along the edge of the wood which lined the approach to the battery, to check any advance that might be made to retake the guns.

Here a little incident happened, which shows how easily a mistake might occur. We were formed in line about 10 yards from, and parallel with the road, but could not be seen from it on account of the brushwood, and we were expecting an advance of the enemy along this road. In a short time, being on the right, I saw above the brushwood the head and shoulders of a man on horseback advancing along the road, which from the cap and uniform I saw, bore the rank of captain in the Federal army. Supposing him to be the leader of the attacking party, an impetuous corporal by my side raised his rifle to take him down. I ordered him not to fire yet, but wait a little. In the meantime the officer rode past a tree which intervened and the corporal was rating me for having made him lose his shot, when the officer stopped, and I heard some one talking with him, and recognised the voice of our lieutenant-colonel.

I immediately went out to the road, and saw the officer and our lieutenant-colonel in conversation. I explained to our lieutenant-colonel the danger the officer was in. The officer acknowledged his rashness and dismounted, and a flag of truce was displayed by way of attaching a white handkerchief to a bayonet which was held up. He was the chief medical officer of the Federal army, and wished to negotiate for the treatment of the wounded.

General M'Culloch, who after the battery was captured had galloped to another part of the field, fortunately at this moment returned. He readily agreed to let the enemy take their wounded off the field, on the strict conditions that they should take nothing else, such as arms, etc., until the result of the battle was known, and that every ambulance party should bear with them conspicuously a hospital flag, and orders were sent along not to fire upon any party bearing a yellow flag.

We were now ordered to secure the guns and such of the horses as had been left unwounded, scour the fields and bushes in the neighbourhood for hidden parties of enemy, and prepare for action in another part of the field.

Immediately in the rear of the battery was a pretty substantial farm-house with extensive barns and out-houses. All the buildings were completely riddled by the shot. I was sent with a small party to search all the houses, in case some of the enemy had taken refuge or hidden themselves there. We found several of the enemy in a hay loft who surrendered as prisoners. I forced the back-door of the dwelling-house which was locked and entered the kitchen. Several cannon shots had passed through it, and the floor was strewn with dust and broken crockery. I examined the other rooms but found nobody. I was about to retire when one of the boys called to me that here was a stair down to a cellar and we might catch some one down there.

I went down, and caught a tartar. A woman jumped up and confronted me.

" What do you want here ? Get out of this," she cried, as she launched out into a tirade of abuse about how their house and property had been destroyed and themselves almost killed.

I desired her to compose herself, as I was only looking to see if any of the enemy had taken refuge there. Looking round the place, I saw a younger woman, a man, and some children, who were crouched in a corner behind some barrels and a large pile of apples.

" Is that your husband ? " said I.

" Yes, he is my husband, and them is my children."

" Oh, very well, we will not molest you further," said I,

calling out to the boys, who were helping themselves to the apples, to desist, and we turned to go upstairs.

"Oh, take the apples," said she, "take a plenty of them; take them all if you like. Are you Lincoln's folk or Jeff. Davis' folk?

"Jeff. Davis' folk," said I.

She then asked if the fuss was over. I said I did not know, but that I thought it would be over at this part of the field, as we had taken the enemy's guns that had been in the front of her house.

"Then burn the pesky things," said she. "My head is split in pieces, and the children has got fits, and my old man has got quite deaf with the big noise of them."

I felt like saying that, considering her gift of speech, a worse thing might have happened to the old man. But the old man, having regained his hearing and a little assurance, asked me as we were ascending the stair if it would be safe for them now to come up, as they had been down there ever since the fuss began. I said it would, but if they heard firing to go down again. They were quite safe in the cellar from any kind of shot, but that a shell, if exploding in it, might have set the house on fire. The old woman was up first, but on seeing the wreck, and looking out and seeing the dead men and horses lying in front of the house, she broke out in a greater fury than ever. Who was going to pay for all this? Who was going to take away them dead folks and dead horses? Was she to have them lying stinking round her house? so that I was glad to get away and join the regiment, which was now forming to proceed to another part of the field.

General M'Culloch now addressed the regiment and said, "You have beaten the enemy's right and left wings, only their centre is left, and with all our forces concentrated upon that, we will soon make short work of it."

Our route was now by a detour, and then to ascend Oakhill and attack the enemy in their rear. We were led by our colonel; the detour was long, and we were to move as quickly as possible. The sun was now intensely hot, and the men were considerably fatigued, but they pressed on. The heavy firing at the centre continued, showing that there was heavy fighting going on. We got to the base of the hill in their rear and began to ascend. The enemy discovered us, and opened fire at a considerable distance. We were pressing up the hill to get to closer quarters, when a ball took me in the pit of the stomach, and for a few minutes I remembered no more.

When I recovered consciousness, I was lying on my back, with the sun pouring into my eyes. I had fallen with my head down the hill, my left hand, which was the wounded one, was under my back. I must have thrown it back to stop me from falling. I felt the wounded hand sore, but no other pain. In trying to move my wounded hand, I felt something trickle upon it. I concluded the ball had passed through my body and had come out at my back, and that the blood was trickling from the wound, and that, therefore, it was all up with me. What my thoughts were I need not say, but I felt no faintness nor pain, except from my wounded wrist. This I gently withdrew from under me, and bringing it before me, saw the wound was bleeding a little, but what had trickled over my hand was water. A sudden flash of hope sprung up, and I ventured to shake myself and felt nothing wrong, and I sprang to my feet. My belt and sabre fell away from me as I rose, but I could not realise that no ball had pierced me, and I examined closely, shook myself, and drew long breaths to be sure that I was all right. I was burning with thirst, and applied to my canteen, but found it was nearly empty, and I observed a hole in it, showing that the ball had passed through it. The cloth covering having got worn off the canteen, the water had got warm with the sun, and it had been that which trickled on my hand. Glad to find I was still all right, I proceeded to buckle on my belt, but found the clasp broken, and the large brass plate in front, on which was emblazoned the Louisiana State emblem of the "Pelican," dented and marked with a ball. It was now evident that the ball had come in a slightly slanting direction, struck the brass plate, and glanced off, passing through my canteen, while the thud on the stomach had knocked the breath from me, and paralysed me for a time. I fastened my belt with a string and started to follow up the regiment.

The cannonade had now ceased, and there was only a slight firing of small arms. When I got up to the regiment I found them sitting down, the battle supposed to be over, and the enemy in full retreat.

We were ordered to remain here until Churchhill's regiment and the Texas rangers should pass on to harass the enemy's retreat and capture some more of their guns, if possible.

It was now about two o'clock, and the men were pretty tired. A party was sent to fill the canteens at the creek, and another party was sent off to attend to the wounded.

We soon afterwards received orders to go back to camp; the battle was over, and we had gained the victory. This announcement was received with loud cheers, and we started back to camp highly pleased with the day's work, everyone, of course, recounting the deeds they had done—some of the boys having slain half-a-dozen generals or put a squadron of horse to flight.

When we got to our camp we found the ground torn up in some places with shot, and strewn with fragments of shells, but not much damage done. (The enemy, in their report of the battle, said they had destroyed the camp.) But there was but little to damage; one or two tents had been burned by the shells, and one or two waggons damaged, but the horses and mules and the greater part of the waggons had been got behind a hill, out of range of the shot. In our bivouac the coffee was standing over the cold fires, just as we had left it in the morning (it seemed an age since that time). We were ordered to stack arms, get something to eat, and then a party to be sent to relieve the one that was attending to the wounded, and have all the wounded brought in and cared for, (the enemy being allowed to attend to their own wounded), and all our own dead to be noted and buried, there being no chance of the enemy annoying us any more at present. We were very hungry and tired, and soon made a hearty breakfast and dinner all in one. Having called the roll and made the details from my company, I went to the scene of the battle of the morning to look out for the missing. After diligent search I accounted for them all, and was glad to find that there was not one killed outright, but 19 wounded—some of whom afterwards died of their wounds.

Stretchers were procured or made out of blankets, and the wounded were carried to camp and put under the best cover we could provide; and the quarter-master, having procured spades and mattocks, the burying of the dead was proceeded with—our own dead first.

The enemy, having some ambulance parties in the field picking up their wounded, and conversation between the parties not being forbidden, our men were so happy over their victory that they were in the best of humour, and cheerfully assisted the enemy's parties in taking up their wounded.

I remembered the young officer whom I had encountered in the morning, and took them to the place I left him, but found he was not there. I could not be mistaken in the place, for the row of dead showed where their line had been formed, and I found some shreds of the flag, which he seemed to have cut or torn up to prevent it falling into our hands. I picked up the shreds, intending to say nothing about the flag, as I feared I might be censured for not having taken it from him. I afterwards found him in the barn of a deserted farm-house near by, where he with some others had managed to crawl. I hailed one of their ambulances, and got him put into it. He was shot in the groin, and it was just possible that he might recover. He was very faint, and did not seem to recognise me. I showed him my wounded wrist and some pieces of the flag; he then recognised me and called me back, grasped my hand, and thanked me.

Having examined the wounded of my company, and the nature of their wounds, I hurried back to camp to make out my report. Having no paper or form, I tore a leaf out of my roll-book, and, heading it with the name of the company and date, wrote under—" Killed, none ; wounded, 19 ; missing, none." This I got signed by the captain, and took to the colonel's tent.

In the tent was the commissary, and the colonel was just in the act of squeezing the last drop of claret out of a demijohn which the commissary seemed to have brought. I cast a longing eye on the tin cup, which was nearly full of claret, and an imploring look on the colonel, as much as to say that I was awaiting orders ; but the colonel did not see it in that light, for he drank it off with seeming great satisfaction, and had not a drop to spare. He then looked at me and said : " Well, have you brought your report ? " I said I had no form or paper to make it out properly, but there was the substance of it, and I handed the scrap of paper to him. He said that would not do ; I must give the men's names and the nature of their wounds. I said I could do so if he would give me paper. He then gave me a sheet of paper and directed me to sit down, and he showed me how to make out the return. There were four dangerously, nine severely, and six slightly. He asked what I meant by slightly. I said I meant not dangerously or severely, but still rendered unfit for duty for a time.   " I don't mean," continued I, " such scratches as that," showing him my wounded wrist ; "we have several such as that, but these I have not counted." He said that was right ; " but," said he, " that is a sabre wound ; how did you get that ?" I told him of the affair, and as I saw that the wine had put him in good humour I thought I might as well ease my mind and make a clean breast of it about the flag, and showed him some of the shreds. He said I should by all means have taken the flag from him, as it would have been an honour to me and to the regiment. I said I could not think to struggle with a man whom I had come upon wounded and helpless ; besides, my company had gone on following up the enemy, and I was in command of it at the time. He allowed there was something in that, but said that I must never in future lose an opportunity of capturing a flag. He said he was well pleased with me for the day, and, looking towards the commissary, asked if he had anything left. The commissary said he had not a drop left, and I judged from his appearance that what he said might be true. The colonel turned to me and said he was sorry that he could not ask me to drink, but I was just to consider that I had got a drink from him ; the honour would be all the same. I came away, thinking that it was rather a dry honour.

As I came out I saw a party of the enemy bearing a flag of truce. They had come to ask for the body of General Lyon, who had been killed in the engagement. The request was granted, and General M'Culloch sent his own spring waggon, furnished with a guard, to take the body as far as Springfield.

The surgeons were now busy operating upon the wounded. The orderly sergeant of the company next to ours had been in civil life a medical man in full practice. He now came forward and offered his services, which were accepted. He was after-wards appointed surgeon, and an excellent surgeon he was. He was known as Dr. C. If Dr. C. is still in life, and this should meet his eye, he will remember his old friend the sergeant of the rifles. The doctors worked late that night. I watched some of the operations ; they were very painful. But what struck me as most incredible was the strange courses taken by the bullets, particularly by the pointed conical bullets.

The surgeon was cutting a ball out of the back of a man's head, which had entered near the eye. I saw that man marching with his company a few days afterwards. It was

certainly imprudent of him to do so, but still he recovered
quickly. The ball had passed round the skull under the skin,
and was cut out at the back of the head without injuring the
bone. Some were wounded in the front of the leg, the ball
going round the bone and passing out at the calf. Some, to
their great annoyance, had got wounds in the back by bullets
striking against trees and glancing backwards. Our first
lieutenant, who had dropped while talking with me, had a
most miraculous escape. The ball had struck him on the one
side of the neck, taking a curve round his throat and passing
out at the other side, laying bare the windpipe, but not cutting
it. The boys teased him, saying the scar would look more like
as if he had attempted suicide by trying to cut his throat, than
that of a wound received in battle.

About eight o'clock Colonel M'Intosh, who had been away
following up the enemy, came riding in, and going up to where
the surgeons were, he dismounted, and throwing off his coat,
said he did not want to take up much of their time, but he
had been hit on the shoulder by one of their d——d canister
shots, and they might see what it was like. They examined
the place, but found the skin was not broken. The shot had
struck and glanced off, leaving a large blue lump. He said it
was painful, but laughed at it, and went through and visited
the wounded.

Guards had now been put out for the night and men detailed
to attend the wounded. I found an empty waggon near our
bivouac, which had been damaged by a shell, and in this I lay
down for the night.

Whether there was anything in the air (which was strongly
impregnated with the smell of powder, as there was not a
breath of wind) I do not know, but I think I enjoyed the
sweetest night's rest I ever enjoyed in my life.

I awoke about dawn greatly refreshed. The morning was
beautiful; there was not a breath of air, and there was still a
strong smell of saltpetre. At daylight everything was quiet.
What a contrast to the previous morning! and I remembered
that many of my poor comrades would not have passed such a
pleasant night. I got up and went to see how they had passed
the night. Some of them had had a bad night and were in
great pain.

The bugle sounded for roll call, and large details were made
to go and bury the remaining dead. Provision was made for

having the wounded forwarded to Springfield, it being now known that the enemy had evacuated that town and retreated northwards.

Arms were now cleaned, and ammunition pouches inspected and fresh ammunition served out. All serviceable arms lying on the field were gathered up, and the captured guns were brought into camp.

The process of burying the dead was toilsome and got on slowly. In many places where the dead lay thick the ground was hard and rocky, and the bodies had to be dragged some distance to where pits could be dug. By the early part of the forenoon the sun got intensely hot, and some of the bodies began to show signs of decomposition, and the flies became intolerable, and the men could stand it no longer.

About midday we received orders to march. The general, I understood, had made arrangements with the country people to bury the remainder of the dead.

As we went out of camp we passed near the place where Woodruff's battery had opened upon the enemy's cavalry. Some dead horses lay there. The flies were in myriads, and the smell was already unbearable.

We marched northward for about five miles and encamped at a place about four miles from Springfield. Here a general detail of the battle was gone into and our losses estimated.

Our regiment had 47 killed and about 180 wounded. Our company seemed fortunate in having only 19 casualties; but then it was small in numbers, being about 80, while the other companies were over 100. It would seem at first the number of wounded was proportionately large to the number killed, but this is easily understood when the number that were merely grazed is looked at, the number hit with skin grazed or clothes cut being greater than the killed and wounded put together, showing how often a man may be hit before the bullet reaches a vital part. What was more astonishing still was the comparatively small number of casualties sustained considering the heavy fire the troops had been under.

The total loss on our side was about 700 killed and about 1700 wounded. The enemy's loss was calculated to be about 1400 killed, about 2400 wounded, and about 200 prisoners. Of the wounded on both sides, about one-fourth would probably die of their wounds, and another fourth would never again be fit for service.

Of the total number of men engaged, there were upon our side between 14,000 and 15,000. The enemy, as usual, made many absurd and ridiculous statements about the smallness of their numbers; but, making every allowance, they could not have had much less than 14,000 men.

It was easy for us to form an idea of the strength of the enemy from the positions they occupied and their plan of attack, and General Lyon was too able a general to leave an advantageous position and attack us with an inferior force when he was provided in every way and could afford to lie and act on the defensive.

The battle, though on a small scale, was considered a good battle. It was well fought throughout, skilfully managed and stubbornly contested on both sides, and lasted eight hours. That it resulted as it did may be ascribed to various causes, of which fortune no doubt formed part. The Federal commander showed no lack of skill, or his troops of bravery. Nothing could excel the bravery of the United States regular troops, who fought on their left wing. What told most against them was their strict adherence to military rigidity and form of discipline, by standing up close and maintaining their line in the open field, making themselves conspicuous marks for the fire of their opponents, who fought in open ranks and kneeled down, forming a less prominent mark.

But the great advantage in favour of the Confederate troops was their practical skill as marksmen. Accustomed, as many of them were from their boyhood to shooting with ball while hunting bears, deer, wild turkeys, and other game in the woods or on the prairies, their certainty of aim was acquired by instinct.

The enemy had slightly the advantage of position. How they came to get this position and the unexpectedness of their attack has been a subject of conjecture and some criticism.

It was certainly never expected by M'Culloch that the enemy would advance from Springfield, where they were entrenching themselves after their retreat from Crane Creek. He never expected to fight at Wilson's Creek. He had not taken that position as an advantageous one for defence, but simply to concentrate his forces for an attack on Springfield. On the night of the 9th of August he had formed the line of march, but did not advance, owing to the rain.

How the enemy got to know our exact location, and how he

got forward during the night and had his artillery planted in such a commanding position as Oakhill on our front and the high table-land on our left, was somewhat of a mystery, and showed that he must have known exactly our movements on the previous day, though he could not have been aware of our intention to advance and attack him on the same night, as, if we had advanced as was intended, the two armies must have met unawares and encountered each other in the night, and the thing would have been a little complicated.

How he had been informed so minutely of our position was a matter of surmise ; but the general impression was that the supposed party of ladies who had ridden through the camp on the preceding day were something else than what they pretended to be, and it was taken as a warning not to place too much dependence upon parties who professed great zeal in the Southern cause.

Be this as it may, I believe this tended greatly to widen the breach between M'Culloch and Price ; at least after this battle they got to greater disagreeance than ever.

CHAPTER XIX.

IT was now known that the enemy had retreated to Rolla, a place about 100 miles north from Springfield, and from which place there was communication with St. Louis by railway, that being as far south as railways then extended.

The whole of the south-western part of Missouri was now cleared of Federal troops, though it was reported that a force was being raised in Kansas.

After moving about and camping in several places in the neighbourhood of Springfield, we camped near a place called Mount Vernon, some distance to the west of Springfield. Here it was evident that we were to remain for a few days. Price's army was not with us, but encamped somewhere in the neighbourhood of Springfield ; it being necessary, in order to obtain forage and supplies, to divide the army and spread it more over the country.

A regular camp was here formed, and we were ordered to resume our regular company and battalion drills. The finer points of our drill accomplishments had been somewhat rubbed off by the rougher and more practical work of the last few weeks. Our companies and battalions turned out in a somewhat diminished form, and the boys, having had a slight taste of the actual, were inclined to look upon such things as drill with contempt, and seemed to think they were now perfect and should not be bored with drill. This was, however, only brought up in a sort of joking way, and drill was persevered in ; and, like a slightly blunted instrument they were soon sharpened up again, and, hardened by toil and trial, they were more efficient than ever.

Their arms and accoutrements were polished and brightened up, which somewhat improved their appearance; but their clothing or uniforms, as they were called, could not be so easily polished up, although they had, no doubt, a uniform appearance so far as being threadbare, and dirt and raggedness made them much alike. Having now some spare time, clothes were washed and mended, and even these got to be improved in appearance.

But what was to be our next movement? Were we to march on to St. Louis or to act on the defensive? We were about 200 miles from St. Louis, with roads obstructed and bridges destroyed, and through a country where the people, if not hostile, were not to be depended upon; our means of transport deficient, and too far from our base of operations to obtain any supplies—and there were but few supplies even at the base of operations. Our men were without clothing or shoes, and the winter approaching, and to march with our small force of about 12,000 men over this distance to attack a large city on a navigable river, where, by the time we got there, an army of 40,000 men and a fleet of gunboats might be waiting to receive us, and with a force in Kansas menacing our rear, to cut off our retreat, probably did not seem to General M'Culloch to be a very prudent movement. We understood, however, that he was awaiting instructions from the War Department at Richmond, with some promise of reinforcements and supplies.

Price, on the other hand, seemed to place great dependence on his political influence. His proposal, we understood to be, was to call together a State Legislature in some part of Southern Missouri, pass an Act of Secession, declare the State out of the Union and joined to the Confederacy, and then march on St. Louis, when all the people in the State would declare in his favour and rally round his standard.

M'Culloch did not seem to have much faith in such a proposal. He knew Price was very popular with such followers as had already joined him, but they were very poor and ill provided; and, although the whole of the southern part of Missouri was cleared of Federal troops, which was said to have been the cause which had prevented them from joining with the South, yet it was still very questionable what the feeling of the majority of the population might be, and therefore he did not care to trust much to outward demonstrations or the assurances of politicians.

It was supposed that these propositions had been laid before the War Department at Richmond, and we remained here awaiting orders.

We had now nothing to do but a couple of hours' drill each day, which was altogether too little for men placed such as ours were. Fine spirited young fellows, hardened and finely trained by the wild outdoor life, privations, toil, and excitement of the last four months, and now placed in a camp which was to them like a paradise, while farmers' waggons came to them every day selling at such cheap rates as quite astonished them such things as milk, butter, eggs, turkeys, common fowls, young pigs, potatoes, apples, peaches, honey, and other things with which this fine country abounded. The men lived in luxury, and the balmy air of the early autumn of this beautiful climate braced them up, and two, or at most three, hours' drill each day, and guard duty but light, was a considerable change from the labours they had lately undergone.

It might, therefore, be supposed that that meddling, mischief-making personage, who, I have no doubt, was at the bottom of this whole affair, would be stirring them up to some wild pranks. These mischievous pranks were of frequent occurrence, although none of them were of a very bad or serious kind, but I had often to take some of the younger boys to task.

It frequently happened on the marches, while bivouacking, that it was a little difficult at reveille to get some of the younger boys up, in order to get their breakfast cooked and be ready to fall in. Being amongst trees or bushes, there was no room to form the company in line, and they were just called together in any fashion, and having answered to their names, and heard any orders or details made, they proceeded to cook their breakfast and prepare for the march.

Some of them, however, being sorely fatigued and loath to get up, would, when their names were called, cry "Here" from where they might be lying in their blanket near the root of a tree, thinking that in the darkness their position would not be discovered, and that they would thus get resting a little longer. This used to irritate me, and when they would cry "Here" without getting up, I would cry, "Where, sir. You are not here, and are marked absent," which was a delinquency which was always pretty severely punished by extra or fatigue duty. In this camp their conduct was quite changed, and having so little to do, they would be often up talking and making a noise long before roll-call, to the disturbance of others who wished to sleep, and these persons had been complaining to me about it. Intending to check the nuisance, I woke up one morning about two hours before roll-call, and heard much talking and laughing. I drew near quietly to listen. I heard the young rascals going through the form of calling the roll, one calling out the names, not only of the company, but of any notables in the regiment or army, while others would answer, accounting for them in some ridiculous way or as characteristic of the personage so called, something in this way :—R. C.— Playing poker; Captain L.—Writing love letters; General Price—Making a speech; T. Gallagher (the name of the sutler) —Watering whisky; R. M'C.—Writing poetry; Lieutenant-Colonel H.—Got the gout; Colonel H.—Got Gallagher (a name given to an article sold by the sutler; J. B.—In the guard-house; W. I.—Away with Indian Sall; Sergeant W.— "Here." "Where, sir? You are not here at all, but you come here saying you are here, whether you are here or not. I will mark you absent." This was too much for me; I could stand it no longer; I rushed in amongst them, threatening all sorts of punishments. The young rascals were all immediately down, and huddled up in their blankets, pretending to be asleep, though convulsed with laughter. Of course I could only caution them afterwards against making noise in the camp between tattoo and reveille and disturbing the rest of others. I liked the boys; they were mere lads between 16 and 20 years of age.

Of the older members of the company, and indeed the whole regiment, the conduct on the whole was remarkably good. They, of course, nearly all occupied good and respectable stations in civil life previous to the war. But the mere fact of them being taken away from steady occupations and regular social habits and thrown into such a varied and exciting life, and divested of all care and responsibility beyond the duties of a soldier, seemed sufficient to justify many in regarding the affair as a frolic and make them give way to excesses and wantonness. While we are lying at this camp awaiting orders I will review our general behaviour from the time we first entered the service, and touch upon one great social evil which there was much temptation to indulge in—I mean drunkenness, and the means which were adopted to check it. It did seem at first that this was going to be a serious matter.

The men of the country of which the regiment was composed were, in general, of sober habits, and except in cities such as New Orleans, which were supposed to be partly Europeanised, drunkenness did not prevail to such an extent as to be regarded as a serious evil. But the fact of so many men taken away from their regular duties, social habits, and responsibilities in civil life, and thrown together in the way I have described, did have its effect, and it began to show at Camp Walker in New Orleans.

Rigid measures were adopted to stop the evil. These were, that the men should be prevented from getting liquor. Accordingly, every place in the neighbourhood of the camp where liquor was sold was shut up. The severest penalties were imposed upon anyone bringing liquor into the camp, and all packages and parcels coming into camp for private individuals were subject to search. Leave of absence from the camp was limited and restricted.

In any company in which a certain number of cases of drunkenness was recorded, the leave of the whole company was stopped for a time. This last seemed a little hard, but it was intended to throw the responsibility on the company in general, and induce them to use their endeavours to keep their members sober. To the drunkards themselves this order did not apply, no punishment or penalty was attached except that they should be kept under proper guard or control until sober.

These regulations were read out in "General Orders," and were at first logically approved of.

It was not long, however, until the futility of such measures became lamentably apparent. Drunkenness did not diminish in any way, but increased at a fearful rate. Men who had always before been strictly sober in their habits were now to be seen reeling mad with drink, and while their comrades would be trying to keep them quiet they would become more infuriated, offering to fight the whole camp individually or collectively, and pouring out torrents of abuse and defiance against the authors of such an order, and some of them I believe not so drunk as they pretended to be, affirming that they never in their life had been drunk before, and did not care for drink, but they intended to show General Tracy or those who issued this order, that if they wanted to get drink they would have it in spite of all the orders and restrictions he might impose.

Such scenes were not isolated occurrences, but were numerous, and it seemed, as some of the boys remarked, that General Orders No.— had set everyone on the spree.

It now seemed that many of the men had taken the order as a gross insult to their honour and integrity; that instead of punishing and restricting the few of the ill-behaved, who were the cause of the evil, they were exonerating them from responsibility, justifying and protecting them, and for their sakes punishing and degrading the large body who wished to be sober, law abiding, and dutiful, and that they were just doing their best to create drunkards.

War was declared against the order by an almost unanimous desire to show the fallacy of it, and things got daily worse. Men who before would have scorned to walk ten yards for all the drink in the city, and who would have denounced and despised a drunkard, were now ready to join in, or at least to wink at, any attempt to circumvent the order, and to do so was regarded with applause.

The men, to show their contempt for an order sought to be enforced without regard to their honour, would mount on each other's backs and climb over the wall at night, and by pre-concerted signals flasks of liquor were thrown over the wall, and any device whereby liquor was brought into camp in violation of the order was regarded as a merit and applauded.

This state of things continued when we left New Orleans. The order, of course, being a camp order, did not go with us, but its evil effects did, and the same policy was continued with no better results; and at Little Rock and Fort Smith we had a good deal of trouble, and some measures were adopted, such as destroying the drink in the neighbourhood, but this had no effect; the more they tried to keep drink from the men the more the men strove to have it, and disturbances in the camp were frequent.

By the rules of the service a sutler's store and canteen should be attached to a regiment. This was considered an actual necessity; but to have such a thing would strangely conflict with the policy which was being adopted in regard to drunkenness.

At length the sober and law-abiding portion of the regiment, which consisted of at least 95 per cent. of the whole, formed a code of resolutions to be adopted as a general principle.

These resolutions affirmed that men were not children, and were able to take care of themselves, and must be held responsible for their own actions, and that drunkards were not entitled to any undue protection or indulgence.

That drunkenness was unmanly and disgusting, and such as made a merit of indulging in it were unworthy of the association of brave and honourable men.

That those who took drink and became quarrelsome or indulged in riot or braggadocio were poltroons or cowards, who dared not in their sober senses give vent to their passions, but took drink to give them "Dutch courage."

That drunkenness was demoralizing and injurious to the service, and should in every way be discountenanced and discouraged; but if suppressed by authority, it should be the drunkards themselves that should be dealt with, without punishing or restricting the liberties of the sober and well-behaved.

That the silly plea of temptation set up in their behalf only tended to make men believe that if they could get liquor they were justified in getting drunk, and that the fault did not lie with them, but with those who sold or gave them the liquor, and that such doctrines tended to weaken men's minds and tempt them to cast off honourable responsibilities, and were destructive to manly resolution and self-respect, and only served to promote drunkenness.

That if a man got drunk and become quarrelsome or riotous he should be immediately seized and bound, and put into confinement, and afterwards punished; no one should be allowed to speak to him, and any one interfering on his behalf or obstructing the police guard in executing their duty, should also be strictly punished; and, further, that the vagaries of a drunken man should never be applauded, or laughed at, or regarded with complacency.

Of course no "General Order" of this kind was issued, but such principles were promulgated as being the feeling and sentiments of the regiment, and these were brought under the notice of General M'Culloch, who expressed his approval in a "General Order" appointing a sutler. The substance of this order was: that he trusted that men such as they had some resolution and strength of mind, and would not sacrifice their self-respect under a plea applicable only to children, and old women of both sexes, that because liquor was obtainable they must needs make beasts of themselves. He would be ashamed to say that a canteen could not be attached to a regiment, or that the regular and lawful use of liquor must be suppressed among the civil inhabitants of the district, because of the weakness of his men, and he did not wish to have such men in his army. He regarded men who must get drunk because liquor was obtainable as despicable sots, unfit for the companionship of respectable men and true soldiers, a nuisance to society, and the sooner they drank themselves off the face of the earth the better.

This manifesto was received with great satisfaction and applause. It was known that "Ben," as the General was called, was not a total abstainer, but a strictly temperate man, and no man knew better how to use and not abuse the subject in question. Although it was not to be supposed that every man was possessed of the same strength of mind, it was universally allowed, and afterwards proved, that to strengthen their minds he had touched the proper chord ; and no better appeal could have been made or a better policy adopted.

This new view of the subject was endorsed and a new system pursued. Drunkards were no longer sympathised with, coaxed or petted, but more strictly dealt with. A sutler's canteen was attached to the regiment, so that liquor was no longer a proscribed or forbidden article. By this, the plea or excuse of a clever or smart trick could no longer be applied to cover the bringing of liquor into the camp, or to getting out clandestinely to obtain it, and the responsibility for good behaviour was left more to the men's own honour and self-respect.

The effect produced was marvellous, few of the men had yet become habituated to drink, and cases of drunkenness became exceedingly rare. If any one did so far forget himself, it was remarkable to see the change in his behaviour, even when drunk ; instead of assuming a bullying or swaggering attitude he would now creep quietly out of sight and try to prevent the thing being known, and seemed to feel ashamed of his conduct instead of boasting of it as formerly. In short, drunkenness almost entirely disappeared, and at this time, after four months' service, I may safely say that as a whole a more sober and orderly set of men could not be found in any sphere of life. There was no doubt always a love for frolic and mischief, but drunkenness was regarded as low and vulgar. Of course there were always exceptions, and some were more difficult to cure than others, and each company generally had their pest.

To show the stubborn spirit of opposition which some men will display in such things, I may mention a little incident which happened not long after the new resolutions had been adopted.

There was in one of the Red River companies a little Irishman, named Dan, who did not quite agree with the spirit of the resolutions. Honour and self-respect he considered all very well in their way, but he did not like such things to interfere with his whisky. He did not so much object to the order given at New Orleans by General Tracy, because if they thought to put whisky beyond his reach they would have to put it a good long way indeed. He was enterprising, and could obtain it; and the more difficulty there was in obtaining it the more delicious and enjoyable it became. He enjoyed the fun of getting it, and liked to boast of it, and it was a common expression of Dan's, "That he wouldn't give a d——n for drink if it did not give him some trouble to get it, but to punish a man because he took a drop of drink he considered a deadly sin."

While we were at Camp Walker, Arkansas, although plenty of liquor could be had at the sutler's canteen, Dan and some others got out of camp one night and went about seven miles to a distillery, where they got their canteens filled, and, of course, got drunk. For this they were punished and put to hard labour at chopping wood, but as two days afterwards we started on the march into Missouri they were, as a continuance of the punishment, ordered to carry their knapsacks on the march. The weather was intensely hot, and the men thus punished suffered so much from thirst, and the demands for water became so great, that the doctor requested that the knapsacks should be taken off. A halt was called, and the men were ordered to take off their knapsacks. They were now somewhat repentant, and gladly took them off, most of them declaring that they would never make such fools of themselves again, while Dan, seemingly disgusted at what he considered their weakness in thus giving in, as it were, stoutly refused to put off his knapsack. He said he would just be d——d if he would put it off; he was able to carry his knap-sack, and he was going to do it. Dan was taken at his word and allowed to carry it; and afterwards, for many a day, Dan trudged along with his knapsack on his back, his trousers rolled up to his knees, his thoughts to himself, scarcely speak-ing to anyone, generally preferring, if possible, to get out of the ranks and walk by himself in the prairie on either side of the road. I never heard of him being in any more drunken scrapes. He would drink, no doubt, but he would do it on the quiet and by himself, as whisky frolics were no longer popular.

In our company we had one incorrigible named Joe, who gave a good deal of trouble. Joe in civil life was a marble-cutter or sculptor, and was a young man of some refinement and culture, and held a good position; but on giving up civil life he seemed to have divested himself of all care and responsi-bility. Joe was not so much of a drunkard as a general delinquent. He had considerable talent, but so little applica-tion that he seemed silly and inclined to glory in making him-self look stupid. He was most obedient and submissive, but would forget, or feign to forget, in five minutes what was told him. He had to be driven to everything. His great besetting fault was absenting himself from the camp and from his duty, and going after women, with whom he seemed to have been a general favourite, and in whose company he probably was less stupid.

At this camp at Mount Vernon Joe got into a very serious difficulty. He was found, as a sentinel, sleeping on his post. This was a grave offence, and was punishable by death; and, had we been in presence of the enemy, this sentence might have been carried out. He was put under a strict guard, to be tried by court-martial.

I may also mention that we had in our company an Irish-man named Tim D., who was a man of a very different stamp from the last described. Tim was a highly respectable man of good education, though he still retained a bit of the brogue. Tim was zealous in his duty, an excellent soldier, and very popular with the company on account of his bluntness and simple good-nature. In civil life he had long been employed as a clerk in the office of a newspaper in Baton Rouge, which was devoted to the interests of the Democratic party, of which party Tim was a devoted adherent. The contemporary and

Q

rival of that paper was devoted to the interests of the " Native American" party, which, as a party, was somewhat hostile to foreigners ; and that paper had for its motto a saying or order, which they maintained had once been given by Washington on some particular emergency, the words of which were, " Put none but Americans on guard to-night," as if implying that foreigners were not to be trusted.

Several of the officers of our regiment had formerly belonged to that party and supported the latter paper, and Tim lost no opportunity when guard duty had become oppressive and the men were tired, or the night was bad, or the post dangerous, to retort on them the words of the motto, and recommend them to "put none but *Americans* on guard to-night," and the good natured banter between Tim as a " Naturalised Foreigner " and some of the old supporters of the " Native American Party " caused a good deal of amusement.

We had been in this camp about three weeks and it was now into September, and we at length received orders to march. The order said " the movement was not a retrograde one," but did not say where we were going to be sent to. In the same orders the thanks of the Congress at Richmond was tendered to the army for the victory of Oakhill, as the battle was called by the Confederates, though by the Federals it was called the battle of Wilson's Creek. Special mention was also made of the gallantry of the 3rd Louisiana Regiment in capturing Siegel's battery.

Our regiment got great praise for capturing this battery, but it seemed to me to be more of a sudden rush and surprise of the enemy than a desperate fight, and I thought their determined and stubborn fight with, and defeat of, the United States' Regulars in the morning was worth three times the praise. It was, however, a valuable capture, and the attack was well conducted by General M'Culloch.

We were to march at daybreak, the captured guns to be taken along, and the whole of our brigade to be under the command of Colonel H. (our colonel.) The line was formed at daybreak, our regiment as usual on the right. Our colonel being in command of the whole brigade, of course was not seen at all by us. Our lieutenant-colonel and major were both absent, and the regiment was commanded by a captain.

The conjecture throughout the army was, Where would we be going to ?—and there were many surmises and rumours.

In marching, when the road was narrow and confined, the troops generally marched in files of two, but when the road was sufficiently broad and would admit of it, they doubled ranks and marched in files of four. This gave greater room between the files and gave more freedom and air to the men. At this place the road was broad and good, and the captain commanding, when giving the orders to advance, intending them to double ranks and form files of four, thought to make a little improvement in the manner of giving the order according to his own notion. So he gave the command :—" By doubling." " Right face." " Forward, march ! "

" To Dublin, by jabers," shouted Tim D. " Arrah, good luck, me boys, we are going to Dublin. Shure the gineral has found out the right place to go to at last."

" Where do you say we are going to ? " cried two or three voices.

" To Dublin, don't you hear? " cried Tim.

" Shut up, you bogtrotter! " cried some of the boys.

" Ah ! ha ! me boys," continued Tim, " when yees gets to Dublin, it will be you uns will be the ' Foreigners ' there, and it will be me that will be the ' Native American.' "

We marched westward, and the supposition at first was that we were going into Kansas, but the programme was soon made known.

The Confederate Government not being able to send reinforcements, or equip the army so as to warrant a forward movement on St. Louis, the arrangement seems to have been that General M'Culloch with his Confederate troops should fall back within the Confederate lines nearer his base of supplies ; that Price should establish his head-quarters at Springfield, and use his political influence in drawing men to his standard, raise as large a force as possible, and more completely organise his army. About 3000 stand of superior arms, which had been captured at Oakhill, were handed over to him. While M'Culloch would also try to augment his army, and be within supporting distance of Price, and still not impoverish the district of Springfield by the presence of his army, but leave all the resources for Price's troops, while the latter should watch the movements of the enemy. Such was the position, as we were given to understand ; but there was evidently some hitch or deadlock somewhere, and there was a good deal of talk and surmise.

Price and M'Culloch were certainly not on very good terms. Price and his army were not in the service of the Confederate States. They took the name of and acted as " Missouri State Troops;" and Missouri had not formally seceded from the Union and joined the Confederacy, and they were thus acting in a manner independently.

No doubt the Confederate Government wished to humour General Price and get his alliance and assistance in checking the advance of the Federals, and, if possible, bringing over to them the State of Missouri ; but from the position in which he stood, they had no control over him or his forces.

I have heard it said, although with what truth I do not know, that the conditions were that Price with his army would join the Confederate service if he were made a major-general and have full command of the Army of the West.

On the other hand, M'Culloch was not sufficient of a red-tapeist or a politician to be much of a court favourite, and his influence at Richmond was not great ; but his known ability for command, and the confidence reposed in him by his army, seemed to convince the War Department that to interfere with him in any way would be bad policy.

However this might be, there was a misunderstanding and mismanagement somewhere, and though the victory at Oakhill had given us control of Southern Missouri, no advantage was taken of it, or obtained from it in the way of advancing.

We marched westward by the way of Sarcoxie and towards the Kansas border, thence southward through a country abounding in lead ore, the land on each side of the road being honeycombed with pits, varying in depth from three to 30 feet, from which the ore had been dug, each in itself being a miniature lead mine. We also passed, somewhere in this neighbourhood, I forget where, numerous small pits from which coal had been taken at two or three feet from the surface.

As we had now no enemy to deal with, the march was not marked by any particular incident. The weather had become rather wet, and the marching got dull.

There had been some few delinquents for various offences sent on to Fayetteville, where a court-martial was to be held, and the only prisoner under guard was the last delinquent, " Joe," of our company, caught sleeping on post, and he was taken along under charge of the brigade guard. There was no guard tent, and the prisoner had just to lie down on the ground at night, and a sentinel stood guard over him. Joe somehow always managed to make out pretty easily, and looked more stupid than ever, but his stupidness was only in appearance.

One wet and cheerless night, after a long day's march, Joe was lying rolled in his blanket alongside of a fallen tree. It was long past midnight, and all around were fast asleep. The sentinel, fatigued after his day's march, felt it hard to keep standing on his feet, and, seeing his charge fast asleep, he sat down on a block of wood beside the sleeping prisoner, placed the butt of his musket on the ground, wrapped his blanket round his shoulders, and leant his back against the fallen tree. The poor fellow, overcome with fatigue, soon dropped asleep, and his hands relaxing the grasp of his musket, it fell down across the body of the prisoner. The musket falling upon Joe woke him up ; he looked around and soon realised the position. He rose quietly, took up the musket, and, taking the post of the sentinel, kept guard until the relief came round. Having crossed arms, he passed the order : " Duty to guard this prisoner," said he, pointing to the sleeping man ; " he is something of a lunatic, and if he awakens will probably want to take your arms and say that he is the sentinel, so you must be on the look-out." So saying, Joe went off to his company's bivouac, got into a tent, and made himself comfortable for the rest of the night, saying, in answer to inquiries, that he had been relieved.

Next morning it was noised around that a sentinel had slept on his post and that a prisoner had escaped. Joe was immediately sent back to the charge of the guard, having obtained but very temporary relief. Joe had a peculiar drawling or plaintive way of talking, and spoke as if half-crying, and on this occasion said he thought he was entitled to some consideration, as he had filled the vacant post which had been left unguarded.

About two days after this we arrived at Camp Walker in Arkansas, which we had left about the end of July, and where we were to rest for the present.

Camp Walker, in Arkansas, though greatly superior in every way to its namesake at New Orleans, was still not a favourite camp, and we trusted we would not be long here. The usual routine of camp life and drill was continued. We here got to learn a little of how the war had been progressing. The Confederates had been successful in general, but the more thoughtful did not consider that this would tend towards an early termination of the war, and that we might look out for desperate work to come unless something turned up. No reinforcements were likely to be forthcoming, except some newly-appointed officers who had been sent by the War Department to fill offices in the Army of the West; but these were very poor reinforcements indeed. These offices were mostly at stations and depots, and were mostly sinecures, and, as was generally allowed, were created more for the benefit of the incumbents than for any actual use they would be to the service.

These appointments were of course to the sons of wealthy men, politicians, and court favourites. They each, of course, held a commission, with a certain rank, by which they obtained the honour of being in the army, and walked about in handsome uniforms without being exposed to the dangers or hardships of the field. Certain of these, with a sprinkling of field and line officers, now sat on a general court-martial being held at Fayetteville to try such cases as had been standing over, and a few days after our arrival in this camp one of their sentences was being carried out, which was a "drumming out."

The culprit belonged to one of the Arkansas regiments, and was of such a depraved character that I do not think they could have imposed a sentence that would have pleased him better. It was a cold evening in October, the whole brigade was drawn out with ranks facing inwards. The prisoner was stripped of his uniform, such as it was, and dressed in a felon's suit, which we thought, as we stood shivering in the threadbare and tattered remains of our thin summer uniforms, would be to him at least a pleasant change. His head was shaved bare and a board hung round his neck with the word "thief" painted upon it in large letters. The fellow was marched along the line between the ranks, followed by a fife and drum playing the "Rogue's March," to which he kept time pretty well.

He walked along philosophically, casting an eye of contempt on the ragged and destitute-looking men on each side of him, as much as to say, "There is not much more to steal from you; I am going to 'fresh fields and pastures new.'" How he had got into the regiment it is difficult to say, as these Arkansas men, whatever other vices they might have, that of thieving was not predominant.

About this time, perhaps owing to a change from a period

of excitement, toil, and activity under a hot sun, to a state of comparative inactivity in a cold, wet climate, without adequate clothing or shoes, quite a number were taken down with fever, said to be some sort of "typhoid fever," and I also was seized with it, and confined to my tent. The poor boys were exceedingly kind, bringing their blankets to wrap me up, contenting themselves to sleep at night two under one blanket that they might spare me one.

While I was ill J. S. came to see me and take good-bye. His trial was over and his sentence passed. He was dismissed from the service, declared to be unfit for it by a mental incapacity brought on by the excessive use of opium. Whether this may have been so or not I do not know. He spoke to me that day more freely and sensibly than since we had left New Orleans, but on taking leave he fairly broke down, and I have never seen him since. About two days afterwards, Joe's sentence was read out on parade. He had completely exhausted the patience of the judge-advocate by his drawling indifference. His sentence was that he was to be sent back to his company, and kept at hard fatigue duty and fed upon bread and water for a period of 60 days. I was annoyed at the absurdity of the sentence, in sending the man back to his company for the sentence to be carried out, and I asked the captain how he thought it could be carried out if the company was on the march. He said the sentence could not be carried out at all, but that such a sentence was quite worthy of the uniformed fools from Richmond, who possessed no better judgment. I could now see that the sinecure appointments by the War Department had caused much dissatisfaction amongst officers of all classes in the active service.

I had imagined myself recovered from the fever, and was up and moving about, but found that I had got up too soon, and was seized with a sudden relapse. I was taken to the officers' tent, the chief physician of the division sent for, and every care taken, but I soon became delirious and remained less or more insensible for several days.

When I came to my senses, I found myself on a good bed in a room by myself, and the surroundings led me to fancy myself back into civil life again, and the exciting events of the past six months all a gigantic dream. On a table on the opposite side of the room was piled a quantity of new clothing and several parcels, but hanging on the wall were my belt and sabre, reminding me of the truth. I tried to get up but found that I was too weak, and just then the door opened slowly, and in came a lad, E., of our company. He was glad when he saw me again in my senses. I asked if this was an hospital, or where, or what sort of a place it was. He said this was some three or four miles from the camp. It was a great big house, built by some strange class of people, but who had deserted it, and it was being used for an hospital, to which all the sick had been brought over, and he had been detailed specially to attend to me. Some few more of the company were here sick, some men of the regiment had died, and a good many were still sick, but the house was big enough to hold half of the brigade.

"But I see you have got a new rig—where did you get that?" said I, referring to a new suit of clothes I saw he had got on. "Oh," said he, "you don't know about that yet. A whole waggon load of things has come from Baton Rouge to us with new clothes, shoes, stockings, shirts, and all sorts of presents and good things, with letters and papers telling all about the battle, and these are yours lying on the table." I told him to hand me the letters. I took the first one, which I saw was from my partner, and was reading it when the doctor came in. He was the same orderly sergeant, now Dr. C., who had volunteered his assistance to the surgeons after the battle of Oakhill. He was now regularly appointed as surgeon of the regiment, which was one wise appointment. He was glad to see the improvement in me, but cautioned me against exerting myself just yet.

At this time, by some new order or regulation, it was made known that a company was entitled to three lieutenants instead of two ; and as our company had at present actually no lieutenant, the first lieutenant being *hors de combat* from the wound received at Oakhill, and the second lieutenant on detached service, an order was issued for the company to elect another lieutenant. A deputation came to me to ask if I still adhered to my determination. I still adhered to my determination and refused to become a candidate, but recommended Corporal G., who was a personal friend of mine, and had distinguished himself at Oakhill, and I was afterwards glad to find that he had been elected.

I was well taken care of at this hospital, and began to recover rapidly.

When I had been here about a week a sudden call was

made for the army to march northward again, the Federals having raised a large army in the Western States, and General Halleck, with a force of 25,000 men, was marching upon Springfield.

Before marching the troops got their pay in Confederate scrip. This was the first pay they had got, and my pay was brought to me by the captain.

I was declared by the surgeon to be unfit to take the field for at least two weeks yet, so I was ordered to remain where I was for that time.

As many of the company as could get away came to visit me before they departed on their second march into Missouri. They were now in good condition, with good warm clothing, shoes, stockings, blankets, and other comforts, which had been carefully got up for them by their friends, and by the ladies of Baton Rouge for such as had no relations in that place ; and the many little presents and kind letters of encouragement and commendations of their bravery had completely set the boys on fire, and they went off on what seemed to be a winter campaign with more spirit than ever.

Sick and tired as I was of the service, I could not help sharing in their enthusiasm, and when I came to open and examine my packet and found in addition to the more substantial necessaries of blankets, clothing, shirts, shoes, and stockings, and many little gifts, besides several affecting letters from mothers who were strangers to me, but thanking me for the care over their boys, I confess I got fired with the same enthusiasm, and became impatient to go and join the company. I mention this to show the great effect that a little encouragement from their homes has upon volunteer soldiers.

In a few days after the army marched I was able to leave my room and take a look round this strange building. It was an enormous building of wood, and seemed never to have been completely finished. It was outside of the limits of the State of Arkansas and the United States, and within the "Indian Territory." It was said to have been built by some peculiar sect of people, having some singular belief or ideas of their own, who wished to establish a colony or settlement, and it seemed as if they desired to be beyond the jurisdiction of the laws of the United States or the State of Arkansas. It was now completely deserted by its founders, although there was evidence of its having been partly occupied not long previous.

Large quantities of apples and dried peaches were lying carelessly on the floors of some of the lower rooms, but there was very little furniture of any kind except tables and seats, of which there were abundance. There were several large halls, furnished with seats, as if for teaching, lecturing, or places of worship.

One wing of this building only had been adopted by General M'Culloch as an hospital, and in it there were over 100 men of the division, being the sick and their attendants.

In this neighbourhood, being just the border of the "Indian Territory," there were few full-blooded Indians; the inhabitants were mostly white or "half-breeds," but were under the jurisdiction of the Indian Government.

The "half-breeds" seemed to be a quiet class of people, fairly civilised, and possessed of an ordinary degree of intelligence. Their houses were mostly log or frame houses of more or less pretentions according to their means. They cultivated Indian corn, wheat, oats, fruit, and vegetables ; but their attention was chiefly turned to live stock, such as horses, cattle, and poultry. I saw few sheep in these parts, but great abundance of pigs, which, as in other parts of the country, ran wild in the woods.

These "half-breeds" came daily to the hospital, the better class of them in their spring waggons, bringing for sale, deer, poultry, butter, milk, eggs, honey, and fruit, which they sold cheap and found a ready market.

One of these half-breeds I noted, whose dress and manner, as well as the superior appearance of his horse and spring waggon, showed him to be a man of somewhat better standing than the generality of the others. With this man I sometimes engaged in conversation, and found him to be a man of considerable intelligence and some education. He brought me a newspaper, which was published in a small town near his residence. One half of the paper was in English, and the other half in the Indian language. This man came to the hospital every morning and I had many conversations with him. He was just about half-blood between Indian and white, but his sympathies were entirely Indian. On his learning that I was not an American but a Scotchman, he became more interested and spoke more freely. He said he had read some books about Scotland, which he liked much. He offered to drive me out to his place if I would go out and stop a night with him, and I agreed to go.

His place was about seven miles out : a good substantial farm building, equal to that of the better class of farmers in Arkansas. His wife was nearly a full-blooded Indian, but spoke English well. He had several children, whom he was taking care to educate.

The house was as well furnished as the generality of such houses are within the States, and bespoke cleanliness and comfort. Food they had in abundance, and we had an excellent supper off some roast venison and wild turkey. In the room I noticed several books, amongst which I observed a volume of " Scott's Poetical Works." He saw me looking at it, and said I would know that book. On my replying in the affirmative, he referred to the " Lady of the Lake," which he said he greatly admired, and went on to recite from memory some parts of it relating the meeting of Fitz James with Roderick Dhu. He particularly admired that part of the poem. He compared the Gaels to the Indians, and the Saxons to the whites in America, and quoting several passages, drew some very fair comparisons.

Just at the time some of his Indian friends dropped in on an evening visit. He introduced me to them. They nearly all spoke English and were more or less educated. He then went on, by way of entertainment, to explain to them the story, and quoting arguments advanced by Roderick in favour of the Gaels as analagous to what might be advanced in favour of the Indians. He became quite enthusiastic and seemed to draw the comparison so well that I reminded him that although I was his guest that night, and that I expected in the morning that he would conduct me safely back to the Confederate camp, I hoped he would not imitate Roderick at " Colintogle's Ford," or some other ford, in demanding me to draw and meet him " man to man and steel to steel." This, as was intended, produced a laugh, and the conversation took another turn.

Of course the war was the all-absorbing topic of conversation everywhere, and that became the principal subject. I found the Indians generally in favour of the South, not so much out of any sympathy, but the idea seemed to be, as my friend said, that if the States were divided into two nations, the independence of the Indian nation would be more strictly defined, and there would then be a Northern nation, a Southern nation, and an Indian nation. Some of the others seemed to favour the South because they considered the South respected the

Indian more than the North, and did not rate him so much in the same class with the Negro. No greater insult could be offered to an Indian than to regard him in any way as compared to the Negro race, and there is certainly but little room for comparison.

I was very much pleased with the general intelligence of the company, to me strange as it was.

The American Indians, no matter how well civilised or educated they may be, are not by nature a talkative people. In this company they spoke with less restraint than I ever knew them at any other time. 'Tis true it was within their own territory and government, and within their own homes; but my host spoke more than all the others put together. He was, of course, the nearest related by blood to the whites, and had been oftener in communication with the outer world. The night was spent pleasantly and all manner of subjects turned over—races, nations, governments, wars, etc.

In the morning my host showed me over a part of his farm and possessions. He had several negro servants at work; whether they were slaves or not I did not inquire. His crops had been gathered in, and he had several houses well stocked with Indian corn, and a good stock of wheat. He had a large number of horses, most of which roamed on the prairies, several cows with calves, and a large number of cattle on the prairie. He had abundance of poultry, and, of course, his share of the public piggery in the forests.

We had breakfast of some good bacon with eggs, and some broiled chickens and prairie hen. Coffee was prepared on my account, the younger members of the family having mush (corn-meal porridge) and milk. For sugar they had maple sugar and a syrup made from the sorgho plant or Chinese sugar-cane, which grows here abundantly.

After breakfast we drove back to the hospital, he taking, as usual, his produce for sale. The country abounded with game, such as deer, wild turkeys, prairie hens; there were also some buffaloes, but these were now getting scarce. My host had a large number of fine buffalo robes, one of which I bought from him, and recommended him to bring in some to the hospital, where I expected he would find a ready market, which he did.

I found my host was a sort of petty chief among the Indians. He was a member of some legislature, and transacted a good deal of business with the whites on behalf of his neighbours.

I asked him about the demoralizing effects of drink among the Indians. He said that in some places it was bad, but in this district and among his tribe it was little known.

As we drew near to the hospital, I asked him about the history of the building and how it came to be erected. He could not very well tell, but it was some kind of people who wished to establish a settlement there. What sect they were of he could not tell, but they were not "Mormons" or "Shakers," as I had supposed, but some kind of Socialistic brethren, who were to be all equal and to have no rich and no poor, and among whom all things were to be held as common property— free and open to all. " But," continued he, " it did not succeed, for, before they had got the building finished, they began to quarrel and fight among themselves, just like at the big Babel which we read about in the Bible, and everyone went away his own road."

He did not think that either Indians or whites had got good enough yet to live together in that sort of way.

We now arrived at the hospital, and I thanked my host most sincerely for his kindness and hospitality, hoping to be able, when peaceful times came, to repay it, which I regret I have never been able to do.

A day or two after this, General M'Culloch came along and visited the hospital. He was on his way to the front to join the army, and I believe had just a day or two before returned from the front. Fifty or sixty miles in a day was nothing for the general to cover, bad as the roads were. I saw that he, like the rest of us, had got a new rig-out, which he stood much in need of. I may here say that General M'Culloch never wore any kind of uniform or sword. He considered the latter was only a useless ornament, and was an encumbrance, and added weight to his horse. He carried only a field-glass and a small rifle, with which he was said to be a deadly shot from his seat in the saddle. He wore a high-crowned felt hat, and a suit of plain clothes, the original colour of which might have been a dark grey, but the last time I had seen him they were rather threadbare. He had now got a new suit of the same kind, and looked quite renovated.

He gave directions that in a few days some waggons would be going to the front, when all those recovered and fit for service would accompany them, forming an armed escort in charge of an officer.

CHAPTER XX.

ABOUT a week after the general's visit two waggons with some valuable stores on their way to the front stopped at the hospital to pick up an armed escort. All convalescents then declared by the doctor to be fit for duty, about 26 in all, mostly young lads, got ready and put their baggage into one of the waggons. I was ordered to take command of the escort, and one of the teamsters, knowing the road, was to act as guide.

It was now November, the weather had become fine again with slight frost. The air was clear, cold, and bracing, and the journey was pleasant. The country was undulating and hilly, and but thinly settled. The roads were rough and narrow and passed through thin forests of oak, beech, and hickory, and, as usual in that country, led by many round-about ways, so that in the whole journey, about two miles would be traversed to make one in a straight line. The entire country seemed to be in possession of pigeons, which were to be seen in millions, feeding upon the beech-mast and acorns.

We at length arrived at the place appointed for us to halt for the night. It was a fine large building, consisting of a centre and two wings, and I found that it was here the men were to rest for the night, while forage for the horses would be obtained at a farm close adjoining.

The waggons were drawn up in front of the building, and the horses taken out, whilst a serious and consequential-looking gentleman, with something of the city cut about him, and seemingly of Irish extraction, came up and inquired for the officer in command of the detachment. I was pointed out to him. He came up, and making an attempt at a military salute, commenced to make a sort of speech, addressing me as captain. I told him to be easy, I was only an orderly sergeant. He did not seem to appreciate the difference but went on with his speech. His mission was to deliver to me the key of the building, which was one of the State schools— a college he called it, and he was the head-master or "Principal."

I assured him that I would see that no damage was done to the property. There was an outside house where the boys might do their cooking, and one of the class-rooms would do for our accommodation, and I requested he would remove from it, and lock away any movables, such as books or other school paraphernalia. But there were but few movables in it; one or two books in a small bookcase in the corner, for which he professed great veneration, and taking down one of them—a copy of "Virgil," he began to dilate upon its beauties. The boys who were now in a frolicsome humour were bringing in their baggage, and seeing the principal with the book, became noisy, crying out that they were going to school again, and began to babble over passages from Virgil.

"Why, captain," said he, "you have got a regiment of scholars."

I told him they were all men of learning and genius, but a most unruly and unmanageable lot, and suggested the use of his birch or tawse to keep them in order.

After passing a few words in Latin with some of the boys he left, seemingly not desirous of going too far into learned questions with them.

On taking a survey of the building I saw it had been got up at great expense, but it seemed to be very little used, although it would accommodate several hundred. I saw no appearance of any population in the neighbourhood to support such a school.

The boys having made fires in the out-house, which was used as a kitchen, got their suppers cooked, and having set aside the forms and desks in the class-room, they lighted a fire, and each selecting a part of the floor for their bed, deposited their robes and blankets. A guard was posted round the house, horses, and waggons in conformity with military rules.

Shortly after this the farmer came in to see how he was to get paid for the corn and forage which he had supplied for the waggon horses. I told him my orders were to sign a requisition, and he would take it to the post quarter-master and he would get paid. I gave him a requisition "form," and told him to fill it up and I would sign it. He said he did not know anything about these things, neither could he read or write, and for all the value of the forage they had got it was not worth the trouble. He sat a while and talked. He was shrewd and intelligent about matters pertaining to the country or his own business. I asked him about this school, and what was the object of putting up such an expensive building where there was no population to support it. He said it was State money for school purposes; they had plenty of it, and must spend it, and it gave pickings and offices to their friends. I thought that rather a strange explanation, although there might be some truth in it, but the building did very well for our purpose in the meantime, and we did not care how it was put there, and we stretched ourselves on the floor and were soon asleep.

In the morning we had an early breakfast, the waggons were hitched up, and we proceeded. Everything was much the same as on the previous day, and at night our halt and quarters were precisely the same as on the previous night, in another of the State schools, similar in every way to the last, and everything about the same, even to the farmer coming to get pay for his forage, who, like the last, could neither read nor write. I did not like this, as I feared that it might be thought that I had appropriated the forage without paying or offering to pay for it. It looked like robbing the farmers, and I was a little annoyed.

"Confound it!" cried I, "what kind of a country is this at all? Every house I come to is a great, large school or educational institute, while the devil a soul can I find who can either read or write. This won't do; if the general gets to know of it, there will be a row at the quarter-master's department. I must get the requisition filled up in the regular way; can you get nobody to do it? Go and get your schoolmaster, surely he can read and write."

"Well, I don't know as he can," said he, as the boys roared with laughter. "You see, stranger," continued he, "them there schools were built to make offices. The State has got plenty of school money, and they build them schools with it. The men gets the job who work hard for the party that gets elected."

"Then do I understand," said I, "that the teachers get

their appointments through political influence, without regard to other qualifications?"

"Well, that's about it, stranger. They has a few questions they ask them about Latin and things, which they knows how to answer, but that is about all they know."

"And how many children will there be attending this school?"

"Not more than a dozen when they are all there."

"But," said I, "there must be more children than that in the neighbourhood, and by the laws you are compelled to educate your children."

"That is true," said he, "but you cannot compel people to send their children five or six miles to school through them woods."

"That accounts," said I, "for so many being unable to read and write, notwithstanding the large schools; but would you not be better to have smaller schools, and more of them, so that the children would not have so far to go to school?"

"That, of course," said he, "would be better for the children, but it would not do for the parties in power and the teachers—they want big schools and fat offices."

"Then," said I, "you have your children going five or six miles to school, so that the teachers may have fat offices."

"Well, that is so, stranger, but people don't bother about it; besides, most people don't care about sending their children to free schools, and if they can manage it at all they send them to private schools. I have three children at a private school at Bentonville, where they board with their uncle."

"Rather than send them to this school," said I; "that will cost you something."

"Well, it does," said he; "but I won't have my children at a free school so long as I can pay for their education."

"Well," said I, changing the subject, "what about this requisition? Can't you get it filled up?"

"Oh, never mind it," said he; "it would not come to much altogether, and it is not worth the trouble;" and he took his leave.

This man, like most of the farmers in the district at that time, though without education was extremely shrewd and intelligent, and seemed to be pretty well-to-do in the world. But I was astonished at the way he spoke of the educational system. That was a subject I had never given much attention

R

to, and I thought it probable that in politics this farmer might be opposed to the party in power, and perhaps he might not be on very good terms with the teacher of the school; certainly he was by no means indifferent to education when he was taking such care, and going to such expense, in the education of his own children.

By daylight we were again on the march, and were now turned northward towards Missouri. We were going by a different route from any we had traversed before, and we saw no track of any of the armies and could learn nothing of what was going on. The people seemed now to be terrorstruck and very reticent ; and there were some reports of the enemy being near and fighting going on, and the sight of armed men seemed to alarm them.

About the fourth day we heard cannonading at some distance on our right, but our orders did not lead us in that direction ; but I thought it best to be on our guard against scouting parties of the enemy.

The following day we came to a station where we were to report. This was a quarter-master's station. The officer in command stated that our division was about 30 miles in front, but he hesitated about allowing us to proceed further as he said he thought the army was falling back. I reported the cannonading we had heard on the previous day. He supposed that would be a detachment of Price's army engaged with the enemy in the neighbourhood of Springfield, and he immediately despatched a courier to the front, and ordered us to rest at the station for the night. In consequence of orders which came to the station during the night, all stores were packed up and waggons ordered to be ready to proceed to the rear. From my point of view I thought the station to be in rather a critical position, and not caring to undertake to fight the enemy's army with my 26 men or be taken prisoners, I proposed to go on at daybreak and join our regiment. He said I should not move until the return of the courier with instructions. The courier returned shortly after daybreak with orders that all stores and waggons should at once proceed to the rear, the party of convalescents should act as an escort as far as a certain creek, and then report to their respective corps. This was not very pleasing to the boys, who wished to get back to join their old comrades. However, the same courier said that the army was returning by forced marches and would be up

with us by to-morrow evening ; "that is," continued he, in a
confidential tone to me, "if the enemy don't cut them off."

I was pretty sure from the cannonading I heard on the
previous day that the enemy must now be south of us, and
that there had been a mistake somewhere, and from the nature
of the orders we had got we stood a very good chance, this
day, of having the train attacked by some of the enemy's
flying detachments ; and, as we had been bouncing about how
we could send their cavalry to the right about, I told the
boys that they would likely get a chance erelong, and they
had got a name which they must maintain.

We kept up a strict look-out all day, but the enemy did
not make their appearance, and on the following day came to
the creek mentioned. Here we came upon Price's army, and
that of course covered the trains, and we returned to join our
own brigade, which was not far behind. We found they had
camped about six miles north of the creek, near Neosheo,
after three days of forced marches. We met with a hearty
welcome, and I took my place in the company.

We remained in this camp over a day, and I got to know
the position of matters.

The plan of the campaign we understood to have been that
Price should take up a strong position in the neighbourhood
of Springfield, where he would act on the defensive, and hold
the enemy in check while M'Culloch would advance northward
and operate upon his right flank and rear and cut off his supplies.

M'Culloch's army had advanced northward as far as Fort
Scott, when he learned that Price had been unable to hold his
position at Springfield, and had fallen back towards Neosheo,
and his (M'Culloch's) army was in danger of being cut off.

M'Culloch, however, was equal to the occasion. He, with
his mounted troops under M'Intosh, hovered on the enemy's
right flank and threatened their rear, and thus covered the
retreat of the infantry until they formed a junction with
Price's troops.

We were ordered to march southward to a more advantageous position.

As was usual and to be expected in those sudden movements
and counter-movements, it was very difficult to keep the troops
supplied with provisions, and for several days there had been
nothing obtained from the general commissary department.
The country abounded with cattle and pigs, which were

slaughtered and cooked by the men, so that there was plenty of fresh meat, but there was nothing to eat with it, there being no flour or meal to make any kind of bread, and it was not the season to get green corn. To supply this deficiency the men had recourse to dry Indian corn and wild pease, with which the country abounded. These they boiled when they could get an opportunity and ate with the fresh beef and pork, but they found these rather poor substitutes for bread.

About the third day after I had rejoined the company I was at the adjutant's quarters handing in some reports in the morning before proceeding on the march. I there saw our captain, the lieutenant-colonel, and the major sitting in conversation with the colonel. I had left my reports, and was returning when I was accosted by our friend Joe, who was with the company undergoing the punishment inflicted on him by the court-martial. The only punishment he was suffering was that he was going along with the company enjoying himself in comparison with the rest of the men, not having to carry a rifle or accoutrements, and having no duty to do.

"Sergeant," said he in his usual whining tone, "I am glad you have come back. The captain and the acting orderly sergeant have been neglecting their duty and have been using me very ill."

"What have they been neglecting or doing?" said I.

"They have been neglecting to carry out the sentence of the court-martial. You know I was to get bread and water, and I have never got a bit of bread, and for more than a week I have never even got a bit of flour to make bread."

The affected manner in which he complained about the sentence not being carried out took me down altogether. I did not know whether to swear or laugh, but a thought struck me. "Come with me," said I, "we will see about this." I took him to the adjutant's quarters, where the officers were still sitting.

"Captain," said I, "here is a man who is upon that report as under arrest. He is undergoing sentence pronounced by a court-martial, and he has complained to me that you and Sergeant T. have been neglecting your duty, in not carrying out the sentence of the court-martial. Of course I have just returned to duty, and know nothing about it."

"What is the sentence?" said the colonel, in a serious and stern tone.

"I have it here in my book," said I, and turning it up read —"That he be sent back to his company and kept at fatigue duty and fed upon bread and water for a period of sixty days."

"And he complains of it not being carried out," said the colonel.

"Yes," said I.

"How was it possible that such a sentence could be carried out in the company," said the captain. "Bread, as understood in the regulations, we have not seen since we left New Orleans, and we have been on the march ever since the sentence was passed, and we could not put him on fatigue duty."

"You might have put a heavy knapsack on his back," said the lieutenant-colonel.

"Then he would have dropped out and been left behind," said the captain, "and that would just have suited him. It is not easy giving fatigue duty for punishment while on the march."

"That I allow," said the colonel, "unless they are put in the rear with the trains, and then they are of no use, as there is no officer over them, and it is doubtful whether it be any punishment at all."

"I would not have minded that so much if they had carried out the other part of the sentence, and given me the bread and water," said Joe in a most affected and pitiable tone.

The colonel looked at him as if he would have cleaved him with his sword, but he restrained himself.

"Oh, I see, Joe," said the lieutenant-colonel, "if we manage to give you the bread, you are quite willing to let us off for the fatigue duty."

"Oh, yes; these long marches are fatigue enough," said Joe in a tone of concession.

The colonel again looked daggers at Joe, and bit his lip.

"How long has the sentence yet to run?" said the colonel.

"About three weeks yet," said I, looking at the date.

"I am sure I wish it was done," said the captain.

"Oh, there is no hurry about that, sir," said Joe, in a tone of the greatest simplicity.

"Hold your tongue, you impudent scoundrel," roared the colonel, "I will soon give you plenty of fatigue duty and bread and water too."

"Thank you, sir," said Joe, in a grateful tone and withdrew.

"Well, that is a cool scoundrel," said the colonel.

The other officers laughed and commented upon the absurdity of the sentence. The colonel allowed the sentence was absurd, but said nothing more.

The bugle now sounded to form line, and I went to fall in the company.

About three days after this we arrived at the position we were to take up, and Joe was sent off with a large detail of men to block up certain roads by felling large trees so as to fall across them, and roll down large stones upon them and place other obstructions, so as to impede the advance of the enemy in that direction. I question much if the officer in command got much work out of Joe. It was no doubt unquestionable that for ordinary offences work was always the best and most effectual system of punishment when it could be properly enforced, but that could only be done at a fixed camp or station where useful labour was required and some proper authority existed to have it enforced, but for such a sentence to be carried out within the company while engaged in an active campaign in front of the enemy was simply ridiculous.

The position now taken up was a very advantageous one. It was upon a stony ridge where the main road leading to the south from Missouri branched off—one road leading to the south and the other branching off to the eastward, the ridge forming the gusset between the two roads.

We here waited the approach of the enemy, M'Culloch evidently intending to rest on the defensive near his base of operations and near his supplies, with his rear secure, while the enemy would be drawn further from their supplies and their base of operations. In this position we could get supplies easily; the camp was dry and healthy and favourable for drill and manœuvring.

Our company had been augmented by some new members who had come from Baton Rouge to join the service. The other companies in the regiment had also been reinforced by new volunteers, and many of the wounded had now recovered and were back to duty, and the strength of the regiment was considerably brought up, and company and battalion drill was actively persevered in.

The enemy advanced to within 12 miles, but did not seem inclined to attack us in this position, while M'Culloch, with M'Intosh and his mounted troops, kept hovering on their flanks, cutting off detached parties.   Almost every day parties of prisoners and horses and waggons were being brought in.

One day a fine capture of about 14 waggons, each drawn by six fine mules, the waggons being loaded with lead, were brought in by M'Culloch.

It seemed that after the battle of Oakhill and while the army was passing through by Sarcoxie in September M'Culloch had contracted with the owners of some of the lead mines there to prepare and supply him with a quantity of lead.   This lead had been smelted and cast into pigs and stacked up ready to deliver to the quarter-master when he should send for it.

When the Federal General Halleck occupied Springfield in November, he got information that such lead, the property of the Confederates, stood there ready for delivery.   Thinking this a splendid prize, he despatched 14 of his best waggons and strongest mules, accompanied by an escort, to bring away the lead.   Whether M'Culloch had been privy to the information given to General Halleck or not I do not know, but Halleck's waggons had been loaded up with the lead and were proceeding towards Springfield when they were surprised by M'Culloch's mounted infantry, the escort made prisoners, and the whole train of waggons turned southward and brought safely into the Confederate camp.   Thus M'Culloch not only recovered the lead, but 14 waggons and over 80 fine mules, which was a considerable acquisition to his transport department.   Up to this time we had lost no prisoners to the enemy, therefore the arms were taken from the prisoners, and they were paroled and let go.

The weather was now dry, cool, and pleasant ; drill being steadily continued, the troops were in splendid condition. Hardened by the campaign, and having acquired a soldierly bearing and habit and some military pride, the constant drill had brought them up to a high state of efficiency, and the steadiness and regularity of their evolutions in company or battalion drill would have done honour to any European troops, while their fighting calibre was already proved.

I could have wished that some of the military critics of Europe could have seen them at this time, if just to show them something of volunteers and what an efficient army can be produced from raw material in a few months, and that a nation has nothing to fear for its defence that can raise an army of volunteers and knows how to treat them and bring them into the field without having their enthusiasm damped or their progress obstructed by fastidious deference to rank, official formalities, and red-tape restrictions.

While here we had an acquisition to our regiment in the form of an old veteran officer of the French army, who had to leave France owing to some political troubles. He had gone to California, where he had resided some time, but on hearing of the war betwixt the North and South, his military spirit was kindled and he longed to join in the fray. His sympathies were with the South, but to get to join the Southern Army was no easy matter.

To get round to the Eastern States by the ordinary route was expensive, and even if that was accomplished, the South was blockaded round, and he would not be able to get across the lines. He therefore undertook to cross the country on foot, passing through New Mexico and the Indian Territory, his only companion being a faithful donkey which carried his baggage, consisting of a tent to shelter him at night and a small commissariat ; for this animal he had a great affection and regard which were reciprocated. Having learnt that in the Army of the West there was a Louisiana regiment, he concluded that there would be some in it of French extraction who would speak the French language. He found his conjectures to be correct, there being one company the members of which were almost exclusively of French extraction. This company bore the name of the " Iberville Greys," and, like our own company, contained a number of very young lads.

Monsieur Challon was every inch a soldier. He had known no other profession, and had been the greater part of his life in the French army. He was quite astonished at the efficiency of the troops, at the precision and regularity of their evolutions, and considered them to be equal to any European forces, and he could hardly believe that they had only been seven months in service.

Monsieur Challon became an attaché of the " Iberville Greys " company, and took his place in the ranks. The rules and customs of the service not being so rigid as to prevent his fellow-soldiers making a little allowance for his years, he soon became a general favourite. But no less a favourite was his companion " Jason," the donkey, which also became an attaché of the company, and a general favourite with the whole regiment.

As it was known that many regiments in the British army had a general pet of some kind in the shape of a beast or bird, the 3rd Louisiana Regiment thought to emulate them by having a pet in the shape of this donkey.

An incident happened, however, which almost got poor Neddy into trouble.

Our lieutenant-colonel, who was well advanced in years, was a venerable looking old gentleman.   He was of a homely, affable disposition, had a pleasant humour, and liked at times to have a little joke with the boys, and was very popular.   It so happened that our new recruit, or attaché, Monsieur Challon, bore a most striking personal resemblance to Lieutenant-Colonel H., so much so that the one was often mistaken for the other; and as in the time of actual hard work within the regimental camp there was little or no difference in dress, mistakes, or pretended mistakes, would sometimes occur, and often when Monsieur Challon would happen to pass a sentinel the latter would salute, believing or pretending to believe that it was Lieutenant-Colonel H.   Of course a good deal of this was done in joke.

His companion " Jason," though possessing a considerable sense of duty, and withal a very intelligent beast, yet was still an ass; and when the more intelligent lords of creation mistook the identity of the two individuals the same mistake might be excusable in the poor cuddy.

It seemed that during the long journey across the plains, Jason had at certain times been allowed to share the tent with his master, and to this he had become somewhat accustomed, and regarded it as a matter of right.   It was therefore not to be wondered at, when he saw the lieutenant-colonel entering or sitting in his tent, that he would by mistake go in and seek to make himself quite at home.

Whether the lieutenant-colonel's ideas of equality and fraternity would have tolerated this I do not know, but it was certain that his rank prohibited it, and he immediately despatched a messenger to the Iberville Greys, informing them that a member of their company, in violation of the rules of the service, in respect to "honour paid to rank," had been intruding into his tent, and that if such a breach of rules was repeated he would impose a penalty on their company, by ordering them to detail a guard for special service at his tent, night and day, to ward off intruders.   Of course the classing of Jason as a member was intended as a little joke at the expense of the company. A few days afterwards the lieutenant-colonel and the major were called off for duty on some court-martial business. They were about to set off, and the major had ridden up to the lieutenant-colonel's tent, where the latter's horse was standing held by an orderly. The lieutenant-colonel came out, but just as he was mounting, Jason came up and looked at him with a marked expression of affection in his countenance.

"There is your friend, colonel," said the major.

"Confound the brute!" cried the lieutenant-colonel, "he will be into my tent again. Here," cried he, addressing the orderly, "go down to the Iberville Greys and give them my compliments, and say that I order them to detail a member of their company to stand guard over my tent till further orders." So saying he and the major rode off.

I have often heard it hinted that among mankind feelings of brotherly love and affection were often attracted towards a source from whence some substantial benefit was likely to flow, or from whence some advantage was to be obtained. Whether this sentiment extends to donkeys or not I do not know, and I would not like to impute to Jason any unworthy motives, nevertheless, there was just the slightest grounds for suspicions of his sincerity.

It so happened that the lieutenant-colonel, not wishing to trust too much to the honour of the forage purveyors, kept the corn for his horse under his own care in a bag in the corner of his tent. Whether this may have in any way influenced the affection of Jason for the lieutenant-colonel I will not pretend to say, but towards the evening the lieutenant-colonel and the major returned. Having dismounted and handed their horses to the orderly, they both proceeded to the lieutenant-colonel's tent. On entering, their surprise may be imagined when they found Jason with his nose in the bag quietly munching away at the corn. On their approach he looked up, cocked his ears, and regarded them steadily for a moment, then munched away. The lieutenant-colonel's anger was now thoroughly roused. When he had given the order in the morning he had given it half in anger and half in joke, scarcely meaning that it would be carried out.

The major reminded him of the order he had given to the Iberville Greys to detail a member of their company to guard his tent, and of his former caution to the company in which he recognised Jason as a member, and probably they had considered that they had fulfilled the order by detailing Jason, and he laughed heartily. The lieutenant-colonel, thinking the laugh was turned against him, was for a moment nonplussed; but, to make the best of it, he called the orderly and told him to go to the Iberville Greys with his order to send a file of men to take one of their members to the guard-house for neglect of duty while on guard in not presenting arms to field-officers. The major, however, in behalf of Jason, palliated the offence by maintaining that Jason, by raising his head and cocking his ears, had made the best substitute for a "present arms" that it was possible for a donkey to do.

The thing passed off as a joke, but Jason had to find security for his good behaviour in future.

Whether General Halleck's army was not of the strength it was supposed to be, or whether he had over-estimated our strength, I do not know, but they did not deem it prudent to attack us in our position; while M'Culloch, knowing the country and every road and pass, with his mounted rangers kept hovering round them, cutting off small detachments, capturing their supply trains, and even threatening their rear; and the winter now setting in, they were compelled to retreat, M'Culloch following them up and harassing their rear as far as Lebanon, the whole Federal army falling back upon St. Louis.

It was not now probable that the enemy would make any further advance before spring, and the campaign of 1861 might be considered at an end, and the troops were ordered into winter quarters.

Winter quarters had been prepared at places suitable for obtaining forage and supplies easily, having regard to other advantages which might be of importance for health, position, or convenience of having them called speedily together in case of emergency.

Price's army was stationed in the neighbourhood of Springfield and other stations in the south of Missouri according to the means of obtaining supplies. M'Culloch's army was similarly placed in the north-west part of Arkansas. Our regiment was stationed at a place called "Cross Hollows," about 18 miles from Fayetteville, a range of wooden houses having been put up for their accommodation. Our company and the Iberville Greys were specially stationed at the town

of Fayetteville as a guard for that place, it being now a depôt
of supplies.

Our quarters here was a large school or educational institute,
which made one imagine that such buildings were favourite
places for quartering troops.

The facts regarding these buildings I found to be pretty
much as described to me by the old farmer.   The sale of public
lands held by the State for educational purposes produced a
large revenue.   Hence the money was expended for educational purposes, though perhaps not in the most honourable or
judicious manner.   Large schools were built without regard to
the requirements or desires of the population, who seldom sent
their children to the public schools ; and it might be as the
old farmer said, that teachers were appointed with large salaries
and nothing to do as a reward for electioneering and getting
the party into power, while the war-cry of education was
sufficient to stifle any attempt at remonstrance, and no one
might dare to utter a word of criticism on anything pertaining
to the system or the means of carrying it out, be it ever so
pregnant with jobbery and corruption.   'Tis true this was in
an outlying district and in a country but thinly settled.

Fayetteville was a town with a population of about 4,000,
pleasantly situated on a high and dry position, surrounded by
hills from which issued many springs of fine water.   This
place being now an army depôt, there were several of our
commissary and quartermasters' stores here, and factories
established for the manufacture of army waggons, gun carriages, ordnance stores, ammunition, etc.   For these places we
had to furnish a proper guard, and our only duties here were
guard mounting and the usual company drill.

Here we passed about two months as if in garrison without
any stirring events.   There were occasional rumours of an
armistice and talk of peace proposals, but all, I believe, without any foundation.   Here we heard of the demand of Great
Britain in the *Trent* affair, which for a time greatly exhilarated the South, although it ended pretty much as was
expected.

In January we had some severe frost and snow, which was
a source of great excitement to the boys, most of whom had
never seen snow before, and only very slight frosts.   They
were soon sliding or attempting to skate on every pond or dub
of water, and snowballing was indulged in to a great extent,

generally between the two companies, when the battle of Oakhill was fought over again.

During these two months, being the dead of winter, there was little or no fighting in any part.

In the Army of the West there was but little change. There was some talk of a correspondence between General Price and the Confederate Government, and that he was dissatisfied at not having been made a major-general; but what had been done we did not learn.

Colonel M'Intosh was made a brigadier-general, which he deserved, and this promotion gave great satisfaction. No promotion had been awarded to M'Culloch, and it was generally allowed that he was too modest or too independent to ask it.

One General Pike, of Arkansas, had undertaken, and had been commissioned, to raise a brigade in Arkansas and the Indian Territory.

The time in winter quarters passed somewhat idly, and as Satan generally finds some mischief for idle hands to do, he made no exception in this case.

The boys did get into mischief, although it was not of a very serious character. It was chiefly confined to throwing stones at pigs or poultry, chasing cats, and similar depredations, for which they were occasionally punished. But their principal acts of mischief were directed against a woman who lived in a rather dilapidated house near to quarters.

This woman, who was supposed to be a sort of grass widow, did not possess youth or beauty to an extraordinary extent. She was past the bloom of maidenhood, and was remarkable for a freckled face, fiery countenance, and red hair; but what she lacked in grace and beauty she made up in loquacity, and between her and the younger members of the two companies there was a perpetual feud. They seemed to take delight in hearing her scolding, and she seemed to take as great delight in being at war with them. This woman came almost daily to the officers with complaints against some of the boys for some damage done to her fences, poultry, cat, or something, and she would insist upon a severe punishment being inflicted. At last she despaired of getting any satisfaction from the company officers, and declared her intention of complaining to the general himself.

Accordingly one day, as General M'Culloch was riding past

on his way into the town, we saw the vixen had got hold of his bridle, and by her violent gestures we could see that she was lodging a serious complaint against the men in quarters. The general, no doubt promising to see to it, at last got away from her.

In the course of the day orders were given for a dress parade, and therefore we expected there would be some order read out in regard to the subject.

When the parade was formed and the usual evolutions gone through, General M'Culloch rode up and said that he wished to say a few words to the men.

We knew what was coming, but we had never heard the general try his hand at making a speech, and it was soon evident that speaking was not his forte.

He began his address something in the usual stereotyped fashion of—" Third Louisiana, I have—you have—I have always found you ready. You have always been first in any daring act ; you have never failed me when I have called upon you. I have now once more to call upon you, and I trust you will be as ready to obey, as what I now wish you to do is— is—well—is," and he pointed in the direction of the woman's house, " is just to let that red-headed one alone," and so saying he galloped off.

The boys laughed and cheered. The general could have said nothing to have pleased them better, and therefore out of respect for the general they all agreed to let the *red-headed one alone.*

CHAPTER XXI.

EARLY in February rumours were prevalent that we were soon
to take the field again, but this time our campaign was to be
in a different direction. We were to proceed to north-eastern
Arkansas, near the Mississippi, and somewhere in the vicinity
of " New Madrid" to operate with the Army of the Centre in
checking the advance of the enemy on the Lower Mississippi
who was now marching on New Madrid and threatening Island
No. 10, and that in a few days we were to march, our first
destination being Pocahontas. This report turned out to be
correct, although we were doomed never to carry out the programme. The order seemed to have come suddenly and unexpectedly.

The distance to Pocahontas was by the nearest route over
200 miles. The roads were very bad, and in some places
almost impassable. There were many rivers to cross, which
in winter were unfordable, and if a spring rise took place on
the Mississippi much of the country would be overflowed, and
it would be difficult for an army to act.

M'Culloch immediately set about arranging for his transport
and survey of the route, and some advanced parties by the
way of pioneers had already been sent forward.

We were not certain whether Price's army was to accompany
us, or whether he had got his coveted major-generalship and
the command of the Army of the West, which was probably
the intended arrangement.

It was getting near the middle of February, and we expected
to receive orders in a few days to march for Pocahontas, when
upon a quiet Sabbath afternoon, while some of the men were
at church a courier galloped up in breathless haste with orders

for the two companies immediately to join the regiment, that Price's army was already across the Missouri line into Arkansas, retreating before the enemy, who had come down upon him suddenly and unexpectedly with an overwhelming force and taken him quite by surprise.

The detachment being without a fife and drum, the bell of the institution had been used at reveille and tattoo and to call the men together. It was now rung violently, and the alarm soon spread over the town and neighbourhood. The men of the two companies were speedily got together and equipped with ammunition, and within an hour were on the march.

When we had proceeded about 15 miles we began to meet the first of Price's baggage-waggons on their retreat southwards. We tried to get some information from the waggon-drivers about this fearful scare, but we could get no other information than that the enemy were 40,000 strong, and more still coming. As we advanced we met the retreating waggons in still greater numbers, and all giving evidence of the sudden appearance and great force of the enemy.

General Price, whose masterpiece in military tactics was retreating, had effected his retreat in good order, and it was generally allowed that there were few generals in the service who could better conduct a retrograde movement and fall back in better order, covering his baggage trains, poor as they seemed to be—and, indeed, much of it did not appear to be worth the trouble—lean oxen, scarcely able to crawl, old waggons, fit only for firewood, half-loaded with stuff of little value. Nevertheless, Price seemed desirous of saving everything, and it was sometimes said by our men that he was proud of his abilities in conducting a retreat, and lost no opportunity of displaying it, and was rather fond of the movement. We were somewhat astonished at this sudden and unexpected surprise.

We marched all night without halting, and at daybreak came up with our regiment, which was already several miles on the way. We then had a rest for about an hour, and we ate a little bread which we had in our haversacks, and then marched on. The roads were crowded with Price's waggons, and also with numbers of waggons of the country people fleeing southward. As the day advanced and we proceeded we found the country to be in a great state of alarm.

People from all quarters, with waggons filled with women

and children and their effects, were fleeing from the district and hurrying southwards. About nine o'clock we met the advance of Price's army, and then the usual bantering questions began to be asked and answered—

" What is all this scare about ? "

" Go on and you will see."

" What are you retreating for ? "

" We have been fighting for the last three days ; you can now go and take a hand."

The only information we could get was that the enemy had an overwhelming force and was driving everything before them.

About 11 o'clock we heard the cannonading and shortly afterwards the rattle of small arms. We now drew off into some fields and prepared for action, while the shells from the enemy were flying thick and bursting over our heads. An aide-de-camp now came galloping up with orders for the 3rd Louisiana Regiment to proceed quickly to the front, adding at the same time that the enemy had captured one of our batteries. We advanced at a double quick, and were soon engaged with a body of the enemy's troops, which, however, quickly fell back, and we again deployed a little in advance. The fire of the artillery and the rattle of small arms all around were very heavy, but of the position or order of battle we could form no idea. We knew that it was an attack by the enemy on the rear of Price's army, but it was difficult to tell which was friend and which was foe.

A large body of cavalry was forming on a ridge at some distance, which, though we could see no flag, were too well appointed to be Price's troops, and we soon saw that they were a body of the enemy. Their object, however, did not seem to be to attack us, as they rode past at a safe distance and proceeded towards our left in the direction in which we supposed our battery had been captured. They seemed to be commanded by a dashing officer, who wore a red feather in his cap, which made him rather conspicuous. We soon afterwards saw them coming swooping down upon our left, not in squadrons but in single column, as if they were going to pass along our front in a parallel line. The defiant audacity of this seemed too incredible for us to suppose they would attempt it, and we looked on expecting to see them make some other movement. But they did not swerve ; they went whizzing past, discharging their carabines as they passed, but at such a distance as to do no

s

harm, getting the fire from the musketry of our regiment without much damage.

"Out in advance, you rifles, and give it to them!" was now called out.

Our company now dashed out in front for about 50 or 60 yards and delivered a telling fire into them, which sent them off quickly, with a good many saddles empty.

Their object probably was to keep us standing there and prevent us getting forward to retake the battery until it could be got away.

Just then we heard a loud cheering in front on our left, which we knew to be from our side. The cause of this we found to be that some of the guns which had been captured had been recovered, as well as one or two of the enemy's guns, which had got entangled among the trees.

It was now for several hours a constant running backwards and forwards, forming line first in one place and then in another, with what object I did not know, and a heavy fire of artillery and small arms, though what losses were sustained on either side I never learned. The advance of the enemy was checked for the time being, and Price's rear was no longer harassed.

About four o'clock all was quiet again, and we sat down to rest and to await orders.

The day had now become bitterly cold and the wounded were being brought in, and the cold causing the blood to flow freely, everything was daubed over, causing the surroundings to look as if there had been a terrible battle instead of a trifling affair which never took a name.

What was next to be done was now the question asked, and we were impatient to know, as we were tired, hungry, and shivering with the cold.

General Price rode past dressed in the full uniform of a general, with a cocked hat and feathers. It was said, perhaps with some sneering, that he rode along in that dress to show that he had been made a Confederate general, in the expectation that the Confederate troops would greet him with a cheer as a token of their approval of the appointment. But I do not think he had any such idea. The troops could be in no disposition to cheer, as anyone of common-sense among them could not fail to see that there had been an egregious blunder made and gross mismanagement somewhere.

We were now ordered to march back to Cross Hollows and take up position there.

The distance back to Cross Hollows was about 14 miles, and the road was blocked up by Price's army, which was retreating in front of us, and the march was tedious.

The head of our company being on the right of the regiment was the usual place for military gossip, and generally the adjutant, with the latest news, and one or two of the officers would get up there and discuss the situation.

The present state of matters was now commented upon. The first question was, Where was General M'Culloch? Neither he nor M'Intosh had been seen, and certainly had not been with us. They were both away in the entirely opposite direction, surveying the route and arranging for the march to Pocahontas, where we had been ordered to proceed, and part of M'Intosh's brigade had already gone in that direction. Then why was this sudden advance of the enemy by the way of Springfield never suspected? Why had this large force come all the way from St. Louis and been concentrating in Southern Missouri unknown to Price, who supposed himself kept constantly informed by his faithful adherents of all that was going on in Missouri? When Price was surprised in Springfield, how was it that the intelligence reached M'Culloch's army at a distance of 50 miles, only about 10 miles in advance of his sluggish ox waggons? These were questions not so easily answered. We had heard that the Federal General, Halleck, was removed from St. Louis and was going to operate against New Madrid, and Island No. 10, where we were going to oppose him.

The last intelligence we had had through Price's army was that he (Price) had full information of the whole of Southern Missouri; that his scouts had been as far north as Lebanon, and that there the roads were impassable, and any immediate advance of the enemy in that direction was almost impossible.

The generally expressed opinion now was that Price had relied upon the loyalty of the country people to his cause, and believed their information, and that he had been misled; and as his credulity and faith in such information had already caused much disagreement between him and General M'Culloch, it was now supposed that the breach between them would be greater than ever, and, probably, Price seeing what had happened, and perhaps not believing that the enemy was in such strong force, had tried first to repulse them with his own army, and have all the glory to himself without calling upon M'Culloch for aid.

Or, it might be that by orders from the War Department, Price with his army had been left to defend the western frontier, while M'Culloch with his forces was drawn off to join the army of the centre, therefore, Price had first tried to repulse the enemy without calling upon M'Culloch for help.

In any case, many thought that the people of Missouri were not so much devoted to the Southern cause as Price had led himself to believe.

Whether any of these conjectures were correct or not I do not know, but such were the feelings and opinions expressed and discussed among the men and officers of our regiment on the dreary march back to Cross Hollows that night. One thing was certain, a sad disaster had happened, and the strong positions to the north of us had been lost. Had we been able to get the position we had held in November, before going into winter quarters, we might have held it against a superior force and checked the advance of the enemy, but that was now in possession of the Federals.

It was but a small part of our army that was here with us. Several regiments had been stationed at different places, and might take a day or two to get forward. M'Intosh's brigade was supposed to be on the way to Pocahontas, and probably 50 miles distant, and the enemy with an overwhelming force right upon us. It was near midnight when we got to Cross Hollows, and a good many of our company had dropped behind, but came up within an hour or two afterwards. The two companies that had come from Fayetteville were pretty well worn out with hunger and fatigue. The distance from Fayetteville to where we covered Price's retreat was fully 35 miles, so that since hurriedly leaving Fayetteville on Sunday afternoon, we had marched 35 miles and manœuvred often at double quick for about five hours, and then marched back 14 miles without food and without rest, except sitting down on the ground for a few minutes.

We soon got into one of the winter quarter houses, and had some rations cooked and eaten, and hoping that the enemy would allow us till the morning to rest, we were soon asleep.

On the first dawn of day we were aroused by the reveille. The boys, sorely fatigued, thought they had not slept five minutes, and the morning was bitter cold. They rose shivering with cold, and while enduring this cold sensation seemed to have a kind regard for General Price, for they wished him, cocked hat, feathers, and all, in the very hottest place which they could think of.

The roll was called and rations procured, and about seven o'clock the men had got their rations cooked and in their haversacks. The regiment was then formed in line ready to take position and await the advance of the enemy.

We had just formed line when a tremendous cheering was raised all along the front. We soon discovered this was caused by the arrival of General M'Culloch; he had come from a distance of over 70 miles. He now rode along the line while the cheering was startling his horse. He already knew the nature of the position at Cross Hollows, and the whole of the troops were placed in order of battle with the artillery commanding the passes.

Cross Hollows was a good position if the enemy attacked by that line of road, and though we knew our force to be small compared to that of the enemy, yet our position was so good, that had they attacked us here we hoped to have made short work of them,—and we certainly hoped they would attack us and get us out of this difficulty.

How M'Culloch and Price met, or how Price explained to M'Culloch the state of matters, I do not know, but as soon as M'Culloch had placed his troops in position, he set off with a small party to reconnoitre the enemy's strength and movements. It was soon ascertained, to our great disappointment, that the enemy had not advanced from where we had left him on the previous day.

It had now come on a severe storm of snow and sleet, and we were allowed to come down from the elevated position we had taken up and stand in the shelter of the valley, but by no means to leave the ranks. While we stood in this position, a gentleman came along and had some talk with us. He had come to meet General M'Culloch and give him some information regarding the enemy.

He told us that the enemy's forces were in two divisions under two generals—General Curtis and General Siegel; that the force we had met on the previous day was that of Curtis, which was about 13,000 strong; that of Siegel, he thought, was about the same strength, but was not with

Curtis, and was advancing by some other route, though the two armies were acting in close conjunction with each other. He added further, that we might wait a long time before either or both would attack us in this position, but they would flank us by advancing by other routes. What this man told us we found out afterwards to be substantially correct.

It had now become bitterly cold, and the sleet froze as it fell, and our clothes were frozen stiff, and the ground was covered with ice.

About four o'clock in the afternoon orders came for us to move, and we were glad to go anywhere, as we would have been frozen to the ground, but the news was not reassuring when we found that our march was to be backwards towards the Arkansas river.

Our march was much impeded by Price's army and cumbersome trains which were in front, and the snow was now falling so thick that we could not see 10 yards in front. After a tedious and toilsome march we reached Fayetteville about midnight, where we were to halt till daylight, Our company soon found its way into the old quarters and rested there. The rest of the regiment found quarters in what had once been a church, but was now turned into a gun and ammunition factory.

It was later next morning before the reveille was sounded— a little longer time was allowed the troops to rest. When the regiment was formed we were marched out and halted on a rising ground near the town. The ground was thickly covered with snow and the whole country round seemed to be in a general conflagration. The large wooden storehouses which had been filled with army supplies were in flames. On this rising ground where we stood, was piled up large heaps of flour and bacon, and every waggon that could be procured was being loaded up with stores to be carried away south to Fort Smith, while the remainder was heaped up on piles of wood like the sacrifices of old, and set on fire—the troops cutting off from the best pieces slices of bacon which they roasted on the point of sticks (the use of sabres or bayonets for this purpose being forbidden), while the heat dried their wet and frozen clothes. It is astonishing what a little thing enlivens men amidst privations. This was an amusement; the everlasting fun was going on, they roasted slices of the new bacon which was really excellent; and for bread, they cut up the bags of flour which were lying about in hundreds, poured some water on the flour and kneaded up a dough. This they drew out by its elasticity, and wound round a stick or ramrod in spiral fashion, and held it over the flames until it was baked and then broke it off the stick. Having eaten what they could, and having filled their haversacks with this kind of bread and bacon streaming with grease, and had their clothes dried, themselves warmed and put into good humour; and having been told by their officers that they were a set of greasy-looking cannibals, while the officers themselves were not a whit better looking, they were ordered to fall in, and the line of march was taken up about 10 o'clock—Price's army having moved on at daybreak.

Thus the large quantities of army stores which had been collected here throughout the autumn and winter were destroyed, to prevent them falling into the hands of the enemy.

We continued our march southward, it being understood that we were to take up a strong position at Boston Mountain, where the whole force would be concentrated.

We had scarcely left Fayetteville when the enemy's cavalry entered it. They seemed to be a bold and audacious corps, and evidently wished to display some dash. Our boys were longing to get a shot at the chap with the red feather, and it seemed once or twice that day that they would have got their wish, for they followed upon our rear and appeared on our flanks. We gave them a few shots, but they contrived to keep pretty well out of range.

This day turned out like the previous one, heavy snow and sleet came on, and a most disagreeable night was passed. Without tents, and the sleet falling, we could only huddle round the camp fires, but sleep or rest was impossible. Next day was equally bad, and it seemed as if winter was just setting in with greater severity than ever, the roads were also in a dreadful condition, being cut up by the trains and the number of waggons transporting stores southward. However, this evening, we got to our destination.

We now got tents, and a camp was formed and a position taken up commanding the road leading to the south, and which we could hold against a force of double our numbers.

It was obvious that M'Culloch was going to adopt the tactics he had done with Halleck's army in the autumn, which was, that he would station his main army in a strong and

well-protected position, where it could not be flanked by
numbers, while with flying detachments he would hover round
the enemy, and, knowing the country better, would cut off
outlying detachments, worry and harass them by cutting off
their supplies, and otherwise weaken them, while he would use
every endeavour to augment and strengthen his own forces,
and ultimately be able to advance and compel the enemy
either to retreat, or attack him in his strong position. In this
he seemed likely to succeed.

What had been the 2nd brigade at Oakhill, in which was
the mounted infantry, was now called the 1st brigade, and
under command of late colonel, now Brigadier General
M'Intosh. The brigade in which our regiment was, was now
called the 2nd brigade, and was under command of Colonel
Hebert of our regiment who was acting as Brigadier, M'Culloch
acting as a major-general over the whole division.

A few days after we had taken up this position, M'Culloch
brought into the camp several army waggons with supplies of
the enemy, and over a hundred prisoners. He and M'Intosh
continued to make raids on the enemy with great success, and
almost every day some prisoners or spoil was brought in.
The enemy's dashing cavalry seemed not to have been wishful
of trying their strength with them.

In the meantime our forces were fast increasing, numerous
detachments were coming from different parts of Arkansas
and Texas, and a large number of men, as "emergency men" had
joined by a rule which had been recently adopted. By this
regulation or order, men were allowed to volunteer into the
service for a short time on a particular emergency such as a
battle, after which they would be allowed to leave.

A large number of such men from Fayetteville, Bentonville,
and other places had joined and were being drilled in to be of
service, and I may say that the system did very well, and
these men were of considerable assistance. 'Tis true a great
many of them had been already drilled less or more as
Volunteers.

General Pike was also said to have raised a brigade of
between 3000 and 4000 men, of whom over 1000 were Indians,
and Price's army was greatly augmented, and he had got
several batteries of artillery, so that it was now supposed that
we would have fully 20,000 men in all, and it was expected
that 2000 or 3000 more would yet be added.

M'Culloch had become very popular in Arkansas and Texas, and his troops had great confidence in him, and men were joining his army, but the great evil was the disagreement between him and Price. This seems chiefly to have arisen from Price paying too much attention to what M'Culloch seemed to regard as idle gossip of the country people.

Price, supposing that he knew something of the enemy's strength of position from information obtained through such a source, would advocate certain movements; while M'Culloch, acting on experience, would place no confidence on any information obtained through Price.

When we had been in this camp for a little over a week we learned that a major-general appointed by the War Department at Richmond was coming to take command over M'Culloch and Price and the whole Army of the West.

Everyone was now on the *qui vive* to find out who our new general was to be. We soon learned that it was to be General Van Dorn, but all that could be learned of him was that he had been formerly in the regular army of the United States, but of his services in the present war there was no record. I asked my friend P., the drum-major, if he knew anything of him. He said he knew him to be a major of cavalry, but he did not know much about him, and he would ask C., who had served under him. C., who was about as careless a fellow as was in the regiment, replied that he did not know much about Van Dorn as an officer, but he knew him to be an excellent hand at playing poker. I asked what sort of an officer he was compared to M'Intosh. He said that as an officer he was not fit to enter a ten-acre field with M'Intosh. Of course there was not a great deal of importance to be attached to this account, as C. was rather an easy-going fellow; still it was not very satisfactory when it was known that he was to be over M'Culloch and the whole Army of the West. Others said he had the name of being a bold and dashing officer, and that when he came he would do wonders and revolutionise matters, which turned out to be the case.

M'Culloch continued to bring in fresh batches of prisoners almost every day, and a farm-house and large barn adjoining were filled with them. They were quite contented, and conversed freely with us on the general questions of the war and politics, but it was impossible to draw out of them anything in regard to the strength or position of their army. As the feeding of those prisoners was a heavy drag upon our resources, and the enemy as yet held none of our men as prisoners to be got back in exchange for them, they were disarmed, paroled, and let go, care being taken that they could give no important information.

In the meantime the enemy, who had advanced to the south of Fayetteville and to within 15 miles of our position, finding us so strongly posted, did not deem it prudent to attack us in this position, and, being so worried by M'Culloch's manœuvres and constant raids and attacks, they had fallen back towards the Missouri boundary and taken up a defensive position.

It was now a common saying among our men that they hoped when Van Dorn came that he would just leave "Ben" (General M'Culloch) alone and he would soon have the whole of the enemy's army brought in by small lots at a time.

But this was not to be. General Van Dorn telegraphed from a distance to stop all retrograde movements, and that the tactics must now be to advance, still pressing on to victory, accompanied by some very warlike expressions.

There was no general order of this read off on parade; we only saw it in the newspapers, for which we believe it was intended more than for the army.

We considered it looked very well on paper, and, though it had not been read off to us, it would no doubt be read in many a drawing-room, where it would be better appreciated.

About the 26th or 27th of February, Van Dorn, who had arrived at Fort Smith, sent forward by telegraph an order for the troops to march on the 1st of March, the men to carry 10 days' cooked rations in their haversacks, and sixty rounds of ammunition.

The idea of ten days' cooked rations to be carried in their haversacks rather astonished the men, and they wondered if new haversacks were going to be issued, as it was known that most of the men could easily eat in one day all that could be crammed into their haversacks. However, they were told to make themselves easy on that point, for it would be something new for the commissary if he could furnish more than three days' rations, and they might rest assured that their haversacks would hold all the rations they would get.

It seemed evident to the more thoughtful that their new general was giving his orders from a distance off a book or map, without much knowledge of the position or condition of his army, the strength or position of the enemy, or the nature of the country in which his army was going to operate.

It may, however, be said in advance, with regard to Van Dorn, that he was no bejewelled, gloved, or carpet officer, and whatever he might lack in the way of forethought, prudence, or military skill, he certainly did not lack courage or personal daring.

As was expected, the commissary could barely furnish three days' rations, and that of a very poor kind. This was prepared and put into the men's haversacks, and what ammunition there was was served out, although it did not amount to 60 rounds to each man; and on the 2nd of March, 1862, the Confederate Army of the West left its position on Boston Mountain to press on to victory, as Van Dorn had expressed it.

Great need it had to press on or it would itself be pressed. No trains accompanied it with tents and provisions; the so-called ten days' rations were all in the men's haversacks about enough for two days; and the weather was a continuance of blinding snow and sleet. It was necessary that we should get the battle over as soon as possible.

Our total force was about 24,000 men. The enemy's force was supposed to be about 26,000 men, but of course the men were prompted by the braggadocial cry of " What of that, one Southerner is equal to three Northerners," and I must say that I was a little amused when I heard that same saying neatly retorted back on them not many days afterwards.

The first day's march was towards Fayetteville. The snow and sleet were blinding, and the roads in an awful condition. We halted for the night, but of course anything like sleep was out of the question.

The second day the weather was somewhat better, and the sun shone out a little. In the early part of the day we heard a tremendous cheering among Price's troops in our rear, and we were made aware that General Van Dorn was riding up along the line. As he came up nearer to us, the cheering became less enthusiastic, and as he passed our regiment an attempt was made to get up a cheer, but it resulted in a failure.

The third day the weather continued good, the sun shone out, and the men's clothes and blankets got dried. This night some corn meal was served out to the troops, but as they had no means of cooking it in any way, it was of little use. This night we were fortunate in getting a good place to bivouac, in a wood where there was abundance of dry leaves, and our overcoats and blankets being now dry, we nestled among the leaves and were soon asleep. This was the first night's sleep we had got since leaving Boston Mountain.

In the morning when we woke up, we found it close and warm, but what was our astonishment when we saw we were all covered over with snow. I had considerable difficulty in getting the boys up. They had on lying down rolled themselves up in their blankets and covered themselves over with leaves, which in turn got snowed over, and then they felt quite snug, and could not or did not want to hear the call.

We were now in the vicinity of the enemy, and the army closed up and moved slowly; and in the morning an aide-de-camp passed to the rear for an ambulance as General Van Dorn had been taken very ill. This was exceedingly unfortunate just on the verge of battle, and this battle going to be fought entirely upon his express command and under his own directions and responsibility, and against the advice of one whom we considered his best general. The aide-de-camp was also inquiring for a doctor.

"Get a bottle of whisky for him," cried the graceless C. in our company, "and that will put him all right."

In the meantime, the army moved slowly and cautiously, and it was evident that no one knew the enemy's position, and the nature of the country was such that a large army might be within a quarter of a mile and completely hid from sight.

The Confederate army, to the best of my knowledge, consisted of two divisions. The first division, of Missouri troops under General Price, numbered about 11,000 men; the second division was under General M'Culloch, and numbered about 13,000 men. This latter division was made up of three brigades. The first brigade, in which were all the mounted infantry, was under General M'Intosh; the second brigade was under Colonel Hebert; the third brigade, called Pike's Indian brigade, was under General Pike. M'Culloch's division had 18 pieces of artillery; Price's division had about the same number, besides some mountain howitzers. The whole army was under command of General Van Dorn.

CHAPTER XXII.

ON the day mentioned, the 5th of March, General Van Dorn being sick, and the position of the enemy not well known, M'Culloch went to the front with M'Intosh's brigade to reconnoitre. Some firing was heard that day, but nothing of importance was done.

On the following day (the 6th) our brigade (the second) was ordered to follow up and support the first brigade and the artillery, which was going to make an attack on Siegel's division.

I must say that I never got what the Americans would call the "hang" of this battle, and I do confidently believe that no one else ever did, whatever way reports may have pretended to place it. It was a mass of mixed up confusion from beginning to end.

About 11 o'clock cannonading was heard in front, and we were ordered to hurry up. When we got up the firing had ceased. Siegel's advanced guard had fallen back.

About one o'clock firing was heard again; this time heavier, and we closed up. The fire of small arms was now heard, and the order was given, "Forward, boys," and we charged up and drove the enemy from their position; but they got off with their guns, leaving one broken axle and a good many dead and wounded on the ground. The order was now given to follow up quick and not allow them to get their guns into position again, but they seemed to have had their next position already marked out. It was very plain that Siegel, or whoever commanded this force, was a very able officer by the way in which he fell back. The broken axle, which had been struck by a shot from one of our guns, we presumed must have been either the axle of a gun or of a limber waggon, and they had under our fire before retreating either replaced it by a new one or taken the carriage to pieces, packed it on to a caisson, and carried everything off except this relic, which they left lying on the road, as much as to say, "You can have that."

About three o'clock they made another stand, and this time the affair assumed more the shape of a general battle. They appeared to make a stand in full force, and deployed on both sides of the road with their right and left wings extended out into the cover of the wood.

More of our division was brought up, including some of Pike's Indians. These were sent into the thicker wood against the enemy's right wing, while we attacked them on the left and centre. The battle was pretty hot here for some time. Siegel's force was mostly composed of Germans, and whether on the right they got scared by the Indians, who kept up hideous yells and war whoops, I do not know, but they gave way and fell back on the centre.

Siegel, remembering Oakhill, had an eye to his guns, and took care to have his artillery well supported. Evidently not wishing to risk a general battle until he joined Curtis, he now limbered up quickly and fell back in good order with all his guns. It was supposed that this was only a part of his division.

We still followed him up. M'Intosh galloping past cried out, "Now, you Louisiana boys, I must have those guns to-night." But Siegel seemed to dangle them before us, as much as to say, "Don't you wish you may get them."

About two miles beyond this there was a shallow, rapid running river, or large creek, through which the road led by a ford, where the water was about a foot deep. There was a wooden bridge a little above the ford, but it had been set fire to by Siegel's men after they had crossed. Siegel had left a rear guard and one or two guns to sweep the ford and annoy us in crossing. We were ordered to get down the bank to the side of the river, keeping out of range of the artillery, and be ready to cross as soon as our own artillery was brought up to cover us. The artillery was soon up, and we were ordered to cross at once, the smoke from the burning bridge partly obscuring the ford. The boys quickly got off their shoes and stockings.

"What is that you are doing?" cried the major. "Whoever heard of men stripping off their shoes and stockings to wade across a stream in front of an enemy's fire?"

"Better be shot than have wet feet this cold night, major."

"Oh, who cares for wet feet?" cried the major.

"We will soon make up the time in marching with dry feet," was the reply, which was true.

By this time they were nearly all over, carrying their dry shoes and stockings, and soon had them on at the other side. The major had entered the water to cross, when a parting discharge of grape from one of Siegel's guns swept the ford, but doing no damage except to the major's horse, which was struck by a grape shot on the knee. At the same moment it was cried out that Siegel's two guns were off at full gallop. The recall was now sounded, and we had to strip our shoes and stockings and recross again. The major's horse stood still in the middle of the stream and could not move, and the major cried out to some of them to come and carry him ashore, but the boys began to laugh and retort on him by saying, "Who cares for wet feet? Try it, major." The water was certainly nipping cold and it was freezing hard. At last one stout fellow carried the major ashore, and one or two of them did the last office for the poor horse by sending balls through his head, and he fell dead in the stream. I confess I felt more pity at seeing the poor horse shot down as he cast an imploring look on his friends, than at all the slaughter I had seen that afternoon.

I could not follow the rest of the movements throughout that evening. There was heavy firing in other parts all round, and we were marched and countermarched in many directions, while horse, foot, and artillery were moving hither and thither. Siegel had no doubt joined Curtis to prepare for the general battle.

After marching back a good long way in the direction we had come, we came to a halt at an open space where a lot of dead trees lay on the bank of a gravelly creek. It was now near midnight, and some large fires were burning, and some prisoners who had been taken were sitting round them chatting away with some of our men.

It was rather amusing to hear the conversation at such a time and under such circumstances; the subject of the present campaign of course being tabooed. It was something like the following :—

Confederate.—Do you know ——— in Chicago? He is a cabinet-maker; he used to have a place at the corner of ——— Street.

Federal.—Oh yes, I know him very well; he is in the same place still. I have a brother who worked for him. One of his sons went down South about two years ago.

Confederate.—Yes, that was Stephen ; I knew him in New Orleans ; he joined the New Orleans Cadets and went off with the 2nd Louisiana.

Federal.—He has other two sons—one of them is with us, the other is a lieutenant in the 5th Illinois, and I think is in Halleck's army.

Confederate.—Does D. and R. still carry on that foundry business there?

Federal.—Yes. D. is dead, but one of his sons carries on the business; another of his sons is in the 7th Illinois—a captain, I think.

Confederate No. 2.—Do you know old ——, that has a large gasfitting establishment in St. Louis. I think it is in —— Street?

Federal No. 2.—Yes ; some of his sons went down South a while ago.

Confederate.—Yes ; two of them came down and started a branch business in —— as agents for their father. One of them is now in our regiment—that is D. ; but B. went North in the spring and could not get back, as the blockade had been put on at Cairo.

Federal.—Well, I knew them both. B. joined the 7th Missouri, and is now with us in Curtis's division.

Confederate.—Are you not of Curtis's division?

Federal.—No ; we are of Siegel's (but a shake of the head here gave warning that that was approaching the tabooed subject).

An order now came to move on again. "Prisoners this way." The prisoners were to be sent to the rear, and we were to march to some other position.

The prisoners rose up, put on their heavy overcoats, while they and our men heartily shook hands at parting, bidding good-bye as follows :—

Federals.—Well, good-bye, boys ; good luck to you, and take care of yourselves.

Confederates.—All right ; we will try to do so ; these are fine comfortable greatcoats of yours for this weather.

Federals.—Yes ; they are very warm, and need it for this weather; good-bye! And away they went in charge of a guard.

As we moved away I could hardly help reflecting on the manner of the conversation I had been hearing and what a strange thing was war, and particularly such a war as this, although that night I had not much time to moralise, but I have often thought of it since. Here was a man in our company who had a brother who a year ago had been a member of our company, but was now in the army opposed to us, and with which we were to engage in deadly conflict within a few hours. Hundreds of instances there were of the same kind, and this not through any feeling or sentiment of their own or sympathy with either side, but merely owing to the location where they happened to be sojourning at the time.

Cold, hungry, and fatigued we moved sullenly along, some of the lads almost sleeping on their feet. We stopped at a place where a strip of wood came to a point. I forget what it was like. Here some big fires were made, and we were ordered to rest till daylight.

All manner of reports were now afloat. Aides-de-camp flying past stopped to tell us that the fighting for the day had been entirely in our favour, and that we had sorely crippled the enemy; that Price had got in their rear, and that they were cutting a road through the woods to effect their escape.

"Then let them go," cried some of the boys who were huddling by the fires vainly trying in the cold to sleep.

"On no," would be the answer; "we have now got in their rear and completely hemmed them in, and we will capture all their supplies, and they have a large stock, and before this time to-morrow you will have more provisions than you know what to do with."

It is true we were in their rear, but they were also in our rear, and they had the advantage of being in a strong position, while, from the rough and wooded nature of the country it was almost impossible to find out how their forces were placed or in what way we could attack them to advantage.

At daylight some waggons came up with flour and corn-meal, but only a very small quantity for each man, and, as we had no cooking utensils, the men had to do the best they could with their small allowance by rolling it into dough upon a stone and sticking it into the hot ashes of the fires, and eating it half-raw, half-burned, and mixed with cinders. It was certainly scandalous that the commissaries in these flying marches and without camp equipage never tried to provide the men with any kind of ready-made bread or biscuit.

Shortly after daylight, scattered cannonading was heard in

T

different directions, and occasionally a pattering of small arms, and we could see parties of horsemen scrambling on the tops of the numerous small hills through the trees and brushwood, amongst whom we could often recognise the figures of General M'Culloch and General M'Intosh. This firing and reconnoitring seemed to have been intended to draw the fire of the enemy's artillery and show their position, but they were too 'cute to reply.

About ten o'clock we were ordered to move forward on the same road that we had fought upon the previous day. As we marched along, some small parties of mounted infantry came out of the woods in exceeding bad humour. They had been engaged with small detachments of the enemy, which had driven them back, and they were crying out for reinforcements. Of course we could give them no satisfaction, and our men only laughed and derided them, and cried to go back and pitch in again. After proceeding about three miles in this direction a halt was called, and we soon saw the 1st brigade which had been in advance, returning, and, of course, we were to countermarch and follow them. Just as the last of the 1st brigade had passed, I observed General M'Culloch riding behind them accompanied by two aides-de-camp. There was something in the general's countenance which betokened no good. I never saw such a change in a man's face. He seemed haggard and worn out with fatigue, but beyond this, there was in his countenance a mixed expression of melancholy, despair and anger, which he seemed to try to hide, for, as he rode past he nodded to our captain, and said in an easy manner, " We are going to take 'em on the other wing."

But it was easy to read through his countenance the expression—" Well, I will do it, but I know it is going to destruction."

" We have got them all penned up now, boys," said one of the aides, " and you have nothing to do but to shoot them down."

" Tell that to the marines," said one or two voices, after they had passed.

Such prattling was thrown away upon our men; they were now too old to mind such chaff; they saw how things were, and they could read in the general's countenance that there was something wrong.

" Where is that Major-General Damdborn, or whatever they call him ?" cried one; " is he still sick ? "

" Oh, no," cried another, " I hear he is all right again."

" They must have got him that bottle of whisky I prescribed for him," said the graceless C. ; " I bet you he and old Price were playing poker all last night."

It had been whispered all round that since Van Dorn had taken command, he had taken part more with Price than M'Culloch, and had become very friendly with the former. Of course Price's political influence in Missouri counted for a good deal at Richmond.

" Shut up, C.," cried another, " I take up for Price, let him be what he may, he will not neglect his duty, or the care or interests of his army ; and if he is fond of retreating, he is not backward in attacking again, and if he gets his army into a fix, he can always manage to get them out of it again."

" And who is to get us out if we get into a fix ? "

" Ben."

" Yes, if he lives."

There was something ominous in this last expression, whether it arose from the strange expression they had observed in the general's face or not, I know not, but it had the effect of damping the conversation and the men marched along in silence.

What was said about General Price was strictly true. He exercised great care over his army, and though a man advanced in years, he was most zealous and indefatigable in his duties, and possessed considerable ability.

M'Culloch had certainly not been well treated, he had been superseded in his command, and placed in a subordinate position, and the army which he had so well managed and led to victory, reduced to wretched starvation, and blindly ordered to advance against a superior force, strongly posted and whose strength or position it was impossible to find out.

We now began to find that the enemy was posted on that ridge forming the gusset where the road leading from Springfield down into Arkansas branched off. It was an extensive ridge, extending for several miles, and might be called an assemblage of small hills and ridges. It was called " Pea Ridge," I presume, from the number of wild peas which grew in the district.

It was somewhere on this ridge that we had been posted in November, while acting on the defensive against Halleck's army but things were now reversed. The enemy held the advantageous position, and was acting on the defensive, and we were the attacking party.

The ridge may be described as something like a triangle—the apex pointing northwards, and terminating at the road which led to Missouri, and along the base were rocky hills and deep gullies, while along the two sides were roads branching off from the Missouri road at the point, one leading to the eastward, which was called the Elkhorn road, from an inn or tavern of that name; the other, leading southward I think, was called the Bentonville road, though of that I am not certain.

Up this latter named road we had driven the enemy on the preceding day, and returned back, and advanced again in the morning, and were now marching back as M'Culloch had said "to take 'em on the other wing."

At about four miles from the point, the distance across the ridge between the two roads might be about four miles, and about four miles from the point, on the Bentonville road, there was between the road and the ridge a stretch of level cleared fields, which indented into the wooded ridge, leaving the high ridge about three miles broad. Of course, this is only a very rough survey, and may not be very accurate.

Across the ridge at this part, the enemy were supposed to be posted fronting northwards. Their right rested on the Elkhorn road, and their left on the level fields between the ridge and the Bentonville road, their rear being protected by rocky hills and deep gullies, while the ridge in front of them being in most places, rugged, rocky, and wooded, was quite impassable for horse or artillery; and their whole force was entirely hid from view by the hills and woods, and would have to be felt for.

The plan of attack seems to have been that Price should attack them on their right from the Elkhorn road, while M'Culloch's division should attack them on the left from the Bentonville road.

Near the edge of the ridge on the Bentonville road we halted, and here the three brigades were drawn up, not in order of battle, but in reserve, ready to act. Here was the 1st brigade, under General M'Intosh. The 2nd brigade, under Colonel Hebert, acting brigadier; and the 3rd brigade under General Pike, with three batteries of artillery of six guns each—the whole division under General M'Culloch.

About noon, orders were given to the 2nd brigade to strip for battle, and I heard the words of the general as he gave the orders to Colonel Hebert :—

"You shall advance with your 2nd brigade, and attack their left wing, and as soon as you have drawn their fire, you shall have support speedily—and good support too."

The 1st and the 3rd brigades and the artillery were ordered to be in readiness to advance and support the 2nd brigade. Blankets and topcoats were thrown off, and we advanced to the attack, General M'Culloch and General M'Intosh accompanying the brigade with the object, no doubt, of observing the position of the enemy after the fire opened, and seeing where the 1st and 3rd brigades could be brought in to advantage.

We advanced by a sort of a farm-road between two rail fences which led across the level fields towards the wooded ridge. In these fields there had been wheat grown which had been reaped in the autumn, and, as was usual in those countries, the wheat had been threshed in the field, and the straw left in large piles on the ground. We had got about half way across, when a battery which had been hid by one of those piles of straw upon our right, opened on us with grape and canister. The order was given never to mind but to push on at double quick—the generals would attend to the battery. Fortunately, the ground upon the side of the road next the battery was something above the level of the road, and the rail fence considerably marred the grape shot. The men bent their bodies, trailed arms and ran along at double quick. They did not require to be told to close up ; that grape shot had a most disagreeable whistle as it passed within a foot or two of their ears, which was incentive sufficient.

We reached the wood without much damage, where we formed again. But just as we had done so, we heard a loud whooping and a great rattle of small arms behind us in the direction of the battery. The battery was soon silenced, and a loud hurrah showed the guns had been captured by the Indians, and our astonishment was still greater when we saw the whole battery with limber waggons and caissons of ammunition in flames. It seemed that the Indians had a great horror of artillery, and being commanded by their own chief, (Standwattie, I think was his name) when they got possession of the guns, they determined, like the old woman at Oakhill, to "burn the pesky things." So, gathering the wheat straw they piled it round the gun carriages and set fire to it, and thus the carriages, ammunition chests, and everything of wood was burned, the guns falling useless on the ground, while the explosions of the ammunition and bursting of the shells made the Indians clear off, thinking the things were possessed by the Evil One, and that even fire would not destroy them. This was so much done, one of the enemy's batteries destroyed, but we had to move cautiously against an unseen foe, who was doubtless lying in wait and ready to receive us. The leaves were not entirely off the trees, but we could see through the woods much better than in summer. The ground was very rough and covered in many places with large boulders, hillocks, and fallen trees.

We proceeded very cautiously in line. The generals seemed to be trying to discover something of the enemy from the tops of little eminences. A few shots from their artillery at a distance in another direction were falling amongst us, but nothing could be seen of their main body. The wood was now getting thicker, and we could not see more than fifty yards in front.

Suddenly something like a tremendous peal of thunder opened all along our front, and a ridge of fire and smoke appeared close before us, and the trees round us and over our heads rattled with the bullets, as if in a heavy hail-storm. Our boys quickly returned the fire. Colonel Hebert, who had been in front on horseback, quickly sprang to the rear, he being caught between the two fires.

The order was now, "Close in upon them, boys—forward!" We knew the Federal arms were better than ours for distant fighting and our object was to keep them at short range.

A desperate battle now commenced. We kept advancing and they falling steadily back. Their fire was very heavy, but strange to say we did not seem to suffer much from it. We had advanced past where they had first opened fire, and their dead lay thick.

They, knowing the superiority of their arms over ours, kept falling back to keep us at long shot, while we followed them up to keep at close range. This was a considerable advantage to us. Our advancing upon them kept us enveloped in the dense smoke, while their falling back kept them in the clear atmosphere where they could be easily seen. Our men squatted down when loading, then advanced and squatted down again, and looking along under the smoke could take good aim ; while the enemy, firing at random into the smoke, much of their shot passed over our heads.

This fighting continued for over an hour, and we must have advanced fully half-a-mile, when we saw the open field in front of our right, but the wood continued still in front of our left. This was caused by us coming out to the corner of the open fields, which were here bounded by the woods on two sides at about a right angle. Here the enemy quickly disappeared from our right front, but they had scarcely done so when a sweeping fire of grape and canister was poured upon us from a battery in the corner of the field. This for a moment staggered our men, but in a state of fury they rushed forward on the guns. Four of the guns the enemy succeeded in getting away, but two were captured. We closed up towards the wood in front of our left, the firing having now ceased, and the enemy had disappeared.

Here we found that a large body of the enemy had been posted, and the battle here had been severe ; the ground was covered with their baggage, and the dead lay thick. They had fallen back, and we had gained their camp and position. The position was one of some advantage, being bounded on one side by a deep gully, across which the enemy seemed to have retreated.

We thought we had gained one victory at least, and the men sent up a loud cheer. It was answered by a still louder cheer of defiance from the wooded mountain-side in front of our left beyond the gully, showing that the enemy was there in strong force, having fallen back to a stronger position where it would be impossible for us to attack them with our present force ; and we began to realise that, as far as we saw, we were but a small force and in considerable confusion or mixed up, and there did not seem to be any movement towards forming us into order again, and inquiries began to be made as to where were the officers, when the sound of a bugle was heard in the rear on our right. The cry at first was that this was the 1st and 3rd brigades coming up to our support; others again said it was no bugle of ours, it was a cavalry bugle and must be the enemy. But where were all our officers? was the question asked all round—not a field-officer of any kind was to be seen. But here come our reinforcements, and all eyes were turned towards a body of troops advancing in the woods on our right and rear from the direction in which we had heard the bugle, and the way in which we expected our reinforcements to come.

The cry of "The enemy" was next called out as they opened fire upon us, and we found we were attacked in the rear, and the enemy had got between us and the other part of our division.

The battle was renewed again and we were fighting in a reversed position and facing back in the direction we had come. After some fighting the enemy was driven back at this point and retired into the wood, but only to return to the attack again and again. They were scarcely driven back when an attack was made on our left and front by a party of the enemy which had recrossed the gully, seemingly with the object of recapturing the two guns, but after a pretty hard fight they were repulsed.

But where were our officers? The highest officer to be seen was a captain. Where was Major T.? Where was Colonel Hebert who was in command of the brigade? Where were all the other colonels and field-officers? We knew some of them were down, but surely not all. No one could give any account. The captain of our company was missing, the first and second lieutenants were not with the company, the first not having recovered from his wounds, the second on detached service. There was now only Lieutenant G. with the company; he was, however, brave and active. He and I consulted with the one or two line officers of our regiment that were now to be seen on the state of matters, but they or no one could give any explanation of why we were thus placed or what we were to do. We had evidently cut through the centre of the enemy's left wing and were between two fires.

The fearful cannonade and distant roll of small arms far upon our left on the other side of the ridge told that heavy fighting was going on there, but why we should be left here, surrounded by the enemy without support and without orders, was what we could not understand. Where were the 1st and the 3rd brigades that should have followed and supported us?

Our conversation was cut short by another attack of the enemy upon our right and rear, this time more determined, but they were again driven back.

The situation now looked desperate, and what was to be done? It was now certain that we were not going to be reinforced. Some cried out that we must stand here and sell our lives as dearly as possible. The two captured guns stood in the field. It was now very unlikely that we would long be able to hold them, and it was suggested that we should spike them, and then try and cut our way back through the enemy on our right and rear; but we could find no spikes in the limber waggon, and the small end of a ramrod was driven into the touch-holes and then broken off and driven in tight with round shot.

This was scarcely done when a battery opened on us from a point far away on our right and rear, and some round shot came tearing amongst us. This battery seemed to be placed near where we had started from at noon, and where we had left the 1st and 3rd brigades and the artillery. This made confusion worse confounded, and our case seemed hopeless. At last it was suggested that this must be one of our own batteries, who mistook us for the enemy, and we held up our colours for them to see. The conjecture seemed to be correct, for the firing was at once stopped, and we were satisfied that our friends were still there, but why they did not come to our support was inexplicable. The enemy was between us and them, but they could not be in very strong force.

A consultation was again held as to what should be done. The four battalions of the brigade had got much mixed up, but still they always managed to form quickly in line without regard to the companies or even regiments being mixed, and it was decided to form up in regular order the remains of the brigade, attack the enemy on our right and rear, cut our way through, and get back to where we had left the 1st and 3rd brigades at noon.

The line was being formed in the field just along the edge of the wood. I was standing in front of our company closing them up, when suddenly I heard a rush or rustling like a storm of wind passing through the woods, and one of the boys cried out to me, "Look out, sergeant." I looked around, and there about 50 yards distant, coming down upon us in full career, was a large body of cavalry. They came on in beautiful order, with their long heavy swords at a guard, their lines as regular as if on parade, and a look of malicious triumph in their faces, which seemed to say, "We have got you now." I had scarcely time to step back into the ranks, every man stood firm, their pieces levelled steady, with the deadly determination of despair, not a trigger was drawn until within 25 yards, when our fire opened—not in a volley, but in a steady continued fusilade. Then down went men and horses. Some horses plunged and reared in the air; others tumbled forward and threw their riders uninjured among our ranks; some of the horses in falling rolled right up to our men's feet, they standing back just as a man at the sea-side would stand back from a large wave that came up farther than the rest. The second squadron, not being able to check their velocity, tumbled over the first, our troops meanwhile keeping up a steady fire upon them. The field in front of us was literally piled up with dead men and horses. The third squadron was seen through the smoke trying to wheel, when I heard several voices cry out, "There he is; down with him." I was looking forward to see what it was, and there was that dashing officer with the red feather, whom we had seen before, falling from his horse riddled with balls, and the broken remnants of his splendid cavalry flying in disorder from the field.

All this happened in less time than I can write it. The smoke cleared away, and the field in front of us presented a scene of slaughter.

Not a word was spoken, not a cheer was raised. Our men stood motionless, seemingly speechless and amazed at their own work.

This gallant though rash charge of cavalry—this firmness of our men as they stood before the threatening avalanche, and poured their deadly fire on them with such earnest steadiness and precision, while the slaughtered squadrons reeled and fell, seemed to me, from a military point of view, by far the most brilliant feat that I witnessed during my experience in the war. Yet, strange to say, I have never seen any record of it mentioned in reports on either side. It was no doubt on a small scale, and indeed very little of the details of what was done at that time and place ever found its way into print.

Of this cavalry all we ever could learn was that it was a regiment got up as a crack corps. It was splendidly mounted and equipped, well trained, and full of dash, and no doubt wishing to record their name in some brilliant charge, and emulate the light brigade at Balaclava, made this onset which resulted in their destruction. And the affair, with the other events which took place on this afternoon at the same place, having no one to report or record them, were lost in the stirring events of the time, and passed over as best to be buried in oblivion.

On the field in front of us many of the men were struggling to extricate themselves from the horses which had fallen upon them.

" Go and help the poor devils," cried some. And several who were unhurt were extricated, and with those who had tumbled into our ranks were made prisoners. But what were we to do with them when we were little better than prisoners ourselves.

Captain G. of a neighbouring company, who was now one of the few officers of our regiment left fit for duty, was suffering from a bad cold, and was extremely hoarse, and the powder smoke having got into his throat, he was coughing violently and almost speechless. He turned to me, and after an effort said seriously enough, " Would to God it was night or reinforcements would come." I remembered the words of Wellington.

The sun was now getting low. I suggested that we should send out some scouts to take a peep round, and find if there was a large body of the enemy on our right and rear. (The cavalry having come from that direction indicated that the enemy must be there in force.) He objected to my suggestion, " For," said he, " I fear that is where so many of our officers have gone and fallen into a trap." There was now a lull, and there was no firing round where we were, but we heard the battle still raging furiously far on our left on the other side of the ridge. The excitement being over, the pangs of hunger set in, and the men were soon ransacking the enemy's old camp but did not find any food. They then went among the slain and rifled their haversacks. A cry went up that they were plundering, but when it was told that they were only taking the food out of the dead men's haversacks, considering their wretched state of starvation, it was excusable.

But now a horseman was seen coming galloping across the fields waving a white handkerchief.

" Here comes a flag of truce," cries one, " we are completely surrounded, and it is a demand for us to surrender."

" 'Tis not," cried another, " it is a captain of artillery from one of our own batteries," and this was correct.

" Is this North or South ? " cried he, as he approached.

" South," was the answer.

" All right.　Is it the 2nd brigade ? "

" Yes."

" Was it you I fired into some time ago ? "

" It was."

He then explained that since the time we had marched off to open the battle at noon, he with the other two batteries had been awaiting orders but had got none.　He had watched the hard fighting throughout the afternoon, but could not distinguish friend from foe.　And it was when we had changed front and turned round to fight the enemy on our right and rear, that he mistook us for the enemy and fired upon us.

He had seen or heard nothing of M'Culloch, M'Intosh, Hebert, or any of the field officers of our brigade, and no orders had come to him or to the other batteries, or to the 1st and 3rd brigades that he knew of.　There was some terrible mistake or mishap somewhere, and he could wait no longer but must gallop back to his post in case some orders should arrive in his absence.

It was now near sunset, and it was freezing hard and getting very cold, and the little water we had in our canteens was frozen, and whether it is from inhaling the smoke of the powder or from the general excitement or perhaps both I do not know, but thirst is generally very prevalent on a field of battle.

The lull in the fighting continued, and no further attacks were made.　The main body of the enemy on our left and front, probably not knowing the weakness of our force, did not seem inclined to come from their strong position and attack us, while it was quite possible for the smaller force on our right and rear to pass across our rear and join their friends.

I again proposed to the officers to go out and reconnoitre on our right and rear, and try to find if the enemy was still in force, but, to tell the truth, my real object was to try and get some water and perhaps something to eat from the enemy's haversacks, which were lying on the ground.　I was allowed to go, but was ordered to take a few men with me so that some of us might get back to report.　I took about 10 men with me and proceeded cautiously.　The men, who as well as myself had an eye to some grub, as they called it, helped themselves from the haversacks of the enemy's dead as we passed on, and within the thicker part of the wood it was not so cold, and the water in the canteens not being frozen, the men decanted it into their own canteens.

When we got near the place where we expected the enemy to be, we saw a wounded man of the enemy sitting on the ground leaning his back against a tree. He was wounded in the leg and unable to walk, and he asked us for some water. Thinking to get some information out of him, I asked him why he asked from us when his friends were close by, pointing in the direction I supposed them to be. He said they were gone, he supposed, to join the main army if they could get past our forces. One of my men brought him a canteen of water and a pretty well-filled haversack taken from one of his dead comrades, telling him at the same time to take care he did not lie, as we were going in that direction, and if he found he told a lie he would shoot him. The man pointed with his hand and said they had gone in that direction, but that was all he could say about them, and he was afraid he would die of cold if left there. We could not help him, but some of the men cut some of the heavy coats off his dead comrades and gave him to wrap round him, still assuring him that they would shoot him if they found he had told a lie. I tried to get some further information out of him but could not.

We left this man and went on a little further, being now more confident. We soon came to a place where a large force had been shortly before. The snow, which lay here and there in patches, was much trampled, and there was appearance of a large body of horse having been there recently, probably that was where the cavalry had assembled before charging us, but all seemed to have gone. Just then we heard firing again where we had left our friends, and we hastened back. The firing was soon over, as it had not been much of an attack. On our way back we passed through the place where the heaviest of the fighting had been. The trees were thickly spotted with bullet marks, but those which had come against us were mostly high up and above the level of our heads, while those that had gone from us, though much less in number, were lower down and within five feet of the ground.

On the way back my men picked up some of the arms from the field—those of the enemy being mostly Enfield rifles, Belgian rifles, and Colt repeating rifles, the two former with raised sights, all set for 200 yards.

We got back and reported what we had seen. It was now pretty certain that the enemy had gone from our right and rear. But all eyes were now fixed on a body of cavalry that

was forming on the fields at a distance on our right. Was
this going to be another charge down upon us ? It was now
getting dark and it was difficult to make out their flag. Some
were sure it was our own men, a part of the 1st brigade. I
knew that they had not come out of the wood where we had
seen traces of the enemy's cavalry ; but far beyond that and
near the place where we had left the 1st and 3rd brigades
at noon. I volunteered to go with my party and reconnoitre,
keeping within the wood. I did not wait for answer, but
started off, tired as we were, but glad to get anything to keep
us in heat. We passed along keeping within the wood until
near to them, when we peeped out, and could see their flag
plainly, and I think for the first time in my life, I hailed with
joy sincere the Confederate flag. We went out towards them,
and two officers rode forward to meet us, when we told them
who we were, and pointed to where the 2nd brigade was.
They started at the gallop towards it, while we followed
leisurely.

When we got back the two officers were in earnest and
serious conversation with the officers of our brigade. The
troops we had seen turned out to be the 2nd Texas Cavalry,
and this was their colonel and another officer that had ridden
out to meet us.

After some serious consultation between them and our
officers it was decided to form up the remains of the brigade
and retire from this position. It was now pretty dark, and
getting the men together was a little difficult. I missed about
24 out of the company, three of whom I knew to be dead,
and five were present wounded, and had got mounted on
horses which had been caught riderless—quite a number of
our wounded, all over the brigade were now mounted on the
fine cavalry horses which had fallen into our hands.

As we left the field the cries of the wounded imploring not
to be left to die of cold was heartrending, and a halt was
made for a party to volunteer to go without arms and attend
to them, taking the chance of being made prisoners by the
enemy. After consulting with Lieutenant G., I gave the
names of the missing, and those I supposed to be on the
ground wounded, and we sent four men to look after them,
Lieutenant G. saying he would take the responsibility without
anyone's orders. I remarked at the time that I feared that
we had now no longer at our head a general who knew his

duty, and could treat with the enemy as at Oakhill on such matters. Lieutenant G. pulled me by the arm, saying—"Hush, man; don't talk that way."

"I will talk that way," said I, bitterly; "I fear the worst for Generals M'Culloch and M'Intosh, and if they are gone there is not a general left worth the name, and has there been anything like generalship here to-day, or throughout any part of this campaign?"

"W.," said he, "you are well off at not being hampered by a commission; if I were as free as you I might talk the same way about this campaign, but let me tell you one thing, and I don't want you to say anything about it to the men, but this is certain—M'Culloch is dead, M'Intosh is dead; they both fell about the first opening of the fire. Hebert is missing, Major T. is missing, every field officer in the brigade is hors de combat. Colonel M'C. is wounded, Colonel M'N. is wounded, and a great many other officers are wounded or missing; and I don't know who now commands the brigade, or even the regiment."

"Where did you hear this?" said I.

"From Colonel ——— of the 2nd Texas Cavalry; and there is said to be more bad news, besides that."

"What is that?" said I.

"The 3rd brigade is broken up, and a lot of them gone away."

"Gone away! How do you mean?"

"Skedaddled, I suppose," said he.

"Well," said I, "if M'Culloch and M'Intosh are gone, good-bye to the Army of the West."

"That is the way," continued he, "that we were not reinforced. The 1st and 3rd brigades, and the three batteries of artillery have been lying idle all day awaiting orders, and no orders came to them, and I suppose Hebert and other officers, going to find out the cause, fell into the hands of the enemy."

"And where," said I, "was the Commander-in-Chief Van Dorn, who should be seeing to everything? Will he be down also, that there was no one to see to how things were going on in this part of the field?"

"Oh, that I don't know," said he; "there seems to be something wrong somewhere."

It was now dark, but the cannonade on our left and the enemy's right was still raging furiously, suggesting that there must be a good many pieces of artillery on both sides. The darkness of the night, the bleak moaning of the cold wind, and the continued roar of artillery would have suggested a theme for a weird romancer, but we saw no romance about it. We felt it bitterly cold, and the heavy fire of the artillery we considered was little more than a gross waste of ammunition.

We now took a position near the Bentonville road to await orders, but we were forbidden to make fires lest the enemy should observe us. A party was sent to bring up our over-coats and blankets from the place where we had stripped before going into battle. They returned with the unwelcome news that everything had been carried off, and we were left without overcoats or blankets, and the night was bitter cold.

We then insisted on making fires, as better be killed by the enemy than be frozen to death. This was then allowed and a guard thrown out. Large fires were made, and the men tried to get a little sleep, but that was impossible, for when their clothes were burning on one side the other side was freezing, and they had to keep turning round like a roast on a spit to keep from being frozen. Darkness had now stopped the fighting and all was still. About two hours after we had lighted the fires the alarm was spread that we were attacked, and some firing was heard, and all jumped up and seized their arms. It turned out, however, to be a false alarm. The cause of the alarm was this: Some of the men, suffering from the intense cold, remembered that they had seen in the enemy's camp plenty of blankets and overcoats, and slipping quietly off returned to the battlefield in the darkness, and having collected some blankets and equipping themselves in the enemy's overcoats they were returning with their booty, when one of the pickets, seeing what he naturally took by their greatcoats to be a party of Federals approaching, fired his piece and gave the alarm, other pickets doing the same, and hence the commotion.

All was soon quiet again, but before they were fairly settled down orders came for the whole force to come round and join Price's army on the Elkhorn road. This, though not more than three miles in a direct line, was about eight miles round by road.

The men got up staggering with fatigue and half-dead with cold and hunger, but it was better for them, as the march would bring heat into them. The column was formed, the prisoners we had captured were spread along between our files, and we marched along doggedly enough. The two prisoners next to me and under my charge were cavalrymen who had tumbled into our ranks when their horses fell. Some attempts were made at conversation as we trudged along, but it was difficult to keep it up; they were in no mood for conversation, neither were we. This was now the second night of the fighting, and the battle seemed to be as far from being decided as ever.

At length we came to a halt. We were relieved of the prisoners, and, as it would be an hour or two until daylight, we might lie down and rest. We lay down by the side of the road. Our company happened to be at a place where some rocks overhung the road, which broke off the biting winds, and we huddled close at the foot of the rocks and dozed a little in a sort of stupor.

At the first appearance of dawn the artillery burst forth again, and we rose up with joints stiffened with cold and fatigue and in no great condition or inclination to renew the fighting; nevertheless, not a murmur was heard, and everyone moved mechanically to his duty.

While we were awaiting orders the 1st brigade and the artillery, who had chafed at having to lie idle on the previous day while we were sore harassed, pushed past us to get to the front, cheering us as they passed and crying to us that we had borne the brunt of the battle yesterday, and they would take it to-day. Brave and gallant fellows were those of the 1st brigade and the artillery, but they had lost their gallant leader, the brave M'Intosh. But where was the 3rd brigade? Some of them, including some of the Indians, came up in broken parties and attached themselves to the 1st and 2nd brigades. But where was the gallant General Pike, the political patriot and the flower of Arkansas chivalry? That question I cannot answer, for I never learned, and it would not do to credit all the strictures I heard passed on his action at the time, although it might be satisfactorily explained for anything we knew.

Our ammunition being nearly exhausted, it was necessary that we should get a fresh supply before going into action, and we were moved forward to a place where we were to get it served out.

We passed over a place where there seemed to have been heavy fighting on the previous day; at least there appeared to

U

have been heavy damage done by artillery. The ground was ploughed up with shot and strewn with fragments of shells; dead horses, broken caissons and waggons, and other debris lay scattered about. At last we came to the wreck of some of the enemy's ammunition waggons, where several boxes of small arms ammunition were lying open and the cartridges scattered about, and the men were told to help themselves. Our company, however, was unfortunate, as the cartridges were all for a larger calibre than our rifles, and no cartridges were found suitable for Springfield rifles. On examining the pouches, however, we found that we had an average left of about fifteen rounds to each man. We took some of the nearest size in our pockets, intending to pare the bullets down if we got time.

The battle was now raging furiously, and our three batteries having joined in, added at least a good deal more to the noise. We were marched hither and thither, and left standing sometimes in the range of the artillery fire and sometimes out of it, no one seeming to know where we were to go or what we were to do. We saw some of the 1st brigade who were not yet led into battle, and did not know the position of the enemy; and there seemed to be no one able to tell them or direct them in any way, and they had just been told to be in readiness and await orders, and they were getting irritated and impatient.

We were at last taken to an open position, where we were told to be in readiness to fall in. Here we could see some distance over where the fighting was going on. There was an open field in front, and in the wood on each side of it and beyond it the fighting was going on; but, except the noise of the firing and the smoke issuing from the trees, we could ascertain nothing. Numbers of the Indians on horseback were flying backwards and forwards in the open field, but, whether they were going messages, or seeking employment, or what they were doing or trying to do we could not find out.

A short distance from us, and on the wooded ridge which bounded the field on one side, our three batteries had taken up positions and had singled out the enemy's batteries and opened fire upon them, and were keeping up a sort of artillery duel; while the enemy, replying to them and knowing there must be infantry near to support them, sent a good deal of their shot our way.

I think there is nothing so galling to troops as to have to stand still under an artillery fire, even though that fire be comparatively harmless, while other troops around them are actively engaged. Our men, however, at the time were too jaded to mind it much. They sat down on the ground, ate up the last of the rations they had taken from the enemy's haversacks on the previous day, smoked, and the sun now shining out warm many of them lay down and fell asleep.

About 10 o'clock the firing from the artillery got very heavy, as also the fire from the small arms, and up to about 11 o'clock the battle raged furiously. We supposed the 1st brigade had now got engaged, and we would be called up immediately; but still there was no appearance of any orders, and several small detachments of troops which we did not know were posted near us also awaiting orders.

Towards noon there was a sort of lull in the firing, and we heard cheering and counter-cheering, and then the fire was again very heavy for a short time. Our men now began to get impatient.

Shortly after mid-day the fire of the artillery again slackened and we noticed the battery nearest to us had stopped firing altogether. Knowing this to be Captain R.'s battery, who had ridden over to us on the previous day, I remarked to Lieutenant G. that if I thought we would not be likely to fall in soon I would go over to him, and see if I could get any news.

" Oh, hang it," cried he, " I believe we may lie here all day. I don't believe Van Dorn knows anything about us, or "——

" Or about anything else, you were going to say," said I, reminding him of his checking my remarks on the previous day.

" Well," cried he, half laughing, half irritated, " I do believe he has not got his army in hand at all, and he is making a regular botch of this fight; away you go, and see if you can learn anything about how things are going; you will see us if we are marched off."

I hastened over to the battery; the men were sitting down on the ground, and Captain R. was looking round with his glass. On seeing me he cried out :—

" Where are you from ? "

" The 3rd Louisiana," said I, " don't you remember yesterday ? "

"Oh, yes," said he, "I remember. Where is your regiment?"

"Over there," said I, "but what is the matter? Are you silenced?"

"Silenced! No, d——n it," said he, "I am just waiting for the guns to cool a little; besides, I am short of long range ammunition; I have given them the last of my round-shot, shells, and shrapnels—I have grape and canister left, but that is of no use at this distance. I have sent to see if I cannot get a supply, or orders, but have got neither. What is your regiment doing to-day?"

"Doing nothing," said I, "standing all day awaiting orders."

"Confound it," said he, "that is what the half of the army has been doing all through this fight. I got no orders; I just came here and took up this position, and pitched in. I silenced one battery down there, and I could do something with yon fellows on the side of the hill if I could get some long range ammunition, but there seems to be nobody to attend to anything!"

I then asked him if he had any idea how things were going.

"No," said he, "I have not; I suppose you know that Ben has been killed?"

"Yes," said I, "and M'Intosh also."

"I tell you what it is, sergeant," said he, "if we gain a complete victory here to-day, which I have my doubts about, it will be dearly bought with the loss of these two men."

I agreed with him, and took my leave.

As I walked back to where the regiment lay, the firing was becoming gradually less. When I got to our company, one or two officers from other companies were sitting with them. I told them all I had heard, and that Captain R. had never got any orders, but took up position and opened fire of his own accord.

What could be the meaning of this? was now the conjecture.

"Perhaps," said one, "Van Dorn is still sick."

"No," said another, "he was all right yesterday."

"I heard," said another, "that Price was killed this morning."

"Oh, that is quite true," said Tim D., "but he is only wounded."

" Oh, Tim, an Irish bull again," and they all laughed.
Tim was a little irritated at their laughing at him, and did
not think it was a time for laughing, and retorted by saying
that they were just laughing for a brag, and wanted to make
believe they were laughing when they were not laughing at
all.

The firing, which had been getting slack on both sides, had
now nearly died away, and there were reports going that
ammunition was about spent on both sides. We now expected
to be called on at once, and some little preparations were made,
but still no orders came.

It was now past one o'clock, the firing had entirely ceased,
and everything had been quiet for the last half-hour, when an
aide-de-camp came along and delivered some orders.

We did not know who was in command of the brigade ; the
regiment was commanded for the time by the senior captain,
and orders were given to the company on the right to fall in,
and the rest to follow the " aide " riding at the head to act as
guide.   We were now countermarched by the way we had
come. This did not look like going into battle, but we were
told that the enemy were retreating by their left flank and
would pass over the ground where we had fought yesterday,
and would likely try to follow the Bentonville road and get
northwards towards Keatsville, and that we were going to cut
them off and capture their artillery and baggage trains. This
seemed likely enough, and if the enemy had been defeated it
was the only way they could retreat, and we would have a fair
chance of at least cutting off their baggage trains. We began
to think that Van Dorn was not such a bad general after all.

We marched along among traces of the battle and through
several passages where the enemy had cut down trees to form
abatis, but never came out to the Elkhorn road. We could
not tell where we were or were being led to, but by the sun I
thought we were making a detour ; and after about two hours
we seemed to be going to the eastwards and getting further
away from the battlefield, and here we began to join with other
parts of the army, and the aide-de-camp left us.

We thought we should be up to near the Keatsville road by
this time if we had been going in that direction. Lieutenant
G. remarked to me that this looked strange ; I thought so
too.

A battery of artillery was moving along before us, the men

sitting on the guns, their faces blackened with powder. We did not know what battery it was, but away before it we saw other batteries and horse and foot moving slowly along. Lieutenant G. went away forward to see if he could gain any information. In a short time he came back saying, "It is now no use to try and say anything else about it. They may call it what they like, but it is a retreat, and nothing else, but don't say anything about it, or there will be a regular mutiny."

CHAPTER XXIII.

THIS movement soon got to be discussed all along the line. It
was denied that it was a retreat, and it was asserted to have
been a victory. The enemy was said to have been beaten, but
that Van Dorn could not wait to cut them off or pursue them,
as he had orders to hurry with his troops to join the Army of
the Centre, on the Mississippi, where we had been preparing to
go when we were hurried out of winter quarters by the advance
of the army we had just fought. It was also whispered that
Van Dorn had fought this battle on his own responsibility and
against orders; that his orders had been that the Western
States were to be abandoned, and the Army of the West was
to join the Army of the Centre at Memphis. Such were the
arguments all along the line.

Whatever might have been the intention it was clear enough
that there had been a shameful piece of bungling and mismanagement, and the discontent and clamour became general,
and everyone was disgusted. One or two companies, which
were composed largely of Irish, being dissatisfied at not getting
to fight it out with the enemy, commenced to fight amongst
themselves, and a regular melee broke out a short distance in
front of us. The rioters were, however, pushed on by those
behind, and not allowed to block up the way with their fighting. As we came up to the place one man was lying senseless
by the side of the path, and another was coolly trying to
straighten the barrel of his musket, which he had bent into
the form of a crescent by striking the former over the head
with it. He was now pushing the muzzle down into the
ground and trying to bend it back again, amidst the laughter
of our boys, who cried out, "Never mind it, Paddy; it will
now do to shoot round the corners."

We at last came to a halt for the night, but our mortification may be imagined when we found that we were quite away from any road, and entirely cut off from our trains or any means of getting supplies, having made a circuit and fought round the rear of the enemy, while our supply waggons, if we had any on the way, must be far away on the other road with the enemy between us and them. Hungry as we were there was no possibility of getting anything to eat for this night. The men were told that they must make it out for another night, and to-morrow we would march to a place where the supply waggons would meet us by another road across the country. The men did not place much faith in the exertions of the commissary, but there was no help for it. They were also worn out with fatigue and want of sleep, and it was now impossible to obtain any sleep on account of the cold. The men had neither blankets nor overcoats, except a few they had picked up on the battlefield.

The place where we bivouacked was rather a sheltered spot, and there was a good deal of dry grass and leaves, and I and a few more huddled close under a large fallen tree, beside which there was a good quantity of this dry grass and leaves. We found this rather a snug place, and free from the cold biting wind, and we were soon asleep. We had slept for several hours when, sometime after midnight, I was awakened by the others jumping up alarmed, and crying to get up quick, as we were lying among rattlesnakes !

We sprang up quicker than if it had been the enemy, when one of the boys declared that he had heard one rattle close to his head ; and the whole bivouac was roused, seizing their arms, thinking we had been attacked by the enemy.

When the cause of the alarm became known some of our comrades laughed at us, and said, " Who ever heard of rattle-snakes being abroad in such cold weather ?" But then it was known that they were very plentiful in this district ; and it was just in such places that they hid themselves in cold weather ; and it was extremely likely that there might be some of them about the old tree. Nothing could induce any of us to lie down again, and the others beat the ground well, in the neighbourhood of their bivouacs.

We stood shivering in the cold, and sleepy, and considered that it was too bad, after all the privations of the last few days, we should be put out of our humble bed by these varmints ; and, being still in fighting humour, we determined upon revenge. Accordingly dry grass and dry branches of trees were got, and packed all round and under the old tree and set fire to, determined to make the place hot for the snakes. This at least warmed us and gave some amusement, while the boys stood round with their sabres ready to slay the first snake that should attempt to come out. None came out—at least, that we saw, although it is possible some may have escaped in the darkness. From what we learned of the place it was extremely probable that such reptiles may have been there, and this warned us to be more careful in future when selecting our bivouacs.

The alarm, however, had done us good; we had had a few hours' sleep, and the excitement had warmed us and caused our blood to circulate, and we stood by the fire and smoked and discussed the results of the late battle until daylight.

When daylight appeared we moved on again. There was no general road but rude bridle paths through the woods, and the country was very thinly settled, and for miles at a time not the slightest sign of a human habitation. How the artillery got along seems a mystery to me, although details were made to clear and make roads for them and get the heavy caissons over bad places. We understood that our march that day would not be a long one and that we should halt at a place where our supply waggons would meet us, and we would rest there a day or two and reorganise. What should be done after that was now the conjecture and topic of discussion.

After a short march, or rather, struggle, through the rough country we came in the afternoon to an open space on the banks of a stony creek, where there was some appearance of the country having been inhabited and where some apologies for roads crossed each other. By one of these roads our supply waggons were expected to come, but there was not yet any appearance of them. However, it was allowed that they had scarcely time to be forward.

Near the place where our regiment rested there were some buildings, including a grist mill, but the inhabitants had all fled, and the farm and mill were deserted. One or two pigs and some poultry, which seemed not to have had the sagacity of their owners, remained behind, and soon fell victims to their simplicity.

The mill was of the kind driven by steam-power, and was

apparently in working condition, and a quantity of Indian corn in ear lay in the building.

A call was made for engineers to get steam up and the mill set agoing, and a number of men set to shell the corn off the husks. The mill was soon at work and a quantity of meal ground, and in a few hours a small supply of meal was served out to each man. The question now was how to cook it; but necessity is the mother of inventions. The creek was a complete mass of stones, granite boulders of all sizes. The men selected stones of a suitable size having a flat or hollow side. These stones they propped up on others, with the flat or hollow side uppermost. In this hollow part they placed their meal, and with their canteens they took water from the creek and mixed up their meal into dough, and the banks of the creek abounding with dead trees they took dry wood and made fires under and round about the stones in order that they would get hot and so bake the mixture into bread.

Along this tortuous creek for more than a mile the stream was lit up with this primitive system of cooking, while here and there pieces of the unfortunate pigs were being roasted on the points of sticks, the grease, by way of economy, being dropped on the bread, while a pinch of salt would that night have been worth a general's ransom. Some had devoured their bread when it was little more than warm through, not admitting their impatience, but declaring that the food was more nutritious that way; and it was just as well for them too, for in the midst of their festival an alarm was got up that we were attacked by the enemy, and what seemed a firing was heard at different parts along the creek. The men immediately left their cooking and seized their arms, but it turned out to be a false alarm, and the cause of it was soon discovered.

The large granite boulders on which they were baking their bread, having got heated, began to expand and burst with violent explosions equal to the report of a musket, and as the creek did not run in a straight line, but was so crooked that very little of it could be seen from one place, the reports were heard in various directions resembling a firing of musketry, and thus caused the alarm. As soon as the cause of alarm was discovered a quick rush was made back to save the bread which with the splitting of the stones was thrown into the fire and often lost or picked up in fragments from the ashes.

This scare, like many others, caused some fun and served

the purpose of keeping up the spirits of the men and adding something to their experience in the way of making bread. This rude and scanty allowance was soon eaten up. The mill was kept going till all the corn that could be procured was ground, so as to give something for the following day in case the supply waggons did not get forward.

As we were to remain here for a day or two, the mill and the houses were appropriated for such as were sick or suffering from severe privation or over fatigue. Our company, remembering last night, determined to keep out of the company of rattlesnakes, and gathered dry branches, grass, and leaves, and made a bivouac among the stones in the bed of the creek. We were cautioned that the creek might rise in the night and flood us out or carry us away, but we preferred water to rattlesnakes, and determined to chance it. Fortunately the creek did not rise, and we got a good night's rest, and those who thought to have a laugh at our expense were disappointed.

In the morning the senior captain present having temporarily taken command of the regiment, each orderly-sergeant or other qualified officer was ordered to send in a report of his company, killed, wounded, and missing, and the number present for duty, and number of rounds of ammunition to each.

My report was made out so far as I knew : killed three ; wounded, seven ; missing, 13, including the captain and four sent to see after the wounded and missing at the place where we had fought on the seventh, and from whom we had no report. Present, one lieutenant, 31 non-commissioned officers and men, and two emergency men.

It was found that the total loss the regiment had sustained in killed, wounded, and missing, was about 270, but some of those were supposed to have straggled and would yet come up.

The emergency men were now allowed to go home, and it was intimated that a party was going to be sent to the enemy's camp under a flag of truce to negotiate for an exchange of prisoners. I applied to get on that party and was selected. The party, as near as I can recollect, consisted of one field-officer and two captains, with an escort of one lieutenant, two sergeants, and 24 privates. The latter were detailed from different companies ; of course some care had to be exercised in the selection of the men for a mission of this kind, and to have them of good appearance, shrewd and discreet.

The party was made up, arms inspected, men and equipments made to show well, and the party set out about three o'clock in the afternoon, intending to reach the enemy's camp before sunset. We found they had fallen back from their former position, and had taken up a position on the Keatsville road, nearer to the Missouri boundary line. It was near sunset when we approached their picket-guard. On seeing the flag of truce a party came out to meet us bearing also a flag of truce.

They insisted on the usual formality of blindfolding being gone through as we passed into their camp. Of course we considered this an absurd formality in a field camp, but, as it was a mere form and no actual blindfolding, we acceded to the ceremony. By the time we got to their general headquarters it was dark.

The officers were received into a marquee, where they had a consultation, and soon returned with the intelligence that negotiations could not be proceeded with that night, but that the truce party would be furnished with quarters and provisions for the night, and negotiations would be proceeded with in the morning.

Some tents were provided for our accommodation, and our party on giving their parole were allowed to accept the hospitality of any mess that would invite them to sup with them. We had abundance of invitations, and they treated us very well, and we spent quite a pleasant night.

In the morning after guard mounting the negotiations took place at the head-quarters of the Federal generals. The front of a marquee was thrown open, and there sat several officers, conspicuous among whom was General Siegel.

General Siegel was a German, and had been, as we understood, an officer in the Prussian army. He spoke with a strong German accent, and seemed to be in remarkable good humour as he thus addressed our officers :—

"Come away, gentlemen, I am very glad to see you. I understand you come to arrange about an exchange of prisoners."

Our officer replied that he presumed that something on this subject had already passed between them and his superiors, and he had only to furnish them with a correct statement of what prisoners we had in our hands; and as he supposed the number they had of ours was about equal, he would like to get a statement of them and their rank, that they might arrange for a cartel of exchange.

A list of the prisoners they had of ours was then produced, and in it were found the names of Colonel Hebert, Major T., the captain of our company and several other officers—the total number being about 265.

We had of theirs about 280, but the proportion of officers was rather less. We had, however, of theirs two lieutenant-colonels.

Our officer now said that he found they had an officer of ours who exceeded him in rank, and he would prefer to transfer to him the power to negotiate with them, and arrange the cartel. But another officer, who I took to be General Curtis, replied that they could not treat with a prisoner, no matter what his rank might be. Our officer then proposed to arrange for the exchange of Colonel Hebert, and when exchanged he could negotiate with them. They hesitated, and, after some consultation, asked what we proposed to give in exchange for him. Our officer said he was a colonel, and they had also a major of ours, while we had of theirs two lieutenant-colonels, which he considered would be a fair exchange for a colonel and a major.

General Siegel, who seemed inclined to have a joke, now replied :—

" I admit that is a cartel acknowledged by the rules of war, but there is one other thing which you must take into consideration. You Southerners say that one Southerner can whip three Northerners, which means that one Southerner is worth three Northerners ; therefore, it will be necessary for you to give in exchange for your colonel three colonels, and for your major three majors."

This sally of General Siegel, which he delivered with the utmost good humour in his German accent, caused a general laugh and applause, in which our officers joined, and who now said they would be willing to forego that distinction at present and be valued upon equal terms.

After some discussion, it was agreed that the two lieutenant-colonels should be brought to the Federal camp immediately and exchanged for Colonel Hebert and Major T. ; and then a general exchange of prisoners would be effected, although I am not sure how it was carried out, as I and several of the escort now asked leave to go and see our friends who were prisoners. This would not be allowed, unless we were accompanied by an officer, as no private talk would be allowed. Oh, certainly not, we wished no private talk, and would be glad to have their officers accompany us. We were permitted to go, several officers accompanying us. We rather invited them to come with us. The prisoners were glad to see us, and hear that they were likely soon to be exchanged. There was a good deal of laughing and joking.

The adjutant of one of the Arkansas regiments was among the prisoners, and he cried out, " I hope you have got an adjutant to exchange for me ; " whilst another cried out, " I hope you have got a corporal to exchange for me ; " and one cried out in a joking way, " I hope you have got a private of the very highest class to exchange for me."

" Oh," said one of the Federal officers, " you must come under Siegel's cartel, and we must have three privates in exchange for you," and there was a good deal of joking of this kind. The men said they were glad that there was a prospect of their being soon exchanged, although they could not complain of their treatment.

A sergeant of one of the other companies of our regiment asked me when I thought they would get free. I told him I did not know, but I thought it would not be long ; but, seeing a Federal officer close by, listening to every word, I continued talking seriously, and told him that he must just submit to it for a few days ; their treatment was not so bad after all. I had seen the food they were getting, and really, as prisoners, they could not complain of it, although, of course, it was not equal to the good living they would have if they were with their regiment, but——

" Oh, stop there," cried the officer as he laughed outright, " that will do for you. I expect our boys will be fat when they come back from such high living as they will be having among the Confeds."

I had to laugh myself, and all around could not help joining. But the prisoners took the hint that they were perhaps just as well where they were for a few days, though, of course, they always tried to maintain that the Confederate army was well supplied with provisions.

We now prepared to take our departure, and the blind-folding process was again gone through, and we were conducted beyond their pickets, where we bid each other good-bye until the next cannon shot, and we made our way back to where we had left our wretched and starving army on the previous day.

As we marched along we could now talk more freely of what we saw and thought of things in the Federal camp. All the others seemed to have learned and observed more than I did. The enemy did not appear to have regarded the issue of the battle as being very favourable to them ; and if as a victory regarded it as a very doubtful one. They could not account for us withdrawing from the field, and could not tell where we had gone, and throughout the afternoon of the 8th and part of the 9th they had been expecting us to attack them from some other point, and as soon as they found that we had withdrawn from their rear they fell back to their present position.

The action of Van Dorn seemed to us inexplicable, and it was privately thought and expressed that he had calculated upon Price and M'Culloch to win the battle for him, and left the actual conduct of the action to them ; and that when M'Culloch and M'Intosh were killed he found the right wing without a leader, although not demoralized, ready and eager to fight ; but, instead of taking command of it himself, he left it standing idle, while he himself remained with Price's division on the left wing instead of looking over the whole field.

It was his first battle, and he certainly could not handle his army after those whom he had expected to do it for him were killed. Such were the comments that were quietly whispered, and perhaps there was some truth in them, though of course they were not spoken openly. And Van Dorn had always plenty to blow his trumpet for him, as a man in power with offices and gifts at command seldom lacks abundance of friends and supporters.

When we got back to the army we were mortified that no supplies had come, and there was now no likelihood or possibility of any coming by that road. What was now to be done ? was the question asked. We were to proceed to Van Buren across the country the best way we could. Price's army had already gone on before us.

Here was a position to be in. The distance to Van Büren in a direct line was about 90 miles. This would have been nothing if there had been anything like a good road and tolerable weather, but to reach it we might have to traverse double that distance. White River and its many tributaries was in the way. There were no roads or bridges; the country was mostly hills covered with scrub oaks, rocks, rivers, and creeks, and very sparsely settled, and so poor, as some of the men expressed it, that turkey buzzards would not fly over it; and the weather had now set in worse than the dead of winter —cold biting winds, sleet, frost, and snow. We had no guide to show us the best way to get through. Price's army had preceded us; but if they did any good by opening a path, they would do us a great deal of harm by clearing the country of everything that could be eaten by man or beast, even to the last acorn, which seemed to be the only thing which the country produced.

But where was the man who had brought the army into this wretched predicament? Van Dorn had not been seen since the third day after we had left Boston Mountain to attack the enemy, and it was whispered that he did not want to show himself to the troops. Be that as it may, I must say that I never saw him until some two months afterwards at Corinth. Had he shown himself to this division of the army at this time, I question much whether he would have been greeted with enthusiastic cheers.

But this was not our business; we had now the march before us, and we must undertake it, without provisions, without tents or cooking utensils, without blankets or over-coats, and our thin clothing now worn and ragged. I have never seen or read either in newspaper or history any details of this miniature Moscow retreat. It was, perhaps, one of those black or blurred pages in history that is unreadable, and is best to be torn out.

We proceeded to scramble along the best way we could, wading through creeks and rivers and scrambling over rocks and through brushwood. At night we kindled large fires and took off our wet clothes, wrung the water out of them, and dried them the best way we could. Occasionally we passed a small settlement from which the inhabitants had fled, but everything had been carried away by Price's army. In the gardens we sometimes found the remains of some turnips or onions, which were eagerly dug out of the ground with our sabres and eaten raw. Everything like military order of march was at an end, but the battalions and companies kept in their places, and discipline was still maintained, although to leave the line in search of something to eat could no longer be strictly forbidden. Several times it was found that we had taken the wrong road and had to turn back. Sometimes we passed through rather better tracts of country which had been settled, but the few settlers had all fled from their homes and the houses were deserted, and everything in the shape of food had been taken by Price's troops.

One day I went into the house of a farm which seemed somewhat of the better class. I found it deserted and completely gutted, and everything in the way of food within or without the house had been carried away, although there were indications of plenty having been not long before. In the kitchen I found a pail containing some apple-parings, off which I was making a hearty meal, while one of our young lads was scraping with great energy the bottom and sides of a very large pot or boiler in which some Indian-meal porridge, or mush, as it is called, had been boiled some days before, and the cook had humanely omitted to clean the pot, and had left some porridge sticking to the sides. I looked down upon the poor boy ; his starved appearance and sunken eyes told how hunger and privation were telling upon him.

"Well, how are you getting on, Andrew ?" said I.

Andrew, who had now polished the inside of the pot and had turned his attention to the outside, where a quantity of the stuff had stuck by the pot boiling over, looked up.

"Sergeant," said he, "I think there is nothing in the whole world so good as just cold mush off the pot. I think if I was to be the president of the Confederate States I would have plenty of cold mush."

"Andrew," said I, "you would perhaps not then be blessed with such a good appetite as you have to-day—but shut that door quick ! "

A tolerably good-looking fowl, which seemed to have escaped from the care of its owner and the tender mercies of Price's men, and not getting its usual food, had seen the door open and like ourselves sought the kitchen for something to eat. But a fowl's necessity is sometimes man's opportunity. Andrew quickly shut the door, and the fowl was a prisoner. Andrew looked at me, wondering if I meant to steal it after the many lectures I had given the boys against anything like plundering.

"Yes," said I, "kill it, Andrew, 'tis a military necessity ; if the owner was here I would pay him for it in full, but we must have it. We will roast it over the camp-fire to-night, and you shall have a good share of it, as I see you are not out of the need of it."

The fowl was soon killed, stripped of its feathers, and cleaned to make it lighter to carry, and we started off with our prize. We had been somewhat in advance of the company, and we just joined them as they came up. Lieutenant G. said that as we had been so fortunate there might be something more to be got, as the country here seemed to be much richer than what we had been passing through for the last three days, and showed some signs of cultivation. He suggested that three or four men should start off on a tour to forage for the whole company.

Four were immediately sent off to get food, "honestly if they could, but at all events to get it." All these sent were known to be good foragers, and if anything existed at all in the country, they would not come in empty. This was now the fourth day since we left the stony creek, and the men had tasted nothing but pieces of raw turnips, onions, and hard, dry Indian corn.

This came on a wretched day, sleet falling which froze as it fell, and every branch and twig was coated with ice, and our rags were frozen stiff about us.

At last we halted for the night, but we had much difficulty in getting fires started owing to everything being wet and coated with ice. Our officers always studied to make the halt for the night where there was plenty of old fence rails or other good firewood, and there was plenty here, and the fires, once started, were easily kept up,

Andrew now produced his fowl, which I chopped in pieces with my sabre, giving him a good piece for his share, and giving some of the weaker-looking boys a piece, which they stuck on the end of a pointed stick and roasted over the fire. We now anxiously awaited the return of our foraging party, and they came in about an hour after we halted. They did not come in empty. Their arrival caused both joy and laughter. It never rains but it pours. They were actually loaded down. One carried two geese, a turkey, a fowl, and a piece of bacon ; another had a young pig and a bag filled with turnips and potatoes, and a haversack full of salt ; the other two carried on two sticks a large boiler which would hold about 50 or 60 gallons, which they had found in the woods, where it had been used for boiling maple sugar or sorgho.

The boiler was set up on stones, water put into it and fire put under it, and the work of cleaning the pig, geese, and fowls was quickly gone through, and they, with the bacon, turnips, potatoes, and onions, were cut up and tumbled in, with salt sufficient.

What a splendid mess they were going to have! Each man generally carried a spoon in his pocket, and they began to sup the broth before it had been boiling many minutes. The snow kept falling, but they did not care; they were now happy, and, as usual, gloom and despondency were quickly turned into joy and merriment. They invited some men from the other companies to dine with them. They packed the wood on the fire, the cauldron bubbled, and they sung songs and danced round it like the witches in " Macbeth."

" Hallo! what is all this noise about?" cried a voice coming up out of the darkness.

" Come away, captain," cried a number of voices, as we recognised Captain R., of the artillery. " Come away and dine with us, captain. Have you got a spoon in your pocket?"

" Ah, that I have, and I will dine with you, too. What is this you have got?"

" Oh, everything, captain—geese, turkeys, pig, fowl, turnips, potatoes—a regular stew."

" Good gracious! where on earth did you get that big kettle?"

" Out in the woods, at a sorgho mill."

"And how did you get it here?"

" Carried it in."

" You are the boys," said the captain; " but that stew is splendid, and I have had a hard day's work. I have got all my pieces forward."

" Caissons and all?"

" Caissons and all," said the captain, " and two extra pieces, but I had to leave two behind."

" Had you to leave two of your guns behind?"

" Not two of my own guns," said the captain; " but I brought away four pieces belonging to the enemy, and I had to leave two of them behind near the stony creek; the roads were too bad to take them along."

" How did you come to get four of the enemy's guns ? "

" I can't tell; I came across them abandoned as I was coming away, and I tailed them on, but found them too much to bring along, and had to cast off two of them, but the enemy will never get them ; I put them where they won't find them."

" Did Price lose any of his guns ? "

" I don't think so."

" Then we have lost no guns at all ? "

" No ; we have gained two."

" And six that were burned and two that we spiked," said we ; " that will make 12 guns that the enemy has lost."

" Of course these two guns may be unspiked," said the captain, " but the six that were burned will have to be remounted, and likely require to be rebored or recast altogether."

" Then they must have had 12 guns that were *hors de combat* when we withdrew from the field. What do you think of this whole affair, captain ? "

" Oh, don't mention it ; I don't understand it at all. But I must away, and thank you for this splendid supper ; it is the best I have had since we came out of winter quarters ; " and he took his leave and went to join his corps.

The men hung round the fire and smoked ; but to get any sleep was impossible ; the sleet still fell, and they had to keep themselves from freezing.

All were glad when morning came, and we moved on again. The remains of the stew, being now boiled into a consistency like glue, the men put into their haversacks, while the grease came through and draggled them so much that some remarked that, if again reduced to a strait, they might boil their clothes and get good soup out of them.

It was well for us that we had got that one meal and some of the stew in our haversacks, for the whole of the next three days we passed through a wild, barren country where there was not a thing to be had in the way of food. The 1st brigade and the artillery having now parted off and gone by some other and longer route where they could obtain forage, it began to appear that we had gone in a wrong direction, and had to turn back on account of some river which we could not cross, and we lost about two days' march.

About the seventh night we halted on the sloping banks of a creek which ran at the bottom of a pretty deep valley. On the near side of the creek there was abundance of dry grass, making a fine place to bivouac; and, what was better, the weather had suddenly changed, and the afternoon and evening were warm and sultry. We expected to get some sleep to-night if the pangs of hunger would allow us. How the other companies were faring we were not sure, but supposed they had just their little chances same as ourselves.

Notwithstanding the wretchedness of our condition, there was throughout the whole of this trying campaign still kept up a continual animation by light merry-making. Joking was always the order of the day. The most disagreeable and trying privations were alleviated and smoothed over by turning them into a cause for laughter. If some became sullen and desponding, there were always some spirits who could by some comical expressions raise the merry laugh and incite good humour, and put animation into the men. At this mood Lieutenant G. was a perfect adept, and could excite mirth in the most trying circumstances.

When we came to a halt this evening things looked bad enough in the way of hunger. The men had a little dry Indian corn in their haversacks, which alone they had been chewing for the last two days. Nothing had been picked up on this day's march, and there was no chance of anything to eat for this night, and the joke was had recourse to again. This time it was to select the fattest man in the company to feed the rest upon, and a good deal of fun was being indulged in about who should be sacrificed, when temporary relief came from an unexpected quarter.

About sunset a stranger on horseback came along enquiring for the rifle company of the 3rd Louisiana regiment. Who could it be? He came up and enquired for a young man who had joined us at Fayetteville while we were in winter quarters. The young man was still with us and all right. This was his father, and he was glad to find his son all right; but he had heard of the wretched state of starvation the army was in, and he had prepared two good large bags of wheaten hoe cake, and laying them across his horse's back, he sought out the army. He had been three days looking for the regiment before he got to us, and he handed the bread to his son. The lad took out about a day's ration for himself, and handed the bread back to his father to divide among the company. This was divided over the company with the greatest care and exactitude, being about half a pound to each man. Never was a morsel higher prized; for of all things for sustaining strength on a long march, I think there is nothing equal to unleavened wheaten bread. And if ever a sincere benediction was bestowed upon a man, it was bestowed upon that old man that night.

It had now out of necessity become a question to be considered by us, as to how the little food we could pick up could be best applied, so as not merely to appease the cravings of hunger, but to sustain strength and enable us to reach the end of our journey.

Some thought it was best to be taken before lying down at night, as the cravings of hunger would not prevent sleep, and while it was being digested, the body was both strengthened and refreshed. Others thought it was objectionable to start on a journey with an empty stomach—especially as we had always been accustomed to take breakfast before proceeding on a march, and by doing that the body was fortified and strengthened for the day's toil.

I resolved to try the latter method, and reserve my bread for the followng morning. So I put it under the breast of my coat, buttoned it up, and having selected a comfortable place among the dry grass, which we now always took care to beat well from fear of rattlesnakes, I felt sure, from the warmness of the night, to get a good night's rest.

Overpowered with fatigue, sleep and hunger fought for the mastery. I was asleep, but that piece of bread stood before me, and I was trying to grasp it. Banquets of the finest food were before me, but somehow I could not reach them.

I found it was no use. I thought I was just wasting the only mild night in which a little sleep might be got. So I rose up, took my piece of bread, broke off about two-thirds of it, leaving a small piece for the morning, and ate it as I thought, in the most judicious and economical way—licking the flour with which it was coated off my black and dirty hands. I then took a drink of water from my canteen, and a smoke, and lay down again, and I was soon into a sweet sleep.

I must have slept about four or five hours, when I was awakened by the rain pouring down in torrents, and a tremendous thunderstorm, and I heard loud laughter, and shouts of "Stand and take it." Stand and take it, indeed, was the only thing we could do; anything like shelter was out of the question.

The camp fires were soon put out, and the water ran down the sloping banks of the creek so deep that many of us had to get up to the high ground at the top. Strange to say, plenty of the men slept on, with the terrible rain pouring on them, and we were stumbling over them as we made our way up to the high ground, picking our way by the aid of the lightning.

The storm continued for about two hours, when it ceased, and the men tried to light fires again to dry their clothes, but found it impossible ; everything was wet, and before any fire could be started, daylight had broken, which gave great relief, as we longed to resume the march.

I may say that the marching during the day was by far the pleasantest part of it, for to pass the nights when it was too wet or cold to sleep was exceedingly trying.

When daylight came, and we were about to proceed on our march, we found we were in something of a fix.

Our line of march was across the creek, and we had not followed the rules, which was that a creek should always be crossed and the troops to bivouac on the far side. This rule had been departed from at this time, because on the far side of the creek there was not for some distance any suitable place for bivouac-ing, besides creeks here were so plentiful, and had to be crossed so often, that if we got on the far side we were not far from the near side of another. However, in this case the meaning or object of the rule was very well demonstrated.

The creek, by the sudden storm, was swollen to a great extent, so that it was impossible to cross, and we could not proceed ; and if the enemy had been harassing our rear we would have been in the same position as the Israelites at the Red Sea. What was now to be done? No other route was possible ; we were pressed by starvation, and no food was to be obtained in the neighbourhood. It would be at least two days before the creek was passable, and if more rain fell it was quite uncertain when we might get across. There was only the remnant or wreck of the 2nd brigade here, but who was in command of it, or whether it had any commander, we did not know, every regiment seeming to act for itself, and every com-pany to act for itself.

After a consultation among the officers of our regiment, it was agreed that the regiment should separate and each com-pany act for itself, and get along the best way they could to Van Buren, and there join again.

Each company then started to shift for itself as they best could. The novelty of the thing was pleasing, as they were now comparatively free. Our company, amounting in the aggregate to 32, proceeded by itself. We had two axes which we carried along for cutting wood for fires, etc., but that was all the company property we had beyond our arms. We proceeded along the creek to see if there was any possibility of finding a place where we might effect a crossing by felling trees so as to fall across it.

We had some splendid fellows for such an emergency, who could handle the axe as well as the rifle, one of whom we called Canada, as he was a native of that country.

Some gigantic trees grew along the edge of the creek in some places, and soon one of them fell across the stream, but it went whirling away with the roaring torrent as if it had been chips. Another and another was cut, but all were carried away.

At length we came to a place where the creek was narrow and the banks high, but there did not seem to be any tree large enough and sufficiently near the bank to fall across, and at this narrow part all were eagerly looking for a tree that would, if felled, span the creek.

"Here, sergeant! here, sergeant," cried Tim D., in great ecstasy, "here is a fine one."

I hastened to where he was. "Where is it?" said I.

"Over yonder," said he, pointing to a tree on the opposite side of the creek, "if we could only manage to get over to cut it."

"You confounded fool," said I, "if we could only manage to get over to it, it would be of no use to us, because we would not want it."

"What is that?" cried some one.

"Oh, it is one of Tim's bulls," said I. "He proposes that we cross the river first, and then cut a tree on the other side."

"Throw him in the river!" cried two or three of the boys.

"Well, now, that was not what I said at all," cried Tim. "I said, There is a fine tree over there, and if some of yees would go over and cut it, we would all get over; and if you would just come and see the tree, you would say yourself that it was a splendid one."

"Then, go over and cut it;" cried two or three of the boys.

At that time Lieutenant G. and Canada, the axe-man, came

up; we looked across at the tree and pondered. "Well, certainly, if any one was on that side to cut that tree it would just fall across and make a splendid bridge. I wonder if there could be no means of getting one man across to cut it."

There was a place a little farther down, where the stream ran through a narrow chasm, where the banks were high on each side, and not quite 30 feet from bank to bank, but there were no trees near the place. It was suggested that we might get one of the tall ash trees, which grew higher up the bank, and carry it down, and raise it on end and let it fall across, and if it did not break it would be strong enough for some active fellow to straddle over upon, and then we could throw him over the axe to cut the tree.

"The very thing!" cried Canada, "and I will volunteer to cross on it." And he was off at once to select a suitable ash tree.

One was soon cut down and trimmed, and all hands carried it to the place, and a hole was dug in the ground with our sabres to put the thick end into, while the men got about it, and with the aid of long forked sticks got it raised to the perpendicular; and it was thrown across, and landed successfully on the other side.

The roaring torrent below looked rather trying to the nerves.

"Here, Tim," cried some of the boys, "go over now and cut the tree."

Tim said he would go, but, as he was no axe-man, he could not cut the tree.

"Then stand aside, you useless bog-trotter."

The end of the tree was firmly bedded, and held tight to keep it from rolling, while Canada straddled across, like Blondin, crossing Niagara Falls on the tight rope. He landed safely on the other side, amidst the cheers of the boys; while another immediately crossed after him, and we threw them over the two axes. Of course, they cried back in a joke, pretending to bid us goodbye, as they were going to proceed on and leave us, but we could not hear them for the roaring of the torrent.

They both set to work with a will and the tree, a very large one, soon fell across the creek, forming an excellent bridge, and in a few minutes all had scrambled over.

We ascended the banks on the opposite side, where we looked back and saw some of the other companies along on the banks, vainly searching for a place to cross. We gave a loud cheer to attract their attention. There was soon a commotion among them, and a cry of—" Hilloa, the rifles are over ! "

We pointed in the direction of where we had crossed, that they might see our bridge and make use of it, and we proceeded on our way.

" Now, don't yees see," said Tim D., " that I was right after all ; you talk about bulls and bog-trotters, but if it had not been for me you would all have been left behind."

" Why, what did you do ? "

" Well, it was my tree that was the right tree, and if it had not been the right tree you might all have been drowned in the river, and then you would have said that I had been right."

The boys laughed, but Tim did not see what they were laughing at. Tim's good nature and simplicity made him always a favourite, and the boys liked to joke with him.

The place where we crossed was away from any road or track, and we found ourselves in a tangled wood without any knowledge of where we were or which was the proper direction to take. The day was dark and cloudy, and we could not tell east from west. The wood was so tangled that we had to cut our way with our sabres. At length we came to a kind of road, which we followed for some distance to a place where it branched off in a fork, but we did not know which road to take ; both were about alike. We here held a consultation about what was best to be done, and it was arranged to divide the company into two sections—Lieutenant G. to take the one half and I should take the other half, and search the country for food.

We therefore separated, taking 15 men each, and branched off in the different roads.

With such a small party I conceived it would not be difficult to pick up sufficient food to sustain us until we got to Van Buren ; but, as we were so much reduced by want, it was necessary to get some relief as soon as possible.

We seemed to have got off the route taken by Price's army, as everything seemed in its wild state, and no appearance of an army having passed, but still no appearance of any inhabitants.

At length we came to some signs of cultivation, and saw a farm-house at a distance, indicating by smoke from the chimney that it was inhabited.

As we went towards the house a woman appeared at the door, the expression of whose face showed that we were anything but welcome. I left my party outside of the fence and went up to the door and began to represent our condition; but she stopped me short and said that she had not a morsel for herself or family, that Price's army had taken everything she had. I rather doubted this, as I saw no traces of an army in the neighbourhood, and I asked her where Price's army was, as we were following it and had lost the road. She said the army did not pass this way, but a party of horsemen came and cleaned off everything she had.

"They would pay you in paper money, I suppose," said I.

"O yes," said she; "they gave me some paper money, but I can't do anything with it."

I knew that Confederate scrip was already at a great discount, and the country people did not want to take it, but they dare not refuse it, and I said that I wished to pay for anything I could get for my starving men, but I would pay in coin and not ask her to take paper money, and I produced some small gold pieces, which I showed her; but I said if she could not provide me with anything we would pass on and not trouble her.

The sight of the gold pieces had a wonderful effect upon her. She pitied the poor men and asked how many were of them. I told her 15. She said she was just making a baking of corn-bread to replace what Price's men had carried away, and in a few minutes it would be ready.

A bargain was soon struck and we were shown into an empty barn, which, she said, Price's army had denuded of its contents, and in a few minutes she brought in a large tray heaped with hot corn-bread and a large pitcher of milk. Nothing could have been more delicious, and it is no use saying how the men enjoyed it while she prepared more.

Having made a most hearty repast, and another batch of corn-bread being ready, the men put this into their haversacks, and I handed her a 2½ dollar gold piece, and asked if that would do. With this she was so highly pleased that she ran and got another pitcher of milk, and filled our canteens with it.

I then asked for the road which led to Van Buren. She said we were a good long way from that road, but her husband, who now made his appearance, said he would go with us, and show us a road that would lead us to it.

He accompanied us about a mile and put us on to a rough narrow road, by which he said we would get to the Van Buren road, near the foot of the mountain, but it was about five miles distant.

We were now in much better condition, having had something to eat and something in our haversacks, and, although we knew from experience that corn-bread did not possess the same strength-sustaining qualities as wheaten-bread, yet it was a great relief, and we were thankful for it, and we proceeded with more spirit and vigour.

Not long after this, three horsemen came riding up behind us, who I could see to be cavalry officers. One of them called out to us to halt. We did not halt, and they rode up to us. I turned round and asked what they wanted.

"I want to know what corps you belong to."

"We belong to the 3rd Louisiana regiment."

"And what are you doing here?"

"Making our way to Van Buren."

"And why are you away from your regiment?"

"Because the regiment was hemmed in this morning by a river and could not get across; they were in starvation for want of provisions, and the companies were ordered to separate, and each try to get to Van Buren the best way they could."

"I understood supplies reached your regiment yesterday?"

"No, nothing like it."

"How did you get over the river?"

"Crawled over on a tree."

"Well, you are are away ahead of your regiment; go back and join it."

"I tell you the regiment don't exist, it is separated into companies, and they are gone in different directions, and I can't tell where they are."

"Is that all your company?"

"No, it is only half of it."

"Where is the other half?"

"In charge of the third lieutenant, and by his orders the company divided and took different roads in order to find something for the men to eat."

"Oh, that is it," said he, "then I order you back to your regiment, it is away behind."

"Well, I refuse!"

" You refuse, do you ? "

" I do refuse."

" Do you know who I am ? "

" No, but I see by your uniform that you bear the rank of a Confederate colonel, and that is enough for me, but I refuse, and will stand the consequences."

" Then I order you under arrest."

" All right ! "

" I see you are an orderly sergeant; what is the name of your company ? "

" Company K—the rifle company."

He made no reply, but turned to go.

" Stay," said I, " you have put me under arrest, you must take my arms, but before I deliver them to you, you will please tell me who you are, and by whose orders I am put under arrest."

" I am Colonel Churchhill, commanding the brigade," said he.

" Excuse me," said I, " but I thought Churchhill was of the 1st brigade ? "

" Yes," said he, " but commanding both brigades at present."

I handed him the rifle which I carried, and as I was unbuckling my sabre belt, I said I had not recognised him, and if I had known it was Churchhill, I might have been a little more civil, but I thought it was some of Price's cow-footed colonels.

The other officers laughed, saying, " How do you take that compliment, colonel ? "

" Oh, never mind your sabre," said he.

" Oh yes," said I, " if I am under arrest I will carry no arms."

He hung the sabre on the pommel of his saddle, and was going away.

" Stay," said I again ; " you are leaving these men without an officer. Who do you appoint to command them ? "

" Let them go and report to their captain," said he.

" Then they must go to the enemy's camp to do that."

" Is your captain a prisoner ? "

" Yes."

" Then report to the lieutenant commanding."

" They will do so at Van Buren," said I, " as that is the first place that it will be possible to find him."

He looked puzzled for a moment, then said, "Very well," and rode on.

The boys laughed, and I was pleased to be relieved from duty, but the boys begged me to lead them all the same, which I of course said I would do. We now considered we were free to a greater extent than ever, and we might have roamed at will for a few days if there had been any inducement to do so. We were also glad to be relieved of some arms and accoutrements, which were becoming heavy to some of the weaker lads in toiling through the rough country, and we would now have one man light, who might carry along anything we might secure in the way of food; and I took the rifle and sabre from one of the boys, who I saw was getting very weak, and he walked along lighter, and said that Churchhill had done a good thing for him anyway.

As we walked along we talked of the incident, and Sergeant L., the fourth duty-sergeant who was with us, thought I had been a little pert in demanding from Churchhill his name and authority, and wondered that he had given it so readily, considering the great difference in rank. I told him that I considered that it was my duty to do so, and it was his duty to satisfy me; and that as he, as fourth sergeant of the company, would now be supposed to be in command of the party, I thought it was proper that he should know that, isolated as we were in a wild country and the enemy near.

"I don't understand you," said he; "suppose they had refused to say who they were?"

"Then I consider," said I, "it would have been my duty to have made prisoners of them, and might have ordered you to cover them with your rifles and ordered them to dismount and surrender."

"I wish you had, sergeant," said one of the boys, "I would have got one of their horses to ride to Van Buren."

"Would not that have been rather a high-handed act?" said one of the men thoughtfully, "seing they were Confederate officers in uniform."

"Their uniforms were not very well defined," said I, "and I have no doubt there are men riding about this country similarly dressed who are not Confederate officers, and I was perhaps wrong in not demanding to know who they were and being satisfied with it before I answered them a single question, considering the wild and lonely place where they met us. Of course I was pretty certain they were all right, but they might have been Federal spies dressed as Confederate officers, and after having told them what I had about the state of the regiment, it would never have done to let them go without knowing who they were."

"Would you have let them go without asking who they were if they had not ordered you under arrest?"

"Certainly not; I would have done very wrong if I had, and might have been court-martialed for it. I saw my error; I had answered the questions out of courtesy, or rather without thinking, but had determined to know them better before they got away. I might, however, have recognised Churchhill, as I had seen him several times before."

"Then," said Sergeant L., "should we be accosted by any other party in the same way, will I demand to know who they are before I answer them any questions?"

"Well, if in the same way, and far from any other force, I think you should; or, if you answer any questions, don't let them away without knowing who they are."

"Well," said he, "you keep the command and talk to them yourself, I don't want anything to do with it."

It was now near dark and we turned into a sort of by-road, thinking we might come to a farm where we might find some place to rest for the night. It was not long until we found we were approaching a settlement of some kind, for we came to a cattle-pen in which we saw a family of fine young pigs. One of these must be secured, and not wishing to raise any alarm by firing, we shut the gate of the pen, leaving a narrow space for the pigs to pass out, where one stood with a sabre while the others chased the pigs through the narrow pass. A blow of the sabre nearly severed the head of one from the body, and it fell without a squeal. While we looked for a place to clean and dress it, I observed the house at some distance, and the surroundings showed the farm to be a substantial one, and I saw lights, showing that the inhabitants were moving about. I thought that perhaps the best way after all would be to go up to the house, tell the farmer what we had done, and pay him for his pig, and perhaps he would allow us to sleep for the night in some barn or outhouse.

I went up and saw the farmer, told him what we had done, and offered to pay him for the pig. He said we were more honest than some of the troops that had passed; but he would not take any payment for the pig, and he allowed us to sleep in a large hay-loft over his stables, where he said we would be warmer than in a barn, cautioning us to take care of fire.

We kindled a large fire, dried our clothes, which were still wet from last night's drenching and to-day's scrambling through the wet bushes, roasted our pig, and with our stock of corn-bread made a hearty supper, and put the rest into our haver-sacks. We then went to the hay-loft, which was warm from the breath of the horses underneath, and we had an excellent night's rest.

In the morning our host told us that three or four nights previous our general, Van Dorn, and his staff occupied the same quarters. He said they put their horses in the stable and then went up to the hay-loft, where they drank whisky and played cards the whole night. He did not seem to have a very high opinion of the general and his crowd, as he called them, and in truth neither had I, but I said nothing, and we moved on considerably refreshed and invigorated.

This day we crossed Boston Mountain, but I do not think it was by the same road that we crossed it in July, though we were not sure, it now being winter and the face of the country very much altered.

I must not omit to say that while crossing the mountain this day, we were sitting down taking a rest in the wood a little way from the road, when one of the boys, pointing towards the road, cried out, "There is Napoleon crossing the Alps." I looked out and observed a tall, stately figure, with a musket on his shoulder, marching all alone with a firm, quick step and soldierly bearing.

There was something so noble and martial-like in his appear-ance that I determined to see who he was. I ran out and called on him to halt. He turned quickly round, and I recog-nized our old friend Monsieur Challon of the Iberville Grays. He was astonished, and glad to meet us. He had got parted from his company by some means, and thought they were on before, and he was hastening on to overtake them. He was much pleased when I told him that I was certain they were still behind, and he came and joined us. I was astonished to see the old man so vigorous, and we walked on together. I asked him what had become of his friend and fellow-traveller, Jason. "Oh, that is the donkee," he said. He said he had left him behind when we left winter quarters, and he had not seen him since. He was very sorry that he had not been with them on this retreat, as he would have been most invaluable, and he would just have liked to have an opportunity of putting in practice a cherished idea of his own, that donkeys could be used with great advantage in warfare. He had, he said, crossed the dry, sterile plains of New Mexico and Colorado with his donkey, where no other animal could have travelled. A donkey, he said, with panniers, could carry easily 150 lbs. They could go anywhere where a man could go; they could be lifted over walls or fences, and could swim rivers; they required no care, but little water, they did not always need grass, but could live on thistles, cactuses, or anything green, which at the same time served them for water. In some parts of the world they were to be had in thousands, and he thought that a thousand or so of them attached to an army marching over a barren country would be most invaluable for carrying water, provisions, or baggage, and he wondered that the English had never adopted or tried the system.

Of course I did not know much about donkeys; but if they were as he described, I certainly thought there might be something in the idea, though I felt a little amused at the idea of a thousand or two of donkeys marching with an army. "But," said I, "looking at the management of this campaign, don't you think that there have been sufficient donkeys connected with it ?"

"Oh yes," said he; "but dem is de two-footed donkee."

We passed the night in an old fodder shed, on the south side of the mountain, where we supped off the remains of the roast pig and corn-bread we had saved from the previous day; but we had picked up nothing in the way of provision that day.

In the morning we moved on again, Monsieur Challon deciding to remain here until his company came up.

There was now a great change in the weather. Of course it was getting well on in March, but I again observed a marked difference of the climate on the north and south sides of the mountain. We seemed to have come at once into spring; the buds were opening; the birds were singing, and there was quite a pleasant change in the atmosphere. This also brought up a still more pleasing reflection; that our time of service was drawing to a close, and the boys were speculating upon what they were going to do when their time was out.

We now got on to the regular road, and the track of an

Y

army was now only too plainly visible—every house was deserted, and everything in the shape of food or forage was carried away, and a good deal of property seemed to have been wantonly destroyed.

We saw some stragglers on the road before us, and we hastened to overtake them, thinking that they might be a part of our regiment, or perhaps Lieutenant G.'s party. When we overtook them we found them to be mostly of our regiment, but not more than a dozen in all, and among them were two of our company, from Lieutenant G.'s party.

Upon inquiring how it was with the party, and why they were separated from it, they said that Lieutenant G. had heard something about some of the missing from our company, and that our 2nd lieutenant, B., was lying very ill somewhere, and some others were also in distress, and he was going to try to render them assistance; and that he had told these two to go and see if they could meet with our party, and tell us not to wait for them, but to push on to Van Buren.

The effects of an army passing over a country distracted by war were now clearly to be seen. Be that army friend or foe, it passes along like a withering scourge, leaving only ruin and desolation behind.

We found it needless to attempt to procure anything like food on the way, and it was only a loss of time and strength going off the road to look for it. We therefore resolved to push on and reach Van Buren as soon as possible, as the road was now plain before us.

At length we drew near to the place. The poor fellows were brightened up with hope, but they were in a sorry plight. They were actually staggering from want and fatigue. Their shoes were worn off their feet, from passing over rocks and boulders, and through creeks. Their clothes were in rags from scrambling through the woods and briars, and burnt in holes from crouching too close to the camp fires in their broken slumbers. Their eyes were bleared and bloodshot, from want of sleep and the smoke of the wood-fires, and their bodies were emaciated by hunger. But now their difficulties were overcome, and their privations supposed to be at an end for the time at least.

It was about three o'clock in the afternoon when we entered Van Buren. The place was nearly deserted, every house and shop were shut up, nothing was to be seen but army waggons

lying about in disorder.   Very few of our brigade had arrived
and they were rendezvousing at a place about two miles below
the town near the river.

Some teamsters were hanging about, and I inquired of them
for the commissary department.   I was directed to a large
corner building, which had been a provision warehouse, owned
by a private firm, but had been seized by the commissary, as a
matter of convenience.   I at once proceeded there.

It was a large store, well stocked with provisions.   A
commissary clerk, in a half-dazed state, was sitting with some
of his friends near the stove.

I went and stated our case, and requested rations for a
party of 18 men, a part of the 3rd Louisiana regiment.

He said he had no orders to issue rations to us, and could
not do it, unless I brought a written order from the post
commissary ; besides, it was past the hour for issuing rations,
and he was not going to begin to do so to anybody.

It was in vain that I represented our case and remonstrated
with him ; he would not move.   I then asked him who was
post commissary and where I would find him.   He gave me
his name and said I would find him at the hotel.   In the name
I recognised one of those political agitators who had been
active in bringing about the secession movement and who had
now got as his share of the spoil a safe, easy, and lucrative
post, where he would be away from any danger and where he
might plunder at will.   " But," continued the clerk in a significant tone, " you may save yourself the trouble of going, for
I know he won't give it."

If ever a devil arose in a man I think one arose within me
at that time, and I do not know what length my rage would
have carried me, when Canada, who was my right-hand man,
pulled me away and advised me to be calm, reminding me that
I was already under arrest for being a little too sharp.

We left the store and went out to the street, where we
stood, not knowing very well what to do.

Just then two officers came up—one of them with his arm
in a sling, whom I recognised as Lieutenant M. of our regiment.
He had been wounded on the first day of the fighting and had
got back by the same route as we had advanced.   He inquired
about the regiment, and when I told him the condition we
were in, he said it would be of no use to go to the post commissary, for by this time of the day he would be so drunk that

he would not know a pen from a pitchfork. " But," continued
he, " if I was in your place I would not want rations for one
moment ; you are in a starving condition ; you are entitled to
them ; the provisions are there, and you have an armed force."

I quickly took the hint, ordered the men to " Shoulder arms,"
and marched them up to the commissary's store and called to
the clerk in charge to attend.

" Have you brought a requisition ? " said he.

" Yes," said I, " in the shape of an armed force," and I
ordered him to take a note of what stores we took.

The clerk, who did not seem to care much what we did if it
did not give him any trouble, refused to take any part in the
matter.

After witnessing his refusal, I detailed six of the men to
take what stores were necessary for their immediate wants.
" But remember," said I, " nothing more than what is actually
necessary for your immediate relief."

" All right, sergeant," was the reply, and the men proceeded
to help themselves.

A barrel of good biscuit was found, from which a bag was
filled. A good supply of coffee and sugar was got, and two of
the best hams they could find, with some small articles, including soap, of which we stood much in need, until the six men
had as much as they could stagger under, which, as soon as
they got away from the store, was distributed more generally
over the whole party, and we made our way down to where
the troops were rendezvousing.

Here had arrived, and were still coming in, the quarter-
master's waggons with the baggage of the campaign as it had
been left at the different places—arms, tents, spades, axes,
pick-axes, cooking utensils, and other camp equipage, with
blankets and overcoats that had been thrown off and left
behind, all tumbled together in waggons or lying on the
ground in confused heaps, without anyone to take charge of
them, and left the prey of the first that came along.

We considered we were fortunate in being here before the
main body of the army, and we quickly set about picking out
what things we could find that had belonged to us, and also
what other things the company stood in need of, as we knew
they would be picked up by those who could first secure them.
We were not sure whether Price's army was here or if it had
gone on down the river.

We secured some tents and blankets, some cooking utensils, and other camp equipage, and I was fortunate enough to find my overcoat, the same that I had thrown off on the 7th when the order was given for the 2nd brigade to strip for battle, with some things in the pockets just as I had thrown it off.

We selected a good place for camping, pitched what tents we needed for ourselves, and stowed in them some for the other part of the company when it came up, and also some blankets and cooking utensils, and, having partaken of a good supper, we retired to rest, and had at last one good night's sleep.

In the morning, there being yet no reveille or camp regulations, one of the first things was to use the soap which we had taken from the commissary and go to the Arkansas river and thoroughly wash our blankets and clothing and our bodies, which were completely ingrained with dirt and smoke. This was a matter of considerable labour, but fortunately the day was fine, and the drying was an easier process than the washing.

After breakfast, having nothing to do, some of the boys watched the road for the arrival of Lieutenant G. and his party. They came up about two o'clock, and were conducted to where we were camped.

It appeared that the army, which after the battle of the 8th had retreated through the country round to the northward and eastward of Fayetteville, had come, on the north side of Boston Mountain, on to the same road by which the trains and the wounded would return from the south side of the ridge, where the fighting had been on the 6th and 7th, and that Lieutenant G.'s party, after we had parted, by keeping more to the west than ours, had come to this road sooner than we, and come up with part of the trains and got information that there were to come with the trains, or by the same road as them, the wounded we had left behind us on the night of the 7th and the four men that we had sent to attend to them, with some other sick and stragglers.

Poor Lieutenant B., who was on the quartermaster's department, was not over robust at best, and worn out by toil and privation, he had completely broken down and had to be left behind. I am not sure whether he died there or not, but I never heard more of him. The other sick and wounded were left at places where they would be cared for in the meantime.

Throughout this and the following day the rest of the regiment got up and the greater part of the division.

Captain G., who was now temporarily in command of the regiment, on hearing of my arrest, said he would see to it at once, and explain matters. Churchhill, he said, was an officer and a gentleman (which he certainly was) and he had no doubt the thing would be put right. He immediately went to Colonel Churchhill, who had just got up the same day, and after a little explanation returned and told me that I was relieved from arrest without censure.

I was glad it was arranged, as I did not know how it might be about my having commanded an armed party to take rations by force while I was myself under arrest, and I reported the matter to Captain G. He said there would never be a word said about that. All the other companies had taken rations in the same way, as everything was demoralized and in disorder in the commissary department, but that would soon be set right.

The work of reorganising was now set about vigorously. Price's army had already proceeded towards the Mississippi River, on its way to join the Army of the Centre. The 1st brigade of our division also proceeded in that direction; but the 2nd brigade, and especially our regiment, was too much cut up and crippled to proceed, until some of the wounded had recovered and the missing stragglers returned, and the prisoners, among whom there were a good many officers, had been exchanged and again joined the brigade.

Our regiment was ordered up to Fort Smith, to garrison that place and recuperate, and wait for the return of the colonel, major, and other officers and men, who were prisoners in the enemy's camp.

We marched up to the fort, and occupied the same ground which we had occupied in June of the previous year, but taking up much less space than at that time. Our force was now reduced to less than 500, or less than half of what we had been when here before. The ordinary routine of camp life was again resumed. Company and battalion drill (things now stale to us) was gone through every day.

We now discovered one of the chief reasons why we were not cut to pieces while fighting so long against a superior force and under such a tremendous fire as we had done on the 7th.

A good many of the men of the regiment, on returning from

the field that evening, had exchanged their arms for those of the enemy; that is, they had thrown down their smooth bore muskets, and taken up the superior arms of the enemy which lay thick on the field. They now began to try their new arms at marks at 60, 80, and 100 yards, but could not hit the marks—the ball passing high over it. It was now found that all these rifles had raised movable sights which were set for 200 yards, and in no case did the sights seem to have been altered. As we had pressed up upon them that day, keeping up to within from 40 to 80 yards, they seem to have omitted to alter their sights, or in the quick and sudden movements amongst the trees and smoke, it would have been rather a difficult matter to always determine the distance and alter the sights to suit. The consequence was that most of their shots passed over our heads, and this accounted for the trees being marked with shot so high up.

This led to raised sights being condemned by us, and they were taken off, and the line of sight set to range with the line of fire at about 70 yards—it being considered simpler and better when the distance was uncertain and constantly changing, for men acting upon the spur of the moment to learn how to aim, high or low, according to the distance as they were now in the habit of doing, than to stop and calculate the distance and alter the sight for every shot.

Raised sights, it was considered, might do very well for sharpshooters, or in circumstances where the object was single and continued fixed, and time could be taken to calculate the distance, and set the sight to suit it; but the hurry-skurry of the battle, in front of an enemy rushing to and fro, was not a very good place for making nice calculations, and movable sights were there quite useless and in the way.

We had been here only some four or five days, when our officers and men, who had been prisoners with the enemy, being exchanged, returned and joined the regiment.

The reason so many field officers were taken prisoners on the 7th was as had been suspected. After the death of M'Culloch and M'Intosh, they had gone, one after another, to communicate with the 1st and 3rd brigades, and find out why they did not come to support us, and they had just walked into that part of the enemy's force which we had cut off and left behind on our right.

They had much to tell of their experience in the enemy's

camp; and what they had gleaned in the way of information was something the same as we had heard before—that the enemy was astonished at, and could not account for, us withdrawing from the field, and was expecting us to attack them again, and if we had continued the fight for a little longer, they would have been completely defeated.

Of this ill devised and still worse conducted campaign and battle, I have seen very few detailed accounts given, and any that I have seen, seemed, from my point of view, to be very evasive and inaccurate.

What the losses were on either side I never learned. I have seen many contradictory accounts, but I doubt if anything like a correct account was ever given. On the part of the south, I am certain it was reported at a great deal less than it actually was. This was no doubt to cover the blunder and satisfy public opinion, but I doubt if any correct estimate could be formed, as there was a large number of emergency men whose names were not on the roll. Some of these were killed or disappeared among the missing, while some remained with the army, and were enrolled as members, and took the place of some of the regular men who were missing.

CHAPTER XXIV.

A DAY or two after the officers and men who had been exchanged had returned to duty we were ordered with all the remaining troops of the Army of the West to proceed to Memphis, Tennessee, and join the Army of the Centre.

We were not to be taken down the river as we had come, but were to march by land as far as Little Rock at least.

The distance by the road to Little Rock was about 250 miles, but 20 miles in a day, if the roads were anything good, was now to us mere child's play, if we had trains to supply us with food and tents and blankets to enable us to sleep at nights.

We left Fort Smith about the 28th of March and reached Little Rock in about 13 days.

When we got opposite Little Rock we learned that the road from there to Memphis was perfectly impassable, and that it was quite impossible to get there by the land route. Price, who was most indefatigable in his exertions, had taken his army that way, but had to leave a large part of his baggage trains, and some of his artillery sunk in the mud in the neighbourhood of " Des. Ark," and since then the Mississippi had risen, and much of the country and the roads were flooded. It was quite evident that the Mississippi must be very high, as the Arkansas river was very high at Little Rock, from the waters of the Mississippi backing up.

There was, therefore, no help for it, and we were ordered to camp where we were and wait until transport steamers could be sent to take us by water to Memphis. We were camped on the north or left bank of the Arkansas river, opposite Little Rock. There was no town or houses on this side of the river, but a large and substantial ferry-boat plied back and forward to maintain the connection of the roads which passed through at this part.

Colonel Hebert, who still commanded the brigade, had with his staff taken up his head-quarters at the principal hotel in Little Rock.

On the day after our arrival I was sent to his head-quarters with reports and a statement of some articles in the way of clothing for the men, which were supposed to be obtainable in Little Rock.

I made myself as clean as possible, as I would be going again into civilisation.

It was late in the afternoon when I got over, and when I presented the papers the colonel looked over them, but said it would be too late to do anything that night, and I might wait until the morning, and he ordered the proprietor of the hotel to furnish me with accommodation for the night.

I was supplied with a good room, but the idea of being under a roof in a carpeted room and soft bed was too much of a change. I could not realise it, and got but little sleep. At every turn in my sleep the soft bed under me woke me up to a sense of my strange position.

In the morning I got up early and had a ramble through the city. The war had not yet seriously affected this place, except so far as the stock of merchandise was concerned. All kinds of Northern or European goods were very scarce and dear—in fact, scarcely obtainable : this was of course owing to the blockade. The traffic in this class of goods seemed to be here now as it was in the South throughout the war, chiefly confined to the children of Israel. These gentlemen seemed to have international communication by some secret system known only to themselves, by which information was transmitted and the integrity of officials weighed in the balance, and the price of that integrity secretly ascertained, and the " goots," as they called the merchandise, found their way across the lines through secret and intricate channels, and were stored away in unfathomable recesses.

Isaac seldom had much of value in his store to sell under the ordinary way of traffic for Confederate scrip ; such " goots," he would tell you, were unknown within the Confederate States, owing to the cursed blockade, but the confidential exhibit of a few gold pieces would often bring from the vasty deep the articles you desired.

At this time, April, 1862, the dearth of Northern and foreign goods had not got to the extreme in the Confederate States, and there were still some to be had, although scarce and dear.

I bought some shirts and underclothing for myself, of which I stood in great need ; and having got a special requisition from the colonel to the quartermaster, I got some clothing for the men of the company, which I got taken over to the camp.

The town was now beginning to fill up with officers, and such privates as could obtain passes were crossing from the camp to the town, to have a look at civilisation and city life once more. But this was cut short by the arrival of the transport steamers, and we were quickly called upon to strike tents and embark.

At this time there came a piece of news which very much damped the spirits of the men of our regiment at least. This was an intimation of the passing by the Confederate Congress, at Richmond, of the Conscript Act, whereby every citizen of the Confederate States between the ages of 18 and 35 was made subject to military duty, and could be called into service; and all troops enlisted or mustered into the service for short periods should be continued in the service.

This was a great disappointment to the men of our regiment, which was altogether composed of men who had volunteered for one year only, and had been mustered in for that period, and were now looking forward to getting home for a little rest after their privations.

There is no question but nearly every one of the men upon recuperating a little after their toil, and spending a few weeks with their friends, would have again joined the service, as nearly every one had done, who had hitherto been discharged on account of wounds or sickness, and had subsequently become fit for service.

The Conscription Act was now the general topic and formed the subject for conversation on the passage from Little Rock to Memphis, and several copies of the act were in circulation. Most of the men emphatically declared that they would willingly serve any length of time as volunteers, but they would never serve in the degraded position of a conscript.

I got a copy of the act and looked over it. I saw that regiments enrolled for one year might, by continuing as they were, remain as volunteers, with the privilege of electing their own officers. That any one subject to military duty, or already in the service, might be exempted by furnishing a substitute; such substitute not being subject to military duty, and approved by the proper authority.

The next clause directly affected my own position, which was that—

"Foreigners, who are not citizens of the Confederate States, and who shall not have acquired domicile, shall not be subject to military duty, and shall be discharged at the expiration of their original term of enlistment, by order of their brigade commander. The question of domicile, however, shall be a question of law, and not to be determined on the oath, or opinion, of the parties."

It seemed to strike me that one of the principal motives for providing this last clause, by which I would be exempted, was to make provision for the carrying out of the preceding clause in regard to substitutes. There were, undoubtedly, a great many men of wealth and political influence within the limits of the prescribed ages whom it would not be politic to press into service, and to exempt the rich would cause dissatisfaction; and they would not be able to find offices for all those possessed of political influence, and if those possessing wealth or political influence desired to purchase substitutes, it would be necessary to have some suitable men to form such substitutes.

The act certainly caused great dissatisfaction among the troops that had been enrolled for one year only. These of course constituted but a small portion of the army, as by far the greatest portion of the troops had volunteered for the war, and it did not affect them in any way, except so far as it might be supposed that in retaining all the troops in the service, and adding as many more as possible, it would bring more men to their aid, and push on the war sooner to an end, if they expected to obtain their object of independence by force of arms. But the volunteers were opposed to the principle of the act, and considered that men forced compulsorily into service were of little value and would only be an incumbrance—and I believe they were right. It no doubt caused a good many who had not yet joined the service, and who were hesitating, to volunteer at once, whilst they had the opportunity of getting into volunteer regiments, but I never knew of a single instance of any of the old volunteer regiments, though reduced to perfect skeletons, being patched up by the addition of conscripts. In fact the old volunteers protested against the admission of conscripts into their corps.

Some of us rejoiced over the idea that it would catch up, and bring into service, these political loafers who had been such rabid secessionists, and who had so bounced about fighting before the war, and aided in bringing it about, but not one of whom had ever entered the army. These demagogues always contrived to evade the duty in one way or another. Some of them who had vaunted that they would go to the enemy's lines and fight, if they went single-handed, did go to the enemy's lines, but not to fight, but to take refuge for fear that they would be conscripted. Others, more of the class of Government minions, managed to get some low office, such as hunting up conscripts, and every small country town or village, far away from the din of war, was filled with those drunken, swaggering loafers dressed in gaudy Confederate uniforms hunting up conscripts. In fact, I believe it took more men to enforce the act than what they obtained by it; and those who were forced into service only had the effect of filling up the hospitals, and I know that out of 7000 who were sent to the Central Army at Corinth, over 3000 of them were on the sick list before a fortnight; but of this I will say more hereafter.

There were also a few of the more far-seeing and broad-minded that could see in the act just a slight advance towards despotism, but of course such an idea could not be breathed openly.

We arrived at Memphis about the 18th of April. Memphis was a good sized city, and, like Vicksburg, Natchez, and other towns on the left bank of the Mississippi, it is situated on high bluffs overlooking the river. It had not, however, been fortified in any way.

Here was assembled a large body of troops who, like ourselves, did not know where they were going. This was a central place, and we were to remain until further orders.

We got newspapers here with all the news and accounts of the war for the last three months. These accounts, however, all seemed to have been carefully prepared by the different newspapers under the most approved Government inspection, and put up expressly for public use. Each paper at the same time boasted of the free and independent way in which they expressed their sentiments, and congratulated themselves and the people of the South on the glorious liberties which they

enjoyed in always having the freedom of the press, the great
lever of human liberty, preserved inviolate.

Some of us, however, knew what the material was composed
of, and just swallowed what we thought was sufficient. Of
course only Confederate successes were recorded. Fort Henry
and Fort Donelson had been taken by the enemy, but then
they were of no use, and their loss would not be felt. Island
No. 10 had also fallen, but that was altogether in consequence
of the river rising to an unusual height; there might be something in that. In one paper a glowing account was given of
Van Dorn's brilliant successes in the west. He had stopped
M'Culloch's retrograde movement and advanced boldly to the
Missouri line, and got into the rear of the Federal army at
Pea Ridge, and was driving them southward before him like
a flock of sheep, although in a later issue it was admitted
that Van Dorn had found out that General M'Culloch and
General M'Intosh and other officers had been killed, and from
want of them his right wing had got somewhat demoralised,
and he had found it necessary to give up the pursuit, and
hasten to join the Army of the Centre. There was also some
accounts of the Federal navy, which was reported to have
been expending its force along the coast, and had taken some
small forts which were of little or no consequence, but it had
now entered the Mississippi, where every ship would certainly
be smashed to pieces by the gallant General Duncan commanding Fort Jackson and Fort St. Philip.

But the latest and most exciting news was the battle of
Shiloh, which had been fought about two weeks previous, in
which the Confederates had gained a great victory, and had
driven the enemy back into the Cumberland River and taken
many of their guns, but by some means they had been obliged
to fall back again to Corinth, where they were now stationed,
and where it was supposed the Army of the West would join
them. Of course those glowing newspaper accounts were
believed by some, but others knew what allowances to make.

Taking the news all in all was not reassuring. The fall of
Forts Henry and Donelson, and Island No. 10, was a great
disaster, and the enemy's gunboats might be expected down at
Memphis, which was not fortified; and if Fort Jackson and
Fort St. Philip, at the entrance to the Mississippi, fell, the
cause might be considered lost, as New Orleans and the whole
of the Mississippi River and its tributaries would be in the

hands of the enemy, and under control of their gun-boats, which seemed to be their chief source of success, and against which the Confederates were utterly powerless. No care had been taken to provide proper defences on the water, although the Confederate territory was largely intersected by navigable rivers, and there was not now another fortified position on the river, although there was some talk of fortifying Vicksburg.

It was now the subject of conjecture whether we were to fortify and defend Memphis, or to go and join Beauregarde's army at Corinth.

Memphis was an important place from its position on the Mississippi, and had railway communication with Charleston, Mobile, New Orleans, Vicksburg, and other places in the South, and if the advance down the river of the Federal gun-boats could be here arrested, the communication to the west by the Arkansas River would still be preserved, which would be lost if the standpoint was made as far down as Vicksburg.

But Corinth was still more important, for here the Memphis and Charleston railway crossed the Mobile and Ohio railway, and from the latter, at a place called Meridian, some distance south from Corinth, lines branched off to Jackson, Vicksburg, New Orleans, and Mobile. If Corinth should fall into the hands of the Federals, Memphis would be cut off from inland communication and be of comparatively little value.

Our conjectures were soon set at rest by orders to proceed at once to Corinth, a great battle being immediately expected, and we were conveyed there, a distance of about 40 miles, inside and on the top of railway freight trucks.

When we got to Corinth we found an immense army assembling to meet the combined armies of Grant and Buel, under General Halleck. It sounded strange to us that this General Halleck, who now held such an important command and over such men as Grant and Buel, should be the same that about six months before had been so out-generaled and driven back upon St. Louis by our poor General M'Culloch with his small force, who never rose higher than a brigadier-general, but fell in battle and his name all but forgotten.

In a few days after our arrival preparations were made for a general battle; the enemy's forces were said to be drawn out in order of battle about four miles from Corinth. A great bustle it was; our army amounted in all to about 110,000 men; the enemy's force was supposed to amount to about 140,000.

After standing in order of battle for several hours in a heavy rain, it seemed doubtful if there was going to be any battle that day, and we were sent back to camp, with orders to be ready to fall in at a moment's notice.

The next day the same thing was re-enacted, but still the fight did not come off.

On the fourth day we were ordered to be fully prepared, because, if the enemy did not attack us, we should advance and attack them, and we were certain the battle would come off this day. When it comes to the verge of battle there is not much pleasure in the suspense, and the men are impatient till the battle comes off, and they were now getting tired of this delay. The wet weather and the constant trampling of horses and artillery had got the place into a fearful state with mud.

We advanced to where the enemy's line had been formed, but found they had fallen back, so it was just the old story— ordered back to camp again. The men were dissatisfied, and grumbled at being called out so often to no purpose; and here I noticed for the first time for several months our old friend Dan. He was not now carrying his knapsack, and whether he still maintained his principles on the whisky question or not I do not know, but he was still as contrary and pugnacious as ever, for he stood out and said he would just be d—d if he was going back to camp. He had come out here for a fight, and he was going to have it. He said he got nothing to eat when he did go to camp, and he was not going to be wearing his shoes going up and forward this way for nothing. I looked at Dan's shoes; the sole was gone off one of them, and the other was torn down on the one side and tied with strings, and his naked foot protruded through it.

Whether Dan was persuaded or coerced to go back to camp I do not know, as our company had to move on.

We found it very different here from what it had been with us in the Army of the West. There we could see and comprehend all the movements; the army was small and well in hand, and the different corps fell into their places quickly and without confusion.

There was a constant changing of positions in this camp; troops were coming in from all quarters. The whole of the Confederate forces, with exception of the Army of Virginia, were being concentrated at this point. A large portion of the army was composed of raw troops and conscripts, who neither could be trained nor wanted to be trained, but lumbered up the way, and for every three or four of them there was a commissioned officer, some wealthy man's son or Government minion for whom the Conscript Act was no doubt in a great measure intended to provide employment, and they had obtained commissions, but they were as raw and ignorant of military matters as the conscripts themselves, and possessed only a fair share of conceit and effrontery.

These gentlemen and their commands, when a sudden call to the front was made, were sure to be in the way, getting jumbled up and in the way of the older corps as they were hurrying to the front, and they had to be placed somewhere to prevent confusion, but in fact the most of them were soon located in the hospital, commissioned officers and all.

For a considerable time after our arrival here it was a continuation of alarms, constantly turning out and forming in order of battle, but never beyond a few exchanges of artillery fire and an occasional skirmish with small arms did it come to anything.

The object of both armies seemed to have been to act on the defensive, each trying to draw the other on to the attack. It was a continuation of feint attacks by our side or repelling of attacks by the enemy, which also turned out to be feints. Of this we were getting heartily tired.

I sometimes thought this keeping of the troops in constant motion and the prospect of a gigantic battle before them was to give them no time for reflection or brooding over the great disaster which had befallen the Confederacy, the news of which could now no longer be kept from them.

This was in the penetration of the enemy's fleet into the Mississippi, the fall of New Orleans, and the whole of the Mississippi River now in the hands of the enemy. All this had occurred in spite of the well-known importance of the position, and the disastrous effects to the Confederacy should it be forced. Its supposed impregnability and the ample means furnished to, and the great confidence reposed in, those to whom the defence was entrusted made the disaster most discouraging.

The news came like a thunder-clap upon the men, and most of them, I believe, regarded it as the death-knell of the Confederacy.

The accounts were of course garbled, and the matter

z

accounted for in the most plausible way, and set forth as of
little consequence and would yet be turned to the advantage
of the Confederacy. The army was now thickly studded
with minions of the Government in the uniforms of captains
and lieutenants, in sinecure offices, in the departments, and in
and out of the hospitals, whose chief business seemed to be to
keep up a show of enthusiasm in favour of the Government,
and drown by arguments and threats any criticism on the
disgraceful management and poor defence of the place, and
every effort was made to divert the attention of the men from
the subject. Of course a good many did not see the importance of the disaster, and were persuaded and satisfied.

A number of troops were now sent off to occupy and fortify
Vicksburg, which it was supposed would counteract the consequences of the disaster to some extent.

It was now into the month of May, and our term of service
was expired, but so great was the commotion, and the expected
battle on hand, that the subject was not brought up. Our
colonel had been made a brigadier-general, and was away from
the regiment. Both Lieutenant-Colonel H. and Major T. had
resigned and retired ; they were both aged men and their
health was failing. The former had not been with us since we
had left winter quarters. The regiment had been without any
regular commander since Pea Ridge, sometimes one captain
and sometimes another commanding it.

On a slight lull taking place in the commotion, the subject
was brought up, and we were told that the regiment would be
dealt with as a regiment, and not by companies as they entered
the service, and therefore the time of service would expire on
the 17th of May, that being the date on which the regiment
was organised.

It was now the 5th of May, and we were told there was to
be a battle on the following day. Whether the intimation of
the battle was to stir up the men and stop any discussion on
the subject I do not know, but a battle was intended, and did
take place to a certain extent.

In the evening the same old order was sent round—three
days' cooked rations, and 60 rounds of ammunition, and be
ready to march at daybreak. The three days' cooked rations
were superfluous and might have been left out of the order, but
the order was carried round and delivered quietly to each
company, which betokened that something was intended.

At daybreak the whole division was under arms and marching to the front; whether the whole army moved or not we did not know. We seemed to be kept well to the right, making way at times to allow the artillery to pass on. About 11 o'clock our company was deployed in front of the regiment, to form a part of a line of skirmishers.

About noon we heard the fire of the artillery, and we were ordered to press up quickly, in the direction of where we heard the firing. Shortly afterwards we heard the crackling of small arms, and we soon came upon the extremity of the enemy's left wing. We were soon hotly engaged with them, they falling back, as usual, and we kept following them up, to keep them at short range.

We were, however, ordered to be cautious, and advance slowly, lest we should come under the sweep of our own artillery, which was firing direct towards the front; while we seemed to have turned their left wing, and were following them up towards the centre. After a short engagement here we were ordered to halt, the enemy in our front having disappeared in the smoke. The firing in our front was now for some time very heavy, though very little of it came our way. After waiting for some time we were ordered to advance again, to press the retreat of the enemy, who were falling backwards towards a swamp in their rear, where they shortly all disappeared—and the battle was over—the artillery still continuing to send some shells after them into the swamp.

On following them we found that there was a part of the swamp where the water was deep and impassable, and over which there was a substantial bridge, newly erected, over which some of our men had passed, while our artillery was raking the woods on the opposite side.

Here was discovered a bit of Yankee enterprise and perseverance. On the opposite side of the swamp much of the timber had been cut down and a portable saw-mill erected; there was also a telegraph station, with line of wire extending northwards, and probably towards their headquarters.

It was now plain to be seen that the enemy had intended to advance their left wing and obtain a commanding position on our right flank, which Beauregard considered to be protected by this swamp, and they had in an incredibly short time brought up and erected this portable saw-mill, felled timber, sawed it up, and erected this bridge. They had got over it about 20,000 men, and some heavy guns, and were establishing themselves in a commanding position. This being known to Beauregarde he awaited the proper time and made this sudden attack. Having captured the guns and driven the enemy back across the bridge, the saw-mill was destroyed, and the bridge burned.

This battle, which was called the Battle of Farmington from the name of the place, was of no great proportions and has been very little noticed. Nevertheless, it was more decisive in its character, and the results of more importance than either Shiloh or Pea Ridge.

The loss sustained by the Federals was stated by the Confederate newspapers to be about 800 killed, and the Confederates about 300 killed. That may have been, but from what I saw on the field, I do not think there was anything like that number. Several hundred prisoners were taken, some fine heavy siege guns, several hundred stands of arms, and a large quantity of camp equipage fell into our hands. The advance of the enemy on our right flank was checked, and they would be compelled to change their tactics in that direction.

We remained on the field for some time awaiting orders. The place where the enemy had camped was being cleared and the ground was strewn with debris. Knapsacks, clothing, newspapers, letters, and other small articles lay scattered about. I picked up and examined some of the letters. They were mostly all headed with some patriotic motto, and a great many printed cards were enclosed or lay scattered about bearing emblematic figures and inscriptions, such as female figures pointing to Fort Sumter with the words: "Sumter first, peace afterwards." Others with the emblem of the Union—the eagle and the motto, "E pluribus unum," with the words: "Fight for the Union and the Union only," and many similar representations, but never one having the slightest reference to the question of slavery.

The field was soon cleared of the guns, arms, tents, and other material which had been captured, and a party was detailed to bury the dead, and we were ordered back to camp again, with the intimation, this time, that we had done all that we had come to do.

As we passed over the rising ground which had been the position the enemy had been trying to gain and occupy, I observed Beauregarde, Bragg, and one or two other generals in conversation. They seemed to be taking a survey of the position. The two former I had known in Louisiana previous to the war. I would scarcely have known them now, they had got so much older in appearance—especially Beauregarde. Two years before when I had last seen him, his hair and beard were black as jet—they were now nearly white.

It had been supposed by some that the Federal army would not advance far from the Cumberland River, where they were supported by their gunboats, which had saved them at the battle of Shiloh; and if the Cumberland river fell, as it was certain to do as the summer advanced, the gunboats would have to withdraw and run down to the Mississippi, and then we could attack them with more advantage, but the advance at Farmington which we had repulsed, showed that idea to be fallacious.

CHAPTER XXV.

A FEW days after the battle of Farmington, an order was
issued to the 3rd Louisiana Regiment, that as their term of
service was about expired, they would now come under the
Conscript Act, and those subject to service under that act
would be conscripted for further service. But in consideration of the gallant services performed by that regiment, and
the high honours which it had gained, the general commanding was desirous that its name should be preserved, and that
it should continue organised as a regiment, and that as a
tribute to the men composing it, they should be allowed the
privilege of re-organising and re-electing their officers, and continue on the same footing with the other volunteer regiments
which had volunteered for the war ; and such of the members
who were not subject to conscription should serve until the 15th
of July, when they would be discharged in terms of the act.

The men had no choice but to accept the conditions ; they
would have liked to have got a week or two to go to see
their friends, but they knew that if the regiment was dis-
banded, they would never get beyond the lines of the camp,
but be pressed as conscripts, which was of all things the most
detestable. They knew that as volunteers they had at least
some little standing and respect, and by having the election of
their officers, had some voice in the general conduct of the
service.

As conscripts they would be serfs, having neither respect
nor rights ; would be domineered over, and kicked about by a
set of puppies appointed by the War Department, men possessing no other qualification for their office, or knowledge of
duty, beyond brazen effrontery, depraved principles, and aptitude for performing any kind of despicable service to maintain favour with or support a party in power.

The men—or at least the most far-seeing of them—saw that the only chance they had of retaining even the faintest spark of that liberty and independence which had been their birthright and boast, was now to adhere together as a volunteer regiment, and they decided at once on a matter in which they had no choice.

The re-election of officers, which was no doubt thrown out as a sop to the men, and in this case was also extended to the non-commissioned officers, was not very gratifying to the officers.   There were no doubt a great many commissions vacant, which, small as the strength of the regiment was, might be filled up, but it was never expected that a re-election would take place.

The officers had served a year in their respective positions, and were now to take the chance of being turned out by a new election, which was exceedingly probable, not from any unpopularity, but on the old cherished democratic principle of rotation in office.

I was on very friendly terms with most of the officers of the regiment, and had whiled away the time on many a dreary night round the camp fires by discussing amongst other subjects political economy in general, and the forms of government of different nations as compared with American institutions as they were called.

This doctrine of rotation in office I held to be peculiarly American, and I did not approve of it, on the ground that it kept always inexperienced men in office, because the incumbents were turned out just as they were becoming acquainted with the duties of their offices.   In this opinion I took my stand almost alone ; nearly all were opposed to me, maintaining that rotation in office was based upon justice and equal rights to all.

When this order for a re-election of officers was issued it in a manner threw all the officers and privates again on an equality.   The officers of course held their commissions and rank, and could retire altogether if they wished ; but they did not consider the system wise or just, and thought it rather a singular way of promotion.

I, in a half-joking way, reminded them of the justice and equitable rights of rotation-in-office principles, but they did not see it just in the same light.

The most of the officers retired and did not offer themselves as candidates for re-election. All the field officers were already gone, and it was plainly to be seen that the high tone of disinterested principle which had been so conspicuous at the original formation of the regiment, and indeed of the whole army, was now considerably modified. Office was now, not only sought after, but it was hinted that, in some cases, it had actually been sneaked after—a thing supposed to be regarded with abhorrence among the volunteers; and it was openly asserted that little cliques had been got up in the different messes of some of the companies by aspirants to a lieutenant's commission.

When the election took place in our company our captain retired, and was not a candidate.

Lieutenant G. was elected captain, and our 1st lieutenant remained as before, but, beyond this, the election was a mere farce. Two lieutenants, one orderly sergeant, four duty sergeants, and four corporals had to be elected; and the whole strength of the company was about 39. Of these eight were to be discharged on the 15th of July, under the act, and took no part in the election, and several were absent on detached service, while several declined to vote after the captain and 1st lieutenant had been elected; so that the voting was left almost exclusively to the candidates themselves. I must say, however, that throughout the regiment, notwithstanding the principle of rotation-in-office, wherever an old incumbent offered himself as a candidate he was invariably elected.

The regiment was now re-organised and new field officers elected—these were elected by the line officers—a new staff appointed; but as most of the other companies were reduced, like our own, the regiment was a mere skeleton.

As I was going to leave, of course, I was not a candidate for the office of orderly sergeant, and this placed me in rather a peculiar position. Not having a commission, I could not retire from the service without obtaining a discharge; and on consulting with the captain and some of the other officers of the regiment, it was considered that I should get a discharge at once, under the clause in the Conscript Act providing for the discharge of aliens at the expiration of their original term of enlistment. The necessary form was made out and signed by the captain, and I went to the colonel and presented it.

Colonel A., who had just been newly elected to the command of the regiment, was a relation of our late respected and lamented General M'Culloch. He had been an officer in the United States army, and was a thorough soldier.

On my presenting the application to him he was somewhat embarrassed, and did not seem inclined to grant a discharge under that clause, which might be establishing a precedent, as it was probably the first that had been applied for, and he would like to have some instructions as to the full meaning of the clause. He pointed out to me that I could claim no exemption as a neutral foreigner, as I had already taken an active part in several battles and had violated neutrality, and referred me to the Queen's proclamation. I told him I had not seen the Queen's proclamation until I had been enlisted and bound by an engagement to the Confederate States for a period of one year, from which I could not resile, and that I had been refused a commission because I would not become a citizen; and I now considered that I had faithfully fulfilled my engagement to the Confederate States, and I trusted they would do the same by me. He admitted that I had done my part well and faithfully, and for that reason he would do the best he could for me, but he said his position was rather a difficult one in the matter. He would not like to be the first to establish a precedent which might be the means of thinning the ranks of the army, as if one discharge was granted under this clause, he had no doubt there would be 30 applications from amongst the different companies of the regiment within a week, which, in the present condition of affairs, would be a very serious matter; and he must get some instructions in regard to this clause. He trusted I would see the justice of his remarks; in the meantime he would do the best he could in the matter, and would lay it before the brigade-commander, and I would have an answer in a day or two.

I asked him what I was to do in the meantime. If the question of violating neutrality was to be brought up in the way he had pointed out, I would not be justified in taking up arms after I was free of my agreement unless it was under compulsion; and, further, what position would I now be in? I was no longer orderly-sergeant. I would not serve in the ranks unless disrated by a court-martial, and could not draw rations except in some capacity. He pondered a little and said that he did not well see how that was to be got over, but the only way he saw I might not like, which was, that he would formally order me under arrest or suspension in the meantime, and unless I could propose some other arrangement, he had no other alternative. I saw no other alternative myself, and agreed. He said all I had to do was to go to my captain and report myself under arrest, and he would explain the matter.

To be under arrest or suspension on such conditions was not considered either as a disgrace or a punishment, but a simple suspension from duty, and as I was under no restrictions, I rather enjoyed it as a relaxation from duty and a holiday. I had now an opportunity of roaming over the extensive camp of the whole army and studying the position.

The object and disposition of the forces under the different generals, as far as I could make out, was to hold the position of Corinth, where converged different railway lines.

In front was a line leading to the north through Tennessee, being part of the Mobile and Ohio railway. This line of course was blocked by the enemy's forces stretched across it. On the right was a line leading through North Alabama and Georgia, on to Charleston. On the left a line to Memphis. On the south in the rear, was a line leading to Meridian, and from thence to Mobile, New Orleans, Vicksburg and other parts in the south.

The centre and head-quarters of the army was at the small town of Corinth, at the railway junction, fronting north ; while the right wing stretched out to the eastward on the Charleston line for about four miles, and the left wing extended to the westward on the Memphis line, for about the same distance; while to the rear along the railway line, southwards, was a reserve force. This is a rough sketch of the outlines of the camp. The tents, of course, were pitched in the most suitable places for the health and convenience of the troops.

To the north, and in front of this, was a defence line which was occupied by an advanced guard. This line was in the form of a semi-circle—the centre being about four miles in advance of the head-quarters, while on the right and left respectively, it rested upon or crossed the Memphis and Charleston railroad. This advanced line was about 14 miles in length, and was constantly occupied by an advanced guard of about 16,000 men, and several batteries of artillery, each regiment taking its turn of guard duty on this line for 48 hours at a time.

Beyond this line, about a quarter of a mile in advance, was a line of picket-stations, and from these advanced posts were maintained.

The whole army was under command of General Beauregarde; and of his subordinate generals, commanding the different army corps, there were on the centre, General Bragg and General Breckenridge; on the right, General Van Dorn and General Price; on the left, General Hardy and General Little. Under these were many major-generals and brigadier-generals without number.

There were no doubt alterations in these arrangements from time to time, but this was about the arrangement as near as I could arrive at.

For me to presume to give any opinion on the merits and abilities of those generals might be deemed presumption, but I may give an outline of the general estimation in which they were held by the troops, as far as I could gather it.

It will be observed that in this war many of the principal officers—both North and South—came from civil life. This may be accounted for by the limited army maintained in the United States during times of peace. There was, however, a large number of young men who had received a thorough military education at West Point or other military training institutes. Some of these joined the United States army, and after a period of service retired from it, and followed some active business or pursuit in civil life, and were often in the engineering department of the United States or some of the individual States, whence they were ready to come to the front in any case of emergency.

General Beauregarde was a native of New Orleans, of French extraction; he had a thorough military education, and was particularly celebrated as a military engineer. He had constructed the defences at Charleston, and commanded the Southern army at the battle of Bull Run. He was brave, skilful, and cautious, and possessed the universal esteem and confidence of the troops.

General Bragg was also a citizen of Louisiana, and had been employed in the Engineering Department of that State; he had been a captain in the United States army, and had served in the Mexican war, but had retired several years before the civil war broke out. He was not at all popular with the men in general, and they had no great faith in his abilities as a leader. He was said to have made rash adventures, trusting to fortune to have them turn out, so as to get the name of daring enterprises, and it was sometimes quietly hinted that he had no regard for any life except his own. This may have been called forth by his unpopularity. He was of a tyrannical disposition, and his treatment of his troops was harsh, almost amounting to brutality.

General Breckenridge had been Vice-President of the United States under Buchanan. He had a military education, but not much military experience; he possessed much general talent and sagacity, he was but an amateur general, but was generally popular.

General Hardy was a veteran officer of the United States army. He was a bold leader and a skilful tactician. He was the author of a book on tactics called "Hardy's Tactics," which were the tactics adopted by the American armies both North and South. He was particularly noted here for making surprise attacks, skilfully planned, upon the enemy's right wing as they advanced their works, so that when any heavy cannonading was heard on our left the remark would be, "Oh, it is old Hardy driving back their right wing."

General Little, I think, was only a major-general; he had a good name, but we did not know much about him in our division.

General Van Dorn, who was our general, I have already referred to. He was a bold, dashing officer, and had rather distinguished himself here in reconnoitring the enemy's position, the very thing he failed to do at Pea Ridge. He would have done very well to command a brigade of cavalry or a flying column of mounted infantry, but he was too rash and thoughtless to have charge of an army.

General Price, or "Old Papa Price," as he was called, was the very reverse of Van Dorn. He had more the look and character of a civilian, but had considerable military talent and experience. He was zealous, plodding, cautious, and exceedingly careful and attentive to the wants of his men, and was very popular. He and Van Dorn seemed to be jointly in command here, and the two, we supposed, would make one very good general if they could only agree.

The whole strength of the army now amounted to about 130,000 men of all arms, but of these about 10,000 were on the sick list, and the hospitals were full, chiefly of conscripts.

A few days after I had been suspended I was with some of the boys digging out a well at a sort of spring a short distance from the company camp, with a view to getting water. Colonel A. happened to see us and came down to the place and called me over to him and asked what we were doing. I told him. " But," said he, " I thought you were suspended, and take care you are not violating neutrality." I said I thought not in merely digging a hole to get water. He laughed and said he supposed I was tired of being idle. I said I was, and asked if anything had been done in regard to my discharge. He said he had laid the matter before the brigade commander and before the judge-advocate, but it would be some time before any answer would be given—in fact, it was a question which they did not wish to bring up at present, and he did not like to press it. He thought I should just return to duty and he would guarantee me a discharge in July, when the other exempts were being discharged, and if I had any scruples about neutrality he would order me to return to duty, and I might go under protest. " I think," continued he, " that is the best arrangement I can make."

" But what about my rank or position in the company ? " said I. " There has been another orderly sergeant elected, and I suppose he has passed his examination and the appointment has been confirmed. He is on detached service at present on the quartermaster's department, but I suppose will return in a few days and take the appointment."

" Who is acting orderly sergeant at present ? " said he.

" The first duty sergeant," said I.

" Oh, very well," said he, " you can go and act over him for the present, and when the orderly sergeant elect comes to take the appointment, I will give you some other appointment of equal rank, which you can fill until you get your discharge with the other exempts."

I thought his proposals fair and reasonable, considering the imperious position the Government had taken and the arbitrary measures they were enforcing. I therefore agreed to the proposal, taking care to have my protest noted.

I returned to duty, though now taking it easier, leaving the first duty sergeant to take the heaviest part of the camp duties off my hand.

The position of affairs continued about the same, the two armies confronting each other ; but it was known that the enemy had considerably increased their forces, and had over 150,000 men, and were throwing up long lines of earth-works, and working up by parallels and closing in around Corinth in the anaconda fashion.

About the middle of May we were apprised of the destruction of the Confederate gunboats (such as they were) on the Mississippi at Memphis, and the capture of that city by the enemy.

This was not altogether unexpected by certain of our men. The gunboats and a considerable land force had been under the command of a supposed daring and skilful personage, Jeff. Thomson I think was the name. He was described as the Swamp Fox, or the Marion of the present war; although some in their scepticism feared that his reputation arose more from popular bounce and newspaper puffery than from any deeds he had ever performed, and since the catastrophe at New Orleans the army had less faith in these newspaper heroes. However that might be, the Confederates were defeated and their few gunboats destroyed, and Memphis was occupied by the Federal troops.

This was another serious though perhaps not unexpected blow to the Confederacy, as it left the Mississippi open to the Federals down to New Orleans, allowing their fleet of gunboats from above to form a junction with their fleet at New Orleans, unless the fortifications at Vicksburg could be got into such a forward state as to prevent it.

Such disasters were now coming on the Confederacy thick and fast, and mostly through the incapacity and failures of officials who had been placed in high command and responsible positions, such officials of course had been favourites of the Government and got their appointments through influence; whilst the newspapers, which of course lauded everything that the Government did, magnified them into heroes before they had in any way been put to the proof.

The axiom that "the pen is mightier than the sword," may hold good in times of peace, but it may be looked at from another point of view and somewhat modified in time of war. The sword then governs and directs the pen, and the latter becomes merely a servant to the former. In other words, the pen may evoke war, but when war is instituted, the pen becomes subservient to the sword.

I have heard in the midst of those desperate times the pen

compared to a clamorous mob, who, in their cry for freedom, sets aside all established rules, law, and order, and subjects everything to their own blind will, and the first thing they do is to set up on high some power or personage who will lay upon their necks a yoke or chain to which they will unwittingly submit, and become to that power the most helpless and abject slaves. But these are political subjects which I know nothing about, and have nothing to do with, and I must return to my duty. I saw a group of men sitting at the back of a tent poring over something which they hid away on my approach.

"Holloa! What is that you have got there, Jim?"

"What?"

"Why that which you are hiding behind your back?"

"Oh nothing but a newspaper, sergeant."

"Let me see it."

"Let him see it, Jim," says another, "the sergeant is all right."

I took the paper and looked over it. I saw it was a paper which had dared to maintain to a certain extent a little independence, and had ventured to criticise in somewhat severe though cautious terms the gross mismanagement of the Government, and the incapacity of some of their favourite officials to whom they had intrusted commands of great importance and responsibility.

There was in it some reference to a special order or message issued by President Davis, in which it described, as a soother to the army, his statement that he had suspended Generals Floyd and Pillow; some of the boys asking me if that meant that he had suspended them by the neck.

This paper also referred to that arm of the Federal service which threatened to crush the South, and that was the naval power; and in an ironical way referred to an assuring order, issued to the Confederate army, that all uneasiness on that point might now be set aside, as the Government had taken powerful measures to check any further advance of the Federal fleet, and for this they had created a Naval Department in the Cabinet, and had appointed a Secretary of the Navy, in the person of a Mr. Somebody, whose very name, the Government organs seemed to think, would soon send the Federal fleet to perdition.

I was agreeably surprised to find that there were still some newspapers which dared to speak their minds, although in somewhat measured terms.

I was told that such a paper dare not be seen in Bragg's division, as it had severely condemned some acts of brutality on the part of General Bragg, which were now the subject of general comment among the men.

It seemed that there were in Bragg's division some regiments of volunteers from Tennessee, and one or two of those regiments were what were called one-year's troops, having volunteered for one year only, and their term of service was now expired.

A great many of the men composing these regiments were men with families. They had made provision for their families when they left their homes for one year. But since that time the State had been overrun by the Federal troops, houses burned, crops and property destroyed and plundered, and families turned out of their houses, and their homes desolated.

These men were of course very anxious about their families, and requested that as their term of service was now expired, they might be allowed to go home for a short time and see their families, and have them taken to some place of security; after which they pledged themselves that they would return to the service.

Bragg peremptorily refused. They then asked for furloughs, part of them only going at a time. This he also refused, and would not grant a furlough to anyone, even if it were to transact business for the others. The whole regiment then laid down their arms and refused duty.

Bragg then brought up a strong force and surrounded them, and then directed a battery of artillery against them, and gave them five minutes to take up their arms and return to duty.

The men sullenly obeyed, each muttering to himself that it would be but little service that he would ever get out of them, and this was true, as the sequel proved.

A good many deserted, but some were caught attempting, or supposed to be attempting, to desert, and were summarily shot without any trial.

The greatest tyrant that ever disgraced a position of power will always have his horde of sycophants to endorse and magnify his every act, and in this case a number, of course, including the Government organs, did extol Bragg for what they called his firmness and decision. But a far greater number denounced it as uncalled-for brutality, and unjust and improper treatment of volunteers. Even Beauregarde, when he came to know of it, was said to have disapproved of it, and considered it unnecessary harshness, and not calculated to promote either the strength or the loyalty of the army. But Bragg at that time was supposed to be fishing for favour at the War Department, and it was hinted that he was trying to undermine and supersede Beauregarde in the command. He knew that this act would raise him in favour at the despotic Court at Richmond. Of course this was only talk among the soldiers, some few favouring Bragg, but more condemning him, and placing implicit confidence in Beauregarde.

Whether this act of Bragg contributed in any way to his being appointed, as he was shortly afterwards, to supersede Beauregarde, I do not know ; but Beauregarde's remarks, that such acts were not calculated to promote either the strength or the loyalty of the army, if he did make them, were to my certain knowledge strikingly correct ; and if such strong measures were necessary, as was asserted by some, the evil effects of them were clearly shown before many days were past.

The numerous disasters which had now come on the Confederacy were mostly incurred by mismanagement and corruption at headquarters. The despotic tyranny of Jefferson Davis and his minions—the Conscript Act and the brutality of Bragg were now beginning to show in dumb silence on many countenances, but of course no one dared to speak publicly, no matter what they might think, and a superficial appearance of spirit and enthusiasm was still maintained, and it seemed to be now, as I have often seen it before and since, that public opinion collectively was one thing, and private opinion individually another ; and nearly everyone of any judgment considered within himself that the enemy getting control of the Mississippi rendered the cause hopeless, and that further fighting was only to gratify a vindictive spirit or vain ambition.

Another piece of news was now whispered through the army which created universal disgust. It was to the effect that the Confederate Congress at Richmond, having heard that the Federal general, M'Lellan, was advancing upon Richmond, after passing the Conscript Act, had passed a bill to pay themselves their wages in specie, which they pocketed, and then broke up Congress and fled from Richmond.

2 A

I may here say in advance, and I think with very good authority, that at this time, May, 1862, the state of affairs hung in the balance, and the total collapse of the Confederacy and the termination of the war would then and there have taken place but for two circumstances :—

First, the sending of Butler to New Orleans by the Federal Government; and

Second, the transfer of the command of the Confederate army, in Virginia, to General Lee.

The brutal tyranny of Butler in New Orleans filled every heart in the South with indignation, and seemed to foreshadow to them what they might expect if they surrendered to the authority of the Federal Government, and roused them to a determination to fight to the bitter end, while the noble character, the able management, and skilful generalship of General Lee and his brilliant successes inspired them with renewed confidence and hope, and prolonged the struggle for nearly three years.

It was a few days after this act of General Bragg that I first observed something like secret disaffection among the troops.

At some distance from the rear of the camp and within the woods there were a spring and a small creek where the men from different parts of the army came for water and to wash their clothes. To this place one evening about sunset I went to wash some clothes. On approaching the place I observed a number of men who had apparently come there for water or to wash, but who were sitting among the bushes near the spring, seemingly in earnest conversation. I could see that they were not all men of our division, but some of them were from other divisions, and could not have come there for water or to do washing. They did not observe my approach, or did not pay heed to it, and I observed that they were discussing the state of affairs and the action of General Bragg, and I heard something like propositions that the whole army should break up in a general row and march off in bands, taking their arms with them ; and they seemed to be sounding the feeling among the different divisions.

I pretended to take no notice of them, but proceeded to wash my clothes. Some of them then began to do the same, and the conversation became more general ; and the affair of the Congress breaking up, after securing for themselves their wages in specie, was brought up, and it was suggested that the

army should now do the same thing. I asked if it was a fact
that the Congress had broken up, when one of them handed
me a newspaper, which was one of the proscribed papers, and
which gave an account of the action of Congress, with some
rather severe criticisms on that "Honourable Body." It also
contained a piece of rhyme which I copied. It ran thus:—

> Cromwell his crop-eared soldiers sent
> Into the Barebones Parliament;
> But, had he lived in modern times,
> When men make laws and love for dimes,
> He would find our Barebones much more docile
> Than Pim or any other fossil.
> Nor had he found a reason urgent
> To call a file of men and sergeant,
> But simply wait a brace of weeks,
> Till Barebones unto Bunkum speaks,
> Till, tabling other claims, those sages
> Had passed a bill to pay their wages;
> Pressed every man to warlike service,
> Except themselves—these statesmen nervous;
> Then had he sent a courier foaming
> To cry, To arms, the foe is coming,
> Our Parliament would, *sine moro*,
> Evanish like a flock of sorro.

From the general tone among the men I could see that
disaffection was pretty far spread, and I would not have been
astonished to have seen a general break-up. But within a
day or two after this, newspapers were abundantly spread all
over the camp, giving an account of Butler's actions in New
Orleans, and his famous, or infamous, order in regard to
treating females as "women of the town" was read out to
every regiment on parade, and copies of the order extensively
circulated.

Butler and his acts were no doubt made the most of, but
from every inquiry there was no room left for doubt as to the
truth of the reports; and in any way his acts and his language
could be taken they could not fail to raise a feeling of indignation, and the most disaffected became satisfied and seemed to
think it better "to bear the ills they had than fly to others
which they knew not of." The feeling of indignation which was
roused by Butler's acts overcame in a great measure the disaffection that had been fast spreading through the army; and
many were roused to a spirit of revenge, while the disaffected
acquiesced, not that they hated Davis and his Bragg the less,
but that they hated Lincoln and his Butler the more.

It was now getting towards the end of May, and no appearance of a general battle, although fighting along the advanced line was getting heavier every day. We were about half of our time at the front; it was about two days on and two days off, and the two days off were always interrupted by various calls to the front in expectation of a general battle.

The provisioning of the army was now most wretched; such articles of food as were stintedly served out were of the poorest quality—moulded cow pease, and some half putrid, hot weather salted beef.

This, however, we did not feel so much, and cared little about the rations served; for, strange to say, in passing backwards and forwards to the front, we went through large mounds of provisions lying along on each side of the railway, broken open, scattered about, and rotting in the sun and rain; barrels of flour, pork, and beef, lying in all directions with the barrel-heads knocked out by the wheels of the artillery striking against them, the contents mixing with the dust or mud, as the weather might be, while the hot sun soon putrified them, and the swarms of flies which covered them might be compared to one of the plagues of Egypt. Here the men obtained abundance in an irregular way, although the manner in which they obtained it must have involved indescribable waste.

Along the side of the railroad were piled up like houses on the side of a street, several thousand large boxes of biscuits, supposed to have come from Charleston. These would have been a great acquisition and relief to the whole army if judiciously served out, but like the hundreds of tons of other provisions that lay rotting there, they were probably sealed up with red tape and departmental officialism.

Whatever was the cause of them lying there, and the army in a state of starvation, we did not know, neither did we care. The treasure which the boxes contained was soon discovered. The butts of muskets, sabres, and bayonets were soon applied to break open the boxes, and the men of the different battalions passing to and from the front hastily filled their haversacks.

This continued from day to day; the valuable biscuits were scattered and trampled on the ground, the rain fell and wet them, and they heated and smoked like the ruins of a line of building under the engine hose after a fire. The men still in going past had a dig at the diggings, as they called the mound, they quarried deeper and deeper into the heart of the pile to get at the dry biscuits, until nothing remained but a long ridge of broken boxes and rotten biscuits.

About this time sickness broke out worse in the camp than it had ever been. The hospitals were already filled with the unhappy conscripts. But now a general complaint broke out in the form of a violent diarrhœa. This was said to have been caused by some transactions, which, if they were as represented, certainly merited the severest condemnation and punishment.

A quantity of molasses was got up from Louisiana. This was an article which was greatly prized, and pure Louisiana molasses, if properly preserved, prepared and reboiled, is a good and wholesome article of food, and was always much used throughout the South, and indeed, throughout the whole of America, and it was now in great demand.

When the first ration of this was issued to our company, I observed that it was a mass of foam—it was then fermenting and beginning to sour. Our men, being Louisianians, knew the article and could detect the defect. The stuff had been mixed with water and the hot weather had caused it to ferment, and it was not only unfit for food, but dangerous to health, and the story came out that the molasses had come in good order and of excellent quality, but the demand for it was so great outside of the ranks that the commissary had sold a large quantity of it for a high price, and then, to make up the deficiency in serving it out to the troops, had added water, and the hot weather caused it to ferment.

Whether this was the case, and whether there would have been any inquiry into the matter, I do not know, but in the thickening of events at this time, and the change of commanders which took place shortly afterwards, it like many other corruptions was soon lost sight of in the general mess.

It was now certain that the enemy had greatly advanced their position. They were approaching by parallel entrenchments. They had now got their works so far advanced and their heavy guns into position that they could throw shells right into the centre of our camp.

The railway to Memphis on our left was no longer of any use ; it was therefore torn up, the bridges destroyed, and the line on our right leading to Charleston was found to be cut off, showing that the enemy had outflanked us on our right.

Our whole attention was now directed to the front, where the enemy commenced a regular bombardment, continuing it from daylight until sunset, with very few intervals, and it was getting heavier every day, our artillery replying with lighter guns from several redoubts in various places a little in advance of the line of our advanced guard.

It was now almost a continued battle, the enemy every day and sometimes at night making attacks upon our advanced line of pickets. They sometimes brought forward batteries of light field guns, and raked the woods in the neighbourhood of our pickets, and frequently made charges with small bodies of cavalry, and sometimes an attack with infantry. In none of these attacks were they very successful. They were generally worsted, and sometimes pretty severely handled.

For their light artillery we did not care a pin. The country was rough, and we lay down behind hillocks and large trees and cried to them to fire away, and some detachments of the New Orleans Washington Artillery generally gave them back their fire with good interest. When cavalry came upon us we got among the brushwood and brought them off their saddles like crows off a fence; and if infantry advanced we fell back upon the reserve, where, if they followed, they got a hot reception, and were driven back with heavy loss.

Nevertheless they still kept advancing their position. The tide of the war was now with them, and they were getting bolder and more confident, and they far outnumbered us in strength. But our men were now in fighting spirit, and the war-cry was "Butler," and they were eager to fight, and had the enemy come out of their entrenchments and fought in fair field the result would have been very doubtful. But they would not come out of their entrenchments and risk a general battle. They kept behind their works, which they continued to advance and hem us in.

The pickets were pushed forward till within speaking distance of each other, and I presume by a mutual agreement the firing between pickets was stopped except when attacks were made by larger bodies, and then the pickets fell back. A war of words was now indulged in between the pickets, and much banter was passed.

The only beverage which our men had as a substitute for coffee was a decoction made from the roots of the sassafras tree, which grew thick in the woods. This we drank, and it was called sassafras tea. It was not an unpalatable nor, I believe, an unwholesome beverage, but it was a poor substitute for coffee. On this the enemy's pickets bantered us much, asking if we had yet dug up all the sassafras trees in the woods, and asking if we would not like some coffee.

We were glad to hear they had abundance of coffee, as we trusted that it would fall into our hands, as we intended to pay them a visit one of those days. So we said. They of course invited us to come. They then asked how about our conscripts, and how Bragg and the Tennessee boys were getting on, and said that some of our Tennessee boys who were now on their side desired to send their compliments to old Bragg.

It was quite evident that they knew much more of the affairs of our camp than we suspected ; but the fact was, numerous desertions had taken place from Bragg's army, and though some were caught in the act and shot, that did not stop it, and desertions were taking place every day from those Tennessee regiments which Bragg had so brutally treated.

On the 26th, 27th, and 28th of May we had been at the front, and during those three days the fighting had gone on almost incessantly. We were sitting down behind a hillock, near one of the advanced posts, when I tried to make a calculation of the number of shots from heavy artillery that were being fired from the enemy's lines. This I made out to be a daily average of about 40,000. The fixed ammunition for each shot was said to cost about 10 dollars, making the expense of that fire about 400,000 dollars daily ; while, at the very outside, the total number on our side killed each day by that fire did not exceed 100, thus costing for ammunition alone to kill each man about 4000 dollars. This calculation I showed to my friend Tim D., who was sitting near me. Tim, after verifying the calculation, said he thought war was all nonsense, and that Mr. Lincoln was very foolish to spend so much money making war, because he could have got them killed far cheaper without war. He knew, he said, plenty of fellows in Ireland, and in America, too, whom Mr. Lincoln could have hired to kill them for the tenth part of that money without making war at all.

On the 28th there was a pretty severe battle, in which one of the Texan regiments of our brigade lost about 200 men, but the enemy were driven back, and they retired within their entrenchments, and a lull took place.

In the afternoon I was sent with a party of 12 men to take charge of an advanced post until six o'clock, when another regiment would come to relieve our regiment and we would get back to camp.

All was quiet in front of our right wing throughout the rest of the afternoon. I thought it was a truce to bury the dead, as between the lines there were a great many dead, and the air was polluted for miles. I did not, however, see any appearance of this being done, and we still heard the distant firing away on our left wing.

The relief party which should have come to us at six o'clock did not appear till about eight o'clock. It was now dark, and when we got back to the main line of the advanced guard the new guard was posted and our regiment was gone and our company with it.

To where our camp was was more than three miles, and the whole space through the woods between us and it was blocked up by waggons, artillery trains, cavalry horses picketed, and other obstructions, and men sleeping on the ground, who would not be over civil if we kicked against or tumbled over them in the darkness. We did not know the proper way, and we could never be able to find it in the dark, and we knew we would have nothing to eat when we did get back to camp. We therefore concluded to seek out a quiet, snug place in the woods and lie down till daylight, and return to camp in the morning, when we could easily account for our absence.

We kept in front of the guard line, where the wood was less trampled, and soon found a snug place under a large oak tree, where we rolled ourselves in our blankets and lay down beside our arms, and were soon asleep.

We slept well, but imagined we heard throughout the night heavy movements, slow tramping of men, and slow rolling of wheels, but what was going on around us we neither knew nor cared.

At early dawn we woke up much refreshed. We heard reveille beating, but that we knew to be in the enemy's camp, and as we did not intend to go there to roll-call we were in no hurry to get up.

We did get up, however, and looked around to find our way to camp, but we could see nobody—all was quiet. We thought we had wandered further into the woods than we had expected, and began to fear that we might fall into the hands of the enemy. On looking round, however, we saw marks which showed where we were, but we found every place deserted. The advanced posts were deserted, and we went to some of the redoubts, but found them also deserted, and dummy guns placed in the embrasures. One of the men now declared that he remembered hearing, on the previous afternoon, one of the artillerymen say to another these words—" We are going to skedaddle from here this night!"

It was now evident that the army had gone, but, where it had gone to we did not know. The situation was novel, and we rather enjoyed it. We went to a rising ground where we could get a good view, and climbed a tree to see the camp and the country around. We saw plainly that all was deserted, and everything was still as death. We then thought of reconnoitring parties of the enemy, but as they did not generally open fire from their entrenchments until about half-past seven or eight o'clock, they would not know of the departure of our army; and, no doubt, it was to deceive them on this point that dummy guns had been placed in the embrasures at the redoubts.

We now started to follow the army, intending on our way to go to the biscuit heap and try to dig up some good biscuit.

As we proceeded along we heard voices and a movement in the wood. We went to the place and saw a number of men, between 200 and 300, who were lying on their arms among the bushes. We asked where the army had gone?

They said away south, by the railway line, towards Ripley. They asked why we were left behind?

We explained that we had been on picket-guard, and slept in the woods instead of going back to camp. I asked if they were the rear-guard?

Some said "Yes," and some said "No," and some told us to "Go on, and ask no questions."

" I bet you I know who these fellows are," said Canada, who was with us, as we left them. " These are some of Bragg's Tennessee men dropping behind to skedaddle to their homes, and right they are."

I thought from their wretched and haggard appearance that they were Bragg's men, and I did not disagree with him in his opinion.

" I don't care," said he, " I will ask the next lot we come to, right out."

" You had better not," said I ; "it is not our business ; we are no rear-guard to pick up stragglers, and we don't wish to give information, as we are bound to do, against deserters, especially men who are to be so much sympathised with as these Tennessee men ; and so long as we do not know what they are, we have nothing to do with them, and we have no business to ask."

" I will give information against them," said he, " but by that time they will be far enough out of reach ; and I will just do it to annoy old Bragg."

We got to the biscuit heap, and after digging deep into the rotten mass we came upon some sound biscuits, which we put into our haversacks. We then went towards the railway junction at Corinth. The whole of the cars and rolling-stock was gone, and much of the track torn up. The houses were not destroyed but empty ; many barrels of beef and pork with the heads knocked out lay along the line. The beef was execrable, but a piece of tolerable pork was picked up which we took along, intending to grill and eat it with our biscuit as soon as we got to the wooded country and away from this abominable place.

We followed the railway southward, and at last got on to the track of the army. We had not gone far when we came upon another and larger body of men lying in the woods. This time there would be near 1000. We at first thought they were the rear-guard, but Canada pressed the question on them. They were quite indifferent and defiant, and said they were going no further with Bragg, and told us if we saw Bragg that day to tell him to come back and see them, and they would make a bargain with him. I quite believe they would, and it would have been a final settlement so far as Bragg was concerned.

They said they were waiting for others who had yet to come and join them. They asked if we had seen many men north of the railway. We said only one lot. They said these were those who had been on the advanced guard, and they were going to hide in the woods there, until the Federals passed south of them and occupied Corinth, and then they would go to their homes in Tennessee.

Throughout that day we met large bodies of men coming

backwards of whom we learned how far the rear-guard was in advance. These men had dropped out of the ranks mostly in the night, and lingered in the woods until the rear-guard had passed, and then made their way back in the opposite direction.

It had always been quite a common thing for men to straggle from the ranks on a march, but they always came up afterwards, and among volunteer troops such a thing as desertion was never dreamt of. But on reasoning with these men that day, they told us that they would sooner have died than done it while volunteers, but the case was now altered. They had served honourably their time as volunteers, but when they were afterwards driven to serve by having artillery turned against them, they considered they were no longer volunteers, or by honour bound.

This was the first instance of desertion that I knew of in the Confederate army, and it was upon an extensive scale. The Confederate Government and their organs tried to underrate it and smother it as much as possible, and especially Bragg's action which caused it. They admitted the loss of a few hundred men who had been left behind; while the Federal General Halleck declared that 15,000 men had deserted and surrendered their arms to him; but this I think was exaggerated. I have no doubt from what I saw that several thousands dropped out and were left behind.

We were in no hurry to overtake the army, as we could get along much easier and pleasanter by ourselves outside of the crowd. We bivouacked by ourselves for the night, and the following day came up with the army, which at last took up a position at a place called Tupelo, about 35 miles south from Corinth, near the Mobile and Ohio railroad.

CHAPTER XXVI.

THE evacuation of Corinth and falling back to Tupelo was disapproved of by the Government at Richmond, and Beauregarde was blamed for it and superseded by Bragg.

There was, however, a great many who considered that any censure on Beauregarde was extremely unjust, and there must have been other reasons for placing Bragg in command. It required no great military knowledge to see that the position at Corinth was no longer tenable or of any great value to the Confederates, except so far as in keeping it from the Federals.

Memphis being irrecoverably in possession of the Federals, it was of no use for communication with that place. The line to Charleston was in possession of the enemy, and that was of no value. There was no communication then left but the line direct to the South, and by moving South to a stronger position on that line, it was held more secure. It would, however, be of some value to the Federals if they could keep the lines to the east and west and to the north open.

Corinth, with the railways cut off, was valueless as a place of defence, and it was certainly not a healthy position. Beauregarde found himself outflanked by numbers, the railways cut off to the east and west, his rear threatened, and his army suffering from sickness. Out of 130,000 men nearly 20,000 were on the sick list. The enemy had advanced their works so as to throw their shells into the centre of the position, and he could not bring them to a general battle, even against his inferior force. The withdrawing of his forces was skilfully executed, and for the troops lost by desertion Bragg was entirely to blame.

Such was the opinion of many military men, and by many it was considered that Beauregarde was altogether too mild and gentlemanly in his disposition to be in high favour with Davis and his cabinet, and the arbitrary measures of Bragg better suited the imperious policy they had adopted.

The quietness of the camp at Tupelo contrasted strangely with the constant alarms and din of battle at Corinth, and it being now June, the shady position of the camp among the trees was a relief from the heat endured in the exposed camp at Corinth. We had no tents, but we had got accustomed to do without them. We made large huts or bowers of green branches, which kept off the sun by day and the dew by night. The weather was now beautiful, with very little rain. The sick began to recover, and the men got their clothes washed and mended, and to add to their comfort, a large quantity of summer clothing arrived to be distributed among them. This did not come from the army bureau, through the quarter-master's department, but from the homes and families of the men themselves. This consignment was greatly augmented by "ladies' associations," which had now become a powerful factor in the administration of the war, and, thanks to the action of General Butler in New Orleans, the zeal now displayed by them was almost incredible. Nothing seemed to be too good for them to sacrifice. Beautiful silk dresses had been cut up and made into tunics for the soldiers. Rich shawls and plaids had been cut up and sewed together and bound to form blankets or wrappers, and seemingly everything which could be applied to the use of the soldiers was turned to account.

Our regiment being from Louisiana came in for a fair share of these articles ; and on the following Sunday morning, when the regiment turned out for parade inspection, they certainly presented a clean and neat, though somewhat fantastic, appearance ; and the pretty pictures, as they called them, on some of their beautifully-flowered tunics was the subject of a good deal of merriment. I could not help contrasting the difference in the men's appearance with the dirty, smoke-begrimed, ragged wretches that they were on the retreat after Pea Ridge.

I think it was on this same morning that we became aware of another acquisition to the army in the appointment of still another Richmond official. It was, of course, a sinecure appointment, to provide for some hanger-on or minion. It was something in connection with the Inspector's Department.

This branch of the service (if service it could be called) was known to be a sort of receptacle for all surplus office-seekers that could not be otherwise disposed of—in fact, a sort of waste-basket in which to throw all superfluities when the lobby got choked up and it became necessary to clear it.

When this poor "critter" came on with his credentials the appointment was to the old stand-by office of "assistant-inspector," with the rank of captain. So many had been appointed to this office that it had become a subject for laughter and joking about. Our assistant-inspector did not, however, regard it in that way. He had too much self-sufficiency, and came on with an air of great importance and pomposity, as one possessing the full confidence of, and having unlimited authority from, the imperial court at Richmond. But, then, what the duties of his office were to be he did not know, and those who appointed him could not tell him.

The officer to whom he had been ordered to report, seeing the nature of the appointment and not knowing where to place the new comer, referred him to the next in command, who again referred him to the next, and so on, and he was bandied about from one corps to another, until he had no doubt got irritated and perhaps his pomposity a little subdued.

In the course of his rounds he had been referred to Colonel A. of our regiment, perhaps on account of the latter's new appointment making him the junior colonel of the brigade or perhaps of the division.

Colonel A., if the junior colonel, was by no means the simplest, and he was equal to the occasion.

He informed the newly-made inspector that he presumed his duty was to inspect the arms of the regiment, and, therefore, as there would be a general inspection on Sunday morning, he would parade the regiment for this purpose.

Our assistant-inspector was now gratified that his position was acknowledged, and he had some idea of what his duties were to be, but he had not the least knowledge of the regular form and performance of an "inspection of arms," and probably thought that it would be like many other duties of sinecure offices—a mere ceremony, and that he would only take a look along the ranks and then express himself highly satisfied. But the colonel looked forward to having a little amusement.

"Inspection of arms" was a part of the manual, and was always done by the company officers before drill, and also by orderly sergeants in all details or detachments before handing them over, and by one of the field officers at a "regimental parade and inspection," which generally took place every Sunday morning when not employed on more important matters. It was rather a pretty performance when well executed. Ranks were opened, bayonets fixed, rammers drawn and dropped into the guns, and the men stood at "order arms." The officer who inspected the arms began at the man on the right, and each soldier, as he approached, quickly brought up his piece into a position for the officer to take it, the butt of the piece resting against his left side, his left hand grasping the barrel forward of the lock, and the muzzle elevated and thrown slightly forward. The officer passed his right hand under the soldier's arm, seized the piece by the small part of the stock, stepped back two paces, examined the lock that it was clean, clicked and worked properly, examined the fixing of the bayonet, then shook the ramrod in the barrel to show that the barrel was empty and clean, and in the old-fashioned musket a sound, clear ring indicated that the barrel was clean and in good order. When the officer satisfied himself that the piece was in good order he stood in his place and threw it to the soldier, who caught it in the air with his right hand, and with one motion came to "order arms." This throwing of the gun by the officer and catching in an adroit way by the soldier had to be done in a particular way like a circus performance, and required a mutual confidence between officer and soldier.

When Sunday morning came the regiment was formed for parade and inspection. When the usual manual had been gone through, it was formed into column by companies, ranks opened, and the order given to prepare for inspection of arms. The soldiers sprung their rammers, dropped them into their guns, and stood at "order arms." "Now, captain," said the colonel, addressing our new inspector, "you will please inspect arms."

The inspector, who was arrayed in a brilliant captain's uniform, with shining buttons and gold lace in profusion, which completely out-did our boys with the pretty pictures on their tunics, now came forward. He looked nervous, and hesitatingly approached the front company, while the colonel preserved a grave countenance. The inspector went towards the centre of the company first, and began to look down at the arms as the men stood at "order arms," but not a man moved, and there was a dead silence—the men had been warned not to laugh.

At length the inspector happened to come in front of the man on the right, where he should have begun at first. The soldier quickly brought up his piece to the position, the inspector started back in astonishment, and a roar of laughter burst from both officers and men. The colonel immediately ordered silence, and, going up to the inspector, asked him if he was not going to inspect the arms in the regular and proper way. The man had to acknowledge that he knew nothing about it, and would have to be instructed.

The colonel, who was a thorough gentleman, undertook to show him, and taking a piece from one of the men, showed him how to examine it, and explaining to him as he rung the rammer in the barrel that a clear sound ring showed that the barrel was clear and sound, and adding, "Let me show you how to go through it. I will do this first rank for you."

The colonel quickly passed along the first rank, taking each man's piece and stepping back nearly four paces, inspecting it and then throwing it back to the soldier, throwing it high in the air and with such precision, and the soldier catching it with such adroitness, that the transfer of the gun from the colonel's hands to an "order arms" by the soldier's side seemed to be one unbroken motion.

The inspector feared to undertake the throwing of the gun, so the colonel told him just to hand it back to the soldier, and hinted to him to be quick, as the parade was lasting too long. He bungled along in any kind of way, trying to get through with it, amongst a good deal of tittering among the men, in which our company had just rather freely indulged, and as they were then the left flank company, they were the last to be inspected. He had observed them laughing, and was no doubt irritated.

When he came to inspect the company the first rifle he tried did not ring, the rammer fell with a heavy thud. "That gun is dirty," said he to the man. The man was silent. The next was the same, and the whole company's arms were reported in bad condition. The captain declined to take the report, and told him to report to the colonel. The colonel coming up, looked at the arms, and asked what he found wrong. He replied that the guns did not ring. The colonel explained to

him that these were Springfield rifles, which unscrewed at the
breach, and therefore could not ring ; but, continued he, when
you go with them on to the field of battle, you will hear them
ring to your utmost satisfaction.

Our inspector had little more to say, and we heard no more
of him. He would, like hundreds of others, hold his sinecure
appointment and draw his pay but keep out of danger, strut
with his sword and uniform about hotels and cafés, visit
private families, and pass among the ladies as a great warrior.

The camp here seemed to be in a good healthy position, and
the health and condition of the troops continued to improve,
but there did not seem to be any appearance of active movement. The enemy made no further advance, and it was now
the general conjecture as to what the next movement would
be. Beauregarde had been superseded by Bragg, and the
troops in general did not like the change.

About the end of June the orderly sergeant, who had been
elected to fill my place, came to take the position, which I
handed over to him, and I got a temporary appointment as
"Acting Assistant Adjutant-General of the Brigade." This
was simply a sort of clerk to the adjutant-general, and consisted
mostly of consolidating reports. The adjutant-general, who had
been fonder of flying about as an aide-de-camp, than attending
to his reports, had let them get very far behind. There was
not much interesting in this work, except that I saw the weak
state of the brigade, composed as it was of skeleton regiments,
some companies not having more than 12 privates "present
for duty," although having the full complement of officers and
non-commissioned officers. Our own regiment had 133 officers,
commissioned and non-commissioned, and only about 166
privates, present for duty, and over 40 of these were going
to be discharged under the Conscript Act. Of course there
were a good many on detached service and on the sick list,
but the aggregate was under 400 ; of course, these officers
were only in name, they had, all under the rank of captain, to
carry rifles and work as privates.

About this time news came about the successes of General
Lee and Stonewall Jackson, in Virginia ; that the Federal
General, Halleck, had gone to take charge of the defence of
Washington ; that the Federal force in front of us, under
General Grant, was being divided for some other movements ;
and as some alterations and improvements were being made in

2 B

our camp, and wells were being dug for a supply of water, it seemed as if we were to remain here some time.

Having got through with my work of consolidating reports, I was ordered to get a list of all soldiers in the brigade who were not subject to military duty under the Conscript Act, and who had applied for discharge, and make out descriptive lists of them and their discharges.

I may here say that ordinary writing paper had now about disappeared, and all the army forms and documents were made of some kind of home manufactured brown paper—something like that used by grocers in wrapping up goods. It was joyful news to the parties when I went to take their height, colour of hair and eyes etc., as they were beginning to fear, now that as Bragg had come into the command, they would be retained under some pretence. But probably Bragg had seen the effects of his former blind policy, and was trying to regain a little popularity.

There was, in the whole brigade, about 130 who were entitled to discharges under the exemption clause of the act, and nearly every one took advantage of it. Our company had a large proportion of exempts—there being five under 18 years of age.

The descriptive lists and discharges were all made out, of course including one for myself, and I was ordered to take the men to the provost-martial and have them sworn. This being done, he signed the preliminary to the discharges, attesting those to be entitled to discharge in terms of an act entitled an "Act for the Better Provision for the Public Defence."

I now took them to the brigade commander, who spent some time in a long lecture, and used many arguments and persuasions, trying to induce them to change their minds and volunteer again for service instead of accepting their discharge, but he could make no converts, although they all promised to return again to service after a short holiday, which, I believe, most of them did,—but not under Bragg. He then signed the discharges, and the order for their pay for service, and an allowance in the way of mile money for transportation to the place where they were enlisted, and a pass to go as far as the lines of the Confederacy extended but no farther.

My duty was now done, and we went to the paymaster and got paid in Confederate scrip, and we were civilians once more.

We now went and took good-bye with our old companions in arms, and got from them many greetings, messages, and letters to take to their friends at home.

I must say that although I was heartily sick of the service, I still felt a little sorry to leave old friends with whom I spent many happy hours, and had come through many privations and dangers; although it was true that there were but few of them left, in that both company and regiment were very much altered.

We got by railway to Jackson, Mississippi, where we parted; those whose homes were in Arkansas, Texas, and Northern Louisiana, going to try to get by way of Vicksburg, while those of our company proceeded by railway to Camp Moore, which was on the New Orleans and Jackson railroad, about 100 miles north from New Orleans, intending to cross the country from there to Baton Rouge.

Before leaving Jackson, however, we heard news which startled us, which was that Baton Rouge was occupied by the Federal troops, and that the town had been bombarded by the Federal gun-boats which had been lying in the river opposite the town, and that, too, without a moment's notice, and that houses had been destroyed, people killed, and women and children driven to the woods in consternation.

This I was astonished to hear. For, although from all accounts nothing could be too diabolical for Butler to do, yet as regarded Admiral Farragut and the officers of his fleet, they were spoken of in the very highest terms for their honourable and gentlemanly conduct even amongst the most fiery Southerners.

Camp Moore was as far south as the line was open; the line between that place and New Orleans being torn up, and the bridges destroyed.

Camp Moore had been a camp of instruction. Camp Walker, at New Orleans, where our regiment had been organised the previous year, had been found to be unhealthy and unsuitable, and the camp of instruction had been removed to this place. It was now used as a rendezvous and training camp for conscripts, and there were now here of those unhappy men about 200; and about half that number of Government-appointed officers, who knew little more of military matters than the conscripts whom they were vainly trying to drill into soldiers.

Of course we considered ourselves veterans, and did not deign to recognise such things as soldiers or officers; but we also knew that this was about the limit of the Confederate lines, and our passes did not take us beyond this, and there might be some difficulty in getting beyond into what was partly neutral territory.

The distance from Camp Moore to Baton Rouge was about 40 miles, and to the neighbourhood of the latter place we wished to go.

We knew that these conscript officers were mighty men when at a distance from the enemy, and they would stand very high on their dignity if we in a humble way asked to get passed the lines. We knew, therefore, that the only way to get passed was by some device, and that we could easily contrive, as we saw that both the men and their officers were perfectly raw, and knew little or nothing of guard or picket duty, and we easily passed the pickets under the guise of a reconnoitring party.

When we got within 20 miles of Baton Rouge, one or two of our party were near their homes, and we called at the house of a gentleman with whom most of us were acquainted, where we learned the particulars regarding the bombardment of Baton Rouge.

The town had been bombarded and considerable damage done to property, but few people had been hurt; the blame lay, not with the Federal fleet, but with the Confederate Government, or rather with a band of miscreants, which, if the Government did not actually organise and direct, they at least tolerated and acknowledged to a certain extent.

These were a band of lawless men who had with a view of evading conscription organised themselves into a body of what they themselves termed rangers or guerillas. They were mounted on horses and armed, but without order or discipline, and under pretence of making raids upon the enemy, preyed upon the helpless inhabitants, and took especial care never to come within range of the enemy's fire. They were obnoxious to the peaceful country people on whom they committed outrages, and the latter on several occasions had accused them of cowardice in bullying over helpless people, but dared not face the enemy.

Some of the Federal gunboats had ascended the river, and anchored off Baton Rouge, and a small body of troops had landed and taken possession of the garrison and arsenal, all the Confederate troops having previously retreated from the neighbourhood. The Federal troops, after formally taking possession, returned to New Orleans, but the gunboats still remained in front of the town, the garrison and arsenal being under the range of their guns, as also the town.

A not unfriendly feeling existed between the officers and crews of the gunboats and the inhabitants of the town, who generally respected Farragut and his officers, and boats passed frequently between the gunboats and the shore; and it seems the officers and crews had been in the habit of sending ashore clothes to get washed.

One afternoon a boat, containing some unarmed men, had been coming ashore on that business, when a band of about 50 of these guerillas, headed by a notorious bully, thinking no doubt to cast off the stigma of cowardice which had been attached to them, hid themselves behind a wall near the place where the boat would land; and as soon as it touched the bank the gang fired from behind the wall at the unarmed men, but fortunately not doing them much injury.

The officers on the gunboats seeing their men fired upon by a force on shore immediately opened fire upon them, but the cowardly miscreants mounted their horses and rode into the midst of the fleeing inhabitants, selecting groups of terrified women and children, into whom they galloped, trampling many of them under foot, supposing that the gunboats would not direct their fire amongst the women and children.

The gentleman who related this to us was a respectable and somewhat substantial farmer who had previous to the war been a strong Union man; but, nevertheless, he had two sons and a son-in-law in our regiment, from whom we had brought letters. He said the country was infested by these scoundrels, and they might annoy us as we went towards Baton Rouge. Five of us were going to within four miles of Baton Rouge, and we were unarmed, but, if we had arms, we would not care for a whole troop of them; and I asked if it would be possible to borrow some arms among the settlers, who were generally well provided with them, and we were boiling with rage at the cowardly villains. He said the guerillas had, in large bands, searched every house for arms, and taken away everything that bore the shape; and this was, no doubt, to make the inhabitants more helpless that they might prey upon them with impunity.

He advised us to wait and have some dinner and then proceed in the cool of the evening, and if we got within seven miles of Baton Rouge we would be beyond the range of the guerillas, as Baton Rouge was now, since the bombardment, occupied by Federal troops, and guerillas never ventured within seven miles of an armed enemy.

We accepted his invitation to stay for dinner, but just as we were sitting down to table one of his younger sons came in and said that some guerillas were galloping up the road and coming direct to the house.

Our host desired us to sit still and he would go out and talk to them ; as there were only five or six of them they would not be very bold or intent on any outrage.

He went out and met them. They were in a fearful state of consternation, and fleeing for refuge. They told a sad story of a terrible defeat, and probable overthrow of the Confederacy. Their army, as they called it, had been that morning defeated and cut to pieces by a large force of the Federal troops, which had advanced from Baton Rouge, and they alone had escaped to tell the tale.

Our host, who had been listening to their sad story, and seeing that their attitude now was anything but hostile, made a motion for us to come out, saying to them that here was a party of men from the regular army who might probably have something to say on the matter.

We were wishful to get a sight of those redoubtable warriors, and came out to the gallery to have a look at them.

Their appearance was anything but formidable—a more scared and abject-looking set of wretches it would be difficult to describe. The day was sweltering with heat. Their horses, lean with bad care and worse usage, were foaming with per-spiration and staggering under them. They themselves, pale and terror-stricken, were shaking from actual fear. On seeing us appear they got more frightened, and seemed inclined to ride off, but I, as representing the captain of the party, ordered them in an authoritative tone to stand still and report the particulars of the battle. It was easy to be seen that these were no leaders of the gang.

I questioned them as to their leaders, but they said that they always took the best horses and had outstripped them in the flight, and they believed that by this time they would be across the Amite River. I then questioned them about the battle. They could give no account of where it had taken place, but that it was somewhere this side of Baton Rouge.

" What was the amount of the enemy's force ? "

That they could not tell, but supposed that it could not be less than 40,000. [We had here to stop the boys from laughing.] They added that the enemy had a great lot of cannons, and asked if we did not hear the firing of cannons.

" How many men did they have killed ? "

That they could not tell, but they knew there must have been plenty.

Further questioning brought out that they had not seen the enemy at all, but had heard the firing of artillery and thought they heard the shot rattling among the trees.

Our host, who knew some of their friends, told them that they had got into bad company, and advised them to go home, and if they wanted to fight for the Confederacy to go and join the regular army like men and give up the cowardly guerilla system, and they went off promising to do so.

Having had dinner and some rest, we proceeded on, two of our party expecting to reach their homes the same night.

The following day we got to within four miles of Baton Rouge, and our party was reduced to two—myself and one of the youngest of the boys, and we wished to go into the town.

The town was occupied by the Federal troops to the number of about 7000 and surrounded by a picket guard; and, although we had our discharges in our pockets and they could not make us prisoners of war, yet we did not want to be arrested by the picket guard and led as prisoners into the town, and, as we considered we were old hands, we would evade the pickets and get past them in some way.

The lad had friends who lived about two miles from the town, and to their house we went. These people were farmers, and were in the habit of driving into the town daily with milk and produce, and they undertook to get the lad past the pickets, and I learned from them that one of the posts was at the wood factory on the river belonging to our business firm.

I then went to the house of a planter which was near the river bank, about half a mile above the factory, and with whom I had always been friendly. He was astonished and glad to see me, and as he had a standing pass he went into the town and brought out my partner, who, owning the works where the picket was placed, had also a standing pass. I then changed my clothes and foraging cap for a suit of a more civilian cut, and walked with my partner into the works, and we walked about as if looking at various things pertaining to them.

The works were stopped and all business at a stand. The guard station was on the river bank, about the middle of the works, and they used the gallery of the office as a shade from the sun and rain. The guard were Germans, ignorant, and could scarcely speak English, but full of importance and swagger. My partner held out a piece of paper to them, and I did the same; the papers looked like passes, and we knew they could not read them, but they knew him to be the owner of the place. We kept looking at things and talking as if on business, and eventually passed on into the town.

As we passed the garrison and ordnance ground, I could see it was filled up with troops and the ground covered with tents. Several of the regiments were on parade at the time. Their troops were not in better training than ours, nor indeed so good, as our old volunteer regiments, but they were much better equipped, and certainly had the appearance of being much better fed, clothed, and quartered.

On our way through the principal street we went into a large café, where a number of Federal officers were assembled drinking and playing billiards, with whom, on terms seemingly of the highest friendship, were several of the same fiery politicians who eighteen months before in the same spot had so loudly advocated secession and war, and pledged themselves to fight and die in the cause. I felt so incensed at their treachery, and having now become bold and pugnacious, that I would certainly have gone up to them and publicly charged them with their treachery and cowardice, but my partner restrained me, and reminded me of the position I was in, and the way I had entered the town, and that it would be necessary for me to go to the provost-martial and report my arrival, and then I should go as soon as possible to New Orleans and get a certificate from the British consul that I was a British subject; this being the way that all foreigners who had not become naturalised citizens of the United States had done, and it was absolutely necessary in those troublesome times.

It was now night; we went home. I stayed that night at my partner's house, and in the morning I went to the provost-martial's office and reported.

The provost-martial asked to see my discharge, which I produced, and he recorded the name. He asked me if I would take the oath of allegiance to the United States. I said no. He then asked me if I would accept a parole. I said no, that I was a British subject and would go to New Orleans and consult the consul. He said it was well that I had reported, as he had been apprised of my having come into the town, and was just going to have me arrested. I then knew that some of the parties whom I had seen in the café on the previous evening had given the information, and I said so to him. He would not tell me who had given the information, but said it was one who had been very active in promoting secession. I asked him if he trusted such traitors. He said no, but he wished to let us know how these advocates of secession had kept their faith. He then asked me about the Confederate army at Tupelo. I said I would give him no information. He then asked me if I had seen any guerillas, of whom he seemed to have an intense hatred. I said I would give him every information I could about them as I did not recognise them as any branch of the Confederate service, or as men engaged in any kind of warfare. I then related the terrible scare they had got two days before, and said they (the Federal troops) would confer a great favour on the peaceful inhabitants for 20 miles around if they would go once or twice a week a mile or two into the country with a few pieces of artillery and fire off a few rounds of blank cartridge, as that would frighten every guerilla from the neighbourhood and drive them away across the Amite River.

He laughed at the suggestion, and asked if the Confederate Government recognised them. I said I could not tell as I had never heard of them until I came within 20 miles of Baton Rouge.

I then left him and took a look round the town, and called on the families to whom I had letters and greetings from their sons and friends in the army, and received visits from old friends who had been members of the company, but who had retired or had been discharged on account of wounds or bad health, among whom was our old major, who had suffered much from the campaign and now looked 10 years older. His son, who had left us when we were mustered into service, was preparing to go and join the company if he could get out past the pickets.

The people of the town in general had not on the whole a great deal to complain of from the behaviour of the occupying troops.

The general in command, General Williams, was a brave, upright, and strict officer, and did not allow any insult or outrage to be committed on the inhabitants, and the notorious Butler had not ventured to go beyond New Orleans.

I had a great desire just to see this personage of whom I had heard so much, for all accounts seemed to agree as to his infamous character.

I looked along the town to see the effects of the bombardment. It had been pretty severe. Large shot-holes were to be seen in many of the houses, and along the street fronting the river they were thickly pitted with the marks of grape and canister, and it seemed a miracle that so few people had been injured.

One gentleman told me that a shot passed through his house and smashed the gas meter, and the gas issued so rapidly that he, with his family, had barely time to get out and escape suffocation. He did not know where to run to for safety; but he remembered that a dry ditch ran along the side of his garden. Into this he got with his family, where he made them lie down, while the shots continued to whiz over them. But in this they were not allowed to remain.

Between the ditch and the boundary wall was a row of beehives, and a shot taking a bee line, as he called it, knocked down the whole row of beehives, and tumbled them with their tenants down into the ditch on the top of him and his family.

The bees, angry at being disturbed, stung most furiously, and they had to get out and run for their lives. Threatened by cannon shot, suffocated by gas, stung by bees, he did not know what to do next. Fortunately the firing then ceased, but he considered himself singularly unfortunate.

About the third day after I got to Baton Rouge, I found a steamer going to New Orleans, and I got a passage on her. The steamer was an ordinary river passenger boat, but carried two light howitzers on her hurricane deck, and a company of riflemen, on account of the guerillas who on one or two occasions had hid behind the river embankments and fired upon unarmed vessels, and it was presumed that the appearance of a gun on the upper deck would be sufficient to frighten them away.

As soon as it became known to this rifle company that I had served in the Confederate army, they were exceedingly friendly, and welcomed me as a soldier, even if I should be a secesh, as they called the Confederates, being a corruption of the word secession. There were two Scotchmen among them, and we talked of the singularity of the position which thus made us enemies and opposed to each other. Many of the other soldiers were intelligent men, and joined in the conversation.

They brought up the subject of the guerilla warfare, which was the cause of them being on the steamer, and accused the Confederate Government of maintaining such a system of warfare. I said I doubted much if the Confederate Government recognised it, and thought they might safely treat as outlaws any they caught, and hang them.

The general question of the war was next discussed. I maintained that, although I had been fighting for the Confederacy against Northern aggression, I was not a votary of slavery. I had no interest in it, or connection with it, but was rather opposed to it, and that a very large number in the South were opposed to it, although on quite different principles from the New England political Abolitionists. Those opposed to it in the South had never yet expressed their sentiments openly in politics, but their influence would soon have been felt, and as the white population increased, the institution would die out of itself as it had done and was still doing in the Middle States.

They most emphatically repudiated the insinuation that they were fighting to abolish slavery; that were such a thing in any way sought to be embodied in the principles for which they were fighting, they would rebel and lay down their arms; and some of them were offended that such an insinuation should be thrown out by me.

Then what were they fighting for? I asked.

"For the Union; to maintain the integrity of the Union, and nothing else." The question of slavery they maintained had nothing to do with the question for which they were fighting.

"Then when you were so wishful to preserve the Union," said I, "why elect a president that was obnoxious to a part of the Union, and whose election might lead to a rupture. Whatever may be the question before us now, there can be

no doubt that the question of slavery, and the election of
Mr. Lincoln as affecting the slavery question, caused the rupture and dissolution of the Union. Would it not have been
more patriotic of Mr. Lincoln to have said, If my election
should tend to endanger the Union, I will rather retire than
be the cause of a rupture or dissolution of the Union ? "

"No, no," they replied vigorously, "that would be conced-
ing to the South the right to approve or disapprove of any
president we might elect. Had Mr. Lincoln been an Abolitionist, it would have been a different matter, and the South
might have had some reason to complain. But, had he been
an Abolitionist, he never would have been elected. His
views on slavery were moderate, and he was opposed to interfering with slavery in the States where it already existed, and
the act of the States in seceding for such a frivolous cause was
unjustifiable."

"I quite agree with you," said I, "in so far as the States
were not justified in seceding. But you must admit that
under the Constitution there seemed to have been no power to
prevent them. And that is the important point that I wish
to come to. The secession, so far as Louisiana was concerned,
was not carried out by the unanimous will of the people, but
by the machinations of a set of scoundrel politicians, some of
whom I now see hob-nobbing with your officers in Baton
Rouge. You are, I presume, now fighting to uphold the
Federal authority. But when the helpless people were crushed
under the feet of those unprincipled usurpers who had possessed themselves of the arsenals and arms, where was the
Federal authority then ? Had one of those ships which are
now lying at Baton Rouge been sent there when these politicians went through their mimicry of secession, the whole thing
would have been crushed in the bud. The people would have
respected the Federal authority, and the integrity of the Union
been preserved. But what is the use of talking of Union and
Federal authority when that authority does not protect the
people, maintain the constitution, or enforce the laws.

"Oh," answered they, "as to the States having the right to
secede that is questionable, and at best only arose from an
oversight or slight omission in the constitution. But it has
all along been the unwritten constitution and a long cherished
principle both North and South. And as to the imbecility
of the Federal authority, that was the fault of Buchanan's

Government, for which Mr. Lincoln was not responsible, for as soon as he got into power he took steps to enforce the Constitution."

"No," said I, "I do not admit that. He got into power on the 4th of March; every day then was adding to the strength of the Secessionists and increasing the danger, yet he took no steps or gave any indication of what steps he would take until after the middle of April, when he issued his proclamation, giving the ultimatum of submission or the sword, which roused the South to a man, and sent into the field the former Union and law-abiding people, who are now fighting the battles of the South."

"Talking of the proclamation," said they, "that was after the bombardment of Fort Sumter. What do you think of that act? Do you approve of it, or did you consider it justifiable?"

"Gentlemen," said I, "I wish you to remember that I think I am speaking the minds of the moderate or Union party of the South, as the sentiment was at that time, and I did not approve of it; because it was a foolish act, and was just playing into the hands of Mr. Seward, who sought to bring it about so as to rouse the Northern people, and I do not consider it justifiable. But still I consider it no more an outrage than the seizure of the arsenal at Baton Rouge, or any other of the arsenals or forts in the South; which had been done without protest or interference of the Federal Government."

At this time the steamer stopped at Donaldsonville, and orders were sent on board to the commander of the detachment, and our discussion was brought to a close, the troops having got orders to prepare to land with their arms.

When I was told this, and saw them preparing, I said to them, in a jocular way, that if it was to fight guerillas they were going ashore, I would be very happy to join them, if they would give me a rifle, just to show them how I was opposed to the barbarous system of guerilla warfare. I was told, however, it was not that, but that upon two sugar estates, a little way down, the slaves had revolted, and refused to work, and they were going ashore to coerce them, and put down the revolt.

I said that if this was the case I would have nothing to do with it, for, although I was a Confederate soldier, I would never take up arms to maintain or enforce slavery!

This, of course, produced a loud laugh, with exclamations of
" Very good for you, secesh ! "

In a short time the steamer arrived at the plantations
referred to, and was run into the river bank and the troops
landed. I thought I might as well go along and see what
would be done. The plantations were right on the river bank
and adjoining each other. The troops were marched up to the
quarters where the negroes were assembled, headed by some
plantation negro lawyers, who were the ringleaders. These
immediately began to set forth their grievances, but the officer
told them he had nothing to do with their grievances. He was
simply there to enforce the laws of the State, and if they
thought that the Federal troops were in Louisiana with the object
of freeing the slaves they were very much mistaken, and if
any of them thought or tried to take advantage of this war to
stir up any revolt or disobedience to their masters they would
be severely punished.

Some of the ringleaders were then seized and put into the
stocks, exclaiming as they went along—" My Got ! Dis is
more worserer dan Jeff. Davis ! " The others were ordered to
take up their hoes and proceed to their work, and the troops
again embarked.

" Now," said several of the men to me, after they had got
on board, " does that look like fighting to emancipate the
slaves ? I think you will be satisfied now that we are not
fighting to abolish slavery."

I said that " whatever might be the cause of the war, or
whatever might be the issue, the act I had seen done was a
very judicious one, and necessary for the present at least."

Any further discussion only led to the conclusion that the
war was brought on by politicians, who were now keeping out
of danger and fattening on the spoils.

When I got to New Orleans I found that the regular consul
was absent on leave, but there was a gentleman acting as
consul. On my producing the necessary testimony he gave me
a certificate, testifying that I was a British subject; but he
informed me that the certificate would be of no use or protection, if I violated neutrality.

I then looked about for a day or two to see the state of
things under Butler's rule.

SECTION IV.

IN THE SOUTH DURING THE WAR.

CHAPTER XXVII.

I soon found that a perfect reign of terror prevailed in New
Orleans. No one was for a moment certain of his liberty.
It was no doubt true that when the Federal troops first
occupied the city, there had been some demonstrations of
disrespect or incivility made towards them. But these did
not proceed from the peaceful inhabitants in general, but from
a number of political loafers and secession spouters, who had
been instrumental in bringing on the war, but took good care
not to join the army, or take part in the dangers of the
hostilities they had created. Instead of leaving the city, and
keeping within the Confederate lines, they preferred to remain
within the Union lines, where they would be free from conscription, and show their zeal and patriotism by hissing and
hooting at the Federal troops, and then if arrested they would
be able to pose as martyrs, by having suffered imprisonment
for the Southern cause.

These people, however, Butler did not much notice except
when one of them, in great braggadocio, pulled down the
United States' flag from where it had been hoisted on the
Mint ; for this Butler hanged him.

This was certainly a rather high-handed and questionable act,
and a good deal was said about it. It took place before I
went to New Orleans, and I never knew the exact particulars.
But I heard it often said that this was perhaps not Butler's
worst act, and that if he had applied the same rope to a
few more of that class, no very serious loss would have been
entailed upon society.

But such were not the class of men that Butler marked out
for his victims. Such men had no substance, and there would

2 c

not be much to be got from them, and they might be converted and become useful to him. He directed his attention
to the more respectable and substantial class, who were
possessed of some means, and from whom something was to
be obtained.

With them it did not require any demonstration such as
hissing, hooting, or groaning to warrant an arrest—a mere look
or smile of irony was sufficient, and it was said that it got to
be that no cause at all was required, beyond the possession of
money, or other portable valuables.

No man, let his conduct be what it might, was certain, when
he rose in the morning, whether he might or might not spend
next night in jail.

I quote a case of which I knew many similar :—

A man is sitting down to breakfast with his family; he is
a merchant of considerable means, and has a store and warehouse
well stocked with goods; while at breakfast a party of soldiers
marches up to his door, and he is ordered to come along.
He is not told of any charge against him, and he is not allowed
to ask any questions. He is taken off to Butler's bastile.
No charge is made against him—no trial, no prospects of
his release. He is suspected of treason, and his arrest is
necessary for the common good. His weeping family are left
behind, a guard is put upon the house, and no one is allowed
to go in or out. The house is of a high class and richly
furnished.

In a few days an official comes along and takes an inventory
of the property, mercantile goods, and house furniture of the
party arrested, which are supposed to be confiscated.

The wife, who has never been allowed to leave the house,
naturally grasps at anything from whence the slightest
information may be obtained, and would eagerly inquire if he
knew anything about her husband. "What was the charge
against him? Where was he confined? Would he get a trial?
How long would he be likely to be confined?"

Alas! he could tell nothing of the charge. These were
terrible times; black treason was rampant. It was no doubt
considered that the arrest was necessary for the public good.
He could not say where he was confined, but most likely he
would be in the casemates of Fort Jackson. He might be
there a very long time; the chance of his release was very
small indeed.

"Good God!" screams the lady; "in the casemates of Fort Jackson! Oh horrible! he will soon die there."

"I can quite believe you, madam."

"O Lord, have mercy upon me! Can nothing be done to save him? Would not money do it? I would sacrifice every dollar I have in the world. But oh! I must save him!"

"Money will sometimes do a great deal; but I fear the case is hopeless. General Butler is a stern man, and nothing will move him. The times are desperate, and desperate measures are resorted to."

"O Lord, help me! Surely something can be done to get him justice. Do tell me if there is any chance. I will not grudge any amount; I will sacrifice all I have."

"Well, madam, I can do nothing for you; but you might try some of those gentlemen who have influence at head-quarters. Perhaps they might be able to do something for you if you go rightly about it."

"Oh tell me who they are and where I might see them!"

"Well, you might see Judge M. at such a place; but don't say that I told you about him, and, mind you, it is a very dangerous thing to go about, and you must make no inquiries, but answer every question he puts to you. It will take a great deal of money, but you must not higgle about that. I don't say that he will get your husband released—that will depend upon the nature of the charge against him; but, if any man can do it, he can."

"When can I see Judge M.?" inquires the lady eagerly.

"Well, the best time to see him will be about three o'clock in the afternoon. Not to-day, because I think he will not be at his office, but to-morrow at that time you might see him;" and, so saying, he takes his leave.

The said official, who has by this time pretty well measured the extent of the distressed lady's means and the depth of her anxiety about her husband, has an interview with the so-called Judge M. and apprises him how the land lies.

The poor lady, after passing a sleepless night, counts the minutes till three o'clock on the following day, and before that hour she is at the chambers of Judge M. After waiting about an hour in the ante-room, she is admitted into his presence.

Judge M., who is "as mild a mannered gentleman as ever scuttled ship or cut a throat," is not, as the word would imply, a dispenser of justice in the legal sense of the term. He was what was known at that time as a sort of passport and pardon broker. He was not in partnership with Butler (as Butler would have no partners—he reserved the whole of the plunder for himself), but he knew Butler's price, and he must extort his commission from his unfortunate clients. He receives the lady in his blandest manner and with extreme commiseration. He explains that the charges against her husband are of a very serious nature, and he fears it will be a very difficult matter to obtain his release; her husband may be innocent— indeed he had no doubt of it, but then information had been laid against him which must be acted upon. He had no doubt that the information had been laid by those whom her husband had supposed to be his good friends, men who professed strong Southern proclivities, and had been instrumental in stirring up this rebellion. It was through such men by means of enormous bribes that information was obtained of those who were sympathisers and movers in the rebellion, and whose arrest and confinement were considered necessary for the public good ; and as such a system of intelligence was kept up at an enormous expense, and no adequate provision was made by the Government for this intelligence department, it had in a great measure to be self-sustaining. Therefore any movement in the matter would be attended with enormous expense. It was no doubt much to be regretted that for security it was necessary to confine political prisoners in Fort Jackson, where their health was so much endangered. It was true that after a certain time they would be sent to Fort Lafayette, at New York ; but if once sent there all hopes of their release might be abandoned.

The poor lady, who is too agitated and engrossed in her husband's safety to see in her counsellor a quondam fiery secession demagogue, or to fathom his drift, half screams out an inquiry of what the terms for his release would be.

He blandly informs her that there is no such thing as terms. The thing would have to be gone about in the most delicate and intricate way, requiring large sums of money for every movement, which of course he was not at liberty to disclose, and she must bear in mind that they were now in the midst of dreadful times. But to cut the matter short, if she would bring to him a sum of say 7000 dollars, he would try what could be done with it; but she must bear in mind that she must keep the matter strictly private and make no comments or inquiries, as the slightest comment would lead to her husband's perpetual imprisonment; and if his release was effected, any remarks on the manner in which it was done would lead to his immediate rearrestment.

The lady takes her leave, and strains every exertion to obtain the 7000 dollars, which she hands to Judge M., who promises to do his utmost endeavours to get her husband released, who after a few days might be set free on taking the oath of allegiance to save his property from confiscation.

This is no overdrawn picture, but an actual occurrence, and several such cases came under my personal observation. I found the reports that had been circulated about Butler's actions were in no way exaggerated.

I was preparing to return to Baton Rouge, when I was astonished to find that I would not be permitted to leave, and that no one was now allowed to go to that place, as it was reported that a battle had been fought there, an attack having been made on the town by the Confederate troops under General Breckenridge.

I thought there could be no truth in the report, as I had left Breckenridge's division at Tupelo, and I saw no appearance of any movement. I also thought it would be a piece of folly to attempt an attack on Baton Rouge, as the place was completely covered by the ships and gun-boats on the river, against which the Confederate forces would be of no avail, and they would be driven back by the fire from the fleet.

Nevertheless, the report turned out to be true. What the results of the battle were, it was difficult yet to know, as there were all manner of rumours. Of course the Butler newspapers described it as a great victory for the Federal troops, but that was a matter of course.

In a few days, however, steamers began to arrive from Baton Rouge, bringing a number of wounded, and a large number of families whose houses had been destroyed, and who were fleeing for safety.

I could never understand the object of the Confederates in making this attack; they could never achieve any success or derive any benefit from it. It seemed to have been a meaningless action, barren of any results, entailing considerable loss to both sides, and redounding in advantage or credit to neither, while it inflicted great injury on the peaceful inhabitants of the place.

On the part of the Confederates it was as unskilfully carried out as it was unwisely conceived. They gained nothing, and had at last to retire before the fire of the fleet, with the loss of a number of men and two pieces of their artillery. Among the former, was said to have been a Major Todd, a brother of Mrs. Lincoln, and brother-in-law of Mr. Lincoln, President of the United States, but who was fighting on the Southern side.

On the part of the Federals, it left their force considerably demoralised, many of their troops had been driven to the river bank, and had to take refuge under the fire of the gun-boats. They lost a number of men, among whom was the brave and respected General Williams, and it led to the evacuation of the place for a time after burning and destroying a large part of the town.

I found it was now impossible to get out of New Orleans. Parties from the country might be admitted in, under guard and surveillance, but no one was allowed to go out, even by sea, to a foreign country, without paying a heavy ransom to obtain the necessary permission and passports to pass the Forts at the mouth of the river, even if any chance of conveyance offered, which was very rare. I have known vessels bound to a foreign port being detained for weeks under the guns of Fort Jackson, on the plea of some deficiency in their papers or passports, and parts of their crews or passengers brought back to New Orleans, and only allowed to proceed after paying enormous sums in the way of bribes.

I would now even have tried to get out of the country had it been possible, but my means were limited, and the business with which I had been connected had been for some time suspended on account of the war. And for all moneys due to the firm, they had been compelled to accept Confederate scrip in payment, and that was now at great discount, and to me in New Orleans altogether valueless, besides, I could not now get to see any of my former partners in business, so I had to make the best of it for a time.

Many of the people who now came into New Orleans were of those who had always been of Union sentiments, and had as far as possible refrained from taking any part in the secession movement, and came to seek protection under the Union flag; but a taste of Butler's rule soon made secessionists of them if they had never been before.

Butler continued his outrages unchecked, and nothing was

now so clearly illustrated as that the most brutal tyrant that ever disgraced humanity had his myriads of obsequious parasites who in the most servile manner obeyed his every command and applauded his most diabolical actions ; and these were the very men who had been loudest in their outcry against tyranny, and the most forward in the championship of men's rights and liberties.

These did not so much exist in the troops under his command, whose duty was only to obey, as in the numerous sycophants who sought offices and favours under his rule, and who could persuade a class of ignorant and weak-minded men who easily become infatuated and are ever ready to prostrate themselves before some idol of their own creation, or to deify a bubble which may float upon the surface of any impure element when stirred up by violent agitation.

Nothing, perhaps, was so observable as the change in the tone of the daily newspapers. Those journals, which had before the war been distinguished by their ultra-secession principles, were now loudest in denouncing the rebellion, and applauding the policy of Butler and justifying the most diabolical of his acts. It is true that these papers may have been coerced by Butler, or bought over and now used as his own organs. There was, however, one honourable exception, the *New Orleans Picayune*, which never had been an ultra-secession paper, and still even under Butler's rule maintained its independence.

Butler continued to hunt for treason, and all material which could contribute to it he confiscated. He found it existed extensively in the vaults of banks, in merchants' safes, in rich men's houses, among their stores of plate and other valuables. It was even said that he dug for it in the graves in the cemetery, under the belief that some of the traitors had buried it there. This, however, I cannot vouch for ; it was only told to me, and it may be an exaggeration.

His headquarters were in the Custom-house, an extensive building of granite, and from a large richly furnished mansion which he inhabited (and which, of course, had been confiscated for treason) to the Custom-house he was driven daily in a splendid carriage, surrounded by a numerous mounted body guard, and with more pomp and display than I have ever seen accorded to a European monarch. He then sat in imperial dignity in his judgment seat, and pronounced sentence according to his undisputed will on the numerous unfortunate wights who were daily brought before him. To see such autocratic power vested in such a man, and the lives and liberties of so many thousands in his hand, and subject to his whim or caprice, seemed to me to be strangely anomalous in a nation which had so long borne the name of being the great seat and home of human liberties.

I had seen this personage only once, as he sat in his carriage at the funeral of General Williams, bedecked with all the feathers and tinsel that could be crowded on to a major-general's uniform, and surrounded by his guards. There seemed to be such an amount of pomp and vanity displayed about his person, which contrasted so much with the ragged and dirt-begrimed generals in the field, that I thought he looked like a vain old jackanapes, and I could not attribute to him all the diabolical cunning that he was said to possess, and I wished to have a closer look at him.

My wish was gratified sooner than I expected, and in a way I did not anticipate.

About this time the inhabitants of the city were secretly jubilant over General Lee's successes in Virginia and the heavy losses he had inflicted on M'Lellan's army, compelling them to retire to a position on the James River. This was represented by the Federal newspapers, not as any repulse, but that M'Lellan was merely making a change of base, and of course no other version of it dare be breathed in New Orleans.

Nevertheless, a portrayal, or caricature, supposed to be cut from some pictorial paper, probably some foreign publication, was shown about among them in secret.

This cartoon represented, somewhat extravagantly, the burning of the supplies and disorderly flight of the Federal army before the Confederate troops, and was headed with this title—" M'Lellan's Grand Change of Base ! "

The secret circulation of this picture was known to Butler, and greatly irritated him. It was strictly suppressed as a treasonable production, and if found in the possession of any one the possessor would be doomed to Fort Jackson.

It so happened that one Sunday afternoon, I was walking with some friends when a heavy shower of rain caused us to seek shelter in a café, where a number of people had taken refuge from the rain. While there some amusement was caused by two dogs, which, following the fashion of the times,

began to fight, and, as they could not both be victorious, at
last the weaker took to flight; and, as fighting was now the
fashionable theme of conversation among those who were not
engaged in it, some jocular remarks were made about the
fighting capacities of the respective dogs. When thinking to
perpetrate a joke I, rather unguardedly, said, in regard to the
dog that was beaten, that he was not beaten, that he was
simply "making a change of base!" This of course produced
a laugh, and I thought I had said something smart.

The rain was now over, and we went out and walked to the
corner of Canal Street, where we stood and talked for a few
minutes.

While standing there a person tapped me on the shoulder
and desired me to speak aside for a moment. I stepped aside
with him, when two others came up, and they told me to come
along with them. I demanded to know what they wanted,
but they told me to come along and ask no questions.

I was taken to the Custom-house, and taken into a large
room in which were a number of those spy detectives and their
menials, the latter mostly speaking with a strong German
accent. Their bounce and bullying swagger knew no bounds.
I took out my pocket-book and tore out a leaf and wrote a note
in pencil to a solicitor whom I knew, and who was an English-
man and well versed in international law, and, I think, was
solicitor for the British consul, and generally attended to cases
of British subjects. This note I requested them to forward.

The name seemed to irritate them, and they sneeringly asked
if I thought that my being a British subject would protect me,
saying that I would find that General Butler did not care for
all the British powers and all the queens and kings in the
world. They then seized my pocket-book, as they had seen in
it treasonable documents in the shape of bank-notes.

I hoped that I would not have to remain overnight in this
place, as this part of the building, which seemed to be the civil
or detective department, was simply horrible. There were
several large apartments like vaults leading off from arched
corridors lighted by gas, all filthy in the extreme, in which
lounged bloated politicians, now holding some kind of office,
and who ordered about a lot of menials, mostly Irish and
Germans, who swaggered, smoked, and drank lager beer, and
eulogised the immortal Butler; while prostitutes of the lowest
class and of all colours prowled round about and in the build-

ing, and I was glad when I was sent round to the military guard-house, where there was at least a little more cleanliness, order, and respect. When I made it known to the guard that I had been a soldier in the Confederate army I was treated with much more respect. I was told by the officer of the guard that I would be taken in the morning before Butler himself, who had all cases brought before him in the first instance, some of which he dealt with himself according to his notion, others he deputed to other tribunals to be disposed of.

In the morning accordingly I was taken before this great personage.

General Butler sat alone in his room dressed in his full uniform and sword. On the table before him lay a loaded revolver, and at the door stood two sentinels, and a number of soldiers in the ante-room, with orderlies in attendance. No one was allowed into the room except those who sought and were granted an audience, or culprits and their accusers.

When I was ushered into the room, Butler was engaged in a game of Billingsgate with an Irish woman, who had obtained an audience to beg a special favour, which was to ask permission to go and see her son, who was within the Confederate lines at Mobile.

Butler, whose greatest accomplishment in his civil capacity as a lawyer and a politician was his proficiency in Billingsgate, had no doubt granted this audience with the view of having a little " set-to " by way of exercising his powers and keeping himself in practice. He seemed to have had his usual sagacity in making a good selection, and he had certainly got a foeman worthy of his steel.

It would be as impossible for me to describe the badinage which passed between the two as it would be unedifying to hear it, but while they were engaged in their war of words I had an opportunity of surveying this Mokanna.

A more forbidding and ill-favoured personage I never saw.

His appearance did not so much portray the cunning trickster, as it betokened a sort of compromise between the proud, semi-sanctified autocrat and the depraved sot.

He had two eyes vastly different in expression. From one, seemed to look out benignity, and from the other, malignity. He might ɒe said to possess a good eye and an evil eye, which he might use according to circumstances. Near to the evil eye there was something like a large, swollen projection on the cheek, which at first seemed to me as if the Irish woman had given him a blow there; but I afterwards observed that it was permanent, and reminded one of the fox's "bag of tricks," in which were stored up, as in a sort of out-house, such infernal devices as could not by nature be admitted within the human brain. It also seemed to serve as a sort of bastion for the demon eye to retreat behind when confronted by the stern gaze of noble sentiment.

His head was large and flabby, and nearly destitute of hair —except a little at the sides, which was just the colour of his epaulets.

He maintained the contention with his opponent with a coolness which showed that in that system of warfare at least his generalship excelled. He lay back in his chair and retorted with a provoking smile of ironical politeness, which acted strongly upon the temper of his opponent, who at length seemed unable to restrain herself much longer, and summing up her patience, and addressing him in a mild, direct way, said—

"Well, now, General Butler, the question is, Are you going to give me a passport or are you not?"

He coolly leant back in his chair and with a provoking smile, slowly replied, "No, woman, I will never give a rebel mother a pass to go to see a rebel son."

She gazed at him for a moment, and then as coolly and deliberately replied : "General Butler, if I thought the devil was as ugly a man as you, I would double my prayers night and morning that I might never fall into his clutches." So saying, she bolted out, passed the sentinels, and disappeared.

Butler then turned his evil eye upon me with a hideous stare, and said : "Well, sir, what do you want?"

I replied that I did not know ; I had been brought here, but I did not know what for.

"Oh no, of course not;" said he, "no one ever knows what they are brought here for, but we will be able to show you before we are done with you. Here, orderly, where is the charge against this man?"

I was about to speak. He ordered me to hold my tongue, but I would not. I said I was a British subject, and would have counsel to attend to my case.

"Oh, a British subject of course," roared he, "I know that they are all British subjects now in New Orleans. The rebels are all getting dressed in the garb of British subjects, or some

other d——d foreign power, but I will see to that. What is
the charge against this fellow ? " said he to the man who had
now come with the charge.

"Treasonable language, sir," said the man in a tone of
servile importance, as he handed Butler a paper.

Butler read the paper over, and then, after an expression of
impatience, handed the paper back to the man, and said :
" Here, take this fellow to Judge B."

The man with a disappointed look, and somewhat crest-
fallen, went with me to Judge B., who occupied chambers in
another part of the building.   I knew now that I was all
right.   I knew Judge B. ; he was a very different man and in
very different capacity from the Judge M. I have referred to.
He was a judge in the proper and legal sense of the word, and
had acted in that capacity in New Orleans previous to the
war.   What part he took when the war broke out I did not
know, but he had the name of being a pretty honourable man.

When I was taken before him, he asked my accuser what
was the charge against me.   The man handed him the paper,
which he read over.   He then asked the man if he had any
further evidence to give against me.   The man said he had
heard me uttering some offensive language about Butler and
his d——d Dutch* minions.   This, however, on my cross-ques-
tioning, he admitted to have been after I had been arrested.

Judge B. then told the man to retire and wait outside until
he would call for him.   He (Judge B.) then asked to see my
certificate as a British subject, and then put a few questions,
but told me that I need not mind to send for my solicitor, and
that it was very likely that my accusers had never delivered
the note.   He then gave me an admonition, in which he told
me to remember the position in which the city was placed,
being a conquered city and under martial law, and reminded
me that, although some of the acts of General Butler might
not be altogether what might be approved of, yet the inhabitants suffered from no outrage, rapine, or plunder from the
troops, as had often been the case with conquered cities.   It
was therefore my duty as a foreigner and a neutral to abstain
from making any remarks which would be irritating to either
party, and he counselled me to be more guarded in my expressions in future with regard to dogs " changing base," or General
Butler and his " German minions."

* All Germans were generally called " Dutch " in the United States.

I could not but admit that his reasoning was very fair, and I did not attempt to advance any arguments. I then asked about my pocket-book, and it was returned to me with about half of the money extracted ; but I might console myself with the reflection that I was very fortunate in getting any of the money back, which was considered a most extraordinary and unaccountable circumstance.

He then called the man and told him to show me the way out, which he did with more civility than he had brought me in. I was quite astonished at having got off so easily. My friends were also astonished. But it seemed to me that Butler, notwithstanding his outward show of disregard for foreign powers, did not on the whole like to meddle with such cases, but handed them over to Judge B.

There was at this time a smart little British war steamer called the *Rinaldo* which often visited New Orleans. She was commanded by a Captain Jewit, or Hewit, I forget which. The Southern party, British subjects, and foreigners in general, held this gentleman in high estimation as one of whom Butler stood in wholesome dread ; and there were many stories current among the haters of Butler—and their name was legion— of the gallant acts of this young officer in cowing down the " Beast Butler," as he was called, and bringing him to his senses on questions regarding British subjects.

There is no doubt that some of those stories were exagge- rated, or perhaps without much foundation ; but there is no question that Captain Hewit was very zealous in his protec- tion of British subjects and very prompt in his actions, and he afforded great support to the British consul, and curbed the overbearing tyranny of Butler and compelled him to respect the rights of British subjects, notwithstanding his outward braggadocio and pretended disregard for foreign powers.

It had always been regarded as a *sine qua non* in the stepping stone to popularity among the lower class of American politicians to maintain a hostile and defiant attitude towards all foreign powers, and particularly towards John Bull. This feeling was confined more to the lower class of Irish and Germans than to native Americans, and it was among the lowest classes that Butler sought and ever could obtain popularity. He therefore strove to maintain an outward appearance of a defiant attitude, and caused his newspaper organs to trumpet forth some pretended instances of his firm and determined policy in dealing with foreign agencies, although his real actions might be very different.

The bitter hatred which existed in New Orleans between the Federals under Butler and the Confederate inhabitants had now become intense.

The Confederate flag was three bars of red, white, and red, and the exhibition of anything representing it was considered treason, and strictly forbidden; and the displaying of something emblematical of this was often done in a vindictive spirit by the Confederates.

Three lines drawn with red and white chalk in this rotation upon a gate or door would cause that gate or door to be demolished by Butler's patriots, and the perpetrators to be imprisoned, or the owner of the property to be arrested. Ladies appeared in the street and in the street cars with three roses in their bonnets, arranged with a red rose on each side and a white rose in the centre. Of course any gentlemanly officer would take no notice of such things, but Butler's sycophants, to show their zeal and patriotism, would go up to a lady and tear the roses out of her cap and trample them under their feet.

I may say, however, that such actions were confined to men who had been made officers under Butler, just because they would condescend to such actions; but such a spirit did not pervade the Federal officers in general.

Butler hung out United States flags over the pavements in the principal streets, while the Confederates, to show their hatred of the flag would step off the pavement or cross the street to avoid passing under it. Butler then stretched strings of flags across the streets from side to side, and latterly placed guards near the flags to seize any person who tried to avoid them, and compel them to pass under them. Ladies, as they were being dragged past under them, would try to cover their heads with their shawls, or put up their umbrellas. In fact, such nonsensical absurdities were carried to such an extreme on both sides, that every day some new amusement was furnished for such as could afford to laugh.

Every kind of business was now suspended, except what was conducted under the directing power of Butler himself, or by those to whom he granted special privileges, for which, of course, they would pay him the requisite tribute. These privileges were only granted to his true and loyal followers, and were something upon the old Roman publican system.

The principal business done under this mandate was speculation in sugar and cotton. The latter being now at an enormous price, and the seizure and confiscation of this commodity belonging to private individuals under plea of some breach of regulations, or releasing it again on payment of an enormous ransom, became a very common practice.

Several paying institutions were established in the city under the direction and control of Butler, among which were two extensive and elegantly fitted up gambling-houses. Such institutions on a small and private scale had not been altogether unknown, but all these had been virtuously put down by Butler's orders.

It was now about the middle of August. The people of New Orleans had been looking forward to an avenger which they expected to come through a desperate source, which was a visitation of that terrible scourge the yellow fever, which, had it come, would have compelled the Federals to evacuate the city, and whichever way that was done, they all knew that Butler would be the first to fly. But the dreadful epidemic did not come, and all hopes and fears of such a visitation now began to subside.

About this time I learned that a large part of the town of Baton Rouge had been burned by the Federal troops, and that all the business premises with which I had been connected, and all the property of our business firm had been destroyed. The cause assigned for this was a "military necessity." The Federal commander, fearing another attack from the Confederates, and wishing to hold the place on account of the garrison and arsenal, resolved to enfilade the rear of the town by the fire from the fleet.

The gunboats were accordingly stationed at points above and below the town, where their fire would converge at a point at the back of the town. This point, to save distance, they made as near to the river as possible, thus leaving within the lines only a part of the city in the form of a triangle.

In order to get a clear sweep for their fire, everything outside of these line was cleared away. Houses, fences, trees, and every other object that would obstruct the range or afford cover to an enemy was burned or cleared out of the way so that the fleet could effectually sweep with their guns every approach to the town. But in the end all this destruction of property was of no avail whatever, for a few days after the

burning was done the river began to fall, and fell so low that
the vessels floated at too low a level to use their guns to any
advantage.

The intelligence of the burning of the town and the destruction of all the property in which I had any interest, and which
I knew would be entirely lost to me, was in such times of
revolution and violence to me a matter of little importance,
but I had been in New Orleans now nearly a month in perfect
idleness, which, after a period of activity and excitement,
became to me exceedingly irksome, and this became more distasteful when I was reminded that I was here virtually
imprisoned and could not get out of the city, and as I was so
completely disgusted with the state of things in the city I
determined to get out of it by some means.

In the meantime the Federal troops arrived in New Orleans
from Baton Rouge, having evacuated the latter place. They
took with them all the movable property which they could
transport, and which they thought could be used in any way
by the Confederates, and without regard to what or who the
owners might be.

Every kind of steamer or boat which could be used as a
transport was seized and loaded up, and sent down the river to
New Orleans. What they could not take with them they
burned or destroyed. The steam ferry-boat, a fine large boat
which would carry several waggons and horses, they loaded up
with plunder to take with them, but in their zeal or greed
they loaded her too deep; and, as if imbued like the inhabitants with a refractory rebel spirit, she determined not to
leave the place for she grounded on the bank, and the sympa-
thizing river falling fast, all their efforts to get her off proved
unsuccessful. They therefore set fire to her, and she was
burned with all her cargo; her owner meanwhile standing at
a point on the opposite side of the river, about three miles
distant, firing at them with his revolver.

I must, however, do the Federals the justice to say that they
gave out at least that they did not carry away those things
with a view to plunder or deprive the owners of them, but
rather for the purpose of preserving them for the owners by
saving them from being plundered or destroyed by the Confederate guerillas, and there was no doubt a good deal of reason
in this. But the practice of seizing private property to prevent it falling into the hands of the enemy, was now coming

to be rather common on both sides, and was painfully unpleasant to those who possessed any substance in the disturbed districts, as no man could say what he could call his own.

There was no conveyance to Baton Rouge by steamers, even if permission could be obtained, which was now out of the question. The only chance, therefore, was to "run the guards," and get to Baton Rouge by land if I wished to get there. With a view to this, I went up to Carrolton, which is a suburb of New Orleans, and was at the extremity of the military district. While there reconnoitring I met with two former acquaintances who were also reconnoitring with a view to running the guards and getting out of the city, and a place was discovered where it was supposed that a passage might be effected ; and by a little cautious manœuvring we succeeded in getting past the guard ; and, after having got a sufficient distance from the lines, we obtained horses and proceeded to Baton Rouge.

CHAPTER XXVIII.

RETURN TO BATON ROUGE—WRETCHED CONDITION OF THE PLACE—OUT OF
THE FRYING PAN INTO THE FIRE—RETURN TO THE ARMY—MILITARY
CAREER CUT SHORT—BATTLE OF CORINTH—WOUNDED AND A PRISONER—
PAROLE AND RETURN TO CIVIL OCCUPATION— CONDUCT OF THE NEGRO
SLAVES — LINCOLN'S EMANCIPATION PROCLAMATION — COMMENTS AND
CRITICISMS UPON ITS OBJECT AND EXTENT.

WHEN I got to Baton Rouge, I found everything in a
wretched state. The greater part of the town was in ruins,
and several fine buildings, besides those burned by the Federals
as a "military necessity," had been burned—whether by
Federals or Confederates I could not learn. Nearly all the
substantial, former residents had left the place. Many of
them having been driven from their homes were living in log
cabins in the surrounding country.

No business of any kind was being done, and hunger and
privation reigned supreme. Our business premises and all
property in which I had an interest had been destroyed. My
partner had removed with his family to a log house somewhere
far out in the country. Most of the houses which remained
were occupied by those who had no right to them. Numbers
of Confederate officers of the home guard class, with airs of
great importance, lounged about with their followers on the
hunt for conscripts, and enforcing the iron rule of military
despotism, with all the official arrogance they could assume.

When I looked upon this state of things, and compared it
with the happy and prosperous state of affairs two years
previous, I could not help reflecting upon the shortness of the
step, from a Democracy to a Despotism; and the condition
into which men possessing what they proudly termed individual sovereign powers may be led, or allow themselves to be
led, by their credulity and apathy.

I now found that by leaving New Orleans and returning
within the Confederate lines, I had only jumped out of the
frying pan into the fire, as far as despotic rule prevailed.
There was only the one consideration, which was, that I was
now on the side I had taken part with, on which I had some
claim, and where I was better known.

But I found my position exceedingly awkward and unpleasant. There was no kind of occupation in civil life to which I could apply myself—all business suspended; and every young and able man of any spirit had volunteered into the army, and those who had hung back and were now being hunted after by the conscript officers, were not looked upon with respect, and although I was now exempt I could not brook the idea of lounging about idle, and I could not get out of the country. I could also plainly see that under a military despotism, such as the whole country was, the best and safest place to be was in the army.

In joining the army again I knew that I was violating neutrality, and forfeiting my rights as a British subject, but I could see no alternative. It was impossible to be in this part of the country without being mixed up in the turmoil, and it was impossible to get out of the place.

I had learned that the old Army of the West was not now under Bragg, and therefore I determined to go and see some of the field officers that I knew, and through their influence I might, on account of my former services, get an appointment in the Engineer corps, either with the army in the field or at some of the fortifications on the river, and with this view I set off to pay a visit to my old friends in the army in northern Mississippi.

When I reached the camp I found that the army had moved from the camp at Tupelo, and had advanced northwards. The large army which I had left had broken up, and a large portion of it had proceeded to the eastward towards Chattanooga, under Bragg. The remnants of the old Army of the West, patched up with some new reinforcements, was still under Price and Van Dorn, and they were preparing to make an attack upon Corinth. It was reported that a large portion of Grant's army had left Corinth and gone to act against Bragg, and Price and Van Dorn were supposed to be able to deal with the remainder.

The brigade, in which was my old regiment, was away in advance, and I learned that at an engagement they had with the enemy at Iuka, they had suffered severely. My old company was much reduced; my old friend, the first lieutenant, had been killed. The captain and second lieutenant, wounded, were both absent from the company, and very few of the officers of the regiment that I knew were left. There was no time at present for me to see any of the field officers, as a battle was just going to begin, and there was no other way for me to do but to join in.

As the proportion of officers of all ranks and classes was very large in proportion to the number of men for duty, it was understood that all officers on the day of battle would arm themselves with rifles, and this was easily done as there was plenty of arms belonging to the wounded men not in use and to be had.

I was joined to a detachment that was bringing up the rear and was a short distance in the rear of the main body.

It was a fine, clear, cool morning, about the beginning of October, that we were ordered to hurry up and join the main body. The detachment hurried up and joined the division just as they were advancing to the attack.

I had no time to look around to see or form any idea of the plan of the battle. We dashed forward at a double quick. The object was, I understood, to break the enemy's centre. The enemy opened a heavy fire upon us, but we kept pressing forward, and they kept falling steadily back. A tremendous artillery fire had opened upon our right and left, and the battle seemed as if it was going to be a severe one. We had just passed over an embankment—whether it was a railway embankment, or a work thrown up, I did not observe, as at that time I was struck on the leg by a ball which caused me to fall.

The men around me were much thinned, and a good many of both sides lay on the ground. I did not like the place I lay in, as it was rather exposed, and I could see that the enemy were not making the same mistake that they had made in former battles, for they were firing low enough now, and I could see the little clouds of dust raised by the bullets as they struck the ground thickly all around me. I tried to get up and walk but could not, so I managed to crawl to a less exposed place, and fortunately I saw a pit, or hole, from which stuff had been dug out to make up the embankment. Into this place I crawled, where I found I was comparatively safe from the fire of either small arms or artillery. Here I tied my handkerchief tight round the wound, which we had often been instructed to do.

I was satisfied that my wound, although painful, was not dangerous, if I could get timely relief.

The battle was now going on furiously, and the artillery fire
was very heavy, though round about the place where I lay it
seemed to have slackened. The smoke had cleared away and
our men seemed to have fallen back from this point. How
long I lay here I cannot tell, but it seemed to me to be a long
time.

At length the firing began to slacken, and I heard cheering
which I knew did not come from our men, and it was evident
that they had fallen back.

It was not until night that I was picked up and carried to
the railway store-houses, which were used as hospitals, and
reported as a wounded reb. There I lay waiting my turn to
get my wound dressed, which was done in the course of time.
Fortunately it was not serious. It had been a spent ball
which had first struck the ground and then glanced upwards.

I was moved into a separate place, or ward, where the rest
of the wounded rebels, or rebs., as they called us, were put.

In the morning I looked around the room, to see how many
there might be in it, and if there was any that I knew. There
might be about thirty in the room, and I saw one that I had
seen before, and had a slight acquaintance with. He was a
captain in one of the Texas regiments. He had been wounded
in the same way as myself, and was sitting with his leg, which
had been newly bandaged, propped up on a box. He was
talking to one or two who were lying near him, and who
seemed to be suffering more. He was venting his rage at a
furious rate on some functionary. I feared it might be some
of the Federal officers, and such abuse might cause bad feeling
and subject us to rough treatment.

"What is the matter, captain?" said I ; "who is that you're
pitching into?"

"Why," said he, "that rash, reckless, little red-headed rat,
Van Dorn. He makes a mess of everything he attempts by
his rashness."

I said I knew he had made a bungle of things at Pea Ridge,
but I thought he had got his name up again while we were
fighting here in May last.

"Yes," said he, "but look at Iuka, and see the mess he has
made here now."

I said I had not been at Iuka, and for this battle I did not
know anything about it. I had just got up as the battle was
going to begin, and was shoved into the column that was going

to advance on the enemy's centre—in fact, I had left the army
in July, and was only back on a visit, and was not attached
to any corps. "But," continued I, "do you know anything
of the plan of this battle or the object of it."

"No," said he, "nor anyone else;" and he was beginning
to give a description of the movements when two hospital
attendants came in under pretence of sweeping the floor,
although it was no doubt to listen to the conversation. We
stopped speaking, and the two fellows, whom I could see were
of the shirker class, seemed not pleased because we had stopped
the conversation, and they began to act roughly towards the
wounded, ordering them to move, and if they remonstrated
they swore at them, calling them d——d rebels. The Texas
captain remarked that whatever rebels might be they would
not insult helpless, wounded men. I remarked to the captain
that rebel or Confederate soldiers would not, neither did I
believe that Federal soldiers would insult wounded men.
"But," continued I in a loud tone in their hearing, "these are
not soldiers; these are cowardly shirkers, who dare not go
into the field, but lounge about the hospitals."

Fortunately at the time some Federal officers and soldiers
were passing the door going out from the next ward where they
had been visiting some of their wounded men. I called to them,
and they looked in.

"There," said I, addressing the Texas captain, "are men
who met us in the field yesterday; they would not insult
wounded men."

"What is the matter?" said one of the officers; "who
insulted you?"

"These two fellows there," said I, pointing to them.

The officers ordered them out, and told us to report any bad
treatment to the superintendent of the hospital. We could
not complain very much of the treatment we got after this.
My wound quickly healed, and in a few days I was able to
move about with the help of a crutch.

In moving about, I met with and entered into conversation
with some of the Federal wounded. Most of them were in
hopes that they would be sent to their homes in a few days.
I found among them one or two Scotchmen, with whom I
formed an acquaintance and through whom I got introduced
to a major, who was also a Scotchman. He was very kind,
and got me put on the list for parole; and as the Federal

army, which here was under command of General Rosencranz, was much encumbered with sick and wounded, I with several others was called up to sign our parole and were allowed to go.

Where the Confederate army had gone to we did not know, but were told it had fallen back towards Holly Springs. Of course we had in the meantime nothing to do with it, and I did not intend again to join, as I had now but few friends left in it, and as I would be for a time crippled, I could with more satisfaction and better grace remain quiet for a time to see how affairs went.

We managed to get an ambulance to take us to Priceville, where we got on to the railway and got *via* Meridian as before to Camp Moore.

I must here remark that throughout this war nothing could exceed the deference that was paid to wounded men, at least on the part of the Confederates. We had no difficulty in getting past pickets. We travelled on railways free of charge. Often hotels would not charge for a night's accommodation— country people were ready to entertain us, and gave us carriages and horses at any time for conveyance, without any charge, and I had very little difficulty in getting to Baton Rouge. I did not, however, remain at that place, but crossed the river and went to the county of West Baton Rouge, where I knew that my partner and some of my former friends had gone to reside.

My wound was now nearly healed, although I continued to walk lame.

West Baton Rouge was an extensive sugar-producing district, and it was now November, the sugar harvest time, and a large crop of sugar cane was ripe and ready to be cut down and manufactured ; and it was stated to have been the desire of both parties that this valuable crop should not be lost, and that the manufacture of sugar should not be molested by either party.

Some landslips had also taken place on the river bank which had broken the embankments, and the country was in danger of being overflowed when the river rose, unless some scheme was devised to keep it back by new embankments.

I now met with some of my old planter friends, among whom was my old friend Mr. C. They told me that I might be satisfied with fighting now, that I had surely got enough of it, and I would be of more service if I would come and give them the benefit of my engineering skill in protecting their lands from overflow, and getting their machinery ready for the manufacture of sugar. There were very few engineers of any kind now to be had, most of them having either joined the service or left the country.

I told them that I thought that was rather cool for their patriotism, but they maintained that self-preservation was the first law of nature, and I was not very hard to persuade.

I may here observe that this district, as well as all the land on the west side of the river, was a sugar-producing district, and consisted almost entirely of sugar plantations and large sugar factories. Throughout this district, the slave population at all times greatly exceeded the white population ; and, after the war had broken out, and a large portion of the white population had volunteered for or had been conscripted into the military service, the predominance of the slave population was greatly increased.

To the everlasting credit of the negroes—not only in this district but all over the South, while the whole country was distracted by war—they never made the slightest show of insurrection ; and never, except in the case of the two plantations on the Mississippi, in July, 1862, which I have already referred to, did I know of even the slightest disaffection, and this I noticed particularly, during this winter of 1862–63, in which I had occasion to go much among them, and I never saw them more orderly or better behaved.

Mr. Lincoln has been spoken of by many in Europe and elsewhere, as the great emancipator—whose generous act in emancipating the slaves in America had earned for him a world-wide fame. But I have sometimes thought that, if some of those who thus lauded him had known a little more of the solid truth, they might have approached the subject with a little more caution.

Mr. Lincoln was certainly opposed to slavery through philanthropic motives, and his philanthropy was of the sincere and genuine kind ; but the measures adopted in his name on which this fame has been based might, if looked into, appear just somewhat questionable from a philanthropic point of view.

The Act amending the constitution of the United States—reconstructing the Union and abolishing slavery—was not passed until December, 1865—eight months after Mr. Lincoln's death, but this dogma of Mr. Lincoln emancipating the slaves, arose from a proclamation issued by him on the 1st of January, 1863.

Far be it from me to detract from Mr. Lincoln any credit due to his name. I believe him to have been a well-meaning man, who wished to do right to all men, an honest, true, and genuine philanthropist, who disapproved of slavery, and was willing to adopt any honourable and judicious means to have it gradually abolished, with due regard to the rights of those who, by fate or fortune, were interested in it, or dependent upon it. And I think I cannot do a greater honour to his memory, than to give it as my opinion, that this proclamation, like others issued in his name, never emanated from him with his cordial approval, and with his full knowledge of its meaning or object.

With regard to Mr. Lincoln's own personal views at that time, I remember reading in the papers a proposal or suggestion he put forth in an address about the autumn of 1862. It was in the form of a grand scheme for the emancipation and colonisation of all the slaves in the United States by a legal purchase out of a fund to be raised according to the increase in the population. I cannot remember the substance of it, but the proposal did not seem to have been favourably received by his cabinet and followers, for it did not take root, and I never heard more of it.

About this time the fortune of the war had again gone with the Confederate arms and against the Federal forces. The latter had suffered some crushing reverses in Virginia, and particularly at Fredericksburg in December, and also in the west by the defeat of Sherman in his advance against Vicksburg; and the fearful wound which had penetrated the heart of the Confederacy, and cut it asunder by the Federals obtaining command of the Mississippi river, had been partially stopped up by strong forts erected at Port Hudson, a place about 18 miles above Baton Rouge, by which the Federal fleet was stopped from proceeding up the river, and by strong forts at Vicksburg, about 300 miles above Port Hudson, which prevented their gunboats passing down. This not only checked communication between the upper and lower fleets, but left nearly 300 miles of the river in possession of the Confederates. Into this flowed Red River, which allowed them free communication with Western Louisiana, Texas, and other parts west of the Mississippi river. The triumph of the Federal arms and the subduing of the Confederate States seemed thus as remote as ever.

On 1st January, 1863, the famous proclamation was issued. On this proclamation I will not presume to pass judgment, but as I happened at the time to be in a locality where its effects would or might have been productive of serious consequences, and its construction was very seriously criticised and commented upon, I will simply state, as near as I can, the substance of it, and the different views expressed in regard to its meaning and object.

The substance of the proclamation, after the preamble referring to the rebellion and the state of the country, was, as near as I can recollect, in these words :—

"I, Abraham Lincoln, President of the United States, by virtue of the authority in me invested, do hereby issue this my proclamation, and do hereby proclaim all slaves within the States or parts of States now in rebellion against the United States to be now, and for ever, free, and all officers employed in the army or navy of the United States are hereby ordered to assist them in every way in their endeavours to obtain their freedom."

It was further stated, by way of interpretation, though I do not remember the exact words, that the slaves were declared free in all States in rebellion, except such parts as were held by the armies of the United States.

This exception would amount to nearly half of the slaveholding territory.

At that time, the feeling of deadly hate between the political magnates and extreme fanatics on both sides had become most intense, and there is no saying to what length their bitter animosities would have carried them. But their power was curbed, and many outrages and cruelties prevented by the more noble and generous sentiments of the military commanders in the field on both sides.

This proclamation was said to have been issued by the authority of Congress as a "military necessity," and I use the words of a Federal officer who stated to me that it would have been more correct to say, "By command of Congress and the Cabinet," and that Mr. Lincoln, when he assented to it, had failed to observe the different ways in which it might be construed.

The fact of it being called forth as a "military necessity," and the significant and positive orders to all officers in the army and navy of the United States to assist the slaves in every way in their endeavours to obtain their freedom, called forth many severe criticisms from both sides. It did not express in any way in what manner this assistance was to be rendered. It did not say that such assistance should be in accordance with civilised customs, or conform to the laws and usages of war.

Various constructions were put upon the meaning of this order—the most extreme being that it was to stir up the negroes to follow the example of the slaves in St. Domingo, and incite them to wreak an indiscriminate slaughter upon their masters and the white population in general within the rebellious States, and that in this they would be aided by the United States forces.

The milder construction put upon it was, that the officers of the army and navy should afford every facility they could in aiding the slaves to escape from their masters, and in rescuing them from any parties who might endeavour to recapture them.

This latter was probably the light in which it was issued by Mr. Lincoln, and the meaning that was represented to him by those who prepared the proclamation and got him to assent to it, and he probably adhibited his signature without looking further into it, or observing the different ways in which it might be construed.

However, that might be, the proclamation caused great excitement and indignation, not only among the Confederates who regarded it in the extreme light, and on whom it acted like a second dose of Butler; but also among many of the Northern Democrats, and it also caused some disaffection in the army and navy, and several officers resigned their commissions. By many, the milder construction was scouted as being absurd, as such an order would be quite superfluous; as an act had already been passed in the Federal Congress declaring that all slaves that should escape from their masters and take refuge within the Federal lines should be free; and an order had been issued to all officers in the army and navy of the United States, to afford them every assistance and protection. This act was passed about three months before the proclamation was issued. Another singular feature in this proclamation was, that it restricted the abolition of slavery to such parts of the United States only where Mr. Lincoln's power did not extend, and where his armies had failed to penetrate, and where he had not the power to enforce it; and in all parts where his power did exist, and where his armies had penetrated and subdued, slavery was still to be maintained.

It was, therefore, in that respect regarded at best as a mere formal or paper proclamation of emancipation, where he knew he had not the power to carry it into effect, and no one could or pretended to maintain that it was done as an act of philanthropy.

To return to the effect and working of the proclamation, allowing it to be recognised, acted upon, and in force.

The parts in which slavery should exist and the parts in which it should not exist were so mixed up and interwoven, constantly varying and uncertain, that it would be difficult to determine which was which, even taking it at the date of proclamation.

Slavery would have still continued either in entire States or parts of States all over the South.

It would still continue in Delaware, Maryland, Western Virginia, Kentucky, East Tennessee, Missouri, large portions of Louisiana and Arkansas, besides the many seaports held by the Federal forces, including Galveston, in Texas, which latter place at the date of the proclamation was held by the Federal forces, and, consequently, slavery would there be maintained and continued, but before the proclamation could reach that place it had been recaptured by the Confederate forces.

Whether the Confederates, when they captured this place on the 1st of January, 1863, might have regarded it as a place in which slavery had been confirmed by Lincoln's proclamation and retained the slaves as slaves, or whether, by the capture of the place by the Confederates, the slaves became entitled to their freedom was a question which, like other things in the proclamation, was a little confounding.

To come more direct to the question. The part of Louisiana in which I happened to be at that time was somewhat uncertain. It was claimed by both sides, but protected by neither.

It consisted of the lands on both sides of the river between New Orleans and Baton Rouge, and on the west side for some miles above the latter place.

The Federals had held it from the time they captured New Orleans in April, 1862, until August, when they evacuated Baton Rouge and fell back to New Orleans. The Confederates had not since occupied it by any force, but some bands of miserable guerillas, pretending to be in the Confederate service, prowled around, while an ironclad Federal gunboat named the *Essex* lay in the river opposite Baton Rouge, occasionally taking a cruise up the river to within safe distance of Port Hudson, but when the river was low, the low country behind the embankments could not be seen or commanded from the vessel.

Sometimes the guerillas would become possessed of extraordinary courage, and they would hide themselves safely behind the embankments and fire at the ironclad gunboat as she passed at the distance of half-a-mile or more. The gunboat would retaliate by firing heavy shot and shell over the embankments and up into the country, indiscriminately destroying houses and property and endangering the lives of and terrifying the inhabitants, who were between the "devil and the deep sea." The people were made unionists by the acts of the conscripting officers and the guerillas, and fled for refuge to New Orleans, where they were made secessionists again by Butler and his acts.

When this proclamation was issued, it was of course treated with scorn and contempt within the Confederate lines proper, but in parts such as this, which were being taken and retaken, or claimed by both sides, if it had been acknowledged and respected, its application would have been a question of some difficulty, for in this district, as I have said, the slave population greatly exceeded the white population.

It might be supposed that the Southern slaveowners would have tried to keep the proclamation from becoming known to their slaves, but they did the very opposite. They produced the proclamation and read it to their slaves. I was present on one or two occasions when this was done.

One, a Mr. L, of West Baton Rouge, called all his slaves up and asked me, in their presence, as a foreigner, a neutral and disinterested party, to read the proclamation, which I did.

He explained to them the construction he put upon it, putting it in the extreme sense, and asked them if they had any desire to rebel, in order to obtain their freedom; for if they had, they need not endanger their own lives or stain their hands with bloodshed, for they were now at liberty to go if they pleased.

The negroes very emphatically, and I believed sincerely, repudiated any desire for any change, and begged of him to retain them under his protection as formerly, and they would be as faithful to him as ever.

Of course, I thought at the time that it was not to be expected that they were likely to make any other reply, whatever might be their inward thoughts. But afterwards I began to joke with some of the more intelligent and leading men among them, and asked them why they did not avail themselves of the opportunity which was offered to them to obtain their freedom so easily.

The reply was :—

"Master, I see no use of us going and getting ourselves into trouble. If so be we are to get free, we get it anyhow. If we not to get it, we no get it; and we think it more betterer to stay home on the plantation, and get our food and our clothes ; and if we are to get freedom, dare we are! But, if we run away, and go to New Orleans, like dem crazy niggers, where is we?"

It may be here observed a good number of the slaves, from both towns and plantations had left their masters, and gone to New Orleans with the Federals—many of them not having run away, but gone with the full consent of their masters ; and after being in New Orleans for some time they, with much difficulty, found their way back to their masters, in a state of great wretchedness and destitution.

Another planter, a Mr. B., read the proclamation to his slaves, in my hearing ; but he put it before them in rather a different way.

He pointed out to them that part of the proclamation which set forth that it was only in such parts of the States as were in rebellion against the United States, that were to be free; and in all other parts, held by the Federal forces, they were still to be slaves.

"This place," said he, " is uncertain. Both parties claim it, and we don't know which Government it is under. If it is under Lincoln's Government, then he says in that proclamation that you are to be slaves ; but if it is under Jefferson Davis's Government, then he (Lincoln) says in that proclamation that you are to be free. So I can't tell you what you are to be until we see which government we are going to be under. But there is one thing that I can tell you, that is, if you are within Jefferson Davis's country Mr. Lincoln says you are to be free, though I doubt it very much, because he has not the power there to make you free.   But if you are in New Orleans or any place within the lines held by Mr. Lincoln's armies, then Mr. Lincoln says you are to be slaves, and there is no doubt about that, because he has there the power to make and keep you slaves.   So there is the proclamation, and you can read it for yourselves, or get any person you like to read it for you, and see if they can make anything else out of it," and he handed them the proclamation.

Of course this was only an ingenious way of showing up the proclamation and turning it into ridicule, but it must be admitted that it was a little open to ridicule.

In January, 1863, the Mississippi River began to rise a little, so that the Federal gunboats could command the country on both sides, and Baton Rouge was again occupied by the Federal troops and the country was now under Lincoln's rule.   This settled the question as to whether the negroes were to be free or slaves in the districts ; not, as one would almost fly to the conclusion, that they were to be free, but on the contrary, strange as it may appear, that they were to be slaves, in accordance with the proclamation, as that part of the country could not be said to be in rebellion against the United States, and had been occupied for some months by the Federal forces, and had never been actually abandoned by them and re-occupied by the Confederate forces.

Of course this allusion to the proclamation is only to show the absurdity of it ; for it was never regarded or acted upon either by the slaveowners, or the slaves, or the United States officers, and only in one instance did I ever hear of any attempt being made to carry out the order even in its mildest form.

In this case the United States officers fell into a trap not very honourably laid, and not laid by any respectable Confederate authority, but by the guerillas and negroes.

The officers of the gunboat *Essex*, which was in the habit of going up and down the river, at a point some 14 miles above Baton Rouge on the west side of the river, on what was considered Confederate territory, saw a party of negroes on the river bank, apparently fugitive slaves, waving to them for

assistance. The commander, in compliance with the order set
forth in the proclamation, immediately stopped and sent a
boat ashore to take them off to his vessel ; but no sooner had
the boat touched the bank, than the negroes ran and hid
behind the embankment, and a party of guerillas from behind
the embankment opened fire upon the boat's crew. But, as
usual with these miscreants, they did not succeed in doing
much damage.

This, however, put a stop to any further attempts to render
assistance to fugitives in that district.

The proclamation, after the first little excitement and
indignation had passed away, became a dead letter ; and,
though not formally withdrawn, was smothered over, and
little referred to within the Federal lines—the Federal
officers seeming to feel ashamed of it ; while within the Confederate lines, and by those opposed to Mr. Lincoln in other
places, it was brought up as a reproach against and a stain
upon his name.

Such was the proclamation to which some would attach such
great magnanimity, and which I would rather not have
referred to, but I think there has been altogether too much
said about this so-called generous act of emancipating the
slaves. While situated, as I was at the time it was issued, I
could not help hearing the comments and severe criticisms
upon it, witnessing the feeling it created, and being satisfied
of its inconsistency, inapplicability, and complete futility, to
say nothing more.

But I only put forth the comments and criticisms as I heard
them, and its operation and effects, only so far as I witnessed
them. Of course there may have been something in it far
beyond the comprehension of my ideas.

CHAPTER XXIX.

THROUGH the occupation of Baton Rouge by the Federal troops, the whole of that country to which I refer was brought within the Federal lines, and the communication between these parts and New Orleans was now less restricted, and I again could come and go to and from the city, still passing as a foreigner and a neutral, and occasionally transacting business for planters who did not deem it quite safe to venture into the lion's mouth.

Many of the planters and small farmers now tried to get their produce to market and have it turned into money, as it was by no means safe on the farms or plantations. It was subject either to be burned by the guerillas, or seized by Butler's speculators, and a good deal of cotton and sugar found its way to New Orleans, though often under extreme difficulties, and even when it got there it was still very far from being safe. The seizure of cotton when landed in the city was the invariable rule. The article commanded such a high price that Butler's officials always contrived to show that some breach of regulation had been committed, and that the goods were liable to seizure and confiscation. These seizures were made with so little regard to law or justice that the artifice of having the produce transferred through the agency of a foreign subject was often resorted to. This might save it from total confiscation; still it was subjected to numerous stoppages and detentions, which could only be got over by the payment of heavy bribes.

Early in 1863 a change took place in the command at New Orleans. Butler left, and his place was taken by General Banks. I am not certain whether Butler was superseded, or whether he retired of his own accord, after having filled his coffers. His departure was certainly hailed with universal joy by the inhabitants, and his administration there should at least occupy a prominent place in the history of that city.

It was supposed by many that his selection and appointment as the absolute ruler of New Orleans was an act of retribution most deliberately planned, and that to punish a proud and arrogant people was the object for which he was sent there. Whether that was the case or not I cannot say ; but if such was really the object there certainly could not have been a better selection made. "Set a thief to catch a thief," is an old adage, and so it may be said "Employ the devil to punish the devil."

Butler could never be regarded as one of the Federal generals, from a military point of view. He ventured but rarely to act in the field, and when he did he showed such incapacity and cowardice that he stood virtually disgraced. All this was counterbalanced by his high proficiency in a war of words, and few dared to bring against him a "railing accusation."

He was not embarrassed by any sensitive feelings. He had no shame and made no secret of his cowardice ; and however incongruous this might be with the title he had assumed as a military general, still, he possessed a great amount of courage of a certain kind, but whether it might be called true moral courage may be another question. He seemed to say, "I am not such a fool as to expose my person to danger. I can manage my point better without doing so, and if I am attacked by the world's censures, I am quite impervious to any wounds from such weapons; whilst I am an adept in the use of them."

If he had no skill or strategy in military matters he certainly possessed both, to a high degree, in political and criminal matters ; and if he could not organise or command an army of soldiers, few could equal him in organising an army of spies and detectives.

The knowledge he acquired of every man in New Orleans, of his business, his means at command, his property in real estate, in money, in merchandise, house furniture, plate, or other valuables ; his sentiments, circle of acquaintances, and everyday actions were truly incredible.

He of course had absolute power, which he did not fail to avail himself of, and he made many harsh experiments.

It was not Butler's maxim that " better ten guilty should

escape than one innocent be punished," but better that ten innocent should be punished than one guilty should escape.

There were, no doubt, many acts and outrages committed by Butler in New Orleans which never went into print or saw the light, and perhaps, many things were said of him which were grossly exaggerated, or never happened at all; and many of his orders, bad as they were, were made more grievous by the way in which they were carried out through his minions.

I may mention one or two things which came especially under my notice.

Butler had a great terror of being assassinated while in New Orleans. He seldom showed himself in public, he travelled to and from his residence in a close carriage, surrounded by guards; and, as a further security to his person, he issued an order disarming the citizens, and commanding all arms of whatever kind to be delivered up before a certain day, and if any arms or weapons were found in possession of any person whatever, or on or within the premises of any person, after that date, without a special permission, such person should be subject to a heavy penalty and imprisonment.

There were perhaps none of his orders that were enforced with such rigour as this, and some of the instances attending them were notable. As an instance of several I knew of, one in particular I may mention, as showing the injustice which may be done in carrying out an arbitrary order through means of a depraved and unprincipled agency—always, of course, in the name of and for the good of the people, as all these orders were declared to be.

A Mr. U., a gentleman of good standing and reputation, who was a Scotchman by birth, but who had been for a great many years a citizen of New Orleans, and greatly respected, had taken no part in the Secession movement, but when the troubles broke out had given up business and lived in retirement.

A short time after this order was in force his house was entered by a party of Butler's detectives, and he was charged with having arms concealed, in violation of the order. Mr. U., knowing the charge to be groundless, told them to search the premises. They went immediately into his back court, turned over some lumber and took out an old fowling-piece, which it was easy to see had been recently put there. This was sufficient, and Mr. U. was dragged off to prison. It was in vain that he protested that he knew nothing of the article being there, and that it had been put there without his knowledge.

Mr. U. was kept in jail until he had paid a very large sum of money by way of ransom.

The information had been given by his negro servant who, probably, instigated by others, had put the article there, and then laid the information in order to get the reward of his treachery. Of such cases there were innumerable instances.

Some of Butler's acts however showed a considerable amount of astuteness and tact, and were less to be condemned.

At the commencement of the war a good many of the wealthy merchants of New Orleans, in order to show their patriotism and zeal in the cause, subscribed large sums of money to aid in fitting out the armies and otherwise promoting the movement. Extensive lists had appeared in the newspapers with the names of those gentlemen, and opposite to them the sums contributed by each, varying from 100 dollars to 10,000 dollars. Butler, having secured one of those documents, and having spotted the subscribers, first carefully and fully ascertained the extent of their means. Then he issued an order in which he most courteously complimented these gentlemen on their liberality, and represented to them the state of misery and privation which had been brought about by the war, and the thousands of unemployed starving people that were now in the city, and other requirements in the city which must be attended to. He then made out another list of these gentlemen's names, and opposite each name he appended a sum which he called upon them to immediately pay. These sums varied a little, according to the extent of means which he knew the parties to be possessed of, but they were generally in proportion to the sum formerly subscribed by the parties to the Confederate cause, and amounted on an average to considerably over double that sum.

These men so mulcted well knew the alternative and paid the sum promptly with the best grace they could afford.

Butler, no doubt, applied the money towards the object for which he collected it, after having deducted his commission for trouble, expenses, etc.

But there was one act of Butler's, for which many expressed their admiration, and it was a pretty fair illustration of setting the devil to punish the devil.

I have often had to refer to a class of men who were prominent in bringing on this war, but whose conduct afterwards was cowardly and disgraceful in the extreme—I mean the agitating political demagogues and swaggering fire-eaters, who took such an active part in the Secession movement, and drowned in their clamorous howl every breath of reason or common-sense. These men, when the war broke out, took especial care to keep out of danger, but what they lacked in courage they made up in shameless effrontery. They displayed their zeal and patriotism by breathing out threatenings and slaughter against Lincoln and his abolition hordes, and often cursing their bad fortune that some important state business, or other cause, prevented them from going to the front, and always hoping to be able to get to the front in a few days, and then it must be up to the very front, to the enemy's very teeth. Somehow they always managed to put off going, until the Conscript Act was passed, and then it was supposed some of them would be caught. But just then New Orleans and a large part of the Confederacy fell into the hands of the enemy and become enclosed within the Federal lines, and within these lines they contrived to keep, where they were safe from conscription. Some of them, with a view to obtaining favour or office, immediately gave in their adherence to the Federal Government and took the oath of allegiance. Others knew they had no chance of favour with the Federals, and in the hope that the Confederates would yet succeed made a great show of their zeal in the Secession cause, and posed as prisoners of war and martyrs.

New Orleans was full of these swaggering braggarts. They strutted about the cafés, acting the part of caged lions, heralding reports of great Confederate victories, and lamenting their stars that they were confined here as prisoners of war, and could not get out to join the Confederate army ; and denouncing and recording the names of those who took the oath of allegiance ; while they themselves were boasting loudly of some gallant feat which they had done in calling the name of some Confederate general at a street-corner, or in a café.

But Butler took little notice of such bladders of wind. He knew they had no money, and there was nothing to be got out of them and were not worth arresting. As they were men something after his own nature, though with less cunning, he knew exactly what to do with them. He allowed them to have their way for a short time. They boasted loudly of their

fidelity to the Confederate cause, and denounced as traitors
such as took the oath of allegiance to the Federal Government. As they were not arrested they became bolder, and
bragged of their defiant expressions. Butler in the meantime
had them all spotted, was ready to pounce upon them, and
suddenly swept down upon them and had them arrested.
Knowing their cowardice he gave them the alternative of taking the oath of allegiance to the Federal Government, and
having their names put on a list and published in the newspapers ; or, to declare themselves enemies to the United States
and go at once and join the Confederate army, and they would
be immediately sent over the lines and delivered over to the
nearest Confederate provost-marshal.

It is needless to say that this put an end to their bounce.
The fear of being sent to that army which they pretended to
have been so wishful of joining made them quake. I did not
hear of any of them being sent across the lines, but some
chuckled at the list in the newspapers of the names of so
many desperate fire-eaters, who had been so suddenly converted ; and it was remarked that, if Butler had made many
thousands of Union men become Confederates, he had at least
made some professed Confederates become Union men, though
it might be doubtful if the Union gained much by the transfer.

This act was regarded as a masterly stroke of Butler's, in
thus dealing with such men ; and it would have been universally commended had he stopped there and carried it no
further. But seemingly acting on the effect of this, he conceived
the idea of following it up by a more comprehensive scheme of
the same kind.

He next issued an order commanding all the inhabitants of
New Orleans, and within his jurisdiction, male and female,
who were not certified subjects of any foreign power, to report
on or before a certain day, at the provost-marshal's offices, or
other places assigned for the purpose, and then and there
declare themselves to be enemies of the United States, and be
registered as such ; or, to take a certain prescribed oath, and
receive a certificate of loyalty. This oath, which was called
the " ironclad oath," embraced many heavy obligations and
penalties which were so utterly repugnant to the feelings and
sentiments of the population that there seemed to be a
universal determination to resist it. Again it was considered
what might be their fate if they registered themselves as

enemies of the United States; or, worse still, if they failed to comply with the terms of the order and not appear; the fear of certain imprisonment for an unlimited period, and total confiscation of property caused many to reflect.

There was also a certain form of oath for subjects of foreign powers, by which they bound themselves to remain neutral so long as their country remained at peace with the United States.

There was nothing oppressive or unreasonable in the "alien oath," as it was called. Neither was it compulsory on aliens to take it, but they were advised to do so for their better protection. So hateful had the name of oaths become that I believe very few did take it, at least of British subjects.

But there were great demands upon the consuls for certificates, and parties were trying to procure evidence to prove that they were aliens, who not many years before would have been offended at being called aliens, and had avowed themselves citizens, having the right to vote.

As for the less fortunate American citizens they were in a sad quandary. As this was the last chance allowed them to take the oath and save themselves, most of them at the last moment succumbed to the terms of the "ironclad oath," excusing and consoling themselves with the idea that on several of the points they maintained a mental reservation.

A large number, however, upheld their dignity and registered themselves as enemies of the United States, which they probably had cause to repent of afterwards, as within a few days an order was issued for them to be put across the lines into the Confederacy, and they were not allowed to take with them any property of any kind, watches or valuables of the smallest kind, not even a change of linen.

The time allowed them to prepare was very short. Their household goods were not confiscated, but the alternative was little better. Many families whose means were limited had to send their effects to auction mart.

The only auction marts now allowed to be open in the city were in the hands of such vultures as followed the army and were privileged by Butler, and the sales were a perfect mockery. An auctioneer brought up a few of his followers, and going up to and closing round articles of the value of over 100 dollars, would cry out, "Who bids?" Bids would be made of one dollar, and knocked down at a dollar and a half, and pass on to the next. Anyone who would dare to bid outside of the circle or remonstrate or interfere in any way would be jostled, thrust out, or arrested and marched off to prison, charged with treason, sedition, or inciting to riot, and the people, who had considered their effects worth over 1000 dollars, might, if they were exceedingly meek and humble, after paying commissions and expenses, receive a balance of 20 or 30 dollars.

There is not the slightest exaggeration in the description I have given of these transactions, and there were hundreds of such sales. Many I myself witnessed.

Such actions were loudly denounced by all respectable people both North and South, but the perpetrators, like Butler himself, had no shame, and if they got the money in their pockets they cared little for the world's censure.

General Banks, who succeeded Butler in the command at New Orleans, was a man of a different stamp from Butler, although not very well qualified to take command of the city in the state in which Butler had left it.

The numerous followers and parasites of Butler did not see so much to admire in him when he had no longer the command. They did not leave the city with him, but remained behind, presuming, now that the lion was gone, they would have the plunder to themselves.

I may here remark that some three years after this I happened to be on board of a steamer at Nassau, New Providence, where I observed some negro boatmen who were alongside throwing over some meat to an enormous shark which they named " Butler." On my asking them why they applied such a name to an honest shark, they said that it was because he kept away all the other sharks from the bay so as to have all the prey for himself, and they found it much safer to have only one large shark than a shoal of smaller ones.

General Banks was a man of milder disposition, and did not find it necessary to lay down any extreme measures or enactments, and he did not himself engage, so far as I knew, in any acts of extortion or plunder. But he was altogether too mild a man to grapple with the state of things then existing in New Orleans.

It was supposed that Butler had sufficiently punished the rebels in New Orleans, and that Banks should act more in the military capacity and take the field and act against the Confederates at Port Hudson, while Grant acted against them at Vicksburg; and, by subduing these two places, would open up again the Mississippi River, and once more cut the Confederacy in two and stop the Confederates from all communication with the States west of the Mississippi; the plan being to advance upon the rear of those places and surround them, and by cutting off their supplies starve them into submission. This might have been easily done as regarded Port Hudson, with the large forces they had at command.

But Banks was not much of a general; he had actually been chased out of Virginia by Stonewall Jackson; but he was a strong abolitionist and that was supposed to have got him the appointment.

The myriads of speculators who had come to New Orleans during Butler's reign, contented then to pick up the crumbs which was all that Butler allowed them, now revelled under Banks, who, though he did not himself plunder, seemed unable to check it in others; and Louisiana, instead of being like the bay of Nassau, having only one large shark, had now whole shoals of them. The great thing sought after was cotton, which had now got to be an enormous price outside the Confederate lines, while within the Confederate lines it was a drug stored up in millions of bales. It was currently reported, and I have good reason to believe that there was some truth in it, that, while Banks was trying to reduce Port Hudson by starvation, some of his own commissary staff, in league with a few of Butler's well-trained patriots, were delivering at certain places for the use of the besieged fort, hundreds of tons of supplies, and receiving in return an equivalent in cotton.

Vicksburg and Port Hudson were also receiving supplies from the West by way of Red River, and it was deemed of great importance that Port Hudson should be reduced so as to enable the gunboats to get up the Red River and stop supplies coming through that source, and an attack upon Port Hudson by the fleet was resolved upon.

Port Hudson was a small town on the left or east side of the river. It was situated upon the bluffs or high banks of the river, which here rise almost perpendicularly from the water edge to a height of about 150 feet. From this place a railway extended into the interior about thirty miles, and previous to the war a good deal of cotton was shipped here. The river in front was rather narrower than the average breadth, being only about three-quarters a mile in width, and on the side next the town was deep and rapid, but on the west side it was shallow, and when the water was low a large sandbank lay bare.   About two miles below Port Hudson there is an island called Prophet's Island, which is the first island met with on ascending the Mississippi.   It is about two miles in length, and situated near the middle of the river, and when the river was high, steamers passed on either side, but the main passage was on the west.

On the bluffs at Port Hudson, overlooking and commanding the river, batteries, mounted with heavy guns, had recently been erected, which debarred the Federal gunboats from ascending, and these forts it was now sought to reduce.

I happened to witness this attack which took place during the night, and was rather an imposing sight, being like a gigantic but grim display of fireworks.   I may give a short description of it as seen from a distance.

The Mississippi had been rising rapidly, and it was known that there were some breaks in the embankments on the west side near Port Hudson, and with some of the proprietors I had been up there inspecting the embankments to see if there was any possibility of preventing an overflow.   While there we became aware of the contemplated attack, and watched the movements.

On the day preceding the attack a number of mortar schooners were towed up the river and anchored on the west side of Prophet's Island, where they could not be seen from Port Hudson.   Towards evening the whole fleet, which had been rendezvoused at Baton Rouge steamed up the river.   This fleet, which amounted to about 16 vessels in all, consisted of frigates and ocean-going gunboats.   As I wished to see the attack, I with one or two others rode over the overflowed land to a suitable place, where we had a good view of the action.   It was dark by the time the fleet reached Prophet's Island, where they remained for several hours at anchor; what they were doing we could not see.   It was getting near midnight.   The night was dark; everything was quiet; not a sound was heard, or a spark seen about Port Hudson, or where the fleet was concentrated, and we were beginning to wonder whether the attack would be made that night, when, suddenly, a rocket went up from Port Hudson, and almost immediately afterwards a great blaze flamed up all along the embankment, on the west side of the river.   This, as it had been intended to do, lighted up the river in front of the forts and disclosed the advancing fleet. Almost immediately afterwards a heavy fire was opened from the mortar schooners, which had in the interval been towed up and anchored above Prophet's Island and within range of the forts, and a storm of shells which showed in the darkness like streams of rockets were showered upon the forts.

The fleet seemed to advance in two lines, keeping two and two nearly abreast. The first was the frigate *Hartford*, Admiral Farragut's ship; and the *Albatross*, which I think was a paddle steamer, but I could not be certain. Next followed the *Mississippi*, a large paddle frigate, and another, which I think was the *Monongahela*. The rest, the names of which I did not know, or don't now remember, followed in quick succession.

It was obvious that Farragut intended to pursue his favourite tactics in not damaging his fleet by lying in front of a fort, but attaining his object, if possible, by sailing past it. The vessels, seemingly under a full head of steam, advanced rapidly up the river, pouring their broadsides into the forts as they passed. But the blazing pine knots on the top of the embankment on the west so effectually lighted up the river that the ships were distinctly seen, and the strategy of passing the forts under the cover of darkness was defeated.

The forts now opened fire upon the ships with telling effect. The *Hartford*, with her consort the *Albatross*, succeeded in getting past, but the next pair were not so fortunate. There was evidently something wrong with them. The plunging fire from the forts at such a short distance and high elevation had penetrated their vital parts. The frigate *Mississippi* seemed doomed to perish in the river she was named after, for keeping too near the western side she grounded on the bank. The *Monongahela* was disabled and drifted helplessly back with the current and fouled the ships which were following. Before she could be got out of the way some of the other ships which had tried to pass up were also disabled, and drifting back with the strong current made more confusion. Farragut, who was now up safe past the forts with his own ship and the *Albatross*, kept signalling for the other ships to follow, but this was easier said than done. The forts were pouring a tremendous fire upon the foremost ships, thus in confusion and foul of each other; while the rearmost ships and the mortar schooners kept up a heavy fire upon the forts.

In the meantime the *Mississippi* lay aground ahead of the

other ships, and in the very focus of the fire from the forts, and could not get off, and she was abandoned.

And here was again displayed that spirit of reckless destruction which was often carried to madness, on both sides, during this war. When they abandoned the vessel they set fire to her. This seemed to me to be at the time a foolish act, when the water was known to be rising rapidly. The flames lighted up the river clear as day, and endangered greatly the advance up the river, and exposed the other ships to the full view and fire from the forts, which was now more deadly than ever. While the *Mississippi* frigate was thus in full blaze her capricious namesake, the Mississippi River, whose sympathies seemed to have again gone with the Confederates, continued to rise and floated her off, and the huge vessel, which was of great length and blazing from stem to stern, swung round and drifted broadside on down upon the vessels below. This made confusion worse confounded, and the whole fleet had to get away from the danger. Disabled steamers were quickly taken in tow by others. The mortar schooners cut their cables and dropped down the river, and all further attempts to pass the forts were abandoned.

It was now about two o'clock A.M. ; we had been watching the proceedings from the upper windows of a sugar factory a little below the place, and as the country was fast being overflowed and the driest part was the road close to the bank, we wished to get down that way before the burning ship drifted too close upon us, as we knew the explosion of the magazine must soon take place, and, though we wished to see it, we did not wish to be too near it.

We mounted our horses and galloped down to a safe distance and waited there. The dim lines of the ships of the disordered fleet could be seen in the darkness as they made their way down the river, keeping out of the way of the burning ship, which seemed to follow them up like an avenging spirit seeking to punish them for their wanton act in setting her on fire.

The firing had now ceased and all was quiet, and nothing was to be seen but the burning vessel as it drifted down the river with the current. Suddenly a tremendous explosion shook the air and filled it with millions of sparks and burning fragments of the vessel, lighting up the country for miles around as if ten thousand great rockets had been sent up, falling hissing into the river and on the land on both sides. In a few seconds all was still, and only a denser darkness caused by the smoke marked the place where the floating conflagration had been.

We now made our way home; of course we could not tell exactly from what we had seen how the matter stood. We knew that Farragut's ship had got past the forts. Whether it was much damaged or not we could not tell. How many vessels got with him we were uncertain : some thought three had passed up, others thought only two. We all knew the frigate *Mississippi* and that it was she that had come to grief, and we had seen other ships disabled and mixed up in confusion and the main body of the fleet getting down the river, chased, as it were, by a dangerous enemy in the form of one of their own ships, which they had set fire to rather precipitately. And I must confess that we were all so disgusted at this wanton habit of burning and destroying property that we wished the burning ship would speed down upon them as a just retribution for such reckless and often quite unnecessary destruction.

My business in this part of the country was now at an end. It was quite plain that nothing could be done to prevent an overflow of the country, while the river continued to rise with such rapidity, and it was now certain that it would continue to do so and remain high for some months. The only thing for the people to do was to remove to higher places, or such of them as had floors several feet above the level of the ground, which most of the houses had, to move all their effects up there and content themselves to live there surrounded by the water, with skiffs or canoes tied at their doors to maintain communication with the dry land.

Most of the people remained in their houses surrounded by the water, thinking no doubt that in these troublesome times they were safer there than anywhere else.

The cattle, like the people, were accustomed to overflows, and generally found their way to the river embankments, where the land was highest. I may here say that the fall of the land away from the Mississippi River was such that in these overflows the water close to the bank would be only a few inches deep, while at a distance of a mile back it would be fully two feet deep.

I had waited up at this place a little longer than I intended in order to see the attack on Port Hudson, and a break had taken place in the river embankment lower down, and I had a little difficulty in getting to Baton Rouge, which I did, however, in course of time and took steamer for New Orleans.

When I got to New Orleans I found the general topic of conversation was the attack on Port Hudson. As might be supposed, each party had their own version of it.

The Federal newspapers represented it as a victory, and columns were headed in large type : " Successful attack on Port Hudson ;" " Farragut at his old tricks again ;" " He sails past the forts."

The Confederate party, in their quiet conversations, triumphed over it as a crushing defeat to the Federals, and represented the fleet as being driven back with heavy damage, and Farragut with his two ships completely cut off and hemmed in on the river between the two strongholds Vicksburg and Port Hudson, and could neither go up nor down, and must inevitably fall into the hands of the Confederates.

The fleet had certainly been defeated and driven back with considerable damage, and Farragut was no doubt in a critical position. But the rats had got into the house, and might do much damage and not be easily caught.

Farragut was a man of great resources and determination. If he had found his position desperate he would have attempted to run down past the forts, for which he could have chosen a favourable opportunity, and it would have been easier to run down with the strong current of the river than to run up against it. If he had fuel and stores sufficient he had about 300 miles of the Mississippi and several miles of Red River navigable for his ships. If the river continued high, as it was now likely to do for some months, there would be a passage for small vessels by way of Atchafalia, by which he might receive fuel and supplies, although no doubt there would be some opposition from the Confederates to be met on that route. But, with that overcome, or if he could hold out for a time, he could effectually stop all supplies being sent into Vicksburg and Port Hudson by way of the river, and, as both these places were being now closely invested on the land side and both short of supplies, they must inevitably fall through starvation.

I did not remain in the country to witness the result, but learned afterwards that the ships *Hartford* and *Albatross* held out and maintained possession of the river until both Vicksburg and Port Hudson succumbed through sheer starvation.

CHAPTER XXX.

FINANCIAL MATTERS IN NEW ORLEANS—INSECURITY OF PROPERTY—DEPRE-
CIATION OF THE CURRENCY—I TAKE MY LEAVE AND GET TO SEA—
CONCLUDING REMARKS.

IT was now getting towards the summer of 1863, and it was quite plain that whichever way the war would terminate the cost was going to be alarming. Whether it was going to result in one or two nations, it was certain that the one or both must be loaded with a crushing debt, which, to redeem, would be almost impossible.

Many of the old standing people of New Orleans and particularly those who had retired from business, and stood as neutral, were considering what was best to be done to preserve their substance, and in what form it would be best to have it put to be safe.

The result of the war was still uncertain. Property was not safe. The city might be destroyed at any moment. There was no security against war risks. No corporation or company was secure. Specie had entirely disappeared. Butler had by an edict declared United States currency (greenbacks) to be the only legal tender. The banks were all shut up— their notes not in circulation, and any that were in circulation not being a legal tender were, of course, classed below the rates of the United States currency. The enormous amount of the United States debt had shaken confidence. Gold and silver being no longer a tender in commerce, became articles to be bought and sold, and were bulled and beared by reports got up of victories or defeats. It was, therefore, hard to get and dangerous to hide, and safe nowhere. Merchandise, or other valuables, were subject to seizure or plunder ; United States bonds or currency constantly depreciating in value and might yet be repudiated.

It was, therefore, sometimes a little amusing to hear the different ideas of what form, in which means or substance, could be best placed to be secure.

One gentleman told me that he had invested in a large lot of Scotch fire-bricks. He said they were fire proof and would not burn, and too cumbersome to be seized or plundered, and if the city was burned they would be in demand to build it up again. Another gentleman, on a similar principle, invested in a quantity of pig iron; another, in a large quantity of building sand; and many similar investments were made, each having his own peculiar idea of what would be safest.

The quotations for gold now ranged from 200 to 250 per cent. premium—foreign exchange still higher and scarcely to be got in New Orleans. Such a rush had been made to turn greenbacks into specie by investing in cotton and shipping to foreign countries that cotton had been run up to a fabulous price, and the shipping of it or any goods to foreign countries was hedged round with high charges, stringent regulations, and restrictions, that it was almost impossible for anyone to do it without having some influence with the officials.

I now determined to make an effort to get out of the country, and having disposed of all my rights, and interests, and claims with my business partners, I, with some others, invested in a small schooner, and having obtained for her a provisional register loaded her for the West Indies.

It would be endless to recount the numerous examinations and stoppages to which we were subjected before being allowed to proceed. Having at length by means of bribes and other devices got a clearance, we thought we had overcome our difficulties, but just as we were about to clear out of the harbour we were boarded by still another official. This was a sort of harbour watchman, whose business it was to take the names of all vessels which left the harbour and report them at the Customhouse. This was a sort of sinecure office, and had been given to an Americanised Irishman, as a sop to the Irish element, which was then in great demand to fill up the ranks of the army. This official assumed airs of great importance. He had discovered that the vessel had a name on her stern, but not the name of the hailing port. He was informed that the vessel was under a provisional register, and therefore could not have a hailing port. But he stood upon his dignity, and probably expecting to get his hand crossed by a five-dollar note he declared the vessel should not be allowed to proceed until she had the name of a hailing port on her stern. Knowing the extent of his power, and that this was all he could demand, a boat was lowered, and a seaman directed to letter on the stern, in the best way he could, the name of the nearest British sea-port, which was Belize, Honduras, where we intended going. This being done, the official had to be satisfied, and we proceeded.

There were still the forts near the mouth of the river to pass, and when we reached them we were warned by a gun to bring to, and ordered to remain at anchor till further instructions came from New Orleans. We dropped anchor, but the current was so strong that the anchor would not bring the vessel up, and she drifted for some distance past the forts. We made every apparent effort to bring the vessel up, and no further warning was given from the fort ; but the vessel continued to drag her anchor. Whether this was observed from the fort or not I do not know, but night came on and darkness closed around, and we were out of sight of the forts, and the wind being favourable we took up the anchor and made sail, and by daylight next morning we were out of sight of land, glad to escape from further detention.

The reason of our being stopped at the forts was, as I afterwards learned, in consequence of orders being telegraphed from New Orleans to stop the vessel.

It seemed that the seaman, in roughly painting the name of the hailing port on the stern of the vessel, found that he would not have room for the whole of the name, " Belize, Honduras," and he was told to abbreviate the last word, and put " Belize, Hon." He being still a little short of room, and being no great artist, had finished it in a rather cramped way, thus : " Belizehon." This the official mistook for " Babylon," having probably heard of the latter place, but not of the former; and he accordingly reported at the Customhouse, as having passed down the river, the " *Rob Roy* of Babylon."

It might have been easily seen that this was a mistake, but official interference was rampant. At that time the atmosphere of New Orleans was pregnant with rumours of the most extravagant kind of some contemplated attack upon the city, from an outside source, through some Confederate agency, and the least unusual movement was construed into a connection with some plot for some raid or attack upon the city. There being in New Orleans no consul for such a place as Babylon, and whether it was on account of this irregularity, or whether there was something ominous in the name, as suggestive of some meditated descent upon the city, by some Rob Roy, or,

2 F

Nebuchadnezzar, I do not know; but, orders were immediately telegraphed to the forts to stop the suspicious craft !

The commander at the forts was probably disgusted at the frequent annoyance he was put to in stopping vessels at the instance of the corrupt officials at the port, and knowing that in most, if not in all, cases it was only a device to extort bribes from the owners or agents of vessels; and having no steamer at hand to follow and board vessels if they drifted past, and he would not be justified in firing into a foreign vessel, if she used every endeavour to bring up, and the anchor would not hold in the strong current. He also knew that the acts and character of the officials would not stand investigation, so he gave himself little trouble in the matter; and this was the way so little notice was taken of us, and we were allowed to slip off to sea.

Having now got out to sea, I felt as if in a new atmosphere, and somewhat relieved at getting away from the turmoil of war, and, what was more unpleasant, the overbearing official tyranny of those in office, and the disgusting jobbery and corruption which seemed to prevail in what was now called the business circle, which had taken the place of the good old substantial and honourable men that were to be found on 'Change in New Orleans before the war.

Here ended my experience and participation in the more stirring events of this war.

I several times after this during the war visited the Confederate ports and had a good opportunity of knowing the state of matters; but, as I confine myself in this narrative only to what came under my own personal observation, I leave history to history writers.

When I got out of the country I had time to reflect upon and review the events of the last three years and the fearful wreck which had been wrought during that time; and, in closing this narrative, I venture to give a very limited expression of the opinions and impressions which experience forced upon me and which have been confirmed by many years of reflection afterwards.

Of course such opinions may be of little value, and can take no place beside the more comprehensive views of men of higher attainments; but, as the impressions which were forced upon me might be forced upon others, if passed through the same ordeal, I give them for what they may be worth.

It seemed to me that the fearful wreck which had been wrought might all have been averted by a little wise and judicious management, had the sober and industrious class of the people—the bone and sinew of the nation—taken a more active part and kept the control of public affairs out of the hands of unprincipled politicians and demagogues. Had the central government been more of a government and less of a party, and executed its functions with a firm hand, instead of pandering for party votes, such a wreck could never have occurred.

That the expression I had so often heard in the early part of the movement, that "there were plenty of sensible and respectable men in the country to overrule the ravings of unprincipled demagogues," was no doubt true; but why they failed to do it, and why a nation of intelligent people should allow themselves to be goaded to destruction upon a shibboleth arising out of a question in which so few of them had any interest was a question for reflection, and seemed to impress me with the idea that for a government to be controlled successfully by the direct voice of the people it is imperatively necessary that the people must be honest, intelligent, and possess a high tone of moral principle and be impervious to flattery; that every man must take an enlightened and independent interest in the government of the country and be ever vigilant and guarded against the insidious wiles of self-seeking agitators and demagogues, who live by agitation and prey upon the credulity of the masses.

That in all countries a certain amount of what may be called the residuum of society naturally exists. These may not be altogether criminal, but of an improvident and idle class, generally termed loafers or roughs; and, although the natural proportion of this class in mankind is but small, the number is greatly increased and their pretensions emboldened by the influence of agitating demagogues; and, though they may still be but a small proportion of the population, they have in politics a great advantage over the industrious citizen. They have no regular business or labour to attend to, and they give themselves up to agitation and politics. Their leaders possess any amount of effrontery, and always put themselves forward in any political movement and take possession of the field, and unless the honest, industrious citizens are constantly on the alert, this element will be certain to gain the ascendency and control nominations and elections; and, for the better accomplishment of their ends, it is a common practice with political tricksters to strangle liberal and broader sentiments by taking hold of public questions and reducing them to narrow dogmas, with two extreme sides, to which public sentiment must adhere *pro* or *con*, allowing no admittance for any side reasoning or inquiry, and the honest, industrious citizen must either follow and support their views and objects or be branded as opponents to all good measures.

Men having business and work to attend to often have little time to attend to political matters, especially when elections are frequent, and they become indifferent and disgusted, especially when they see at the head of political movements men of depraved and worthless character.

That those whose business it is to maintain order and enforce the laws, and also those whose business it is to adjudicate and execute the laws, when they obtain their offices and positions through the influence of such an agency, too often swerve from a strict sense of duty and seek more to please such as have a control or influence in elections than to administer justice with a firm and impartial hand.

That there is no chain so heavy or yoke so oppressive as that which men will unwittingly place upon their own necks, or bend their necks to receive, while being beguiled and led along by liberty shriekers under their pretended banner of freedom.

As to any opinion I formed of the chief actors in this war —if we take the political body, presidents, cabinets, and congresses—I could say very little for them, either North or South; in fact, I knew very little about them, and I would not like to become security for the honesty of any of them. Perhaps the most honest man among them all was Mr. Lincoln himself.

I confess I never had any great regard for Jefferson Davis. I considered him a little too much the type of the extreme Southern politician, with a little tendency towards the autocrat. A man of considerable talent, unbending will, and great ambition; and I cannot help thinking that he prolonged the war long after he saw that the cause was utterly hopeless, when he might have made terms which would have saved tens of thousands of lives, and saved hundreds of thousands from untold misery. And it seems strange to say that the first to

ask for terms was General Lee, a man whom it may be safe to
assert was the greatest hero of this war, whose undoubted
bravery and high attainments as a general and a leader were
unquestionable, and on whose noble character no one could
cast a stain, but who could not stand by and see his brave
followers die of starvation.   Lee I considered to be the greatest
general of the war and Farragut the man who struck the blows
most fatal to the South.

While I never could see much to commend or admire in the
political personages on either side, I think there was something
to admire in the indomitable energy and determination displayed by the combatants on both sides, from the generals to
the private soldiers.

What seemed to me as the most striking feature in this war
was the aptitude of the volunteer system in raising upon the
nucleus of the standing volunteer companies and bringing into
the field in an incredible short time a large and effective army,
and the zeal and general bravery displayed by the citizen
soldiers.

Whatever may be said by European critics about inefficiency,
lack of training, and armed mobs, I still think that there were
some things which might be worthy of a little attention.
Should it ever be the fortune of any of those critics to see an
army cut into remnants and dashed into confusion, mixed up
and scattered, but the troops still uniting as if by mutual
attraction forming a front without regard to parade precision,
sustaining charge after charge and still fighting and holding
their own, he might say that they were defeated but they did
not know of it.   Yet those troops remained masters of the
field ; whereas, some troops, schooled to observe and maintain
as a *sine qua non*, a higher degree of military order and
precision, might have become disconcerted and considered all
lost and fled in confusion.   I have sometimes thought that
one of the chief causes of the success of the Confederate troops
was the alacrity with which they would form up into line, in
a temporary rough and ready way after being driven into
confusion by some sudden cause or movement in a rough or
rugged country and maintain the battle in that position,
while, as soon as opportunity afforded, every man would fall
into his place in the company, the company to its place in the
battalion, and the battalion to its place in the brigade, and
order regained in a short time.

That the troops were not drilled up to the finest points of military precision is certainly true, but most of them had good practical training, and I cannot say that I ever saw them suffer seriously from the want of the finer points.

With regard to mismanagement I must admit that I saw and experienced plenty of it; but this seems to be a necessary accompaniment of all armies, and, I suppose, has been a prominent feature in almost every war on record.

But this does not arise through any inefficiency or want of training of the officers or men, but generally proceeds from some political influence and from misunderstandings among the higher functionaries, and much mismanagement often arises from overmanagement through too much official-ism or through complicated and overstrained regulations in the different departments—particularly in the arrangements for transportation, where there seems to be always great mismanagement.

It has often been asserted by the exponents of human rights and liberties that certain cherished principles inherited, maintained, and contended for by a nation or people, can never be put down by force of arms—that the land may be overrun and held in subjection by a military force, but people imbued with certain inherent principles will never be subdued. They would fly to the mountains and fastnesses, and every rock, stump, and copse would have its rifleman, until they were utterly exterminated. This has, no doubt, been proved to be true in many instances throughout history.

It might be said that in this war such doctrine was proved to be fallacious. But I think for such a doctrine to hold good it is necessary that the principles contended for must be inherent, deep rooted, and universal, and it may not always do to accept as genuine sentiment what may be blurted forth by leading demagogues who may have thrust themselves forward as the champions of the people, and by the combination of a certain number hold the rest of the people in terror and subjection and only allow certain sentiments to be uttered.

I do believe from what I observed that this last was to a considerable extent the state of things in the South; and in a very large portion of the population no deep-rooted principle existed; and though they took up arms promptly, and fought manfully, it was not so much to maintain any inherent principle as in a moment of passion they sought to separate themselves from a people which they imagined had grossly insulted them, and from a Government which they considered had treated them badly, and had forfeited all claims to their respect and allegiance, and provoked them into war. And, with a great portion of them, at least, the question was more a quarrel of the moment, which had been brought about by the machinations of politicians on both sides, into which they had got unwittingly plunged, and could not avoid, than to maintain any fixed principles, or redress any long-standing wrongs or grievances.

The class I refer to were the respectable, industrious class, the rank and file who did the fighting.

As to the political body, who did the talking, what their actual principles or pretended principles were I do not exactly know, and, like many others, considered it in the midst of the violent quarrel of the moment to be of little importance; but certainly there were few among them of that kind that would fly to the mountains and rocks and fight until totally exterminated.

It seems to me that there can be no better proof of this than the way the war terminated, and the incredibly short time in which the fabric was cemented up, the wreck and damage repaired, and the enormous debt wiped off, or brought within controllable bounds, and things restored to their former conditions, and the nation more powerful and prosperous than ever; and rancorous hate dispelled from the minds of the great body of the people and confined to only a very few narrow-minded partisans on either side, and who it is to be hoped, from the desperate experience so dearly bought, will not likely again be allowed on that or any other question to exercise such influence over the minds of the respectable body of the people and lead them on to destruction.

It may be asserted, and with some truth, in regard to the way in which order was so soon again restored, that the institution of slavery, which led to the war no longer existed, and there was no longer any cause for dissension. But had that institution been embodied in a deep-rooted inherent principle, universally cherished and maintained, and it was for that principle alone that such a large body fought so long and so vigorously, it would not have been so soon set aside and forgotten.

There will, no doubt, always remain a spirit or sentiment of sympathy or admiration for the one side or the other, but that will never take the form of party feeling.

I believe that any admiration evoked for the Confederate movement, or any fame which may pass to posterity, will attach, not to the cause or principle for which they were said to be fighting, but to the determination and bravery displayed by those who fought the battles ; and if we accept what I think has been rather unjustly paraded before the world, as the only principles involved in the cause for which they fought, it might be a little difficult to account for the existence of such a brave spirit in men possessing no other principles, and appear somewhat contrary to moral reasoning.

But I confess that I am not skilled in political questions, high military science, or human philosophy, and I do not put forth these closing remarks to be accepted as any authority, but only as the simple opinions which I formed from what I saw and what took place around me.

I have tried to give, in the best manner I can, a brief account of what I observed and experienced in this quarrel and war, and, though in a crude and imperfect style, I believe I could give no truer account were I put into a witness box and examined before a commission or committee ; and if those who may take the trouble to wade through my bad diction should find anything to interest or amuse them, I shall be much gratified.

AIRD AND COGHILL, PRINTERS, GLASGOW.

Library of Congress Cataloguing in Publication Data

Watson, William.
Life in the Confederate Army.
(Collector's library of the Civil War)
Reprint. Originally published: New York: Scribner and Welford, 1888.
1. Watson, William.
2. United States—History—Civil War, 1861-1865—Personal narratives, Confederate.
3. Confederate States of America. Army—Biography.
4. Soldiers—Southern States—Biography. 5. Soldiers—Scotland—Biography.
6. United States—History—Civil War, 1861-1865—Participation, Scottish.
I. Title. II. Series.
E605.W34 1983   973.7'82   83-4724
ISBN 0-8094-4296-5 (library)
ISBN 0-8094-4295-7 (retail)

Printed in the United States of America

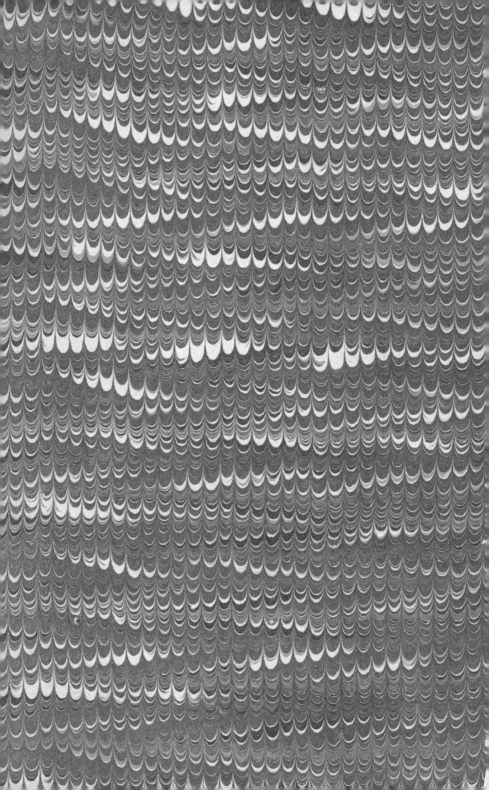